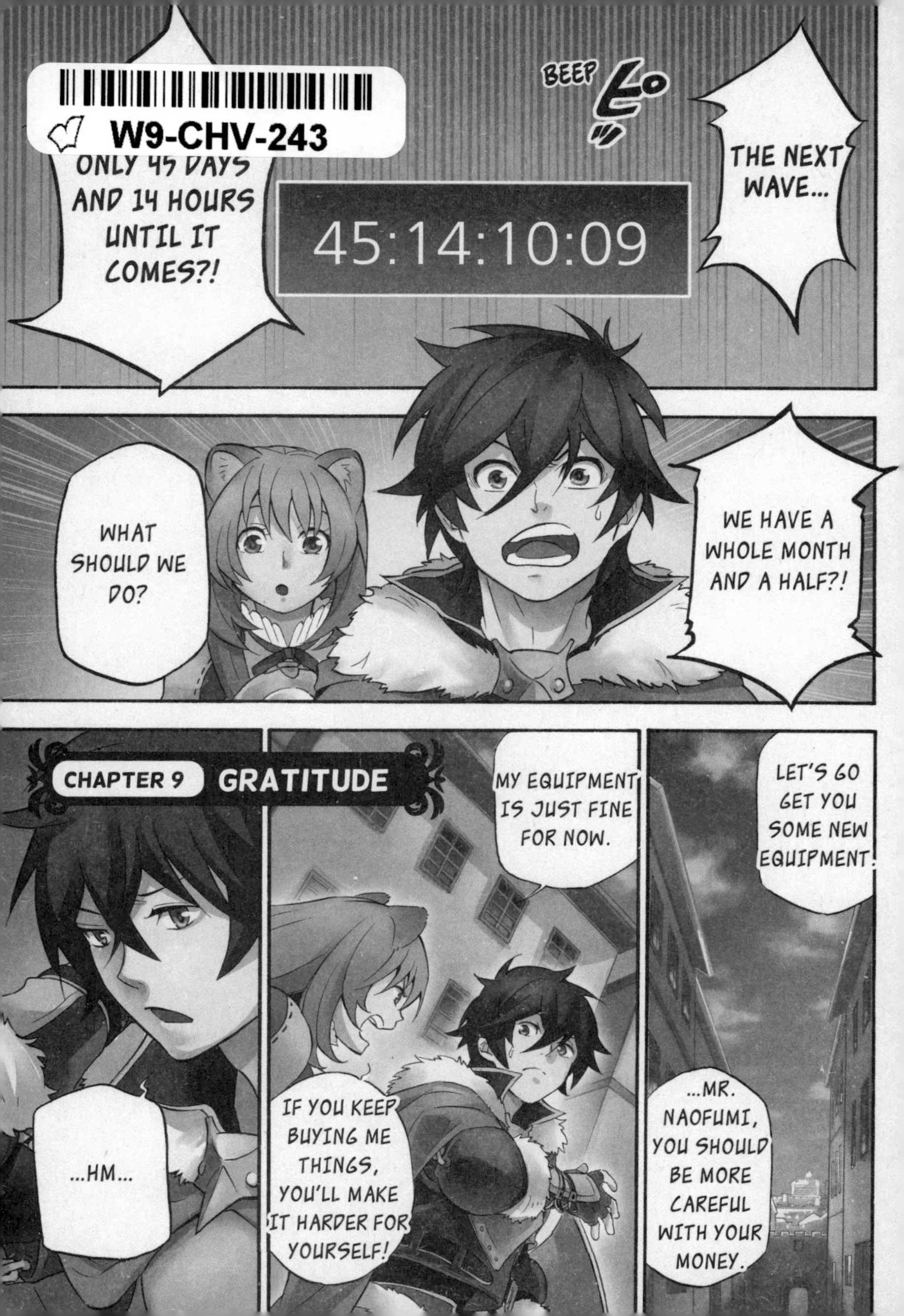
BEEP
THE NEXT WAVE...
45:14:10:09
ONLY 45 DAYS AND 14 HOURS UNTIL IT COMES?!
WE HAVE A WHOLE MONTH AND A HALF?!
WHAT SHOULD WE DO?
LET'S GO GET YOU SOME NEW EQUIPMENT!
...MR. NAOFUMI, YOU SHOULD BE MORE CAREFUL WITH YOUR MONEY.
MY EQUIPMENT IS JUST FINE FOR NOW.
IF YOU KEEP BUYING ME THINGS, YOU'LL MAKE IT HARDER FOR YOURSELF!
CHAPTER 9 GRATITUDE
...HM...

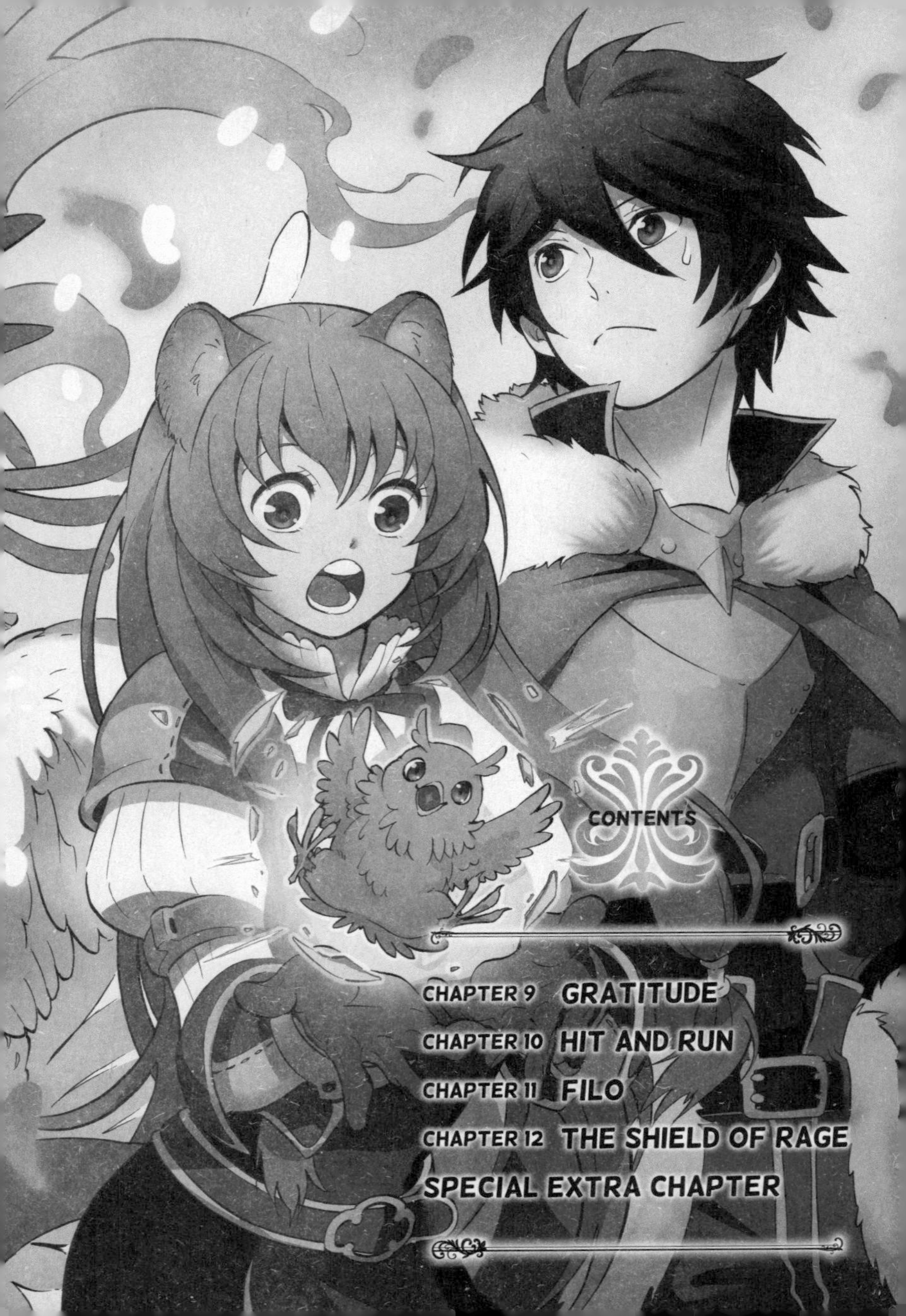

CONTENTS

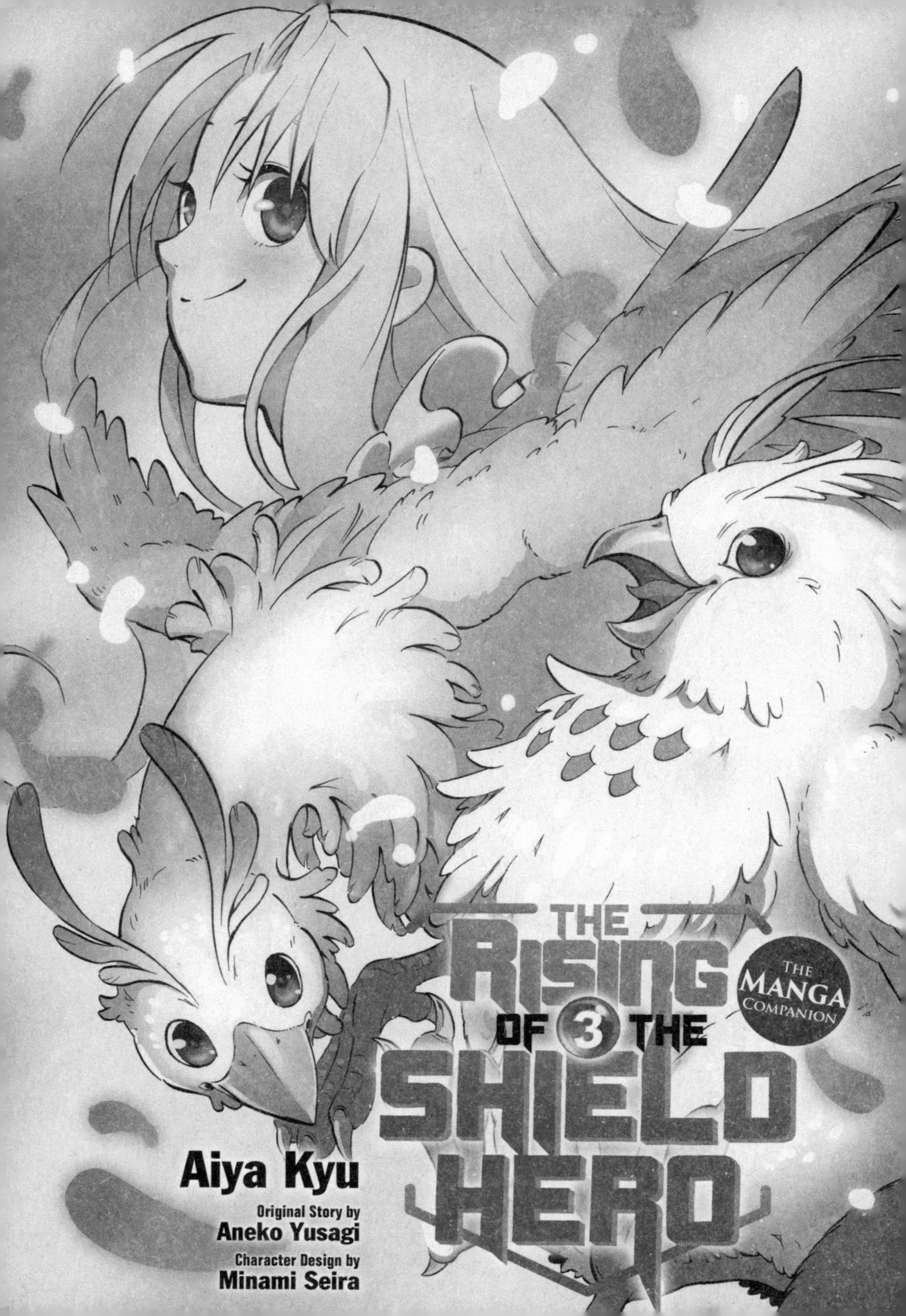
THE RISING OF THE SHIELD HERO
THE MANGA COMPANION
3
Aiya Kyu
Original Story by
Aneko Yusagi
Character Design by
Minami Seira

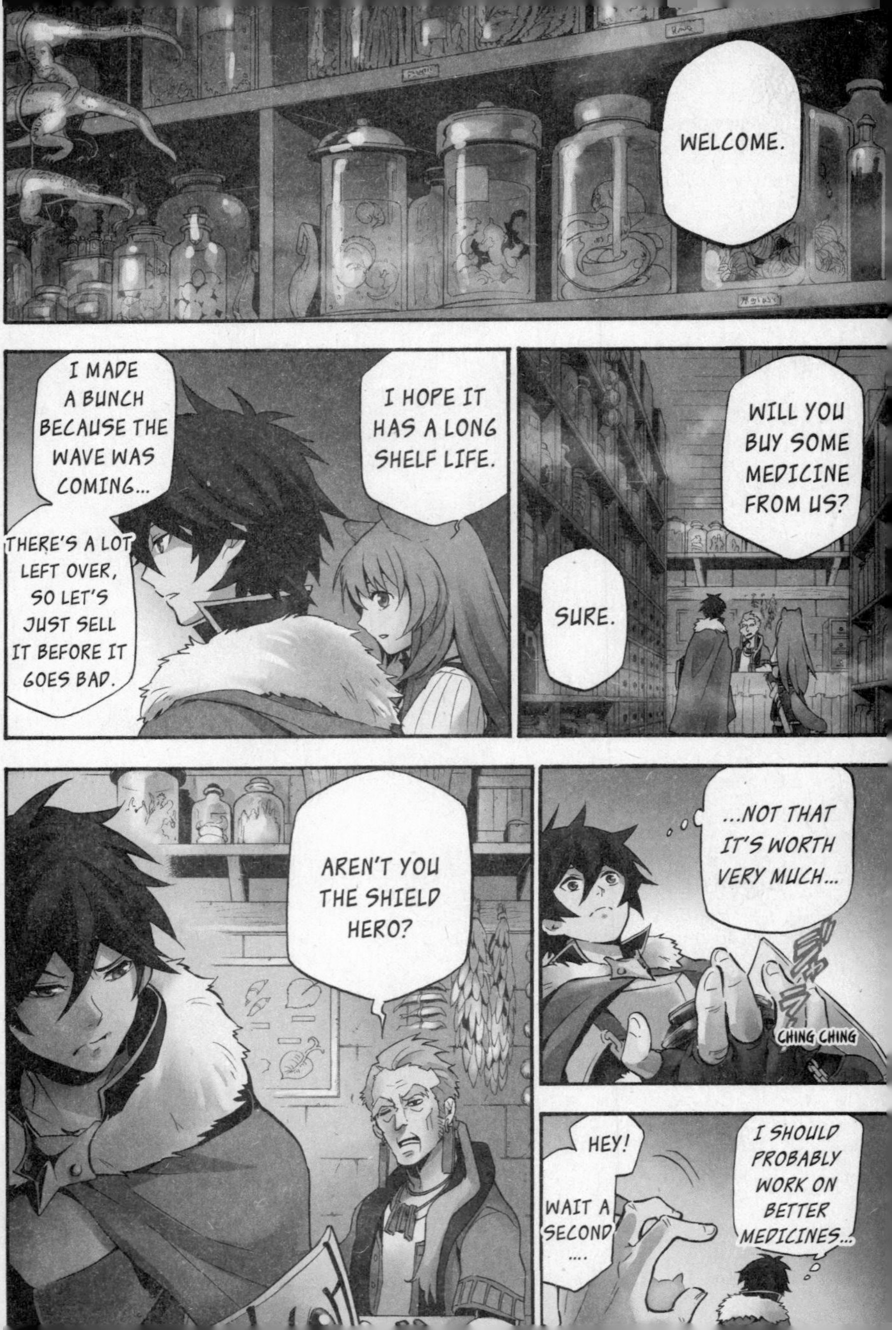
WELCOME.
WILL YOU BUY SOME MEDICINE FROM US?
SURE.
I HOPE IT HAS A LONG SHELF LIFE.
I MADE A BUNCH BECAUSE THE WAVE WAS COMING...
THERE'S A LOT LEFT OVER, SO LET'S JUST SELL IT BEFORE IT GOES BAD.
...NOT THAT IT'S WORTH VERY MUCH...
CHING CHING
I SHOULD PROBABLY WORK ON BETTER MEDICINES...
HEY!
WAIT A SECOND ....
AREN'T YOU THE SHIELD HERO?

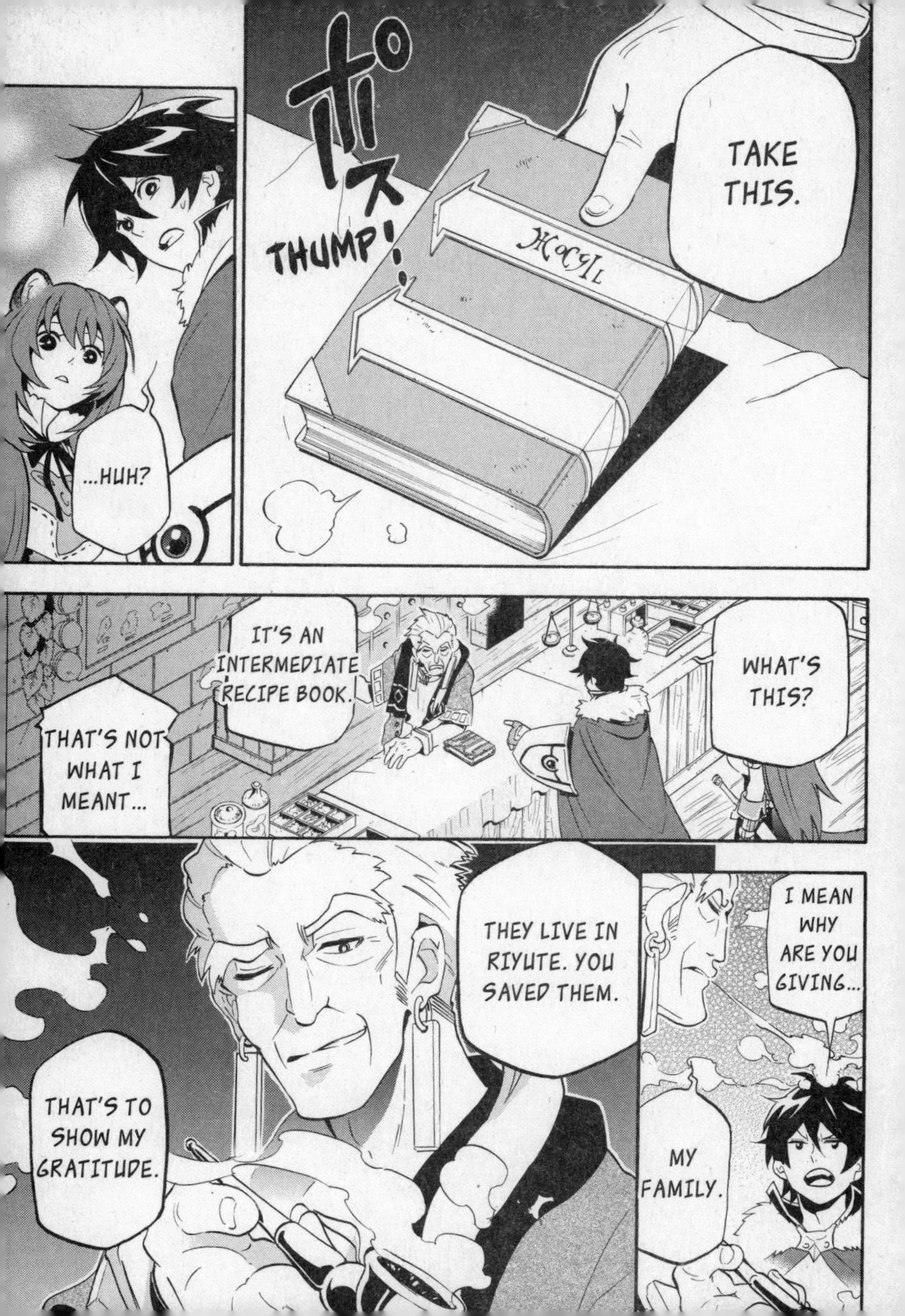
TAKE THIS.
ポス
THUMP!
...HUH?
WHAT'S THIS?
IT'S AN INTERMEDIATE RECIPE BOOK.
THAT'S NOT WHAT I MEANT...
I MEAN WHY ARE YOU GIVING...
MY FAMILY.
THEY LIVE IN RIYUTE. YOU SAVED THEM.
THAT'S TO SHOW MY GRATITUDE.

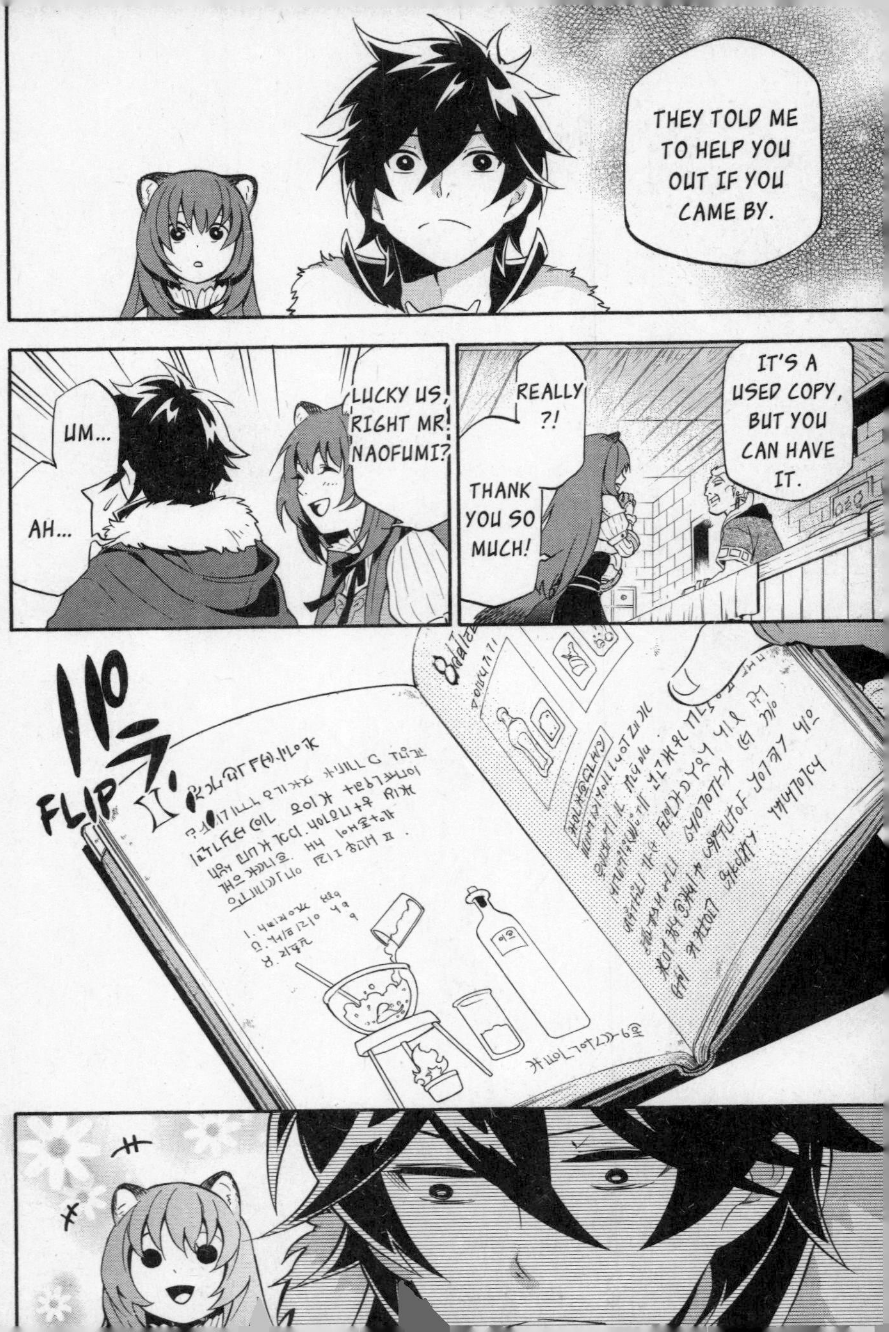
THEY TOLD ME TO HELP YOU OUT IF YOU CAME BY.
IT'S A USED COPY, BUT YOU CAN HAVE IT.
REALLY?!
THANK YOU SO MUCH!
LUCKY US, RIGHT MR. NAOFUMI?
UM...
AH...
FLIP

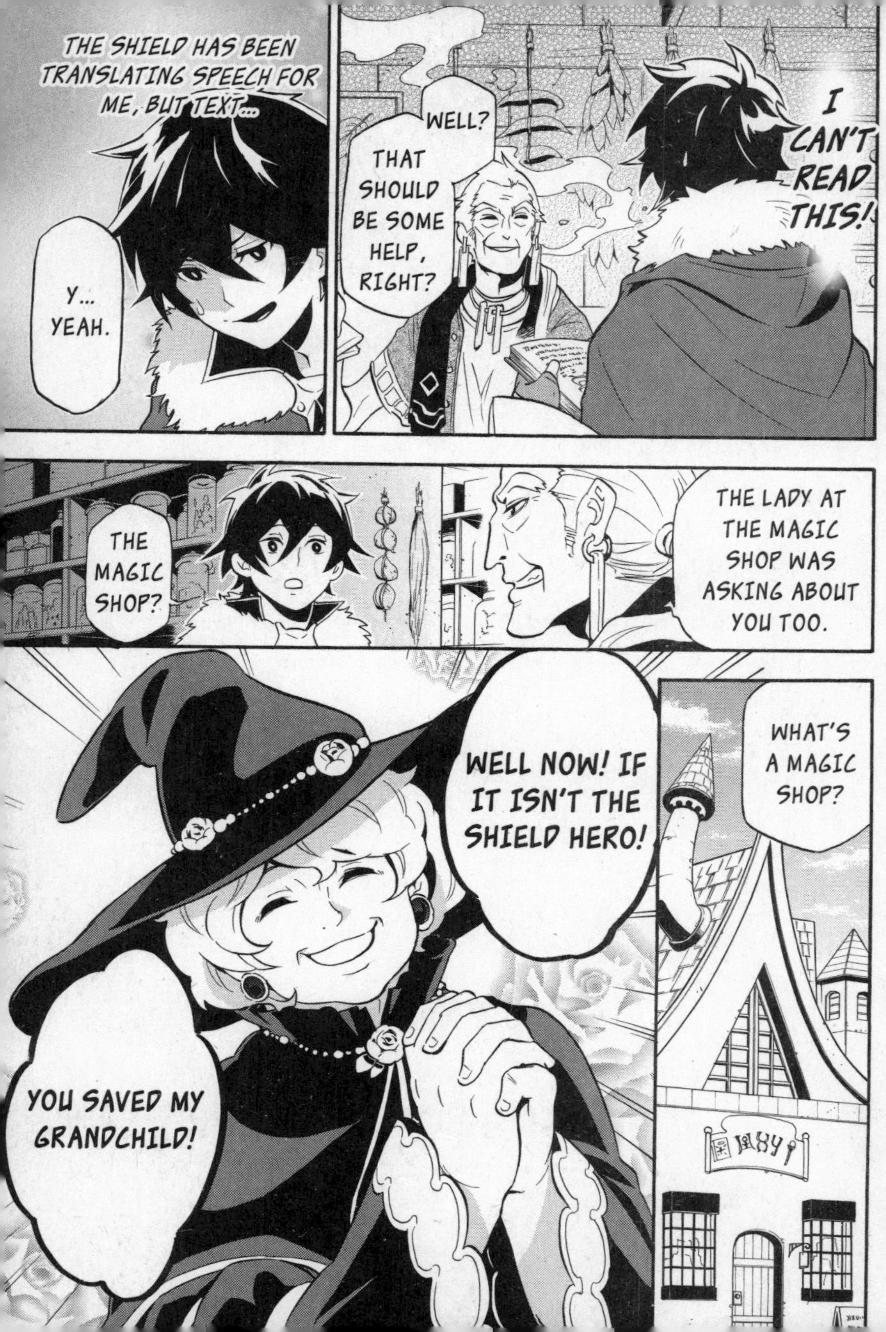
I CAN'T READ THIS!
WELL?
THAT SHOULD BE SOME HELP, RIGHT?
THE SHIELD HAS BEEN TRANSLATING SPEECH FOR ME, BUT TEXT...
Y... YEAH.
THE LADY AT THE MAGIC SHOP WAS ASKING ABOUT YOU TOO.
THE MAGIC SHOP?
WHAT'S A MAGIC SHOP?
WELL NOW! IF IT ISN'T THE SHIELD HERO!
YOU SAVED MY GRANDCHILD!

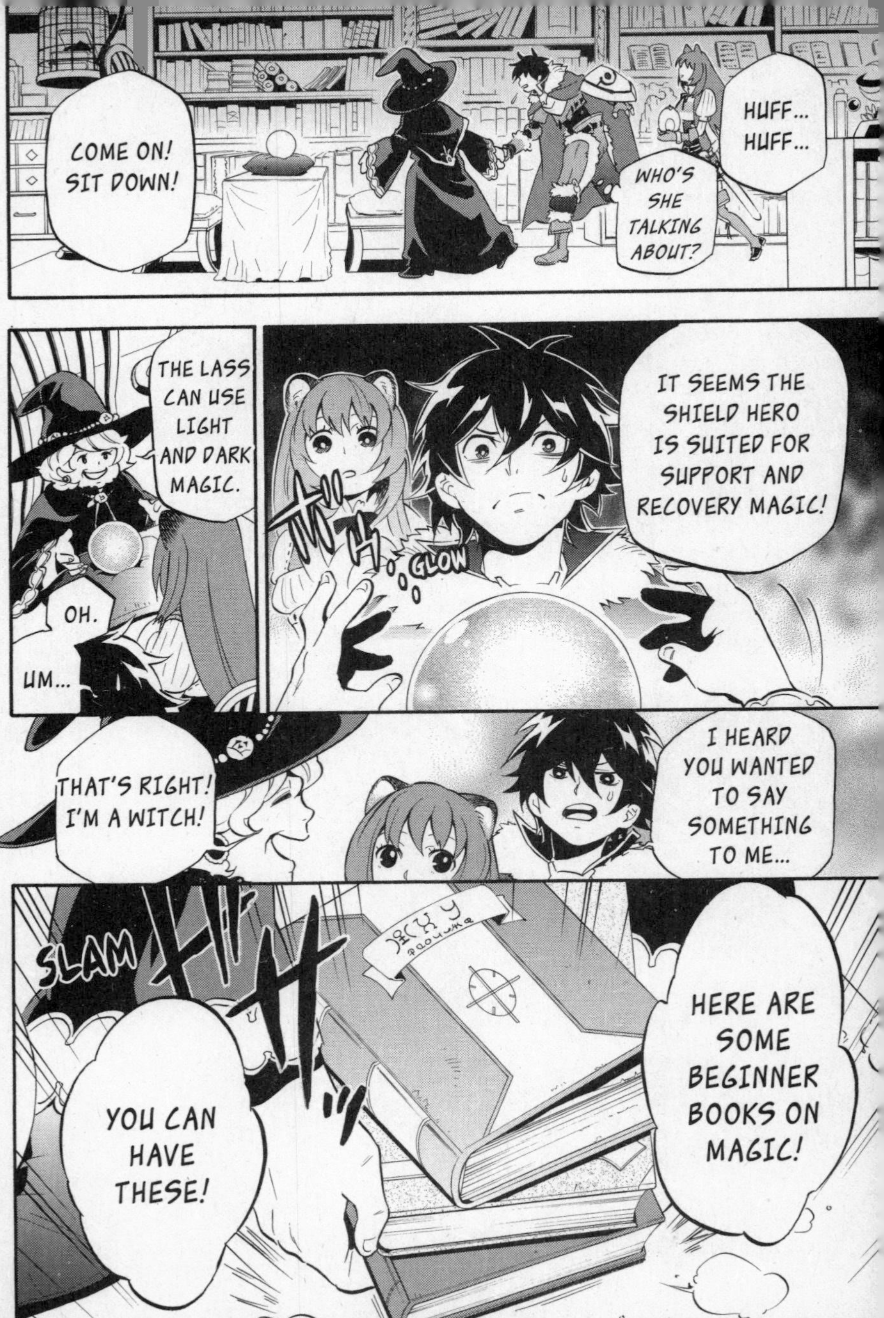
HUFF... HUFF...
WHO'S SHE TALKING ABOUT?
COME ON! SIT DOWN!
IT SEEMS THE SHIELD HERO IS SUITED FOR SUPPORT AND RECOVERY MAGIC!
GLOW
THE LASS CAN USE LIGHT AND DARK MAGIC.
OH.
UM...
I HEARD YOU WANTED TO SAY SOMETHING TO ME...
THAT'S RIGHT! I'M A WITCH!
HERE ARE SOME BEGINNER BOOKS ON MAGIC!
SLAM
YOU CAN HAVE THESE!

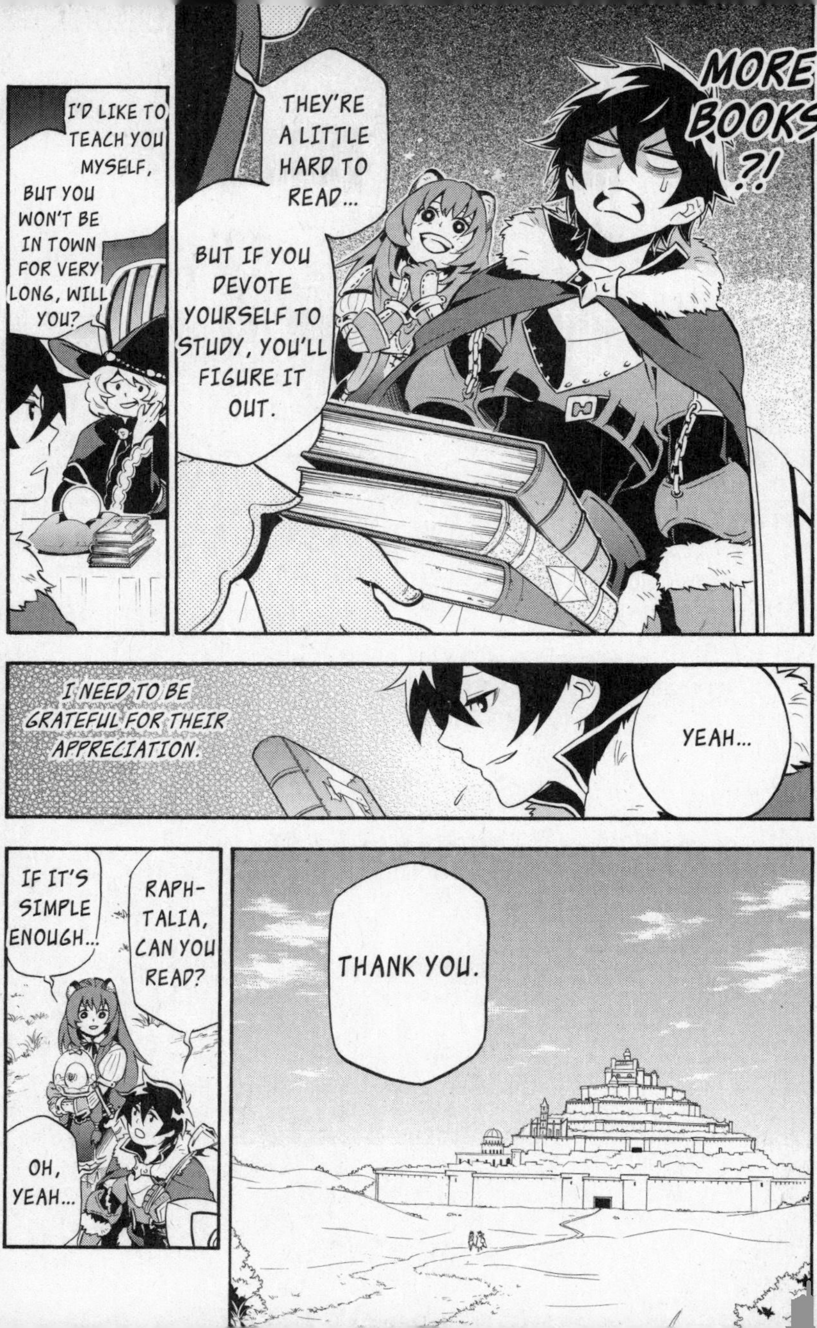
MORE BOOKS ?!
THEY'RE A LITTLE HARD TO READ...
BUT IF YOU DEVOTE YOURSELF TO STUDY, YOU'LL FIGURE IT OUT.
I'D LIKE TO TEACH YOU MYSELF, BUT YOU WON'T BE IN TOWN FOR VERY LONG, WILL YOU?
YEAH...
I NEED TO BE GRATEFUL FOR THEIR APPRECIATION.
THANK YOU.
RAPH-TALIA, CAN YOU READ?
IF IT'S SIMPLE ENOUGH...
OH, YEAH...

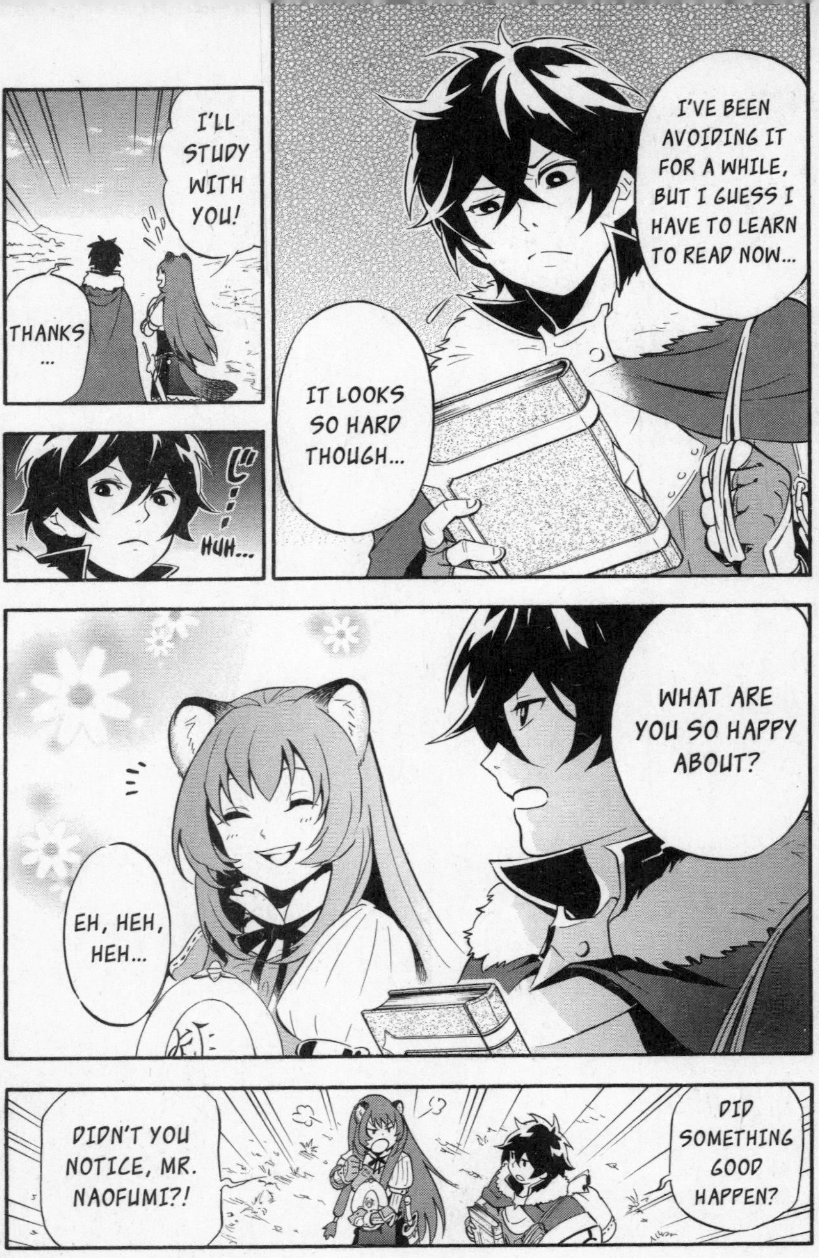
I'VE BEEN AVOIDING IT FOR A WHILE, BUT I GUESS I HAVE TO LEARN TO READ NOW...
IT LOOKS SO HARD THOUGH...
I'LL STUDY WITH YOU!
THANKS ...
HUH...
WHAT ARE YOU SO HAPPY ABOUT?
EH, HEH, HEH...
DID SOMETHING GOOD HAPPEN?
DIDN'T YOU NOTICE, MR. NAOFUMI?!

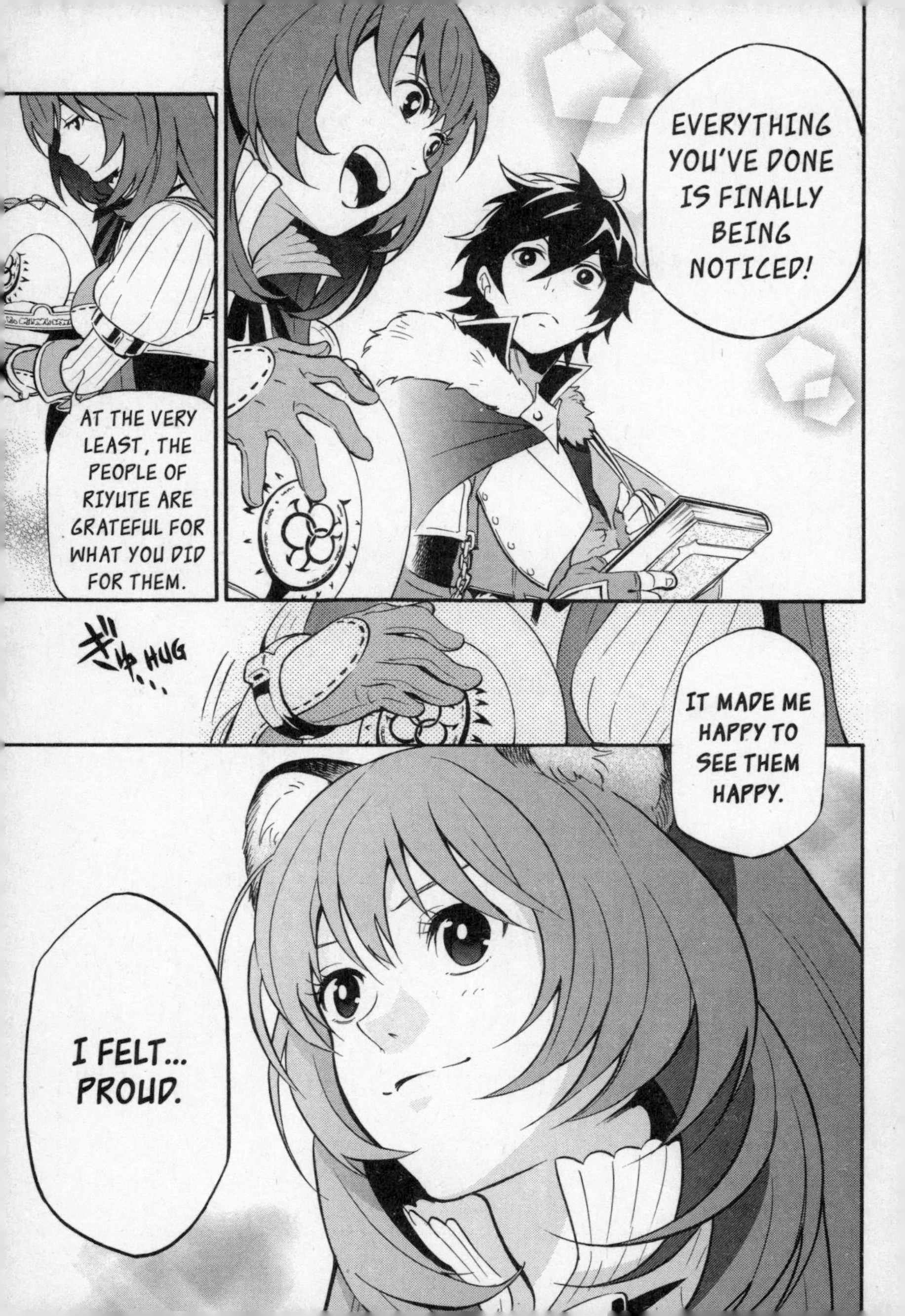
EVERYTHING YOU'VE DONE IS FINALLY BEING NOTICED!
AT THE VERY LEAST, THE PEOPLE OF RIYUTE ARE GRATEFUL FOR WHAT YOU DID FOR THEM.
IT MADE ME HAPPY TO SEE THEM HAPPY.
ぎゅ HUG
I FELT... PROUD.

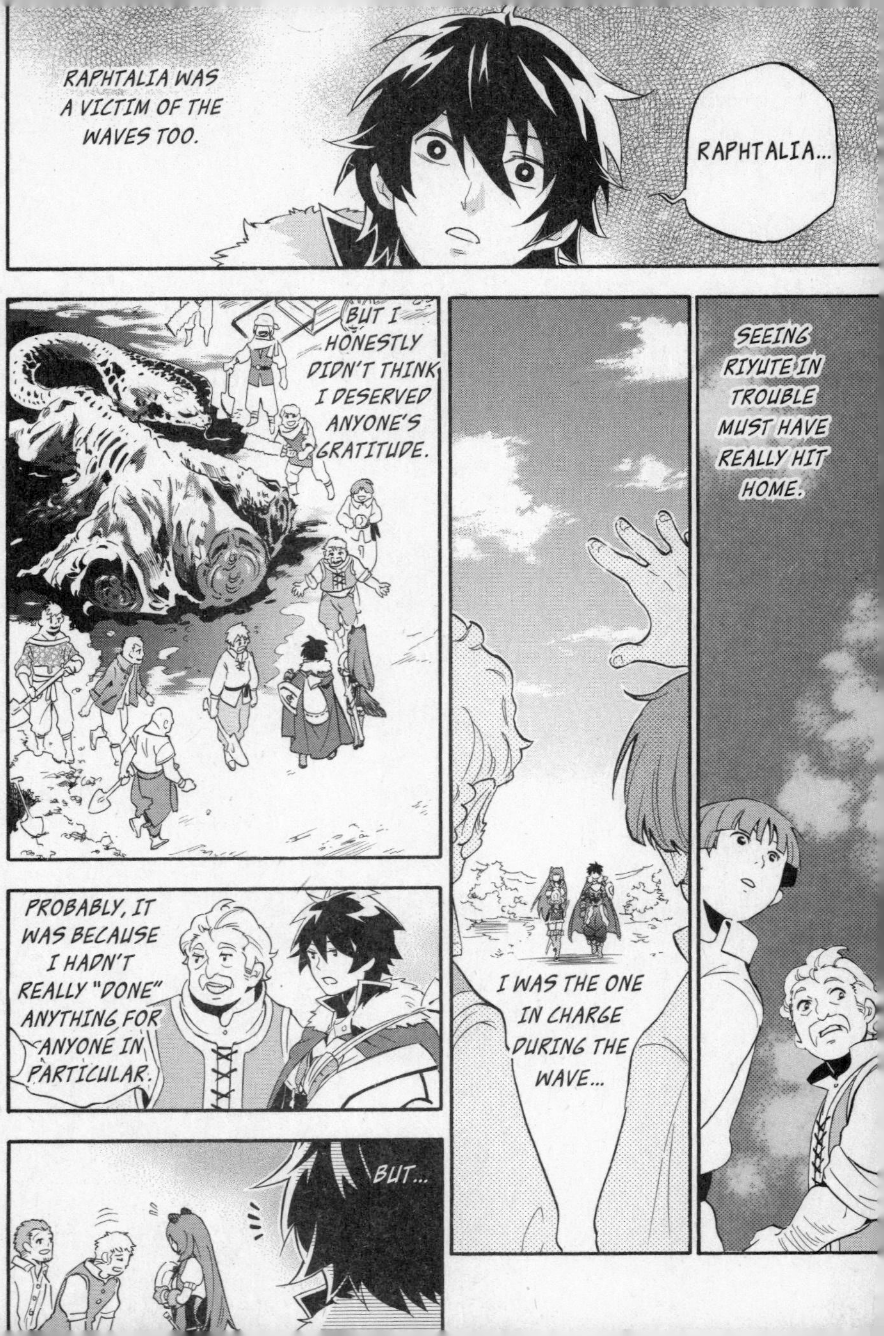
RAPHTALIA...
RAPHTALIA WAS A VICTIM OF THE WAVES TOO.
SEEING RIYUTE IN TROUBLE MUST HAVE REALLY HIT HOME.
I WAS THE ONE IN CHARGE DURING THE WAVE...
BUT I HONESTLY DIDN'T THINK I DESERVED ANYONE'S GRATITUDE.
PROBABLY, IT WAS BECAUSE I HADN'T REALLY "DONE" ANYTHING FOR ANYONE IN PARTICULAR.
BUT...

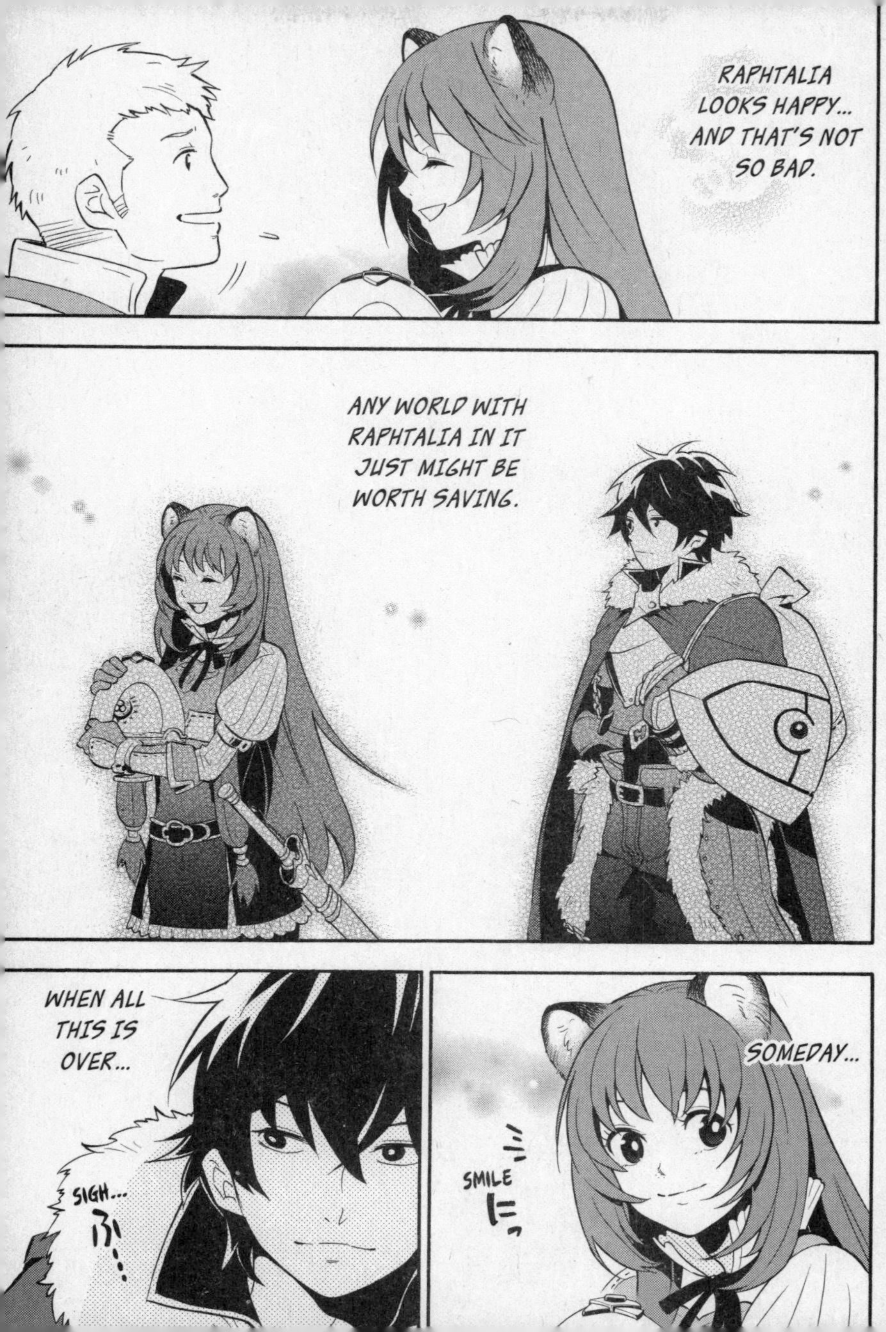
RAPHTALIA LOOKS HAPPY... AND THAT'S NOT SO BAD.
ANY WORLD WITH RAPHTALIA IN IT JUST MIGHT BE WORTH SAVING.
SOMEDAY...
SMILE
WHEN ALL THIS IS OVER...
SIGH...
ふ…

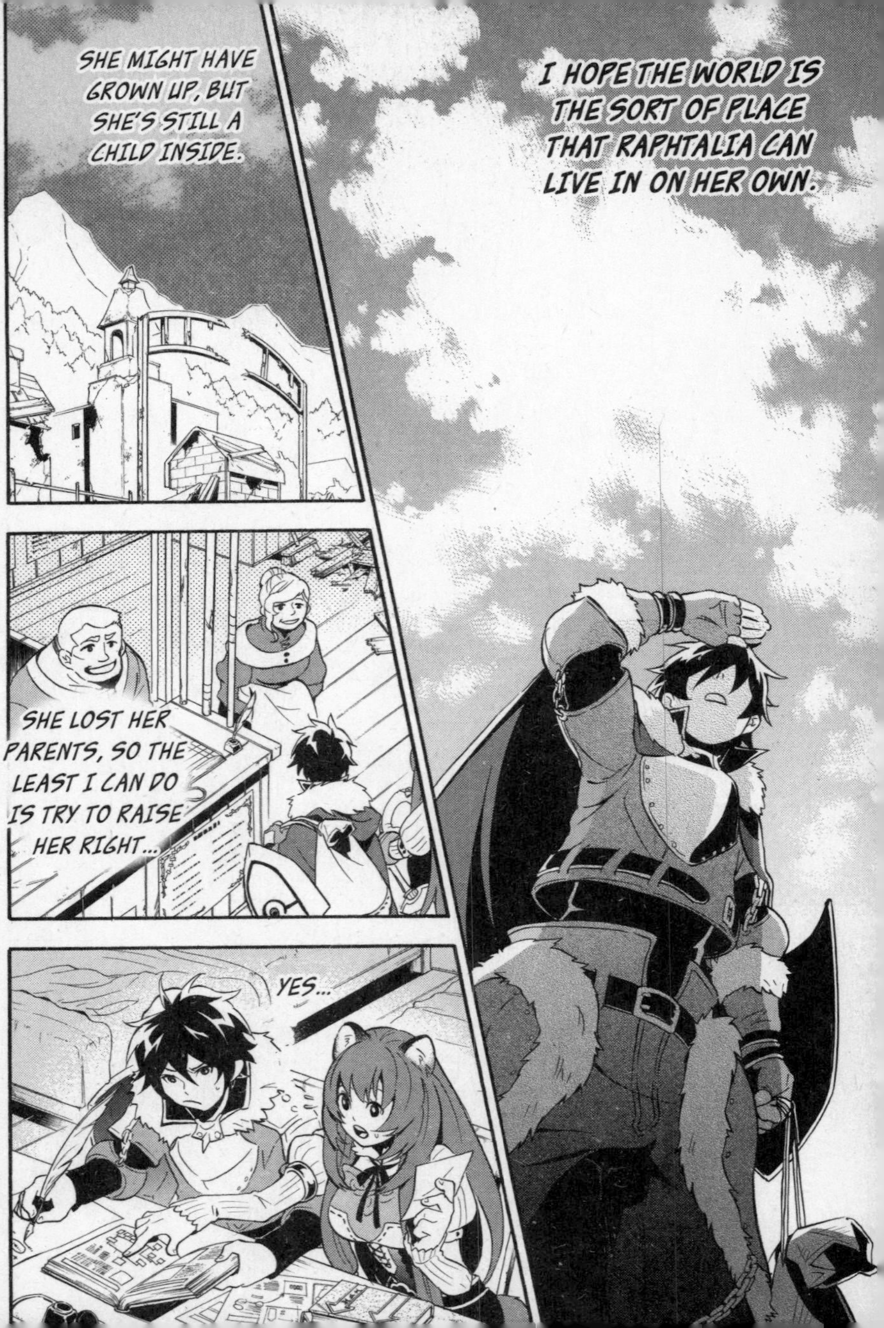
I HOPE THE WORLD IS THE SORT OF PLACE THAT RAPHTALIA CAN LIVE IN ON HER OWN.
SHE MIGHT HAVE GROWN UP, BUT SHE'S STILL A CHILD INSIDE.
SHE LOST HER PARENTS, SO THE LEAST I CAN DO IS TRY TO RAISE HER RIGHT...
YES...

THAT'S WHAT THESE FEEL-INGS ARE...

CRACK

CRACK

CRACK

LOOK! THE EGG!

WHAT?

...MI...

HM?

MR. NAO-FUMI!

CRACK!

CRACK

CRACK

THE EGG IS HATCHING!

CRACK

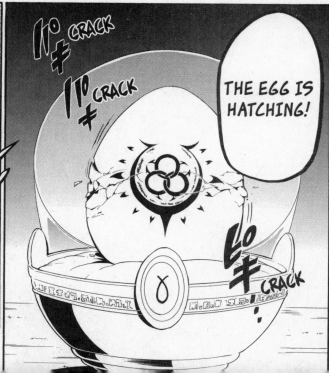

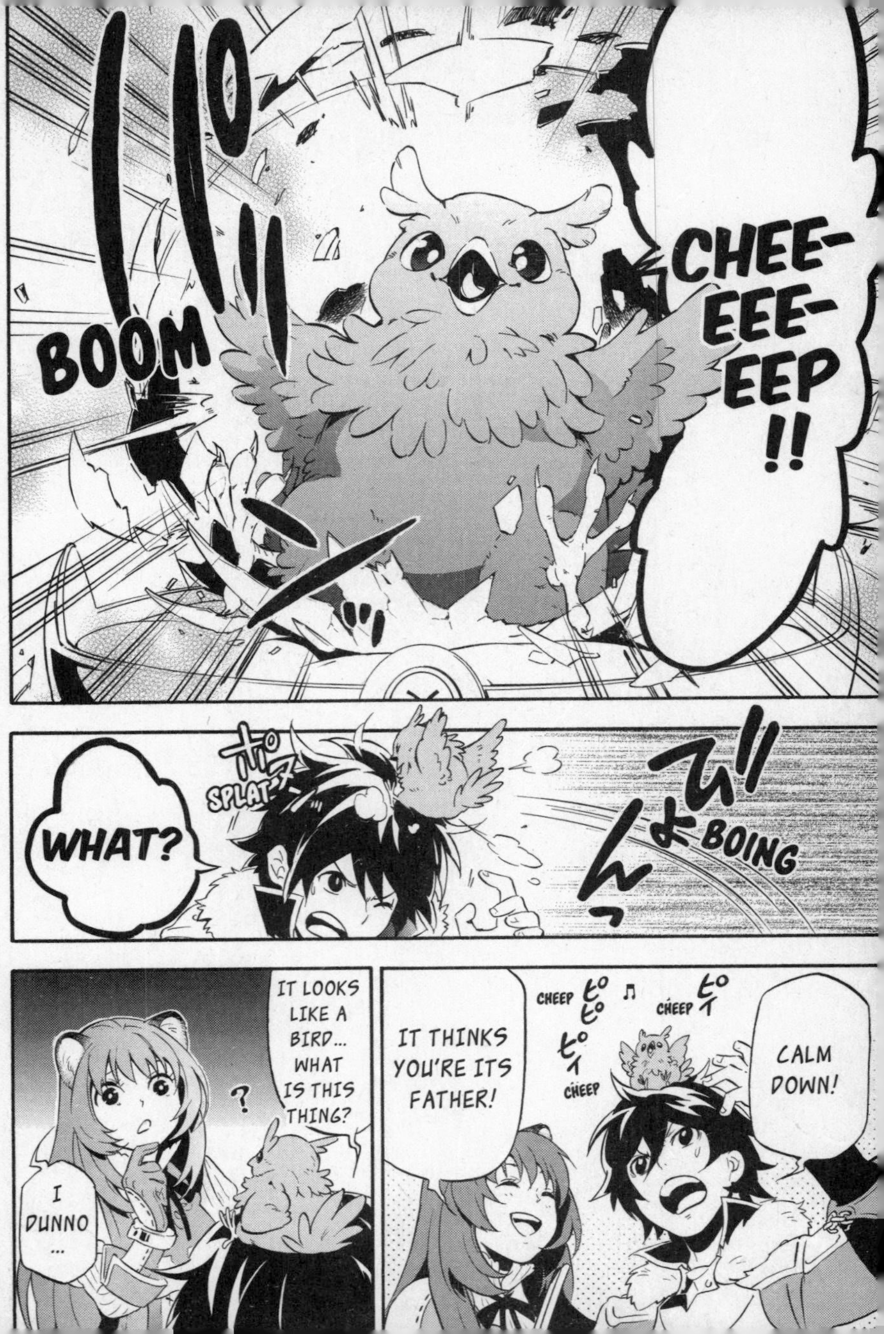
CHEE-EEE-EEP!!
BOOM
BOING
SPLAT
WHAT?
CALM DOWN!
CHEEP
CHEEP
CHEEP
IT THINKS YOU'RE ITS FATHER!
IT LOOKS LIKE A BIRD... WHAT IS THIS THING?
?
I DUNNO...

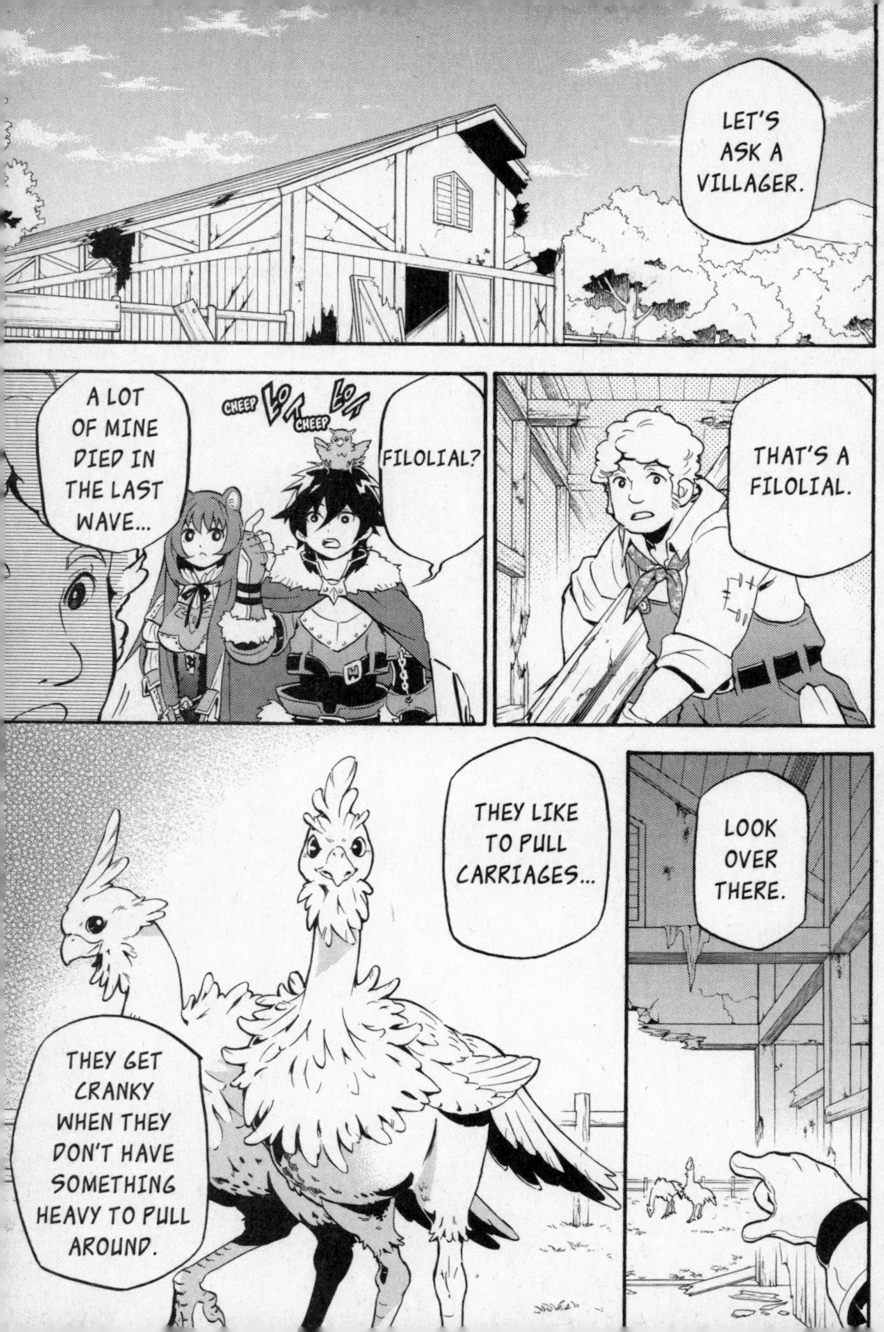
LET'S ASK A VILLAGER.
THAT'S A FILOLIAL.
FILOLIAL?
CHEEP CHEEP
A LOT OF MINE DIED IN THE LAST WAVE...
LOOK OVER THERE.
THEY LIKE TO PULL CARRIAGES...
THEY GET CRANKY WHEN THEY DON'T HAVE SOMETHING HEAVY TO PULL AROUND.

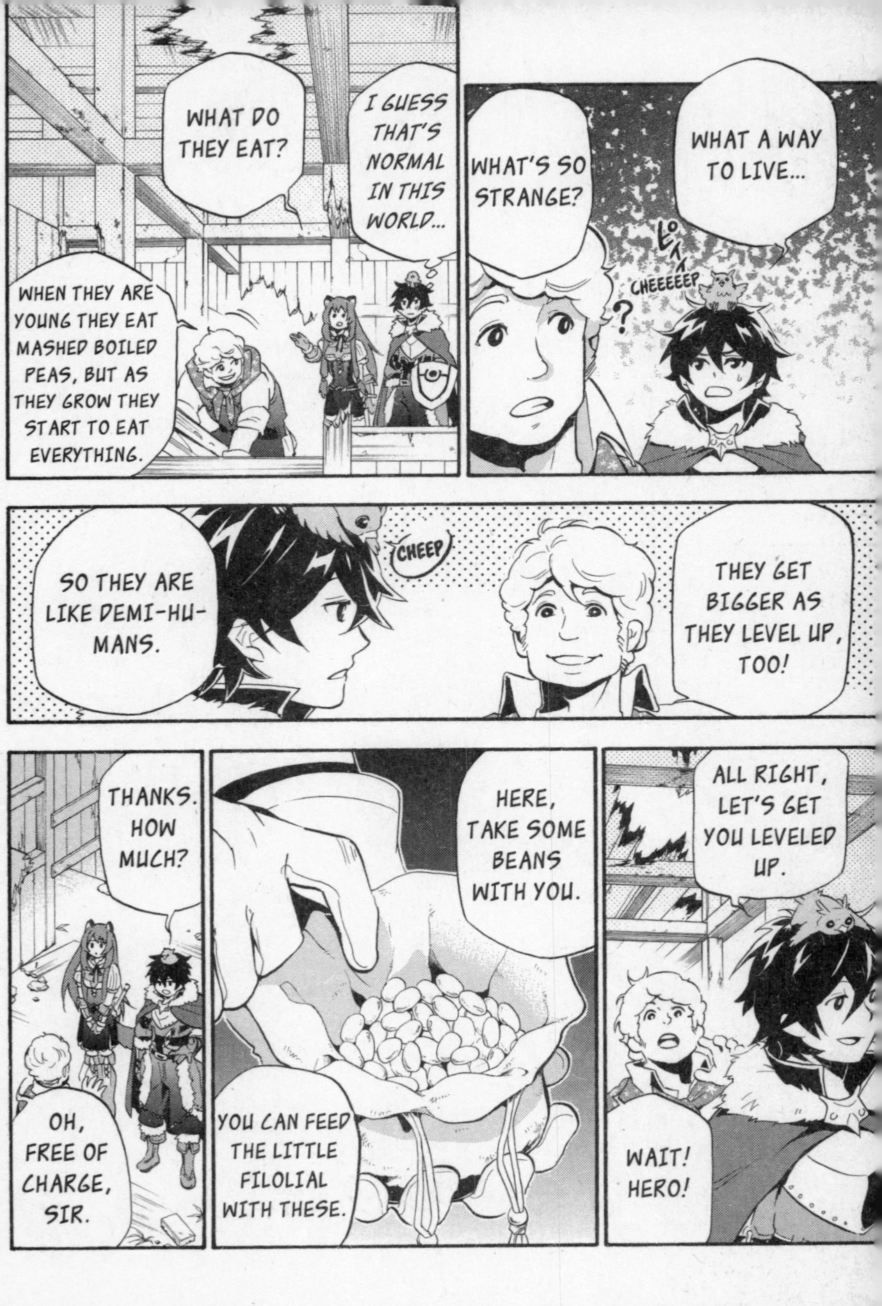
WHAT A WAY TO LIVE...
WHAT'S SO STRANGE?
CHEEEEEP
?
I GUESS THAT'S NORMAL IN THIS WORLD...
WHAT DO THEY EAT?
WHEN THEY ARE YOUNG THEY EAT MASHED BOILED PEAS, BUT AS THEY GROW THEY START TO EAT EVERYTHING.
THEY GET BIGGER AS THEY LEVEL UP, TOO!
CHEEP
SO THEY ARE LIKE DEMI-HUMANS.
ALL RIGHT, LET'S GET YOU LEVELED UP.
WAIT! HERO!
HERE, TAKE SOME BEANS WITH YOU.
YOU CAN FEED THE LITTLE FILOLIAL WITH THESE.
THANKS. HOW MUCH?
OH, FREE OF CHARGE, SIR.

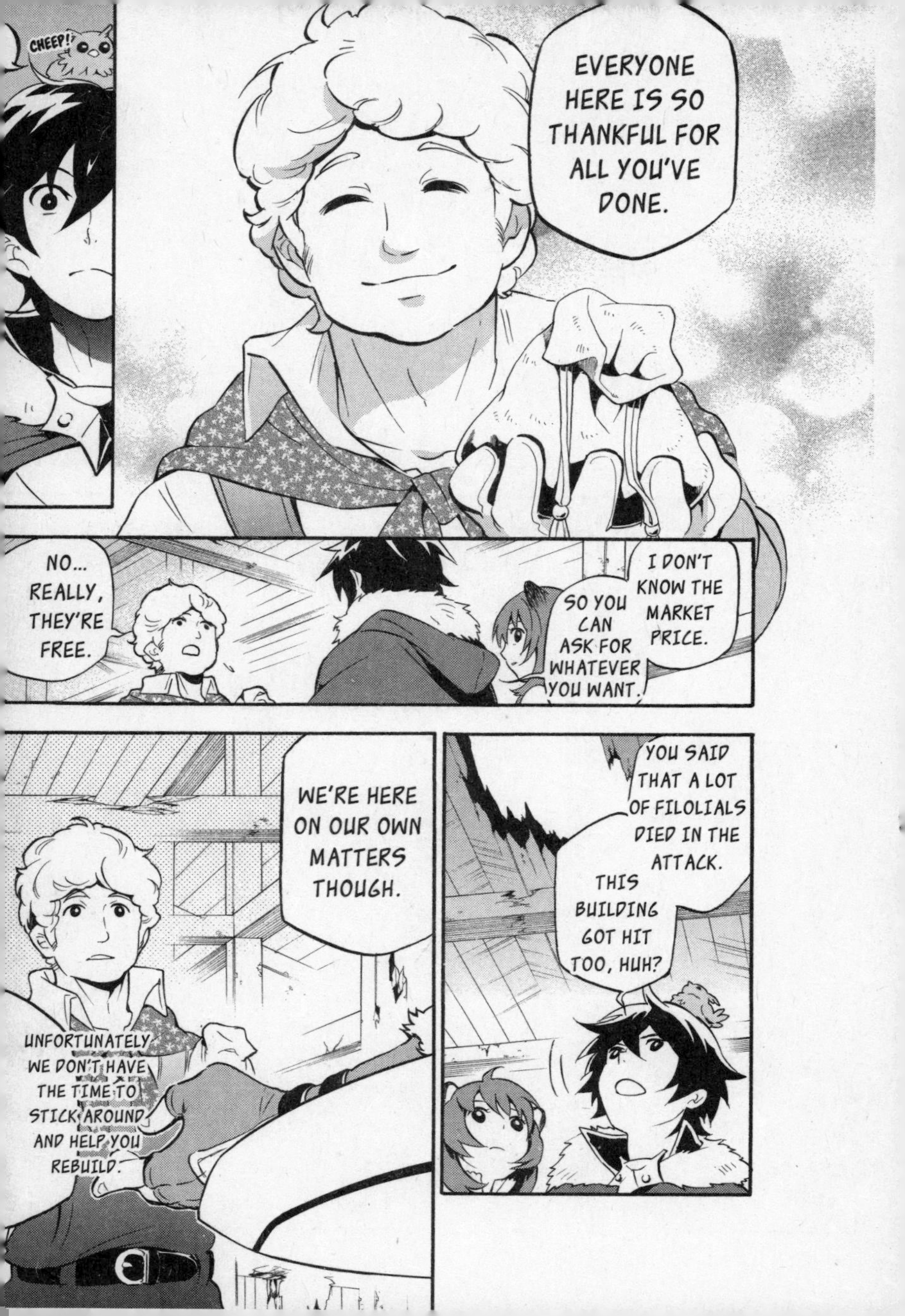
EVERYONE HERE IS SO THANKFUL FOR ALL YOU'VE DONE.
CHEEP!
I DON'T KNOW THE MARKET PRICE.
SO YOU CAN ASK FOR WHATEVER YOU WANT.
NO... REALLY, THEY'RE FREE.
YOU SAID THAT A LOT OF FILOLIALS DIED IN THE ATTACK.
THIS BUILDING GOT HIT TOO, HUH?
WE'RE HERE ON OUR OWN MATTERS THOUGH.
UNFORTUNATELY WE DON'T HAVE THE TIME TO STICK AROUND AND HELP YOU REBUILD.

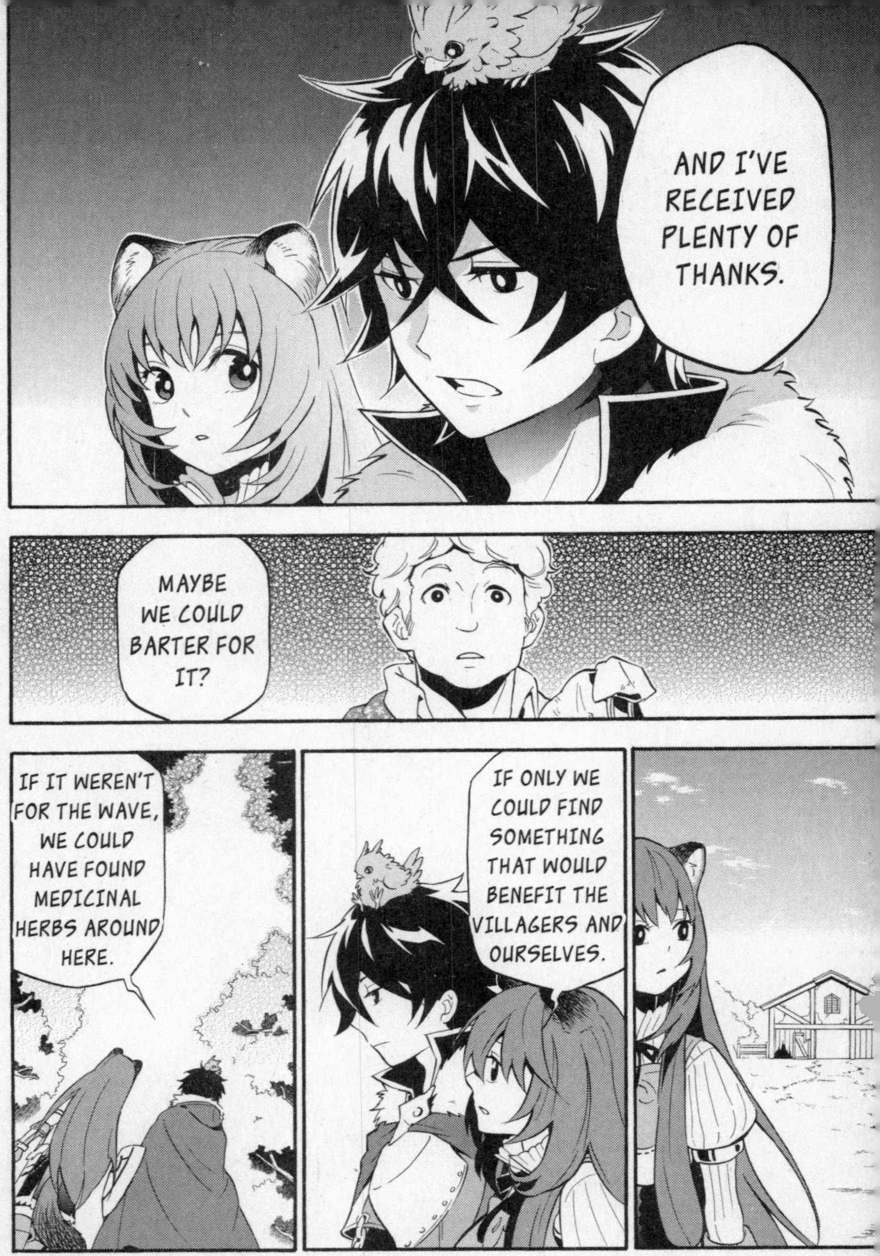
AND I'VE RECEIVED PLENTY OF THANKS.
MAYBE WE COULD BARTER FOR IT?
IF ONLY WE COULD FIND SOMETHING THAT WOULD BENEFIT THE VILLAGERS AND OURSELVES.
IF IT WEREN'T FOR THE WAVE, WE COULD HAVE FOUND MEDICINAL HERBS AROUND HERE.

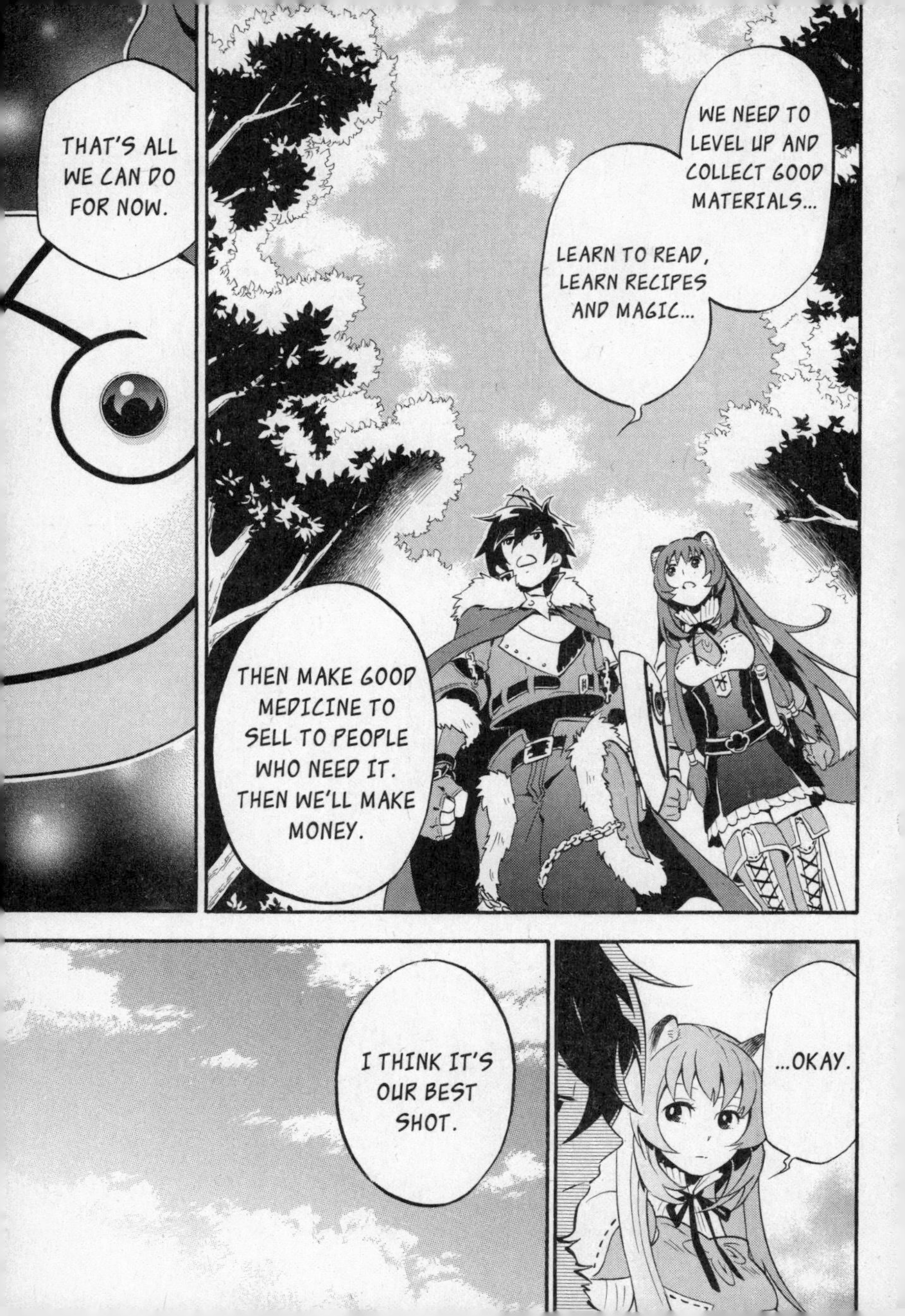
WE NEED TO LEVEL UP AND COLLECT GOOD MATERIALS...
LEARN TO READ, LEARN RECIPES AND MAGIC...
THEN MAKE GOOD MEDICINE TO SELL TO PEOPLE WHO NEED IT. THEN WE'LL MAKE MONEY.
THAT'S ALL WE CAN DO FOR NOW.
...OKAY.
I THINK IT'S OUR BEST SHOT.

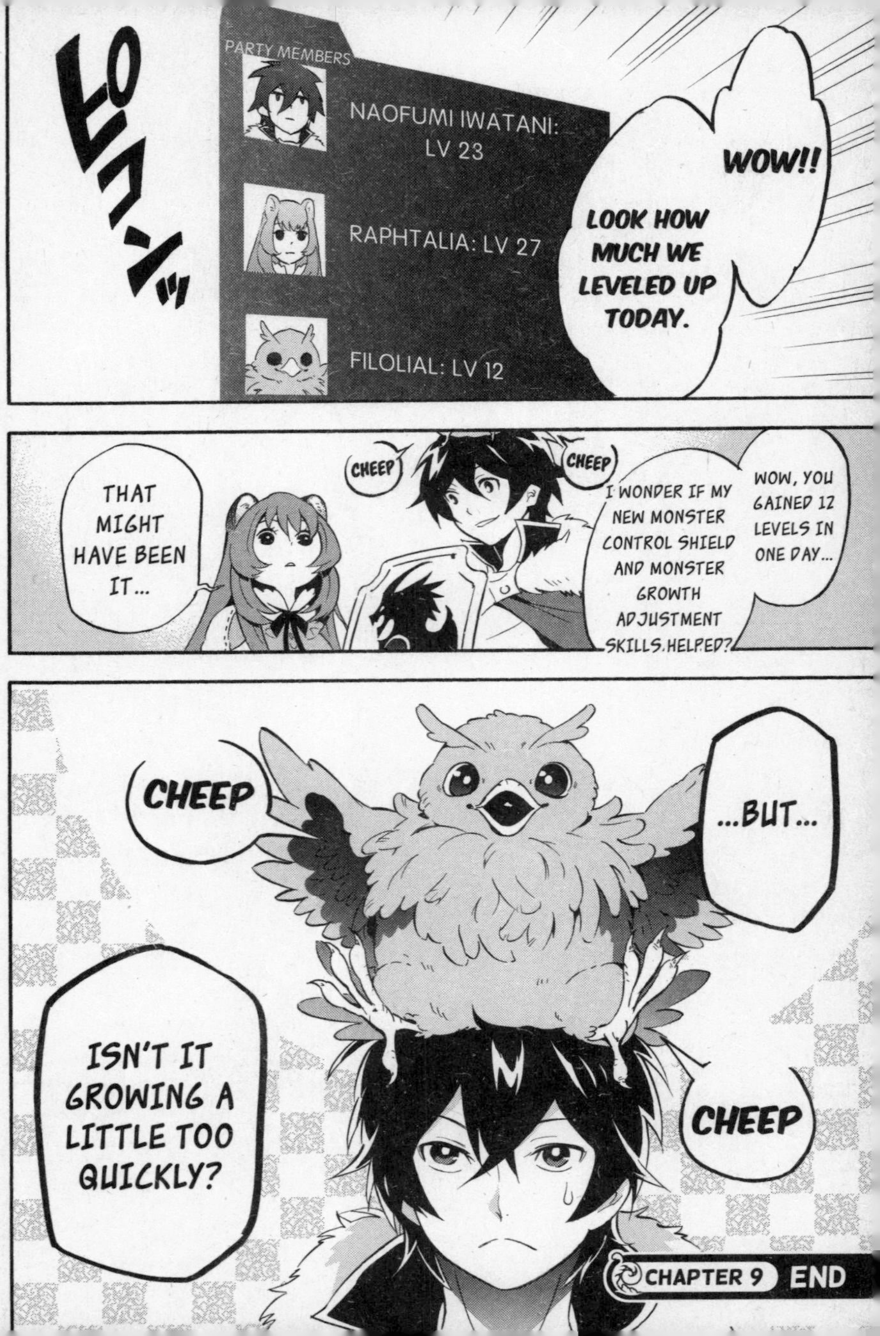
WOW!!
LOOK HOW MUCH WE LEVELED UP TODAY.
PARTY MEMBERS
NAOFUMI IWATANI: LV 23
RAPHTALIA: LV 27
FILOLIAL: LV 12
ピコンッ
WOW, YOU GAINED 12 LEVELS IN ONE DAY...
CHEEP
I WONDER IF MY NEW MONSTER CONTROL SHIELD AND MONSTER GROWTH ADJUSTMENT SKILLS HELPED?
CHEEP
THAT MIGHT HAVE BEEN IT...
...BUT...
CHEEP
CHEEP
ISN'T IT GROWING A LITTLE TOO QUICKLY?
CHAPTER 9 END

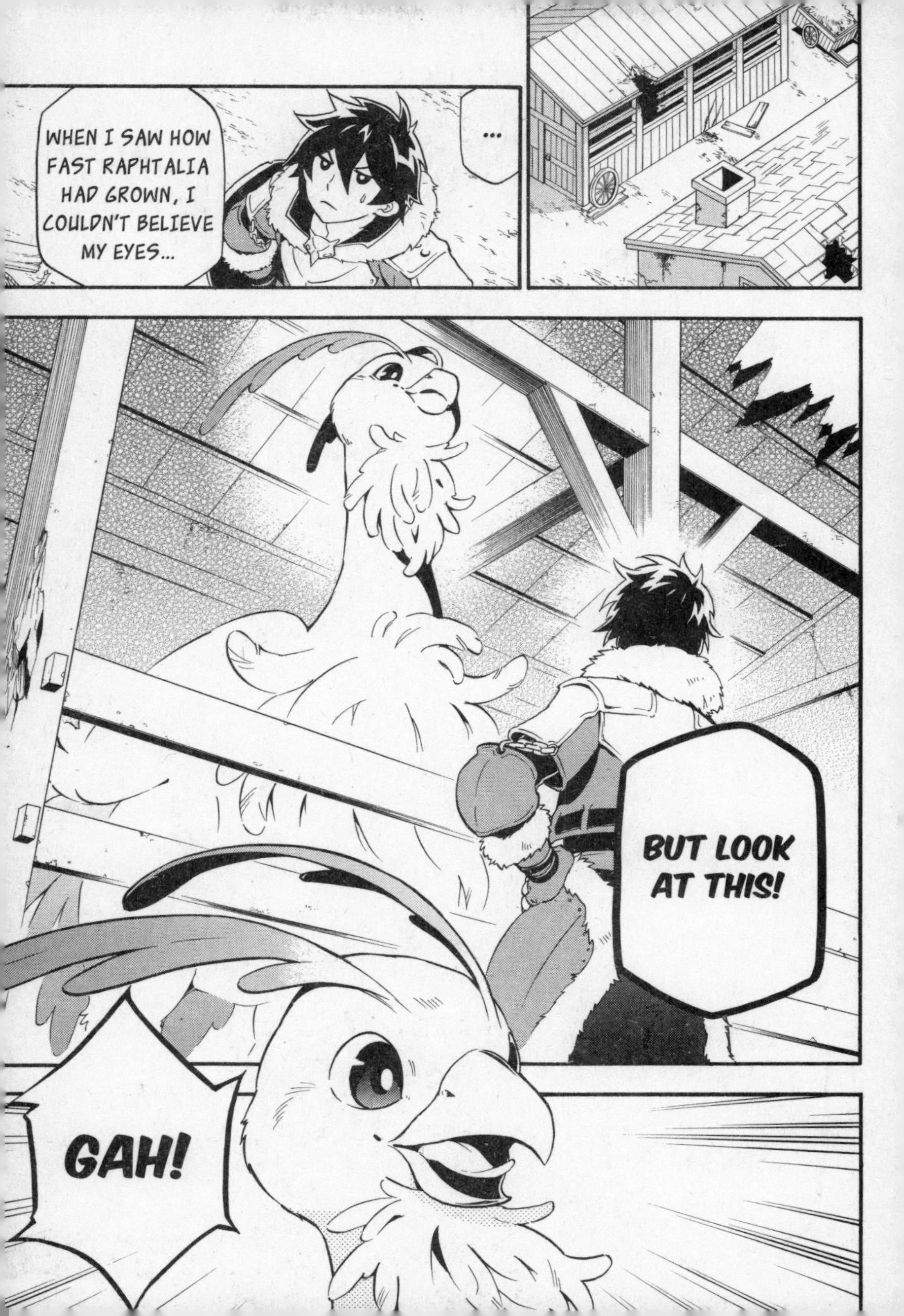
...
WHEN I SAW HOW FAST RAPHTALIA HAD GROWN, I COULDN'T BELIEVE MY EYES...
BUT LOOK AT THIS!
GAH!

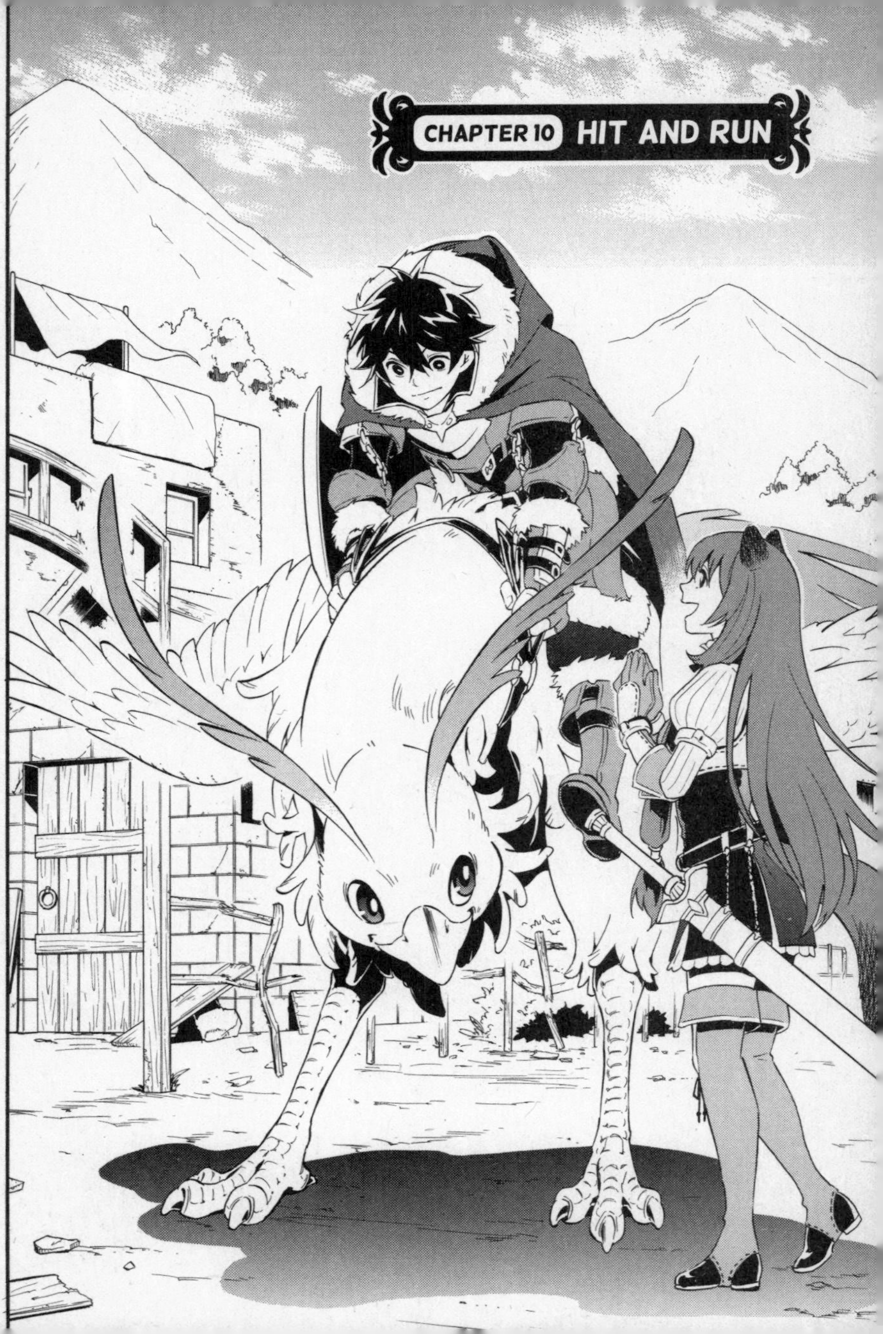
CHAPTER 10 HIT AND RUN

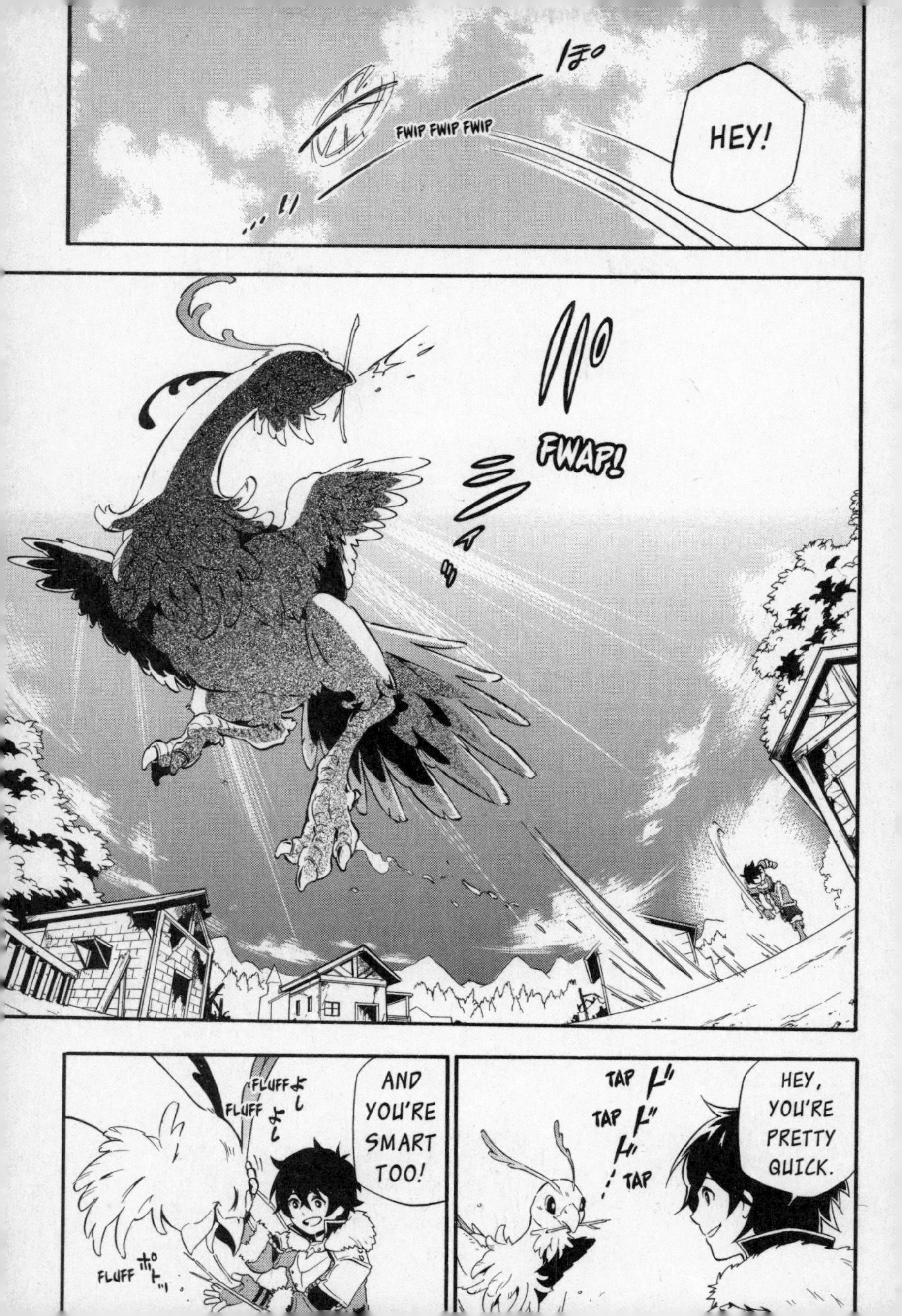

HEY!
ぽ
FWIP FWIP FWIP
...!!
パ
FWAP!
HEY, YOU'RE PRETTY QUICK.
TAP
TAP
TAP
ド
ド
ド
AND YOU'RE SMART TOO!
FLUFF
FLUFF
よし
よし
FLUFF
ポト

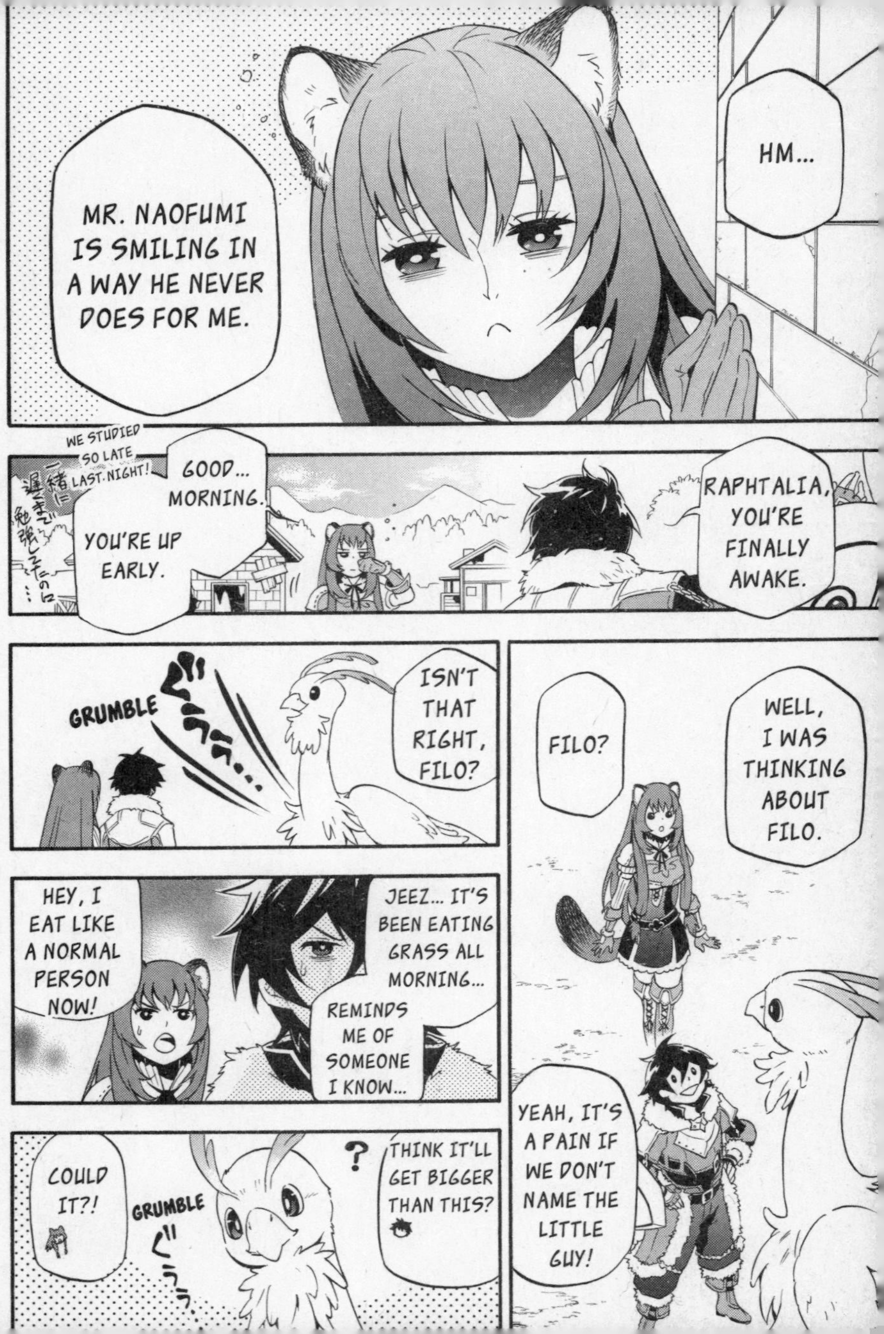
HM...
MR. NAOFUMI IS SMILING IN A WAY HE NEVER DOES FOR ME.
RAPHTALIA, YOU'RE FINALLY AWAKE.
GOOD... MORNING.
YOU'RE UP EARLY.
WE STUDIED SO LATE LAST NIGHT!
一緒に遅くまで勉強してたのに…
WELL, I WAS THINKING ABOUT FILO.
FILO?
YEAH, IT'S A PAIN IF WE DON'T NAME THE LITTLE GUY!
ISN'T THAT RIGHT, FILO?
GRUMBLE
JEEZ... IT'S BEEN EATING GRASS ALL MORNING...
REMINDS ME OF SOMEONE I KNOW...
HEY, I EAT LIKE A NORMAL PERSON NOW!
THINK IT'LL GET BIGGER THAN THIS?
?
GRUMBLE
COULD IT?!

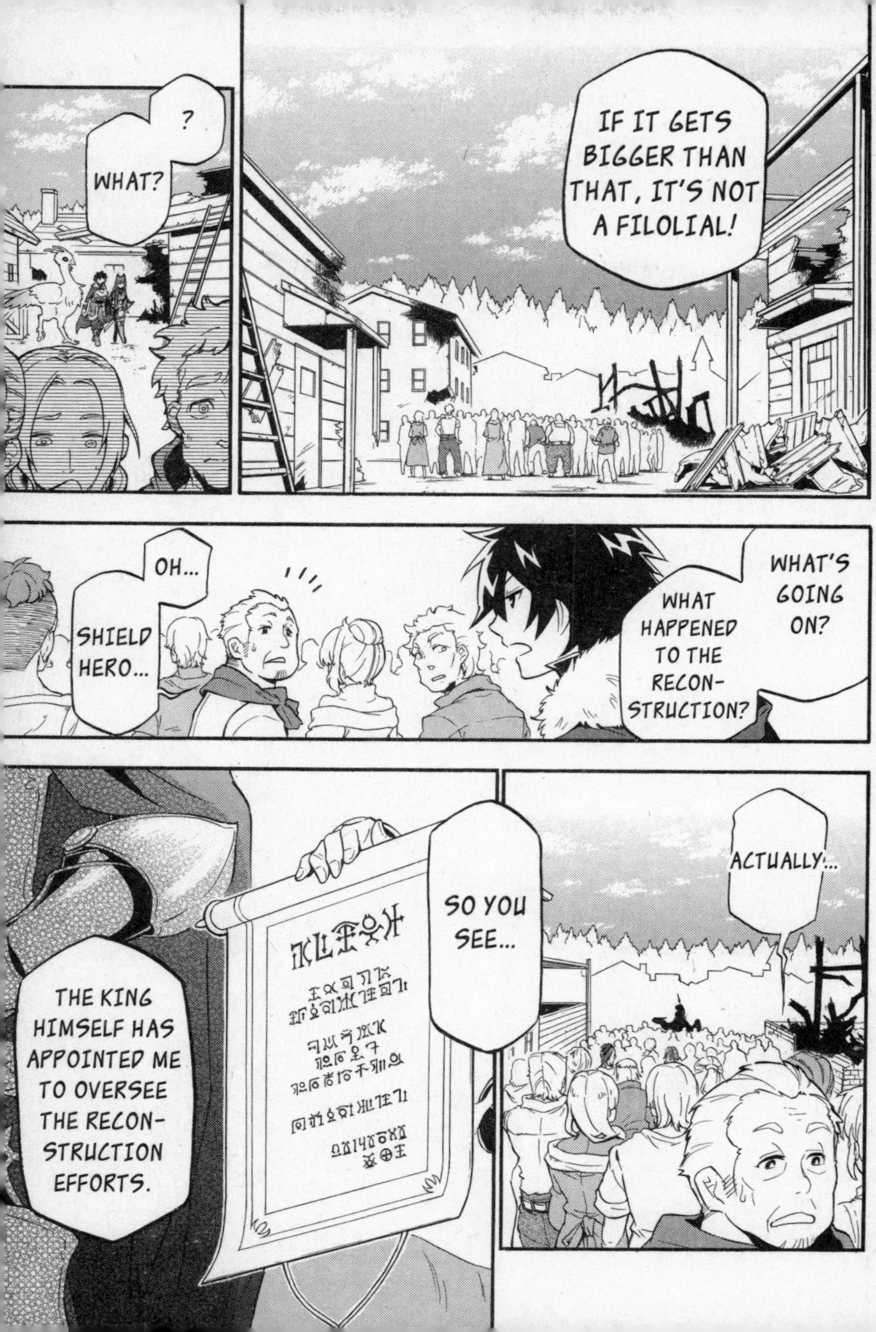
IF IT GETS BIGGER THAN THAT, IT'S NOT A FILOLIAL!
?
WHAT?
WHAT'S GOING ON?
WHAT HAPPENED TO THE RECON-STRUCTION?
OH...
SHIELD HERO...
ACTUALLY...
SO YOU SEE...
THE KING HIMSELF HAS APPOINTED ME TO OVERSEE THE RECON-STRUCTION EFFORTS.

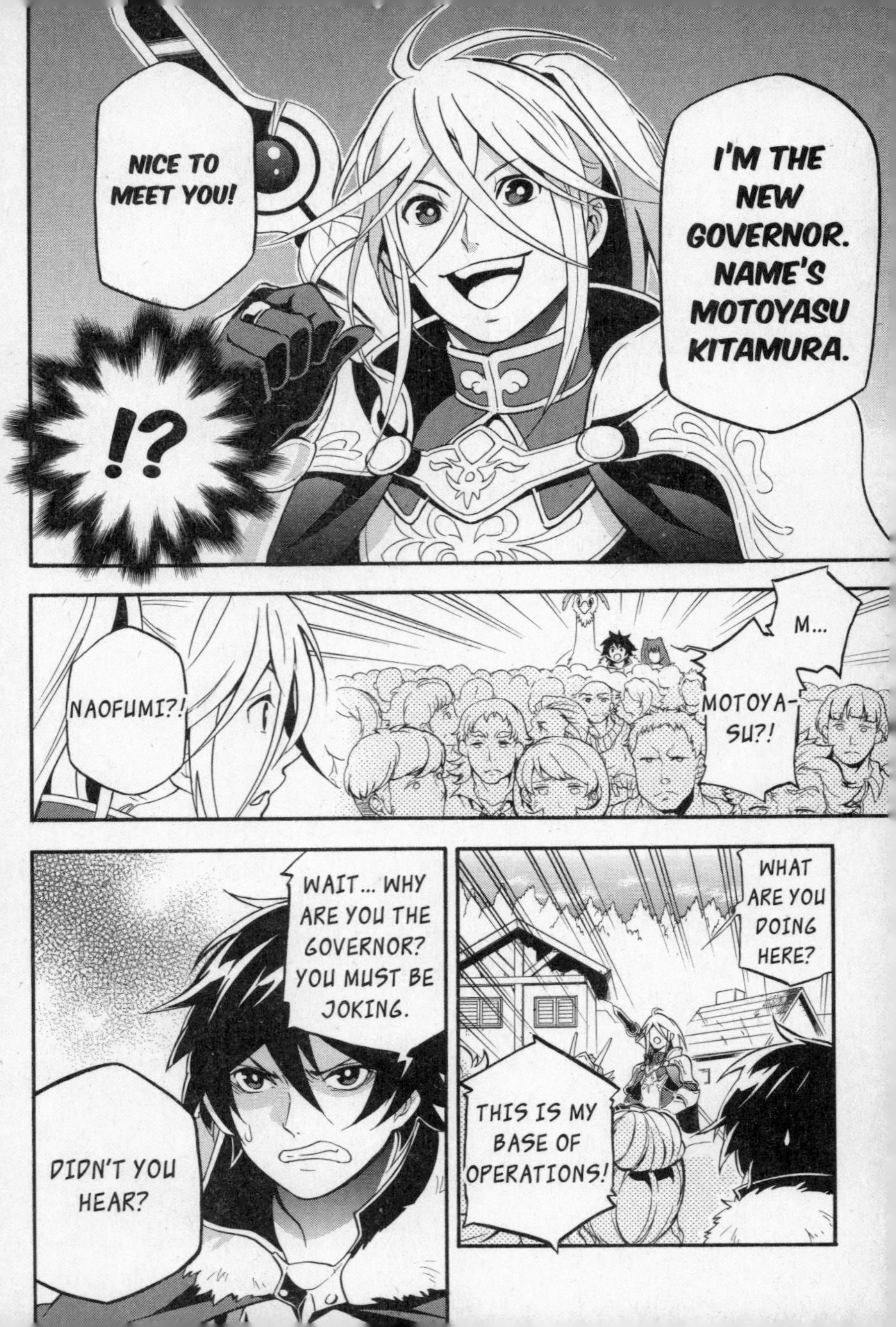
I'M THE NEW GOVERNOR. NAME'S MOTOYASU KITAMURA.
NICE TO MEET YOU!
!?
M...
MOTOYA-SU?!
NAOFUMI?!
WHAT ARE YOU DOING HERE?
THIS IS MY BASE OF OPERATIONS!
WAIT... WHY ARE YOU THE GOVERNOR? YOU MUST BE JOKING.
DIDN'T YOU HEAR?

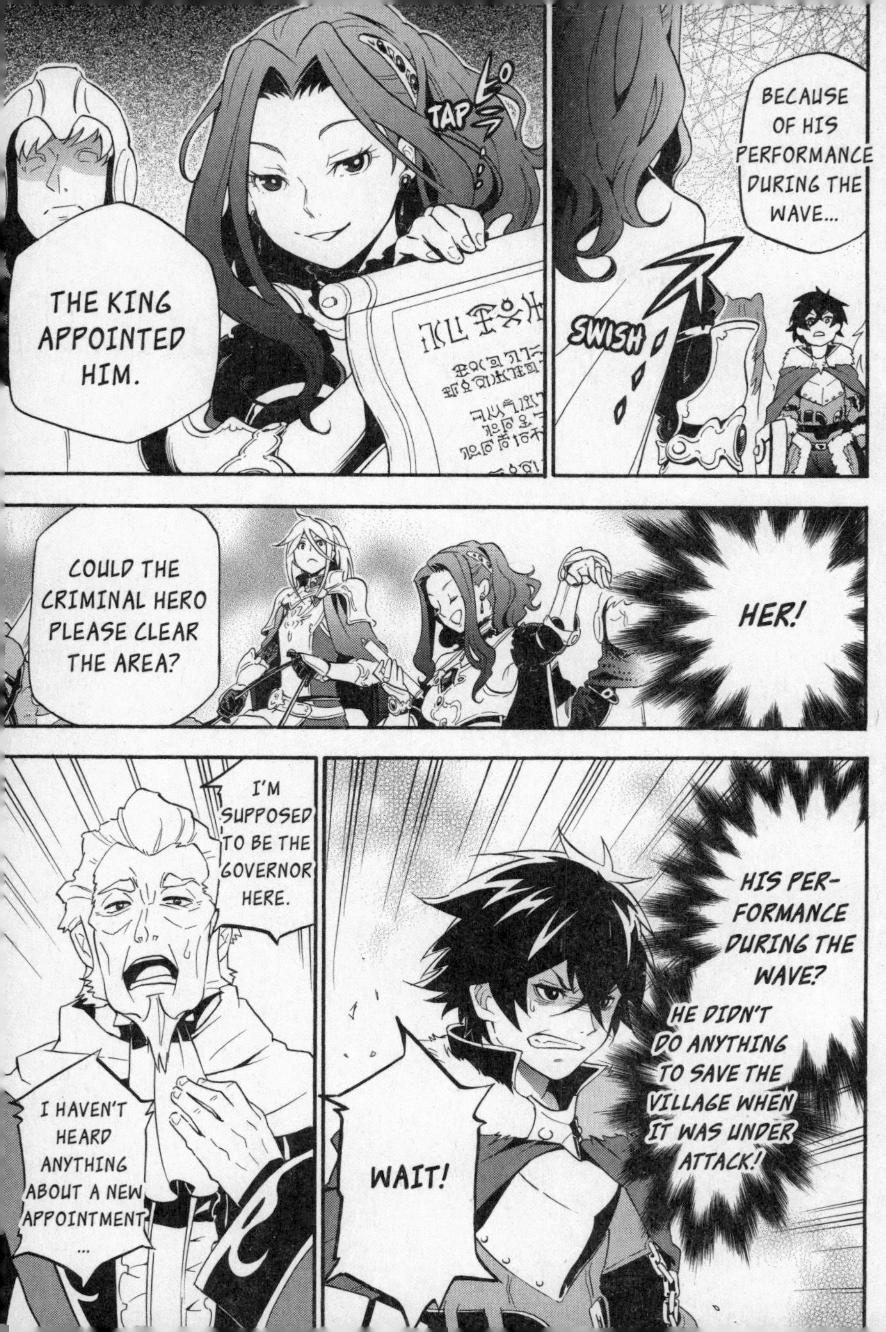
BECAUSE OF HIS PERFORMANCE DURING THE WAVE...
SWISH
TAP
THE KING APPOINTED HIM.
HER!
COULD THE CRIMINAL HERO PLEASE CLEAR THE AREA?
HIS PER-FORMANCE DURING THE WAVE?
HE DIDN'T DO ANYTHING TO SAVE THE VILLAGE WHEN IT WAS UNDER ATTACK!
WAIT!
I'M SUPPOSED TO BE THE GOVERNOR HERE.
I HAVEN'T HEARD ANYTHING ABOUT A NEW APPOINTMENT...

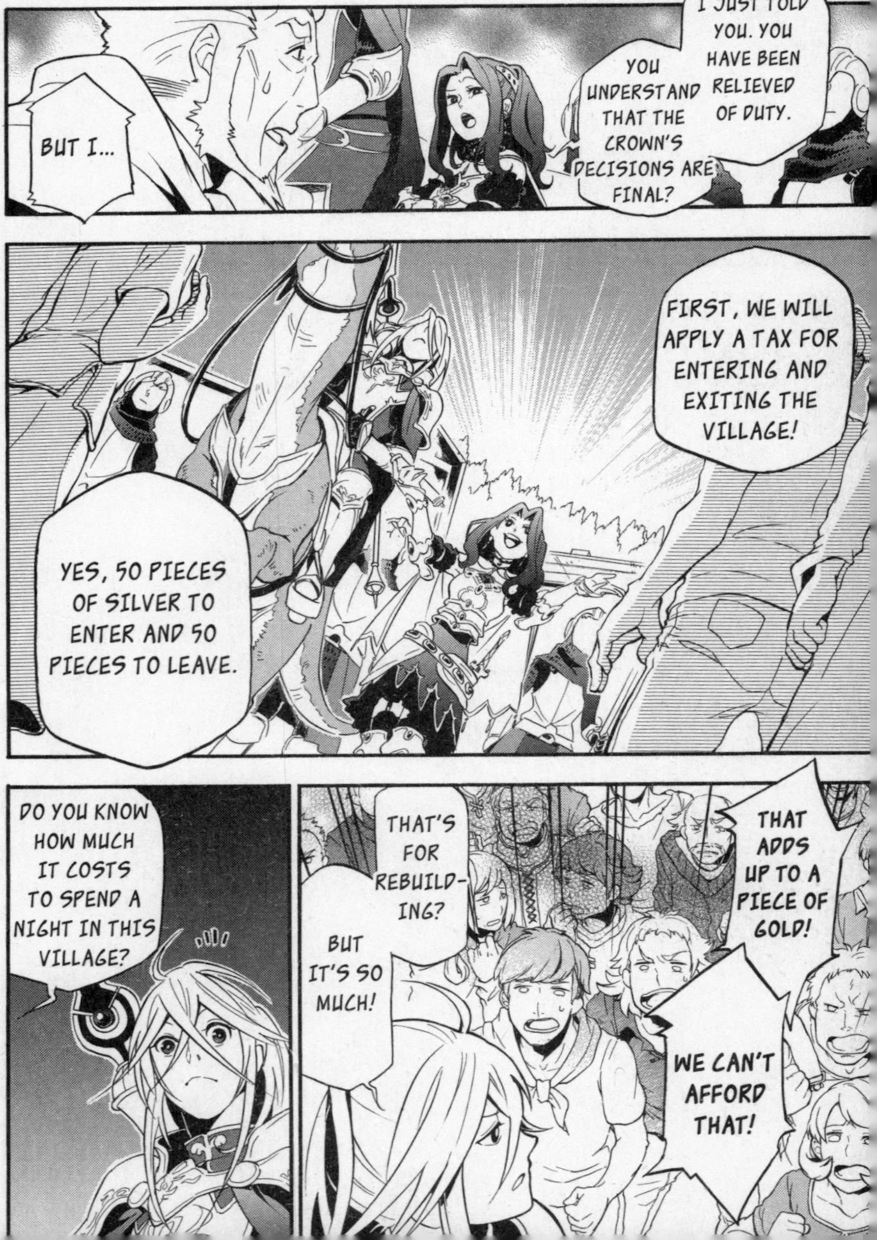

I JUST TOLD YOU. YOU HAVE BEEN RELIEVED OF DUTY.
YOU UNDERSTAND THAT THE CROWN'S DECISIONS ARE FINAL?
BUT I...
FIRST, WE WILL APPLY A TAX FOR ENTERING AND EXITING THE VILLAGE!
YES, 50 PIECES OF SILVER TO ENTER AND 50 PIECES TO LEAVE.
THAT ADDS UP TO A PIECE OF GOLD!
THAT'S FOR REBUILD-ING?
BUT IT'S SO MUCH!
WE CAN'T AFFORD THAT!
DO YOU KNOW HOW MUCH IT COSTS TO SPEND A NIGHT IN THIS VILLAGE?

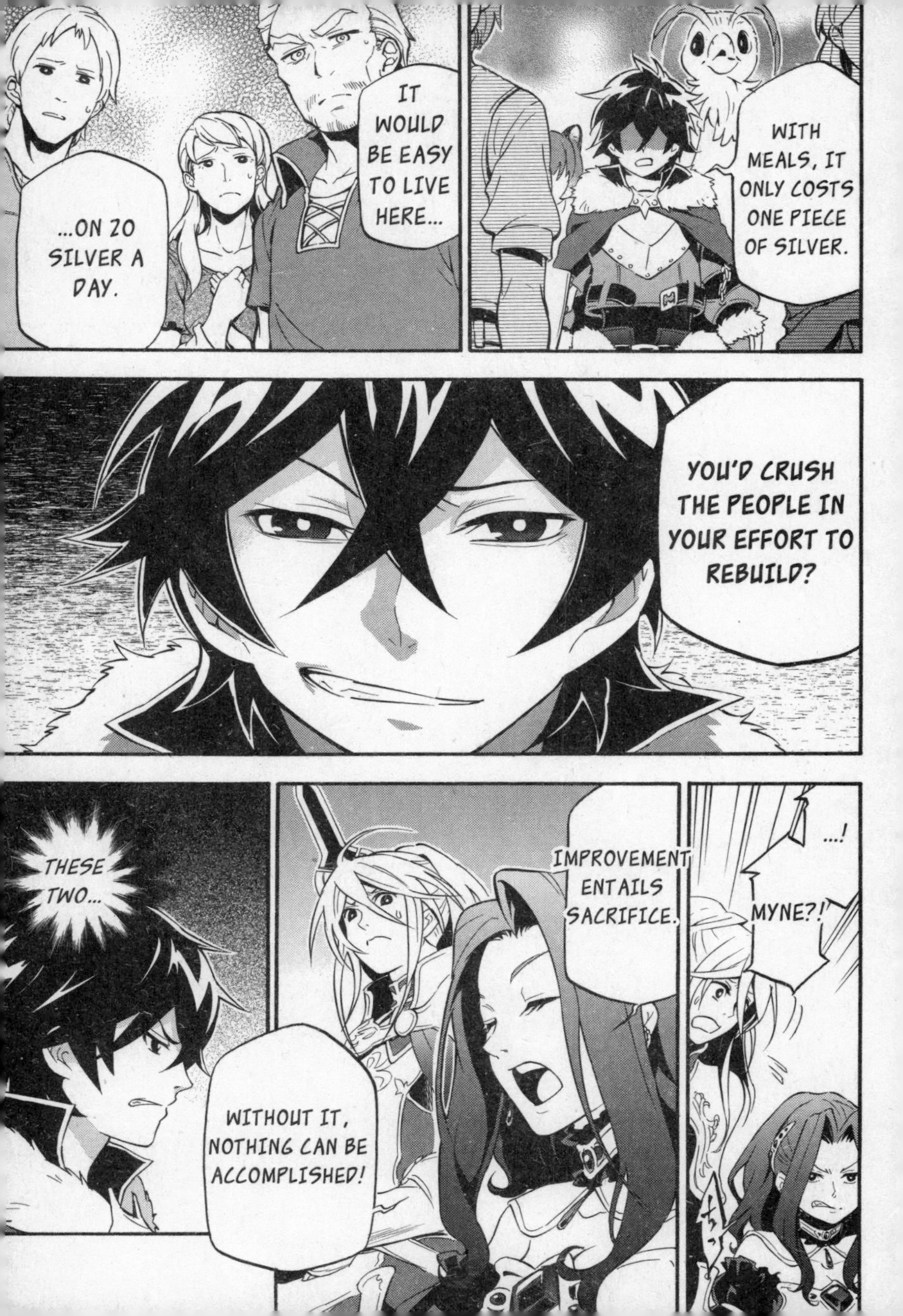
WITH MEALS, IT ONLY COSTS ONE PIECE OF SILVER.
IT WOULD BE EASY TO LIVE HERE...
...ON 20 SILVER A DAY.
YOU'D CRUSH THE PEOPLE IN YOUR EFFORT TO REBUILD?
...!
MYNE?!
IMPROVEMENT ENTAILS SACRIFICE.
WITHOUT IT, NOTHING CAN BE ACCOMPLISHED!
THESE TWO...

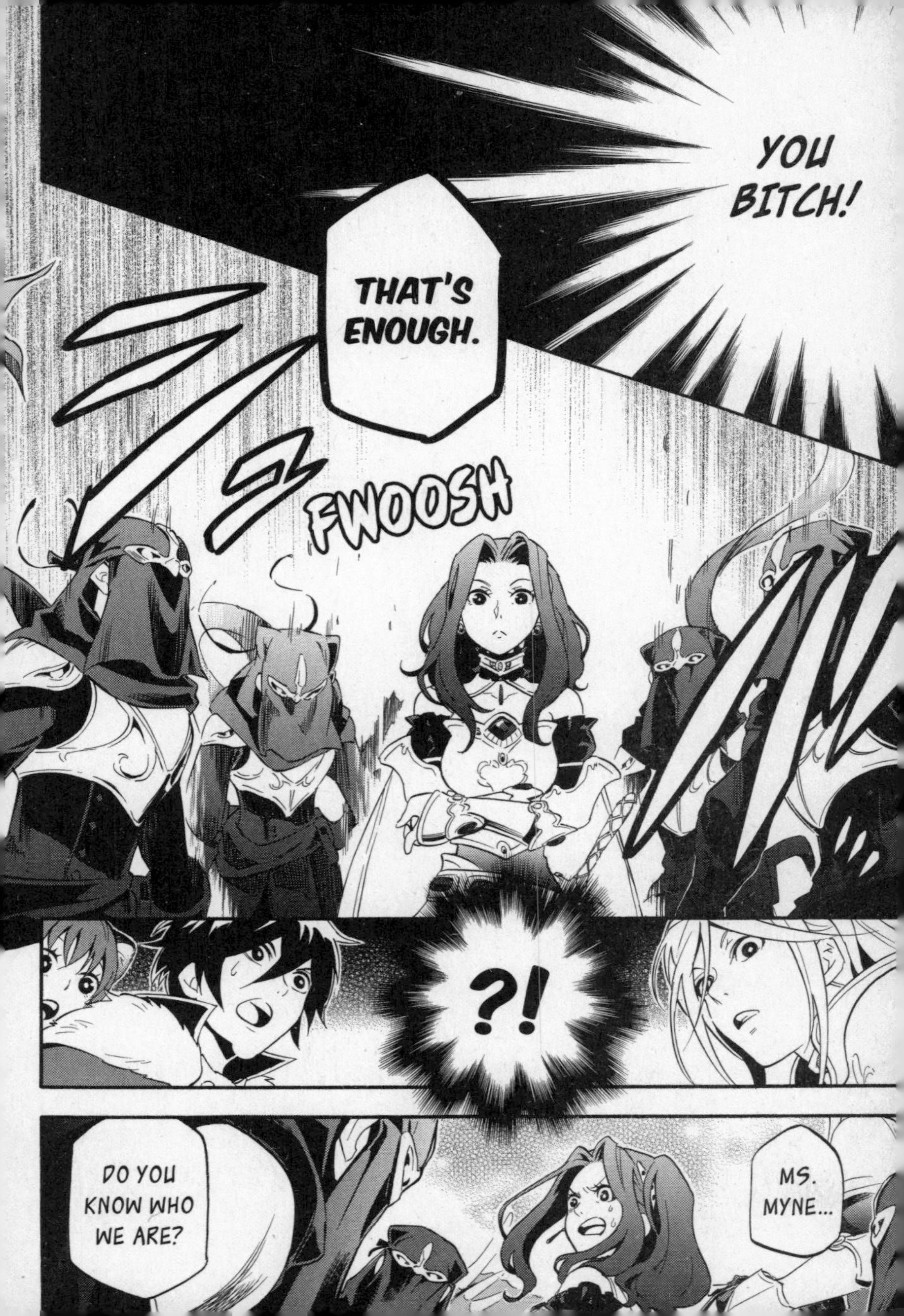
YOU BITCH!
THAT'S ENOUGH.
FWOOSH
?!
MS. MYNE...
DO YOU KNOW WHO WE ARE?

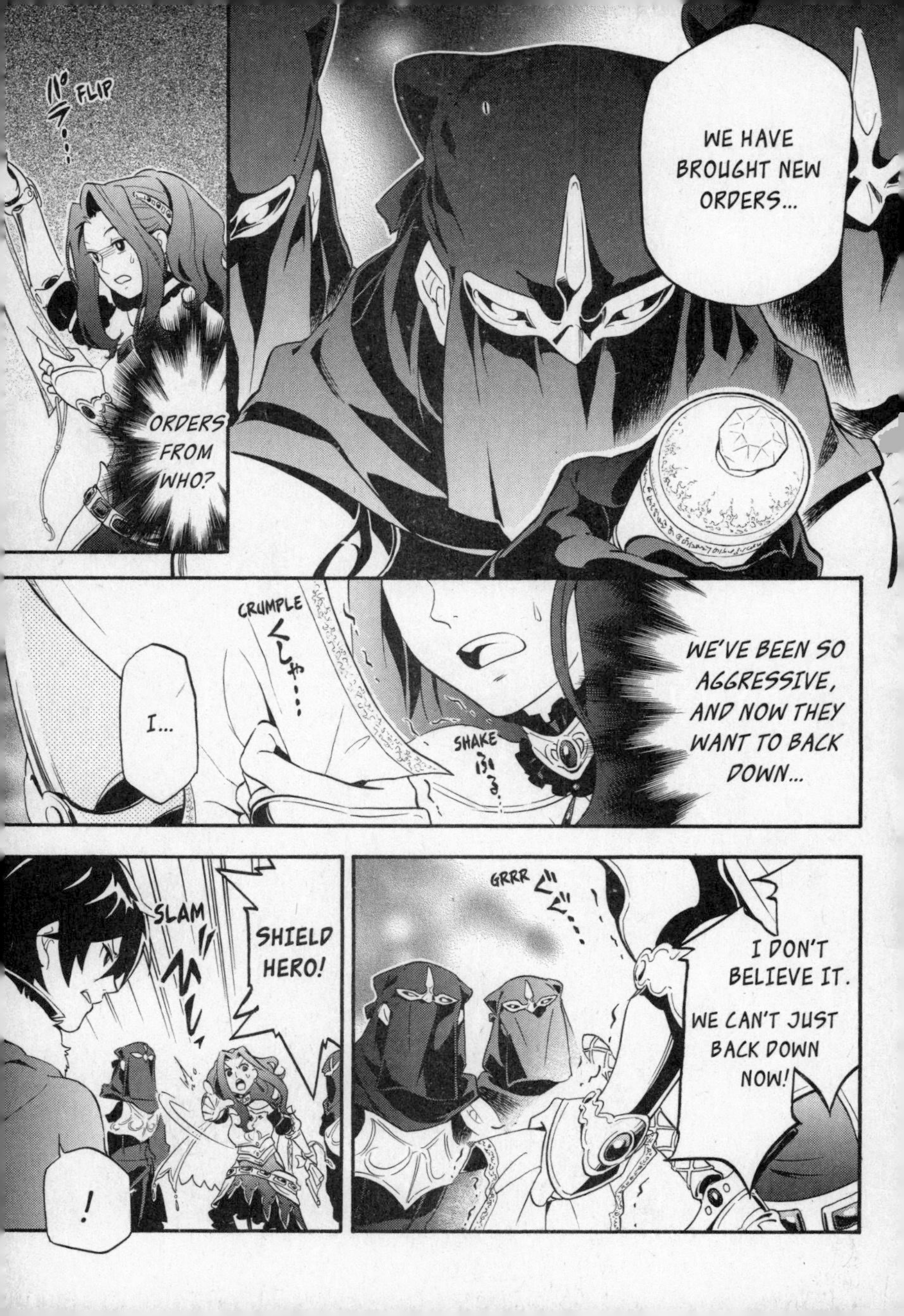
WE HAVE BROUGHT NEW ORDERS...
FLIP
ORDERS FROM WHO?
WE'VE BEEN SO AGGRESSIVE, AND NOW THEY WANT TO BACK DOWN...
SHAKE
CRUMPLE
くしゃ...
I...
GRRR
I DON'T BELIEVE IT.
WE CAN'T JUST BACK DOWN NOW!
SHIELD HERO!
SLAM
!

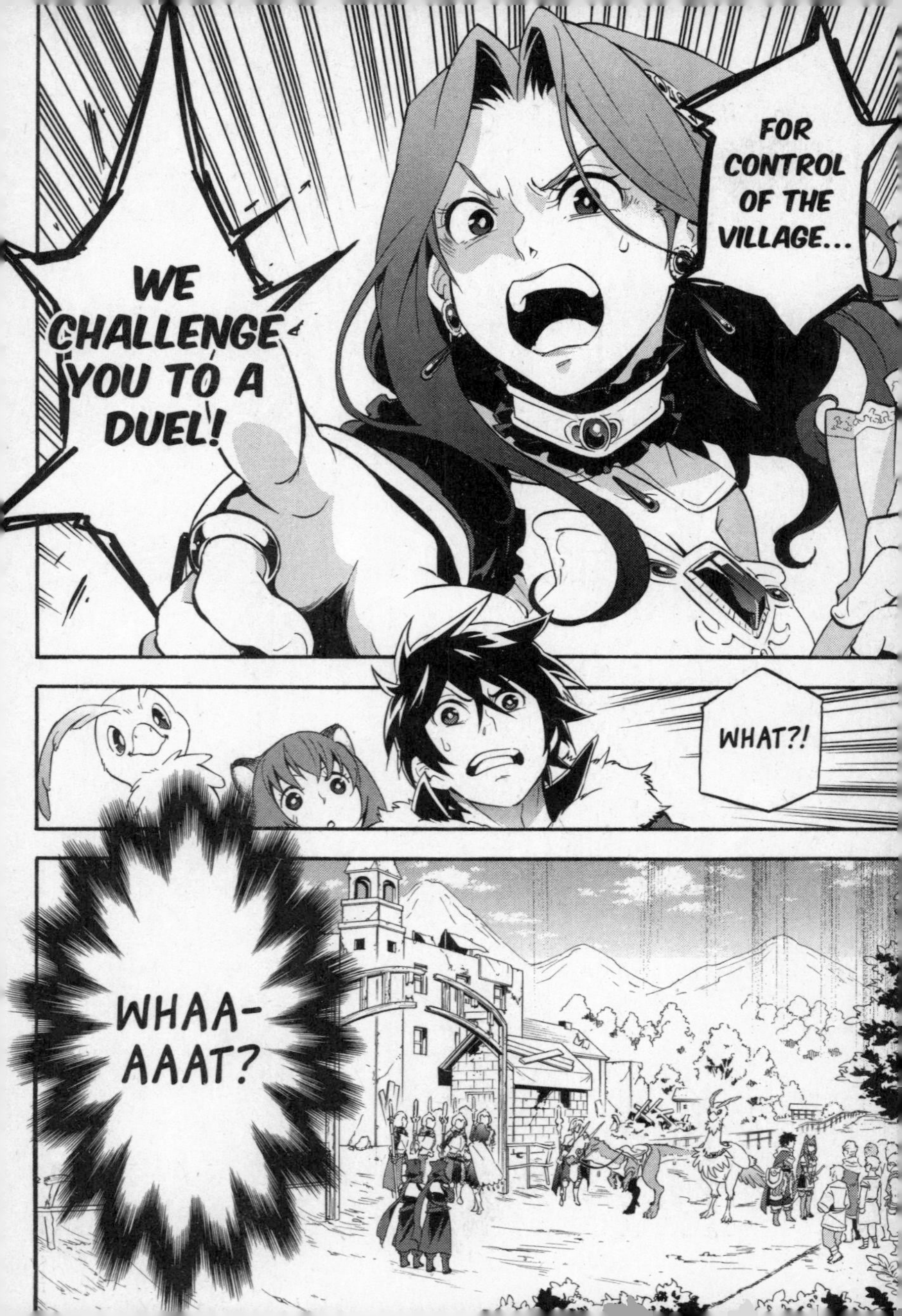
FOR CONTROL OF THE VILLAGE...
WE CHALLENGE YOU TO A DUEL!
WHAT?!
WHAA-AAAT?

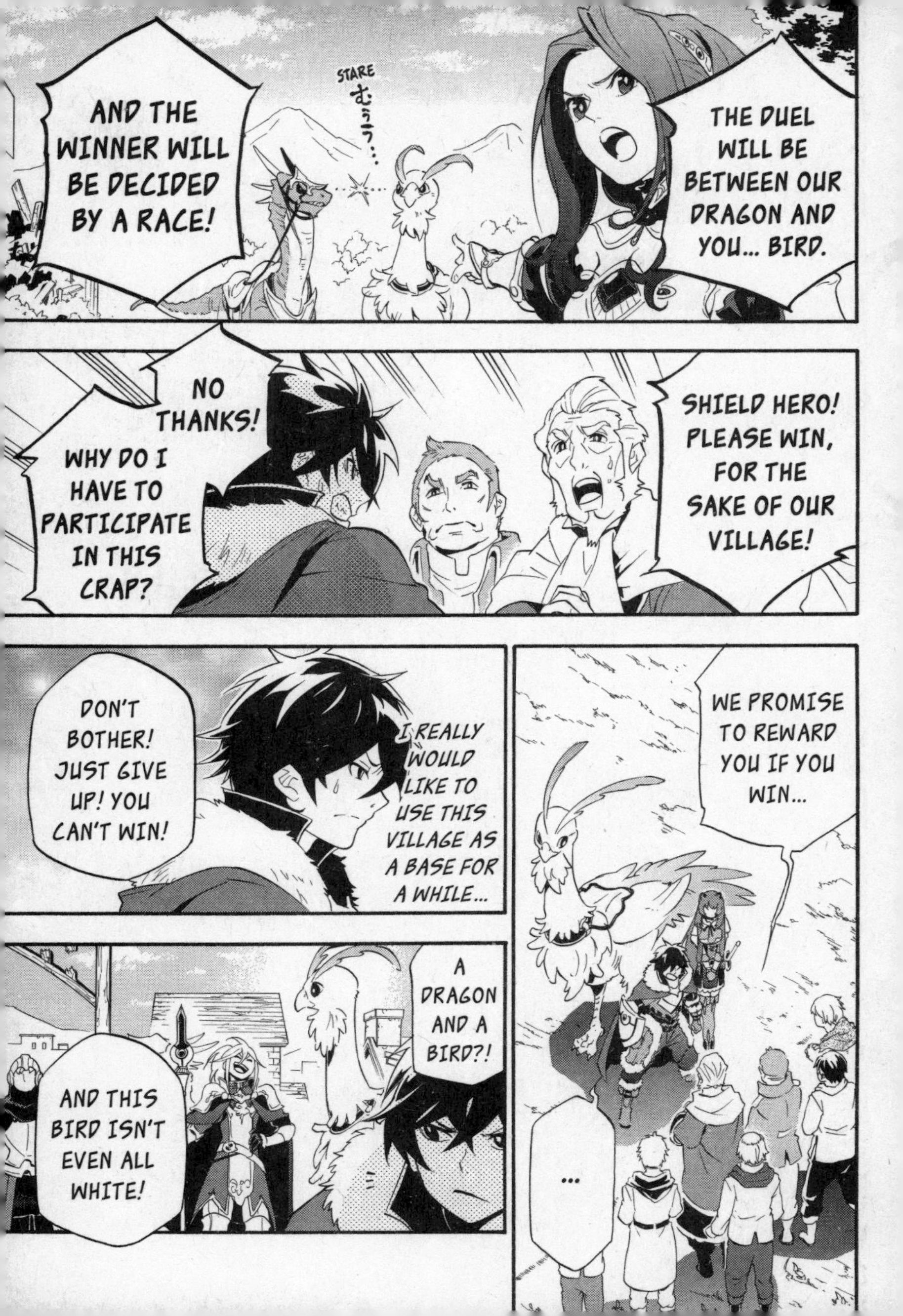
THE DUEL WILL BE BETWEEN OUR DRAGON AND YOU... BIRD.
STARE
AND THE WINNER WILL BE DECIDED BY A RACE!
SHIELD HERO! PLEASE WIN, FOR THE SAKE OF OUR VILLAGE!
NO THANKS!
WHY DO I HAVE TO PARTICIPATE IN THIS CRAP?
WE PROMISE TO REWARD YOU IF YOU WIN...
...
I REALLY WOULD LIKE TO USE THIS VILLAGE AS A BASE FOR A WHILE...
DON'T BOTHER! JUST GIVE UP! YOU CAN'T WIN!
A DRAGON AND A BIRD?!
AND THIS BIRD ISN'T EVEN ALL WHITE!

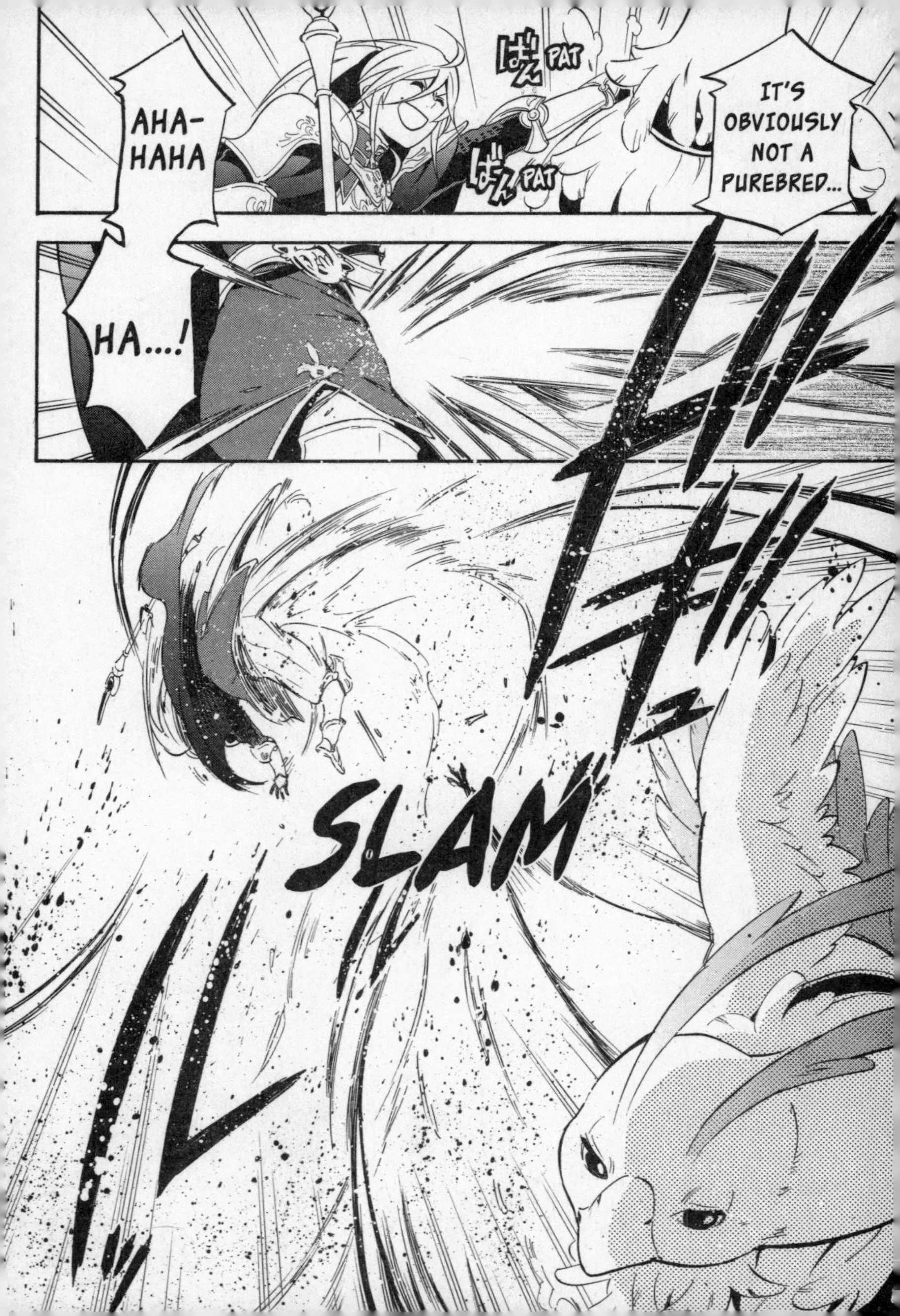
IT'S OBVIOUSLY NOT A PUREBRED...
ぱん PAT
ぱん PAT
AHA-HAHA
HA...!
SLAM

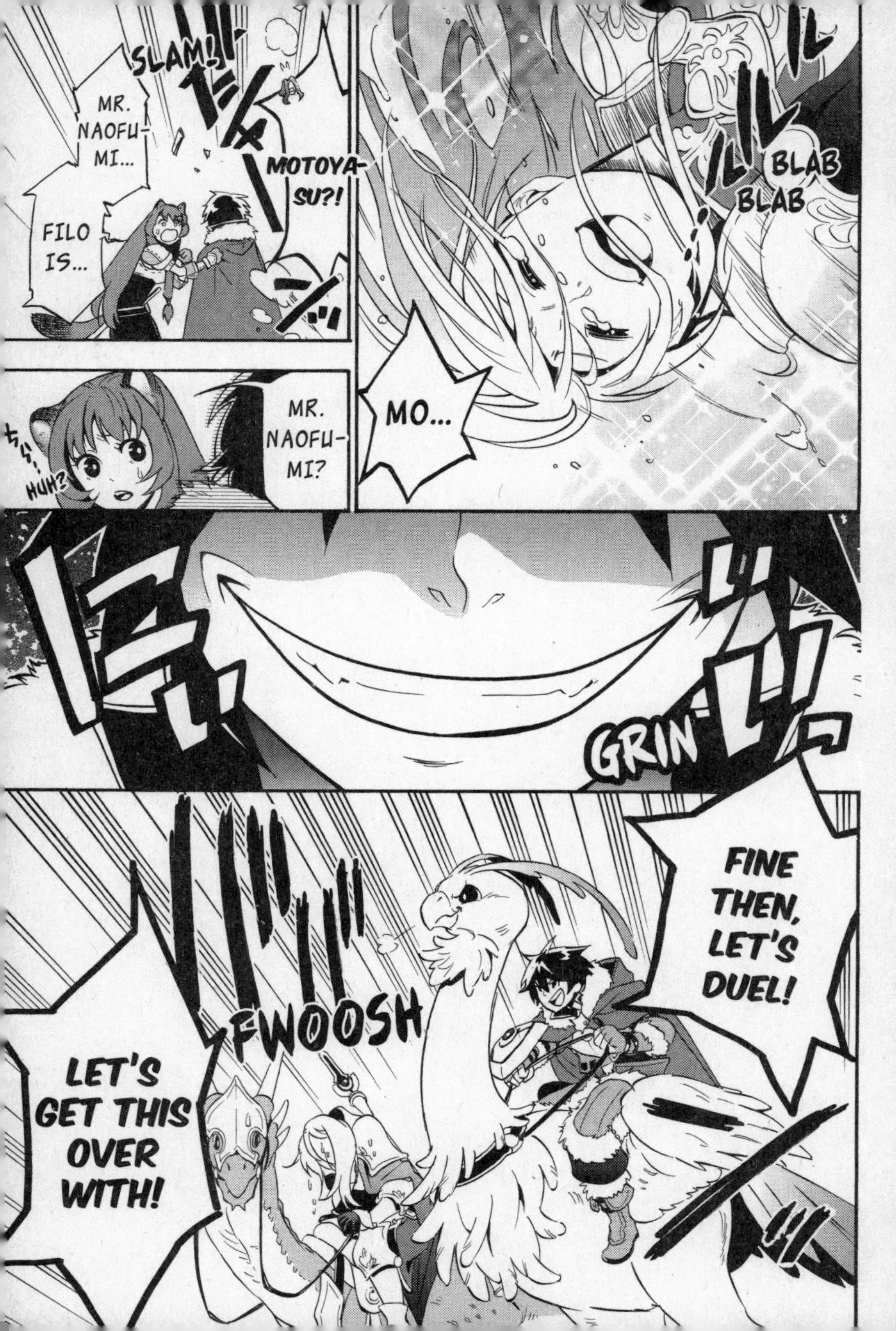
BLAB BLAB
MO...
SLAM!
MOTOYA-SU?!
MR. NAOFU-MI...
FILO IS...
MR. NAOFU-MI?
HUH?
GRIN
FINE THEN, LET'S DUEL!
FWOOSH
LET'S GET THIS OVER WITH!

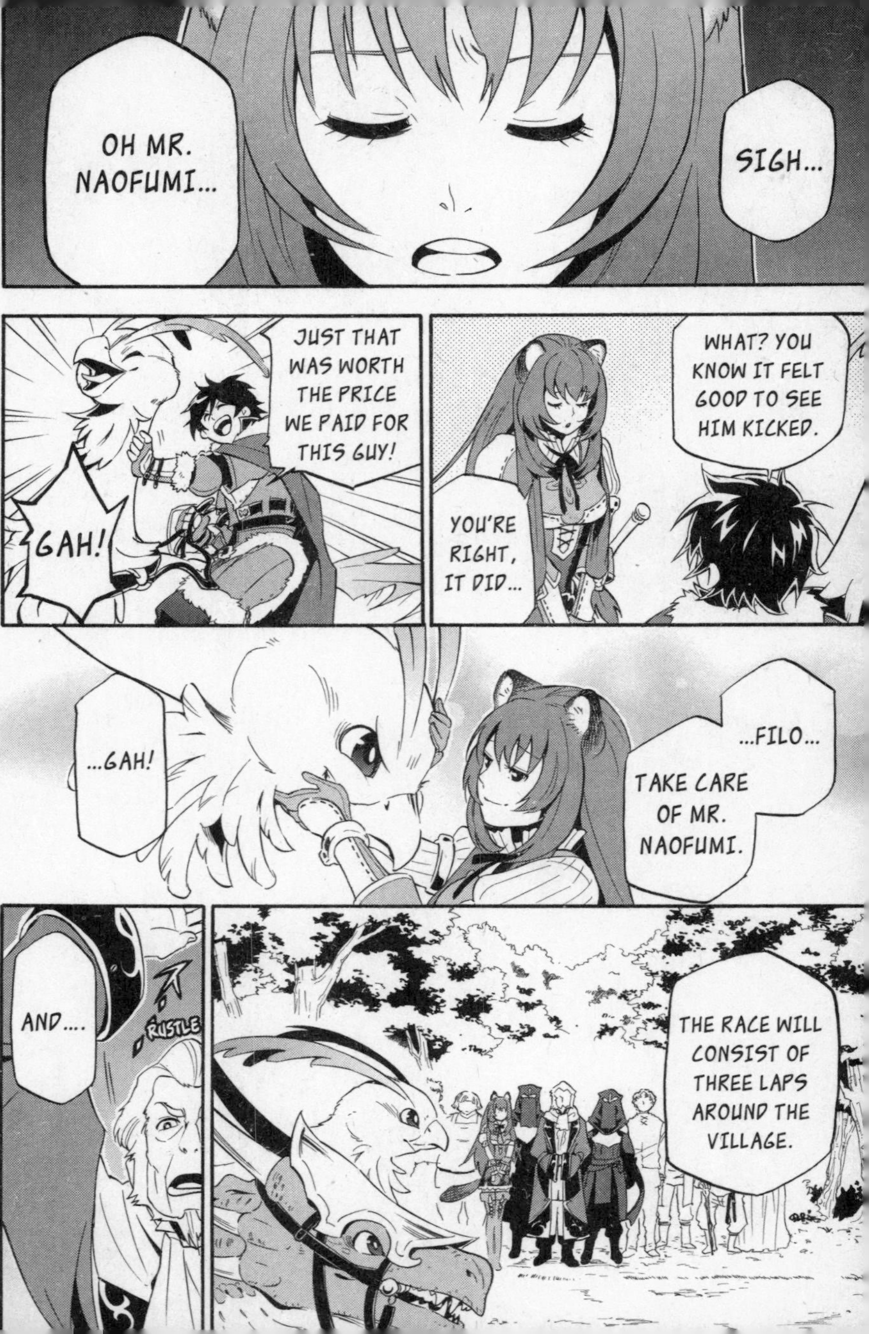
SIGH...
OH MR. NAOFUMI...
WHAT? YOU KNOW IT FELT GOOD TO SEE HIM KICKED.
YOU'RE RIGHT, IT DID...
JUST THAT WAS WORTH THE PRICE WE PAID FOR THIS GUY!
GAH!
...FILO...
TAKE CARE OF MR. NAOFUMI.
...GAH!
THE RACE WILL CONSIST OF THREE LAPS AROUND THE VILLAGE.
AND....
RUSTLE

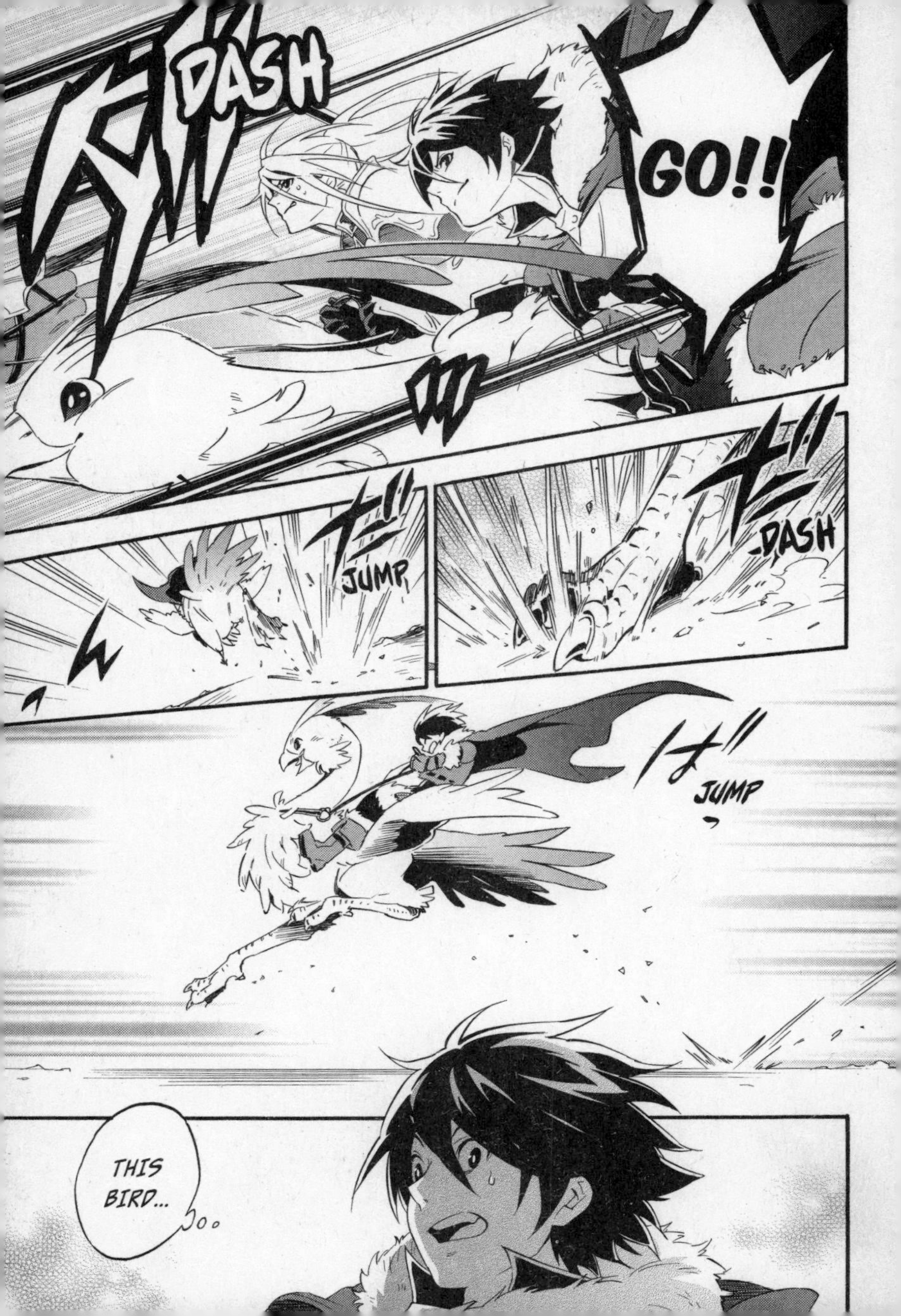
GO!!
DASH
DASH
JUMP
JUMP
THIS BIRD...

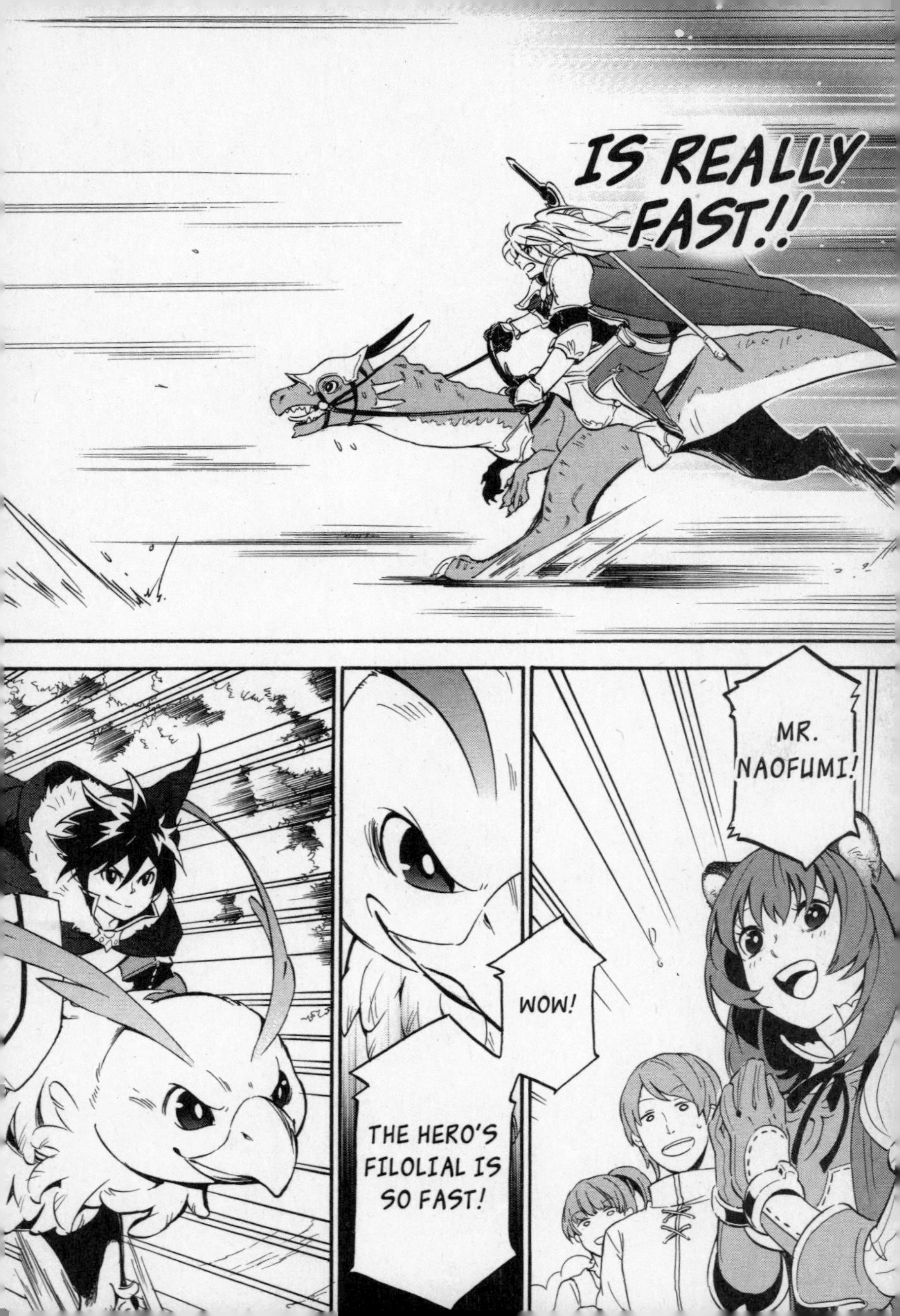
IS REALLY FAST!!
MR. NAOFUMI!
WOW!
THE HERO'S FILOLIAL IS SO FAST!

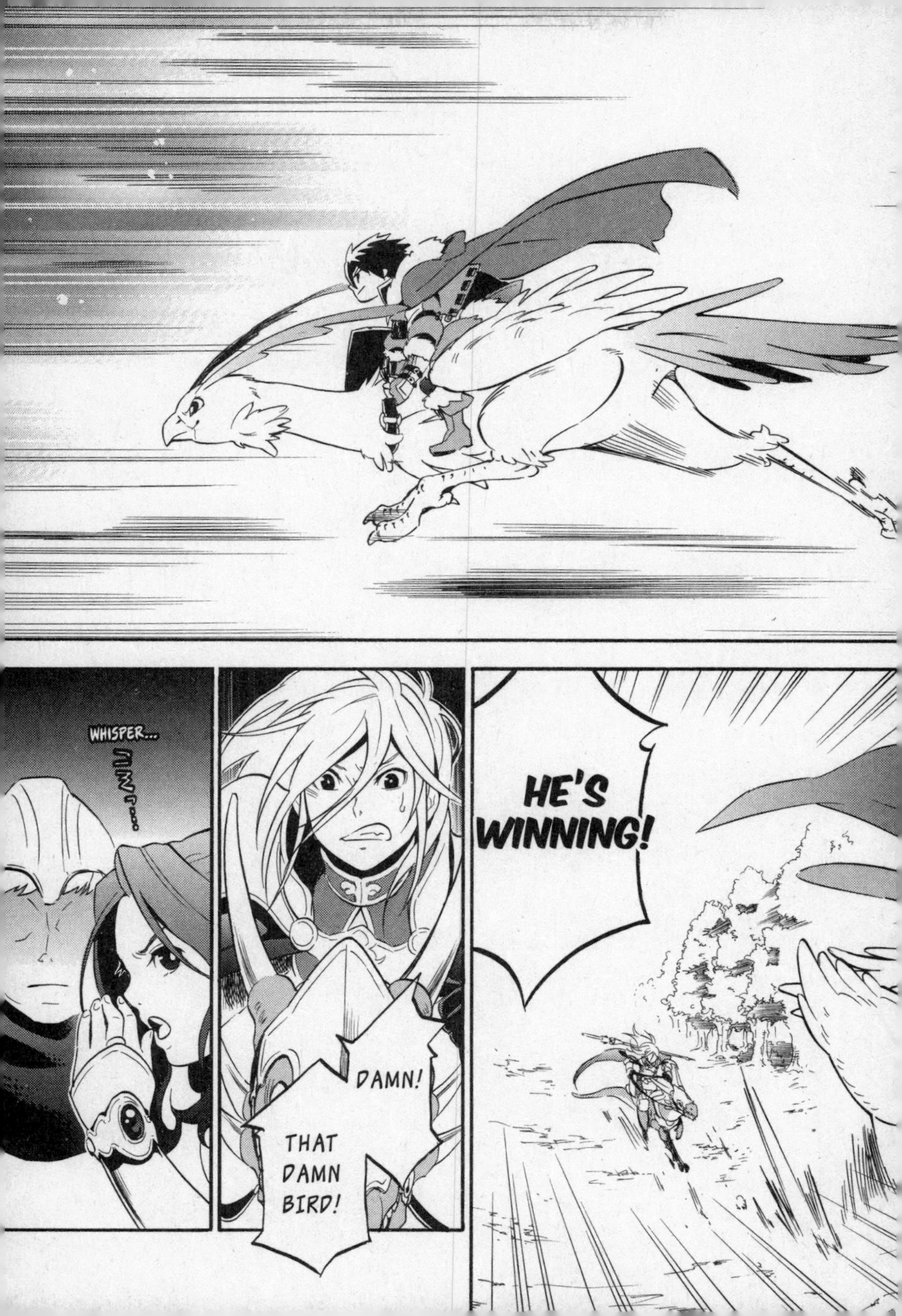
HE'S WINNING!
DAMN!
THAT DAMN BIRD!
WHISPER...

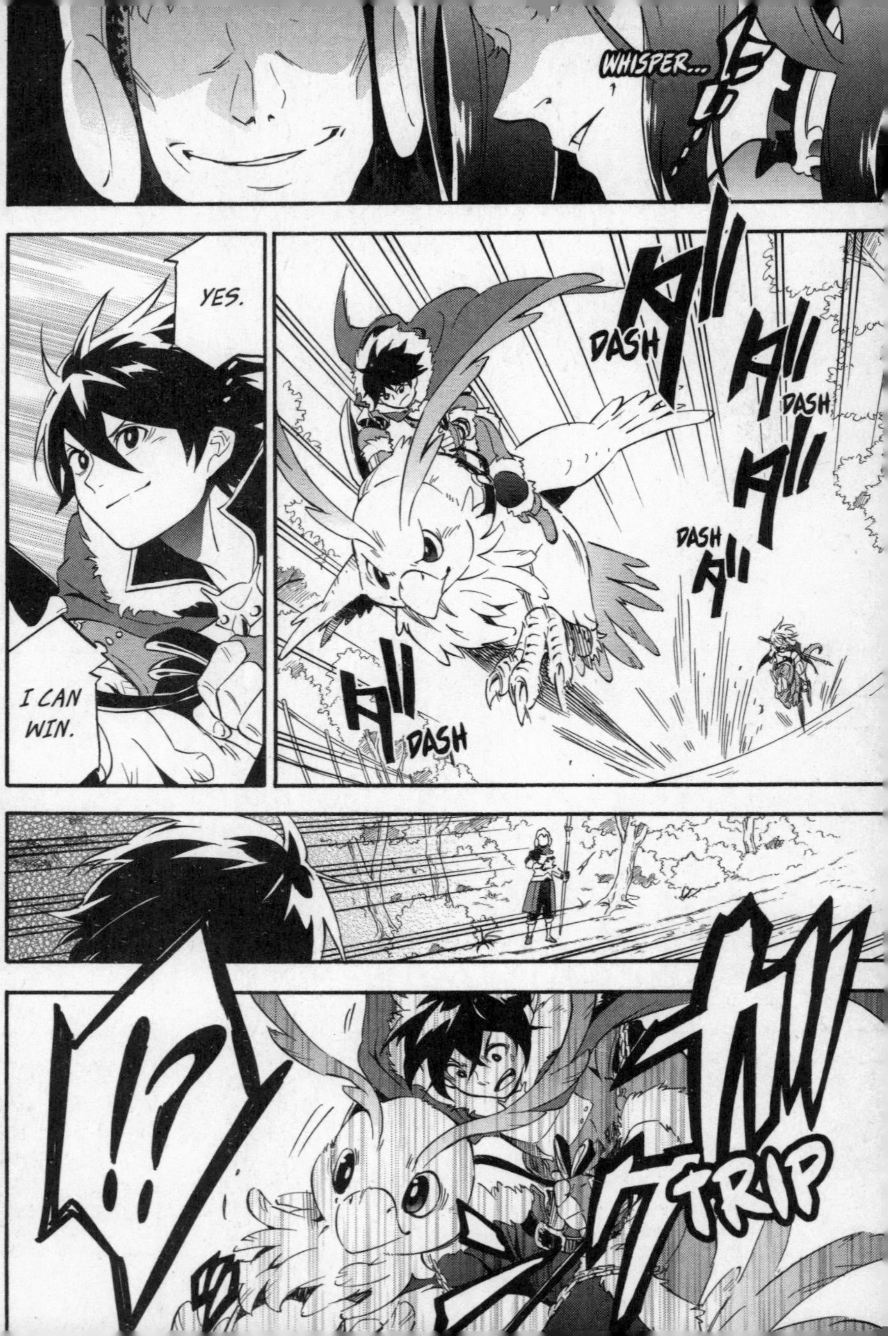
WHISPER...
DASH
DASH
DASH
DASH
YES.
I CAN WIN.
TRIP
!?

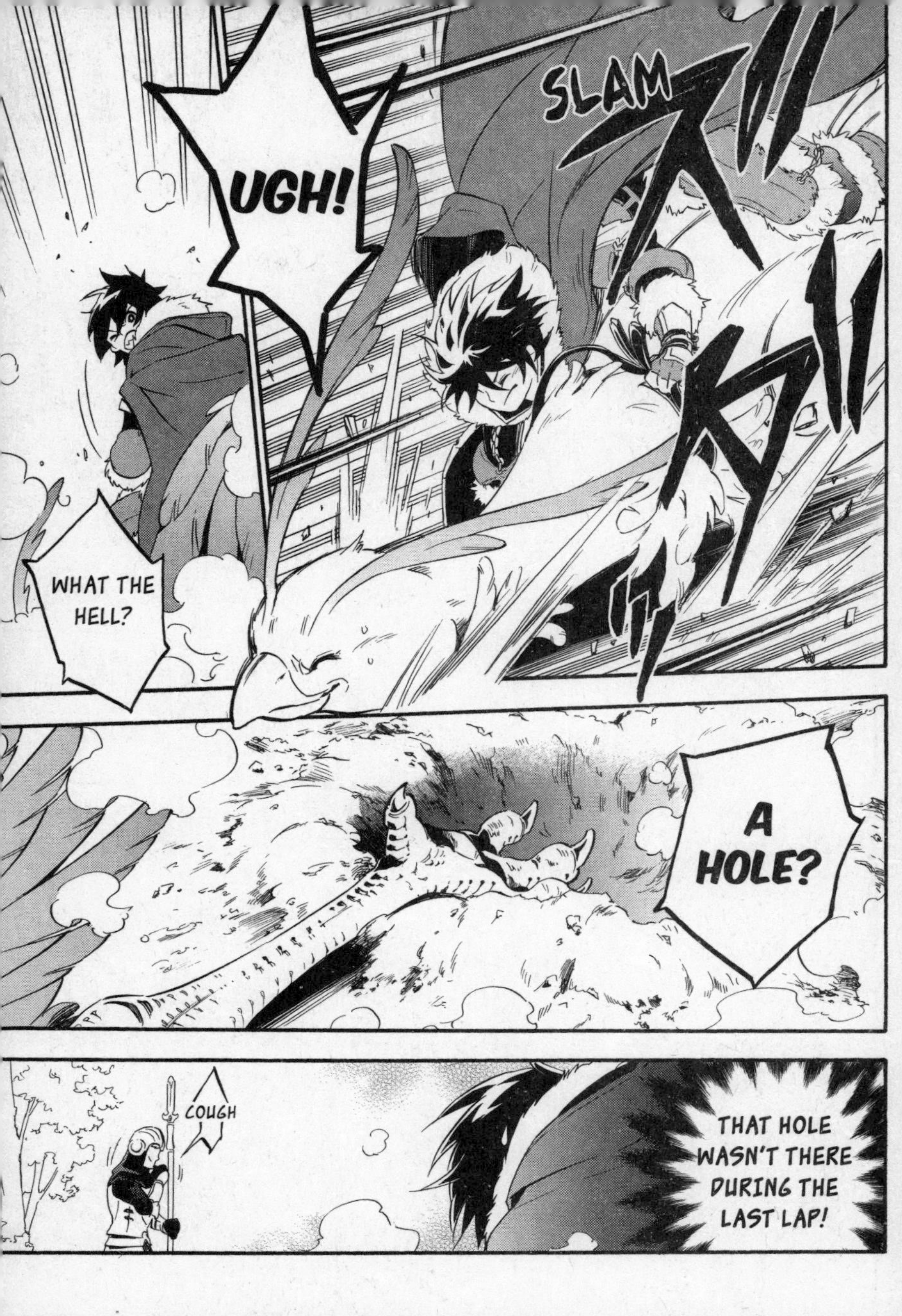
SLAM
UGH!
WHAT THE HELL?
A HOLE?
THAT HOLE WASN'T THERE DURING THE LAST LAP!
COUGH

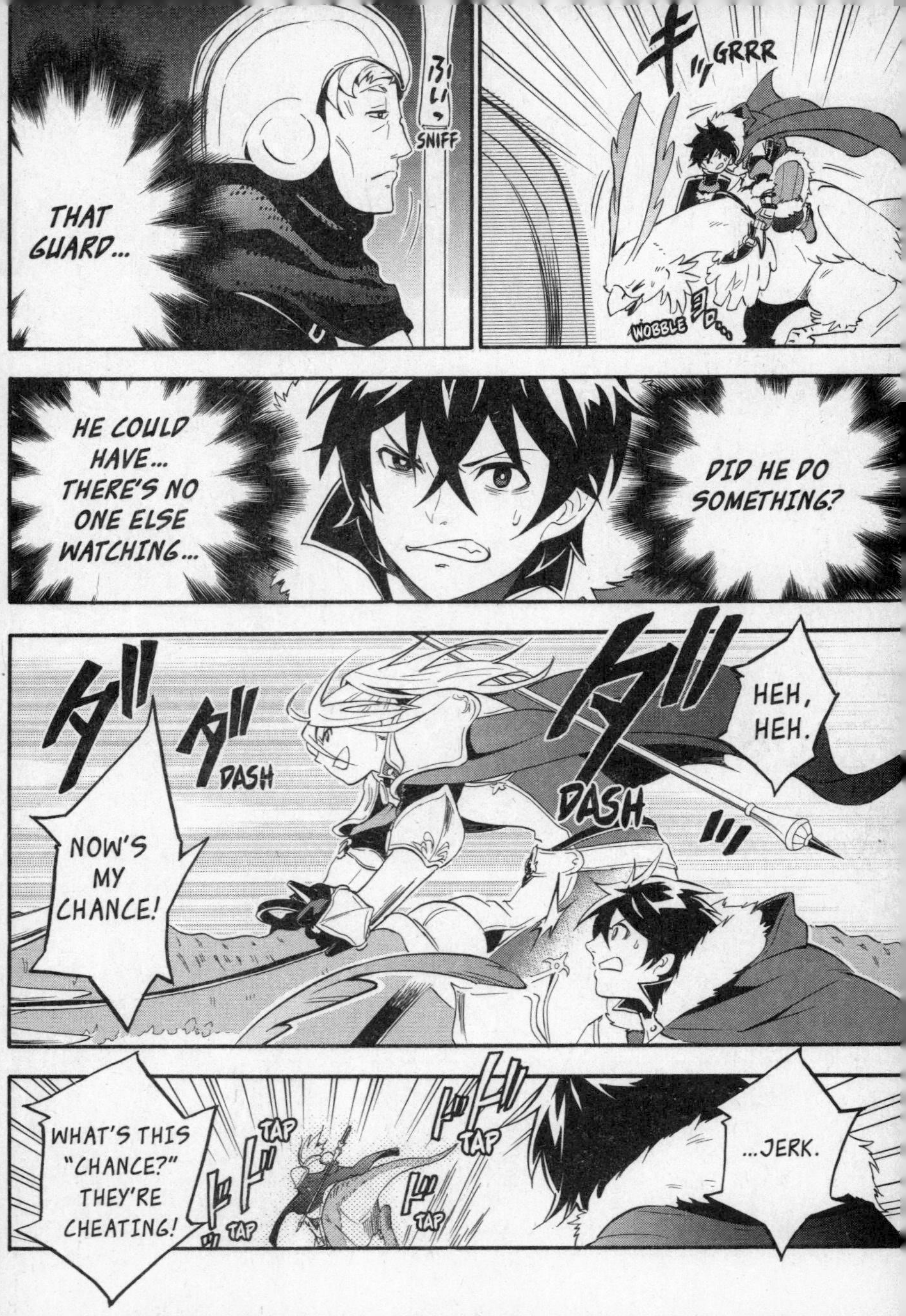
GRRR
WOBBLE
SNIFF
THAT GUARD...
DID HE DO SOMETHING?
HE COULD HAVE... THERE'S NO ONE ELSE WATCHING...
HEH, HEH.
DASH
DASH
NOW'S MY CHANCE!
...JERK.
TAP
TAP
TAP
TAP
WHAT'S THIS "CHANCE?" THEY'RE CHEATING!

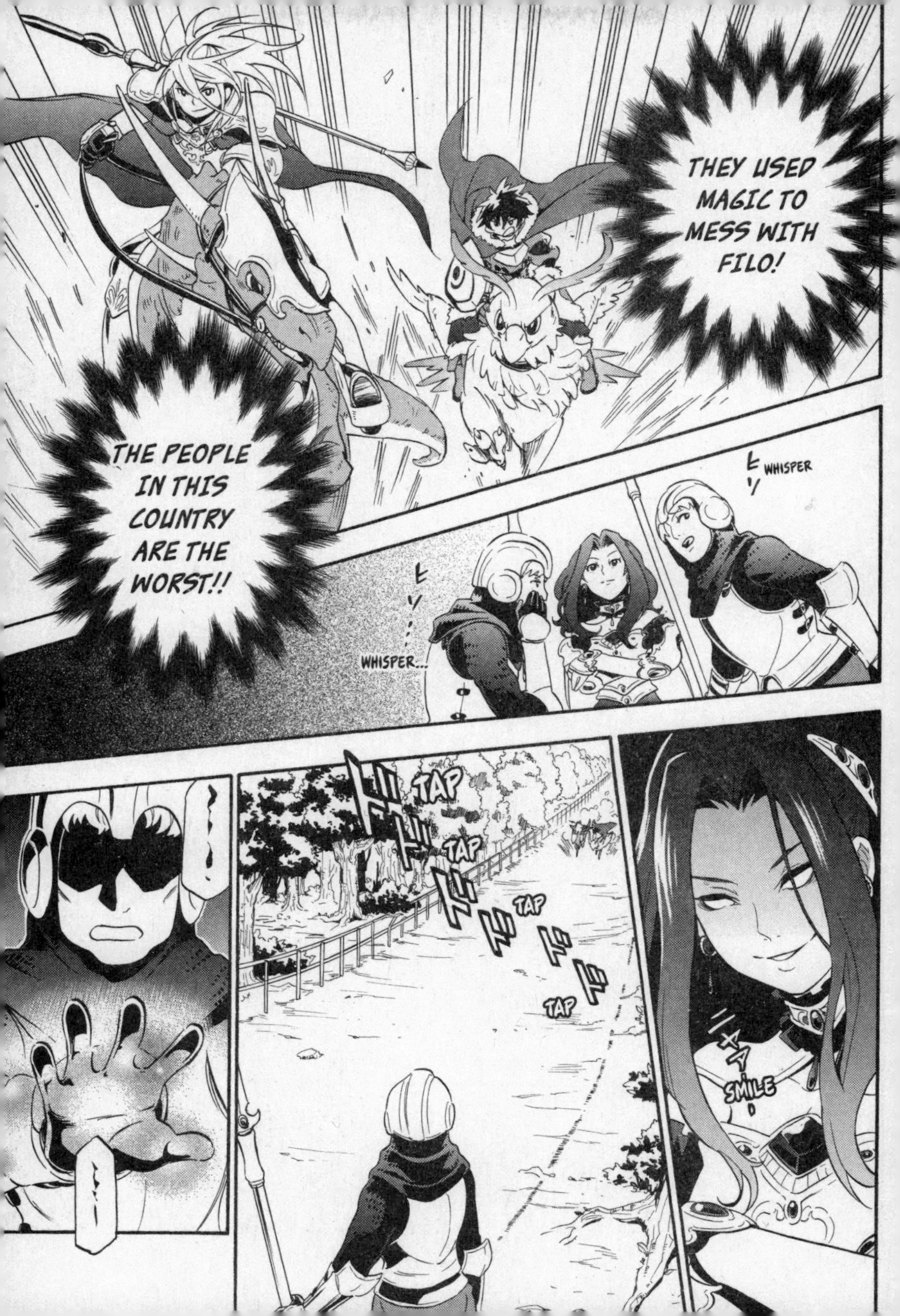
THEY USED MAGIC TO MESS WITH FILO!
THE PEOPLE IN THIS COUNTRY ARE THE WORST!!
WHISPER
WHISPER...
SMILE
TAP
TAP
TAP
TAP

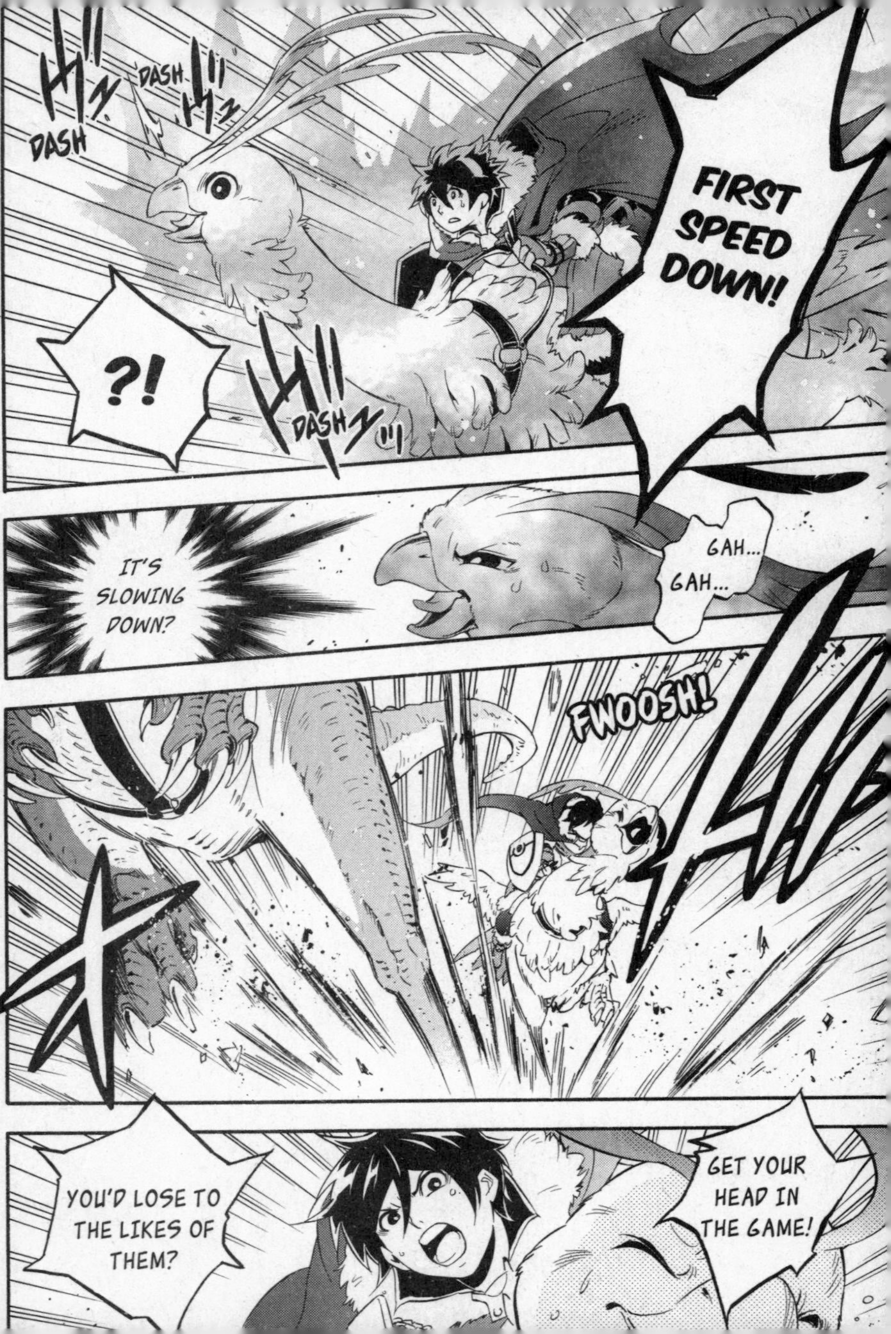
FIRST SPEED DOWN!
DASH
DASH
?!
DASH
GAH... GAH...
IT'S SLOWING DOWN?
FWOOSH!
GET YOUR HEAD IN THE GAME!
YOU'D LOSE TO THE LIKES OF THEM?

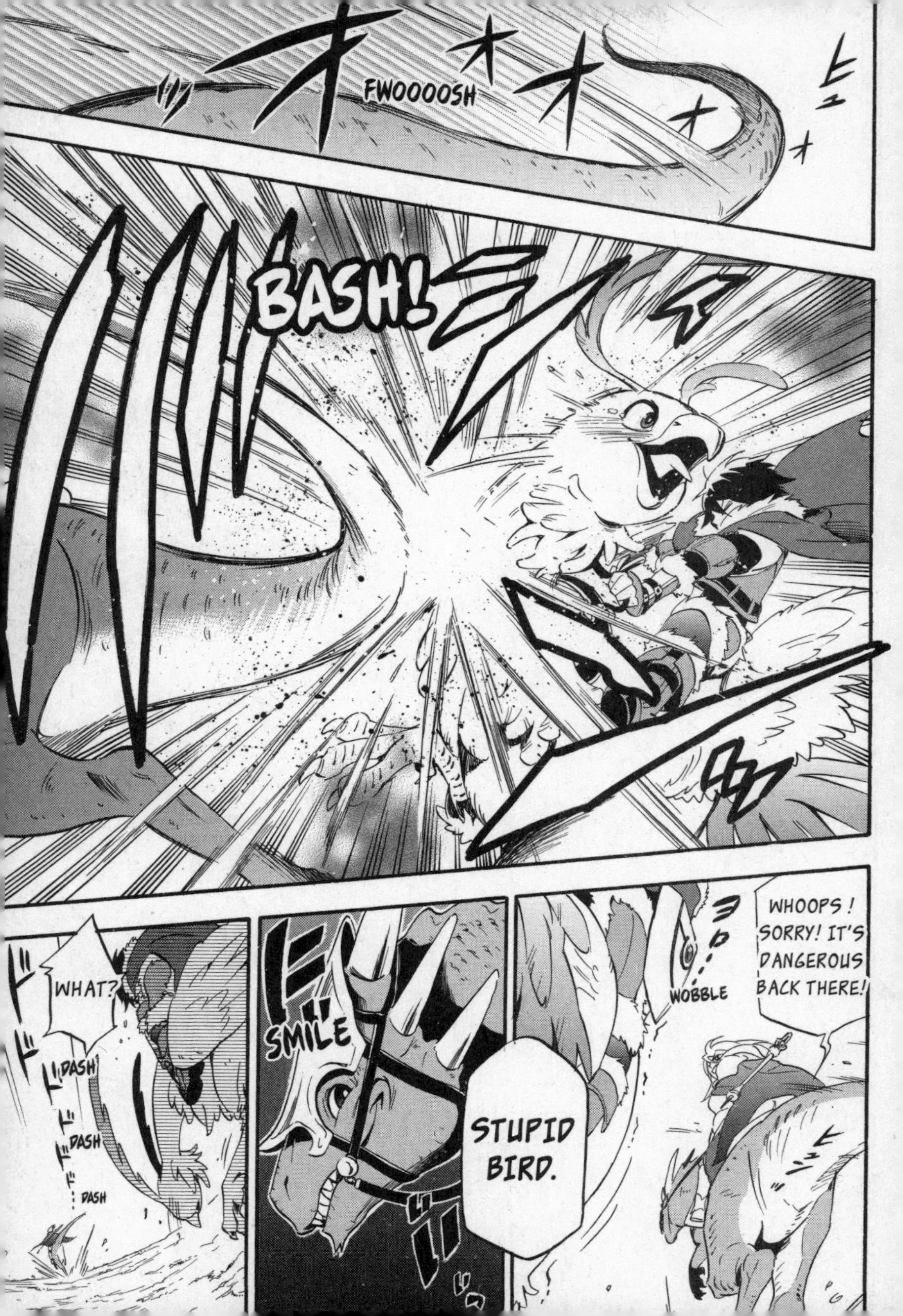
FWOOOOSH
BASH!
WHOOPS! SORRY! IT'S DANGEROUS BACK THERE!
WOBBLE
SMILE
STUPID BIRD.
WHAT?
DASH
DASH
DASH

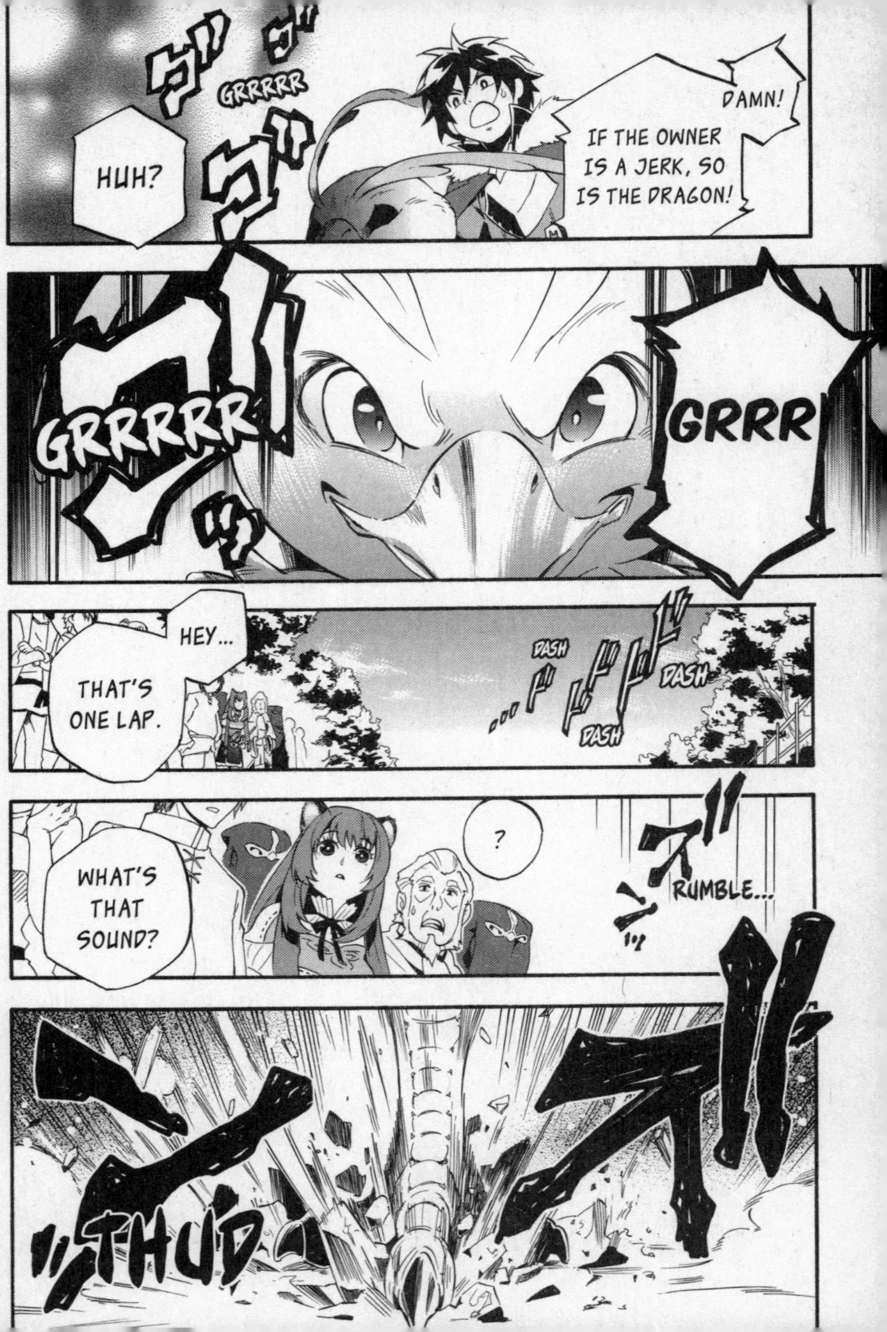
DAMN!
IF THE OWNER IS A JERK, SO IS THE DRAGON!
GRRRRR
HUH?
GRRR
GRRRRR
DASH
DASH
DASH
HEY...
THAT'S ONE LAP.
RUMBLE...
?
WHAT'S THAT SOUND?
THUD

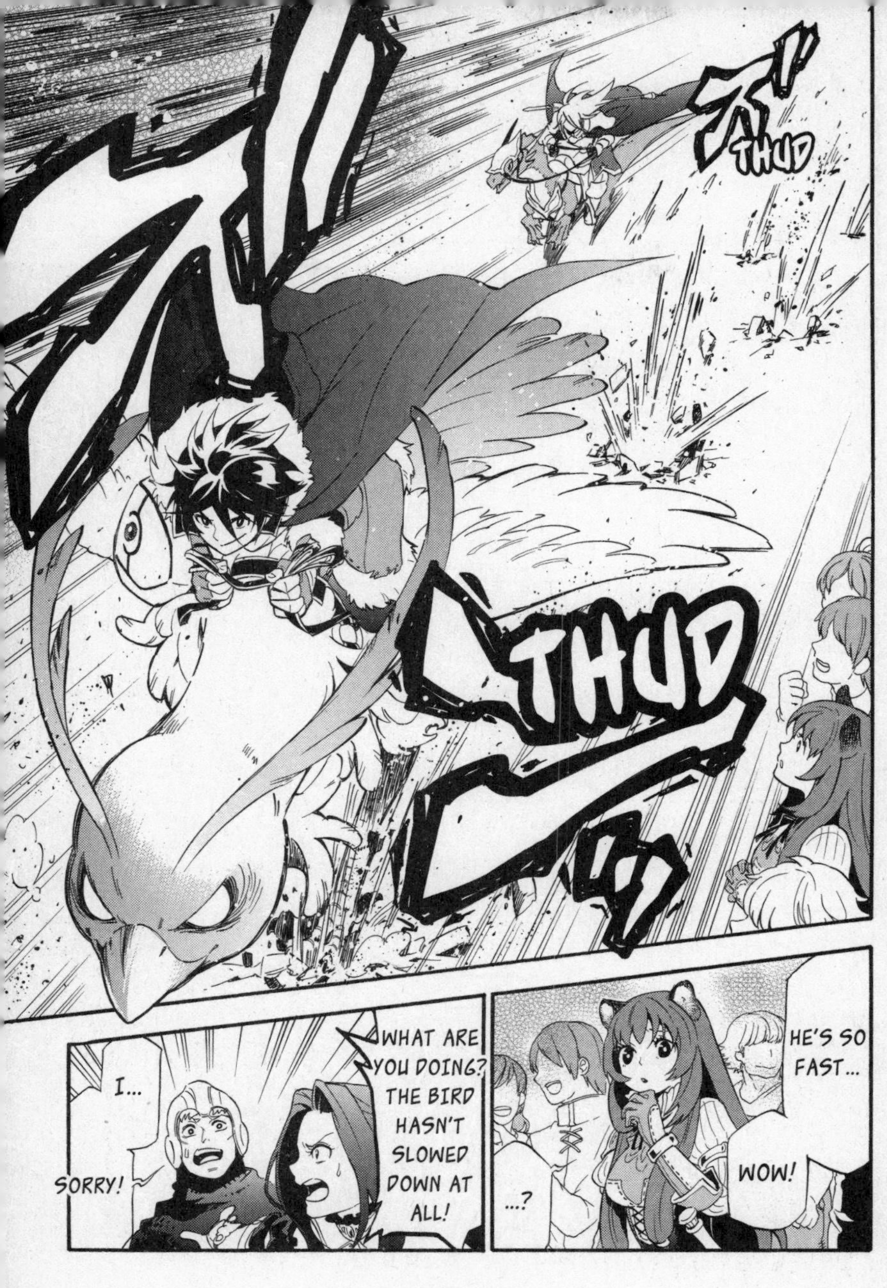
THUD
THUD
HE'S SO FAST...
WOW!
...?
WHAT ARE YOU DOING? THE BIRD HASN'T SLOWED DOWN AT ALL!
I...
SORRY!

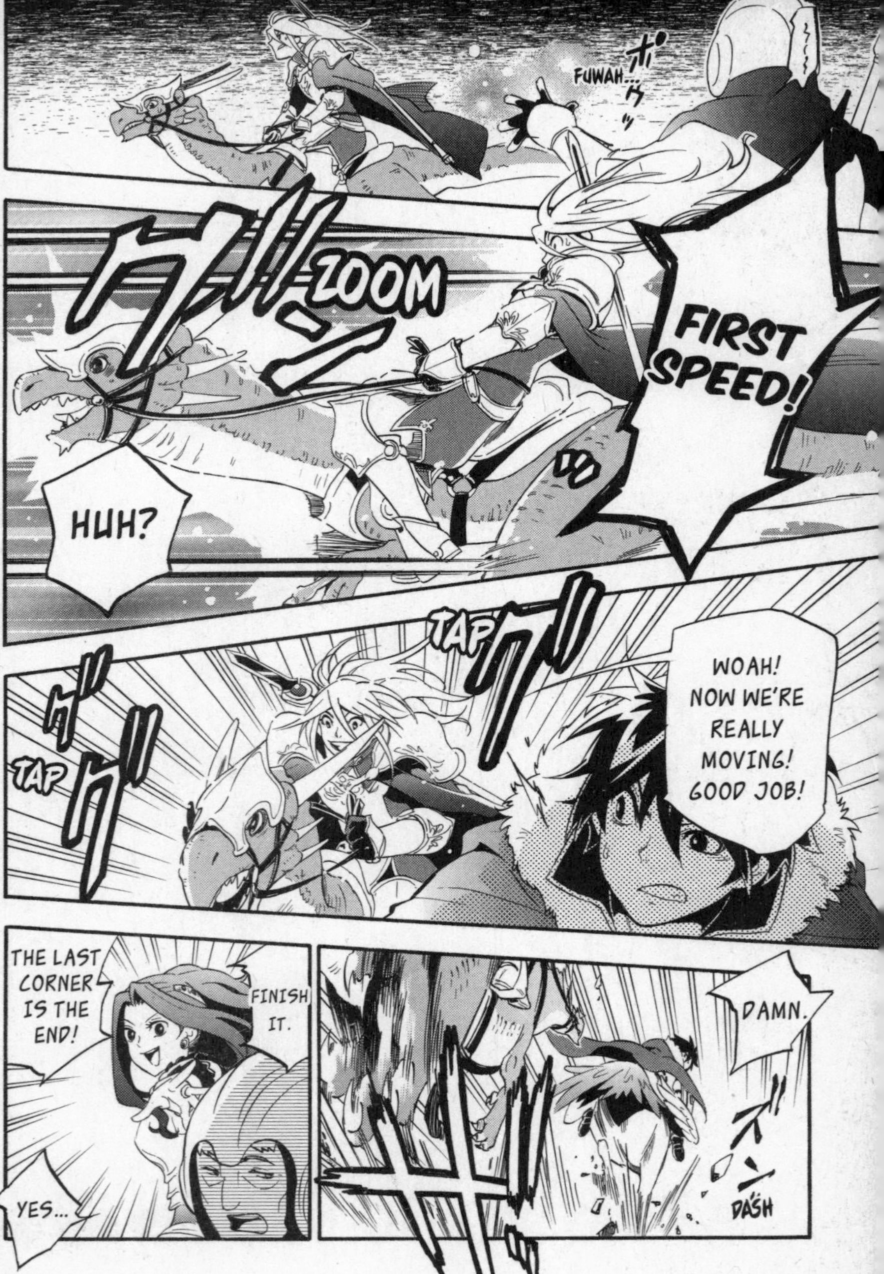
FUWAH...
FIRST SPEED!
ZOOM
HUH?
WOAH! NOW WE'RE REALLY MOVING! GOOD JOB!
TAP
TAP
DAMN.
DASH
THE LAST CORNER IS THE END!
FINISH IT.
YES...

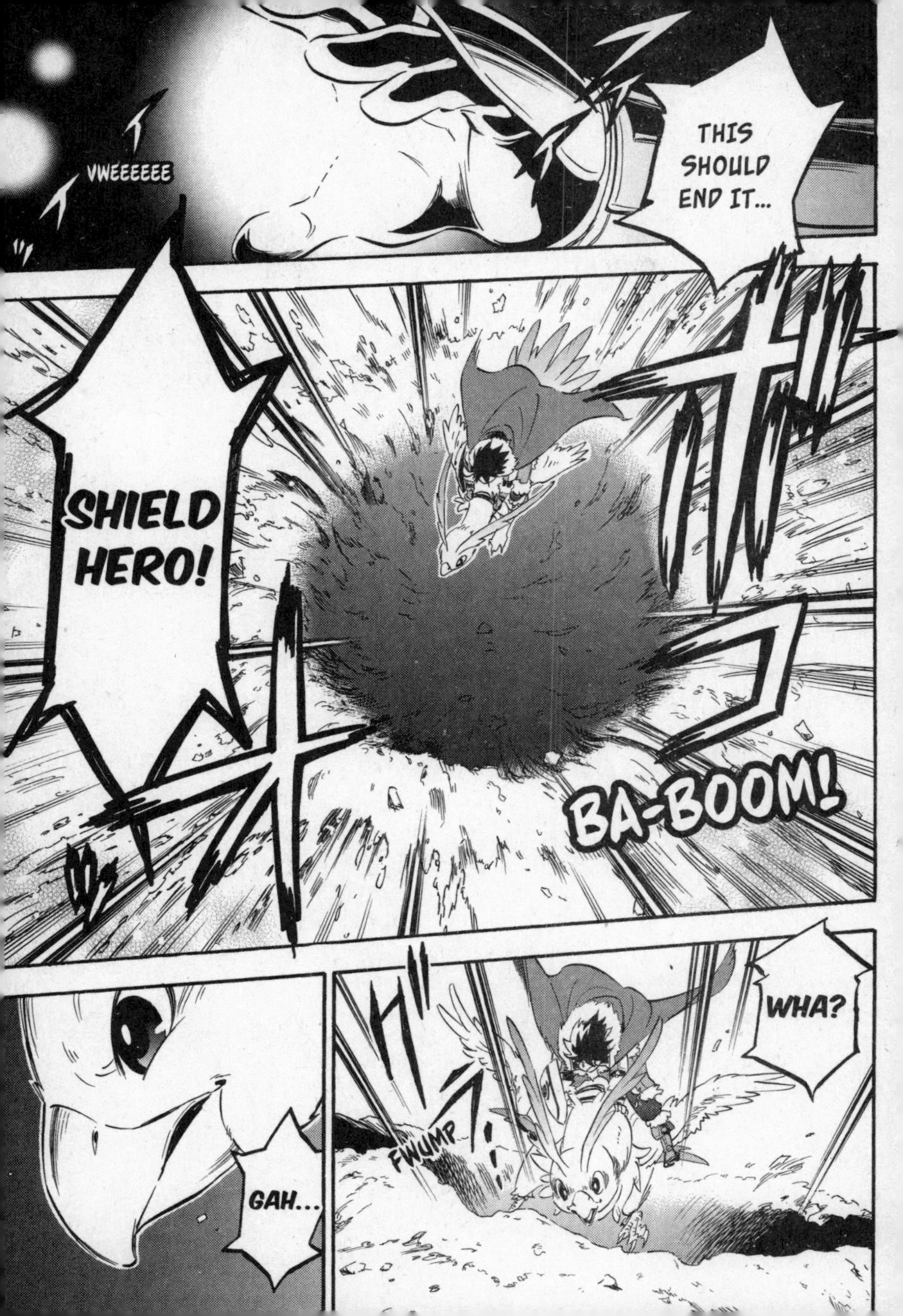
THIS SHOULD END IT...
VWEEEEEE
SHIELD HERO!
BA-BOOM!
WHA?
FWUMP
GAH...

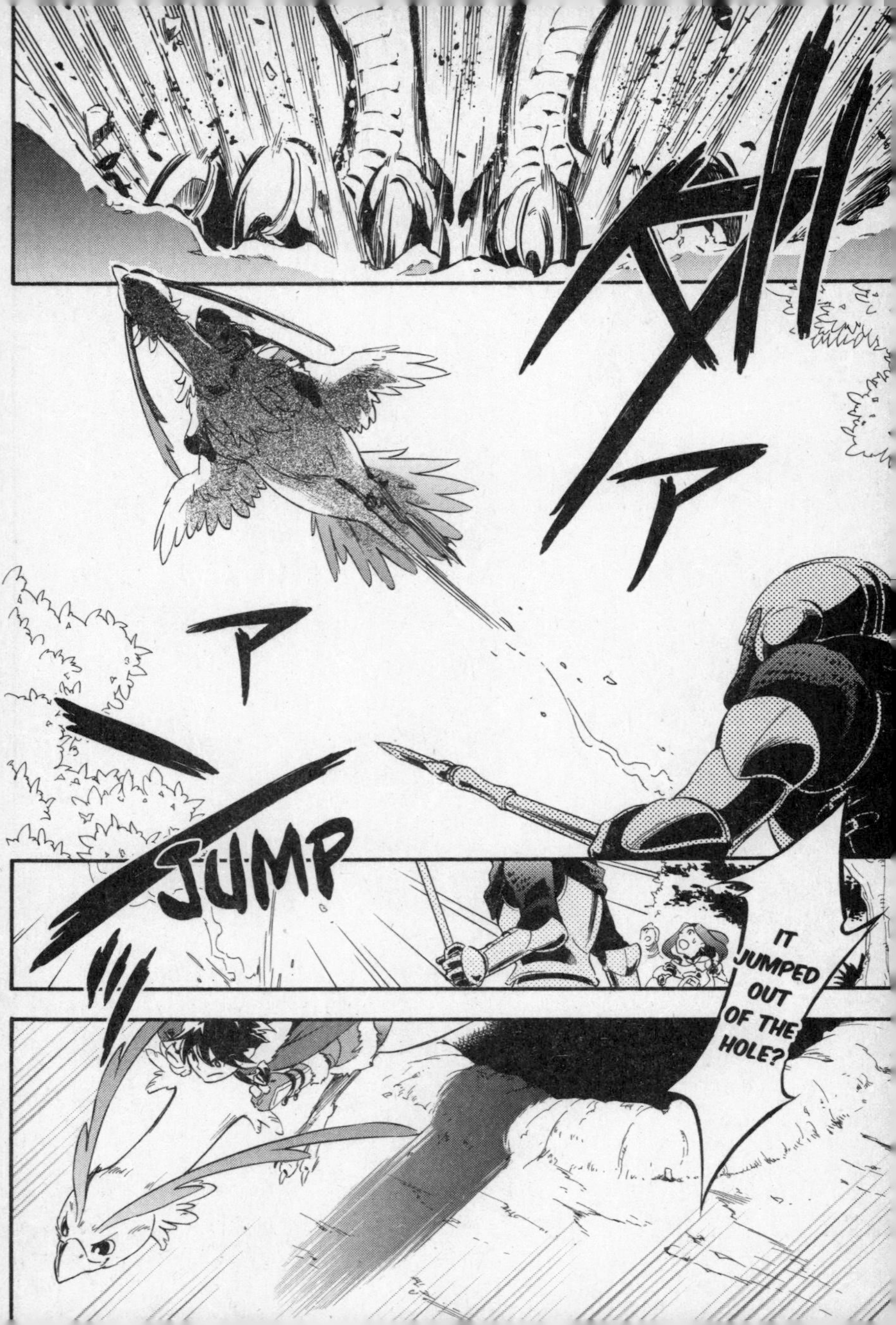
JUMP
IT JUMPED OUT OF THE HOLE?

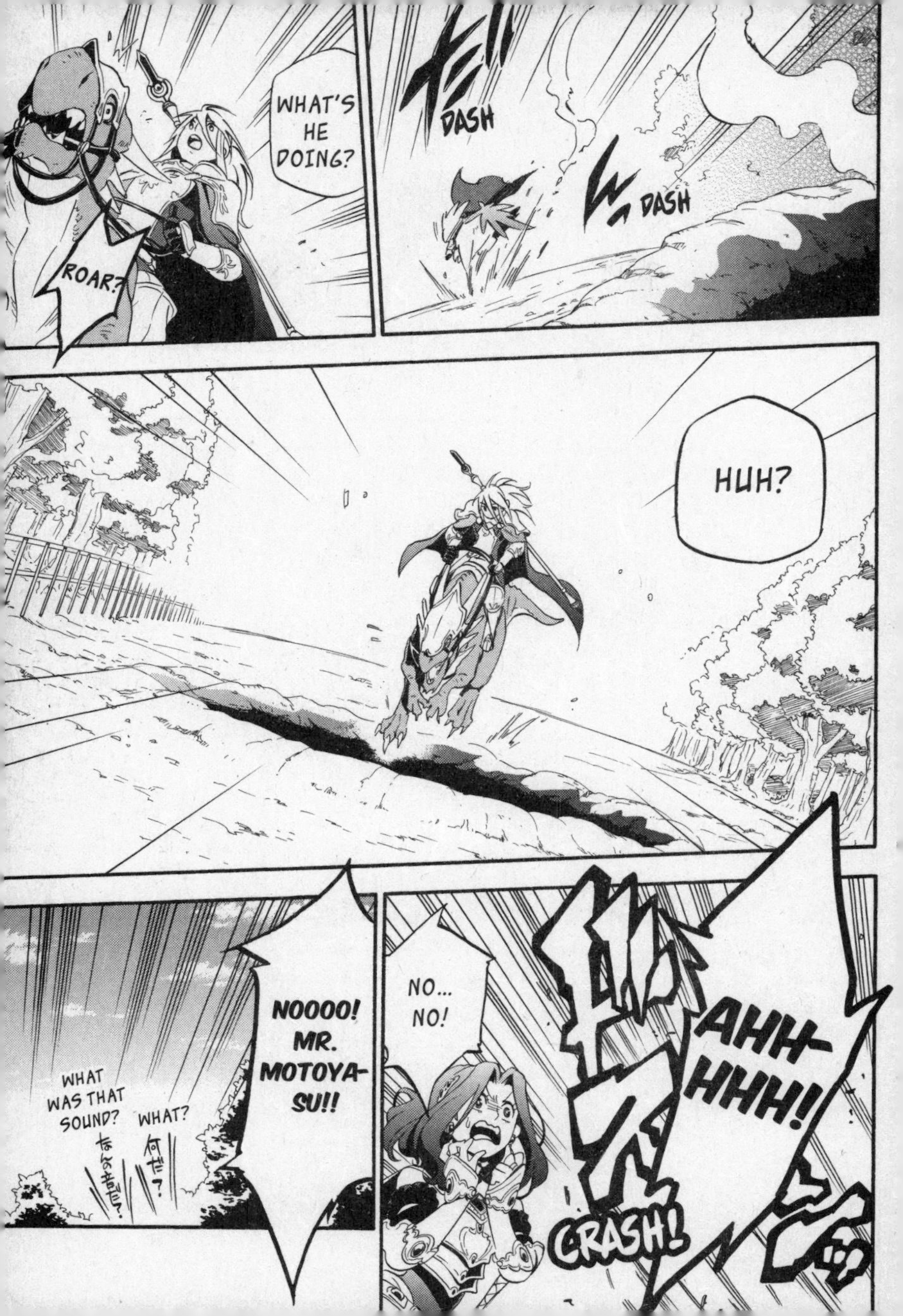
DASH
DASH
WHAT'S HE DOING?
ROAR?
HUH?
AHH-HHH!
NO... NO!
CRASH!
NOOOO! MR. MOTOYA-SU!!
WHAT?
何だ？
WHAT WAS THAT SOUND?
なんの音だ？

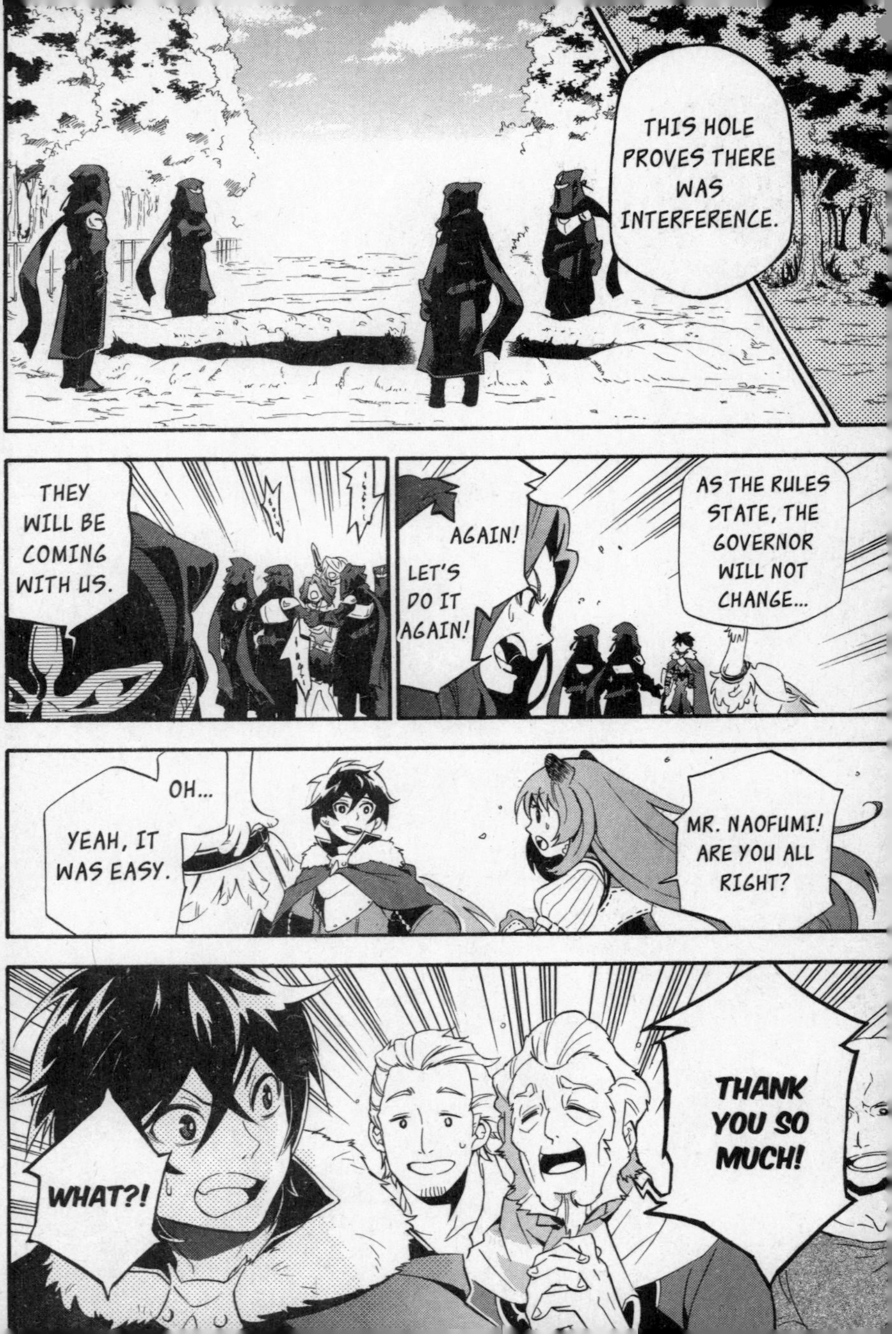
THIS HOLE PROVES THERE WAS INTERFERENCE.
AS THE RULES STATE, THE GOVERNOR WILL NOT CHANGE...
AGAIN!
LET'S DO IT AGAIN!
THEY WILL BE COMING WITH US.
MR. NAOFUMI! ARE YOU ALL RIGHT?
OH...
YEAH, IT WAS EASY.
THANK YOU SO MUCH!
WHAT?!

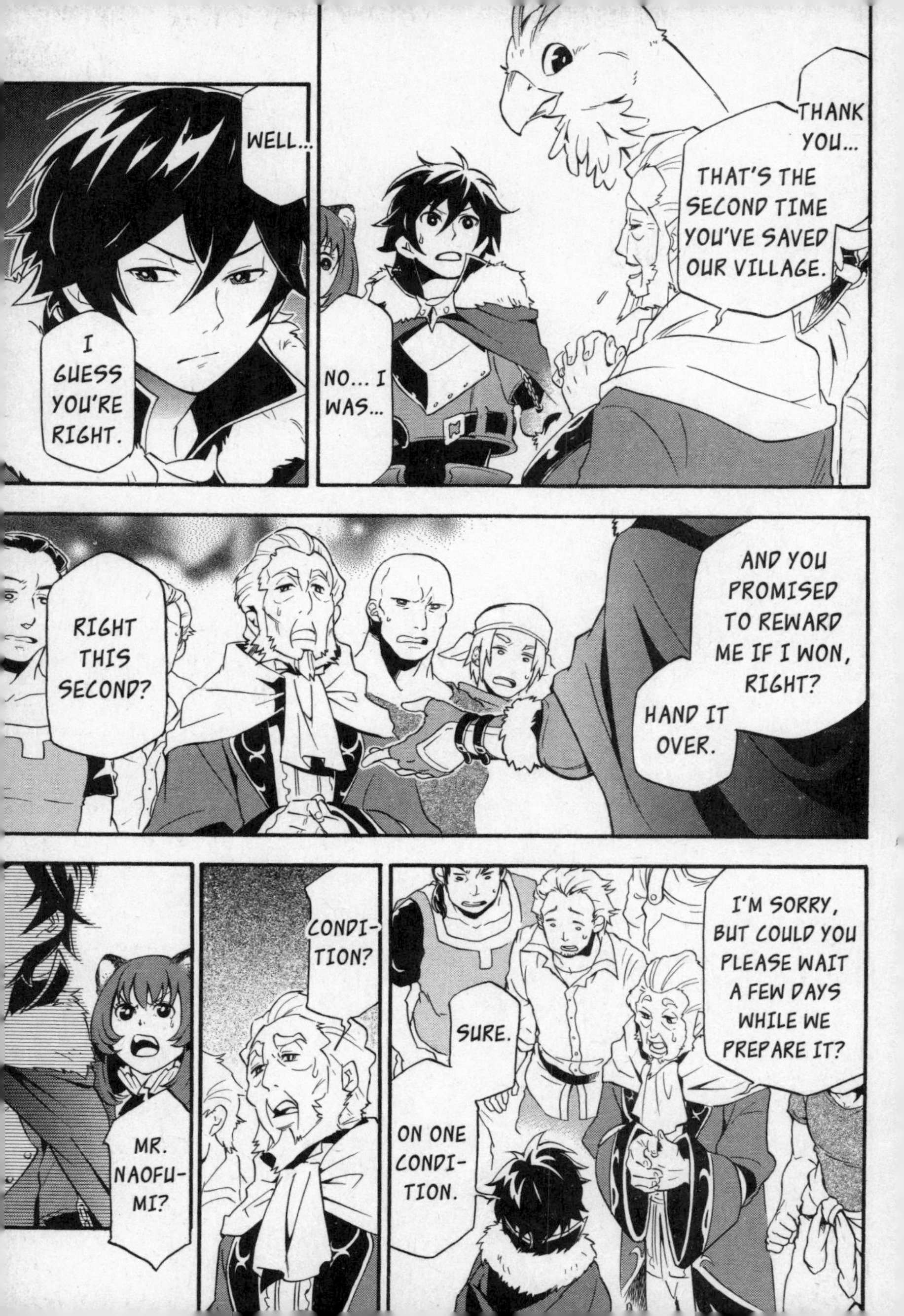
THANK YOU...
THAT'S THE SECOND TIME YOU'VE SAVED OUR VILLAGE.
NO... I WAS...
WELL...
I GUESS YOU'RE RIGHT.
AND YOU PROMISED TO REWARD ME IF I WON, RIGHT?
HAND IT OVER.
RIGHT THIS SECOND?
I'M SORRY, BUT COULD YOU PLEASE WAIT A FEW DAYS WHILE WE PREPARE IT?
SURE.
ON ONE CONDI-TION.
CONDI-TION?
MR. NAOFU-MI?

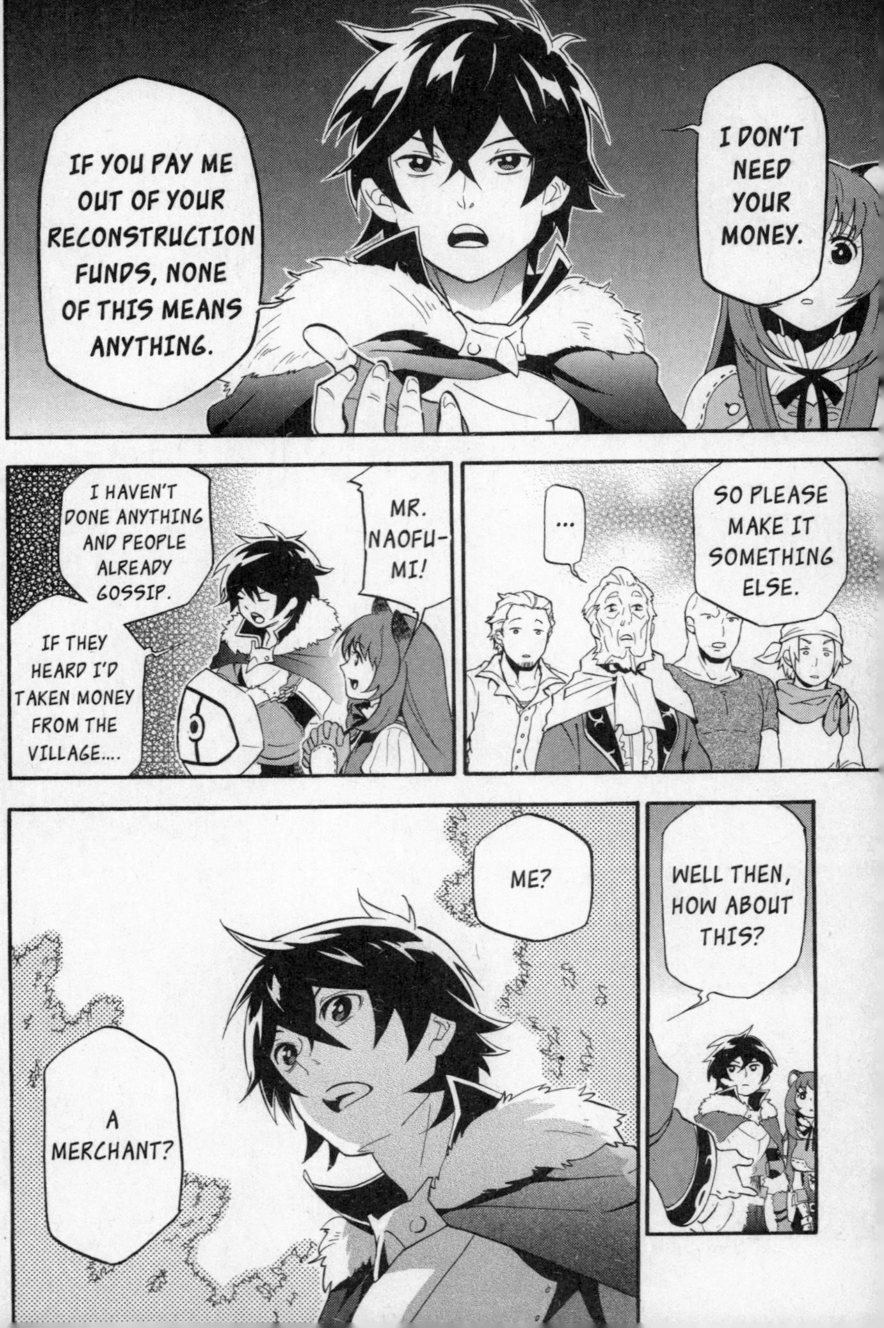
I DON'T NEED YOUR MONEY.
IF YOU PAY ME OUT OF YOUR RECONSTRUCTION FUNDS, NONE OF THIS MEANS ANYTHING.
SO PLEASE MAKE IT SOMETHING ELSE.
...
MR. NAOFU-MI!
I HAVEN'T DONE ANYTHING AND PEOPLE ALREADY GOSSIP.
IF THEY HEARD I'D TAKEN MONEY FROM THE VILLAGE....
WELL THEN, HOW ABOUT THIS?
ME?
A MERCHANT?

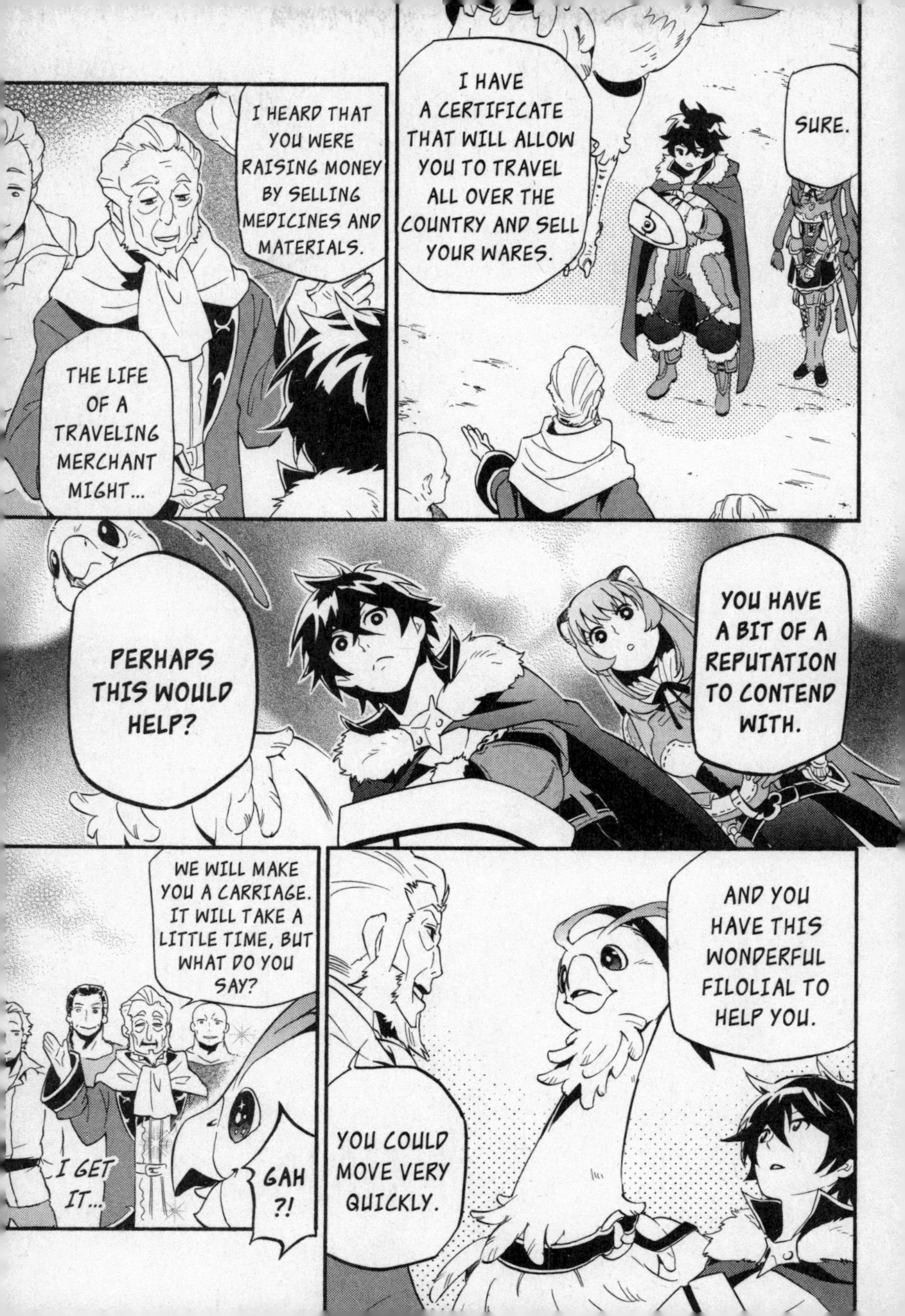
I HAVE A CERTIFICATE THAT WILL ALLOW YOU TO TRAVEL ALL OVER THE COUNTRY AND SELL YOUR WARES.
SURE.
I HEARD THAT YOU WERE RAISING MONEY BY SELLING MEDICINES AND MATERIALS.
THE LIFE OF A TRAVELING MERCHANT MIGHT...
YOU HAVE A BIT OF A REPUTATION TO CONTEND WITH.
PERHAPS THIS WOULD HELP?
AND YOU HAVE THIS WONDERFUL FILOLIAL TO HELP YOU.
YOU COULD MOVE VERY QUICKLY.
WE WILL MAKE YOU A CARRIAGE. IT WILL TAKE A LITTLE TIME, BUT WHAT DO YOU SAY?
GAH ?!
I GET IT...

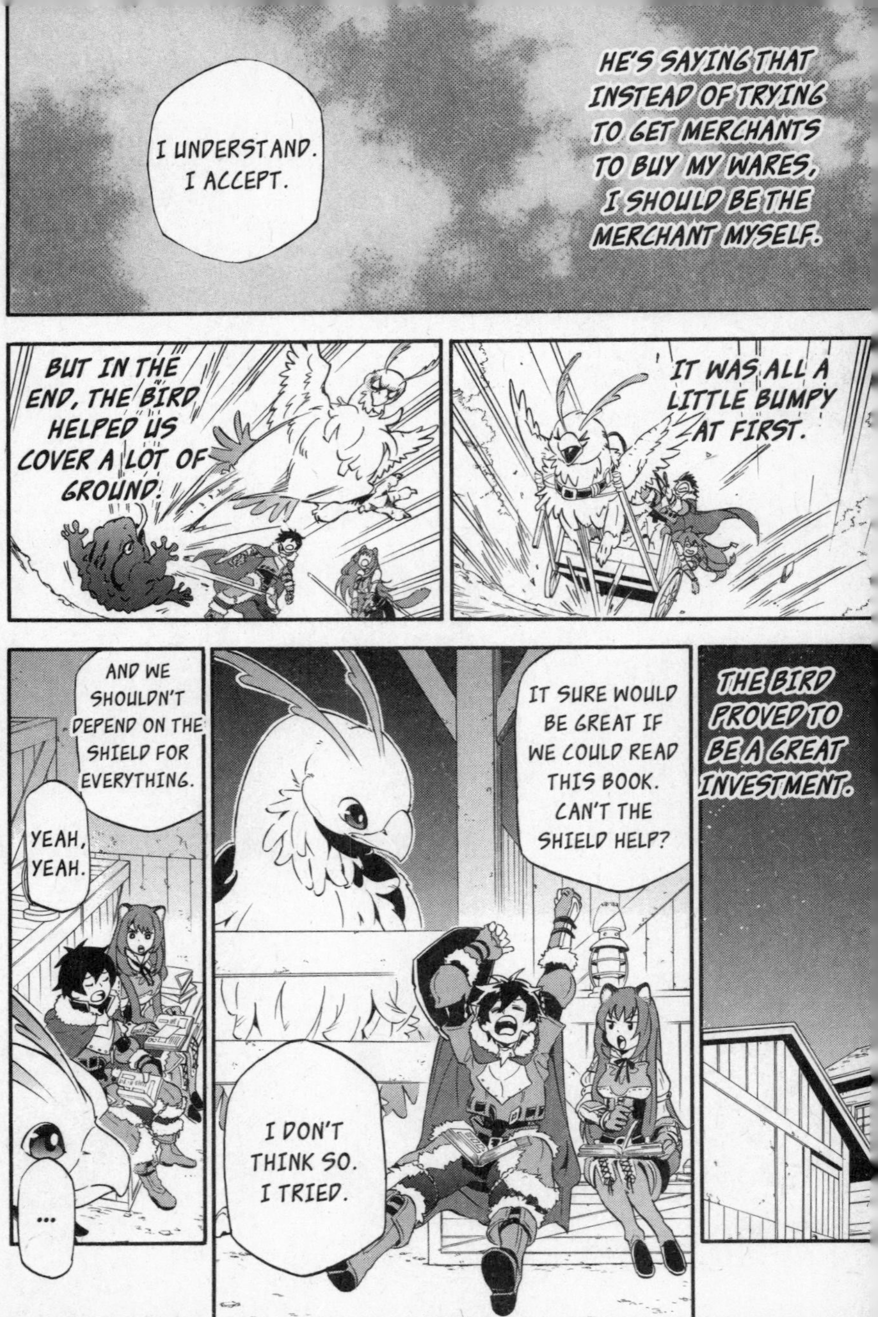
HE'S SAYING THAT INSTEAD OF TRYING TO GET MERCHANTS TO BUY MY WARES, I SHOULD BE THE MERCHANT MYSELF.
I UNDERSTAND. I ACCEPT.
IT WAS ALL A LITTLE BUMPY AT FIRST.
BUT IN THE END, THE BIRD HELPED US COVER A LOT OF GROUND.
THE BIRD PROVED TO BE A GREAT INVESTMENT.
IT SURE WOULD BE GREAT IF WE COULD READ THIS BOOK. CAN'T THE SHIELD HELP?
I DON'T THINK SO. I TRIED.
AND WE SHOULDN'T DEPEND ON THE SHIELD FOR EVERYTHING.
YEAH, YEAH.
...

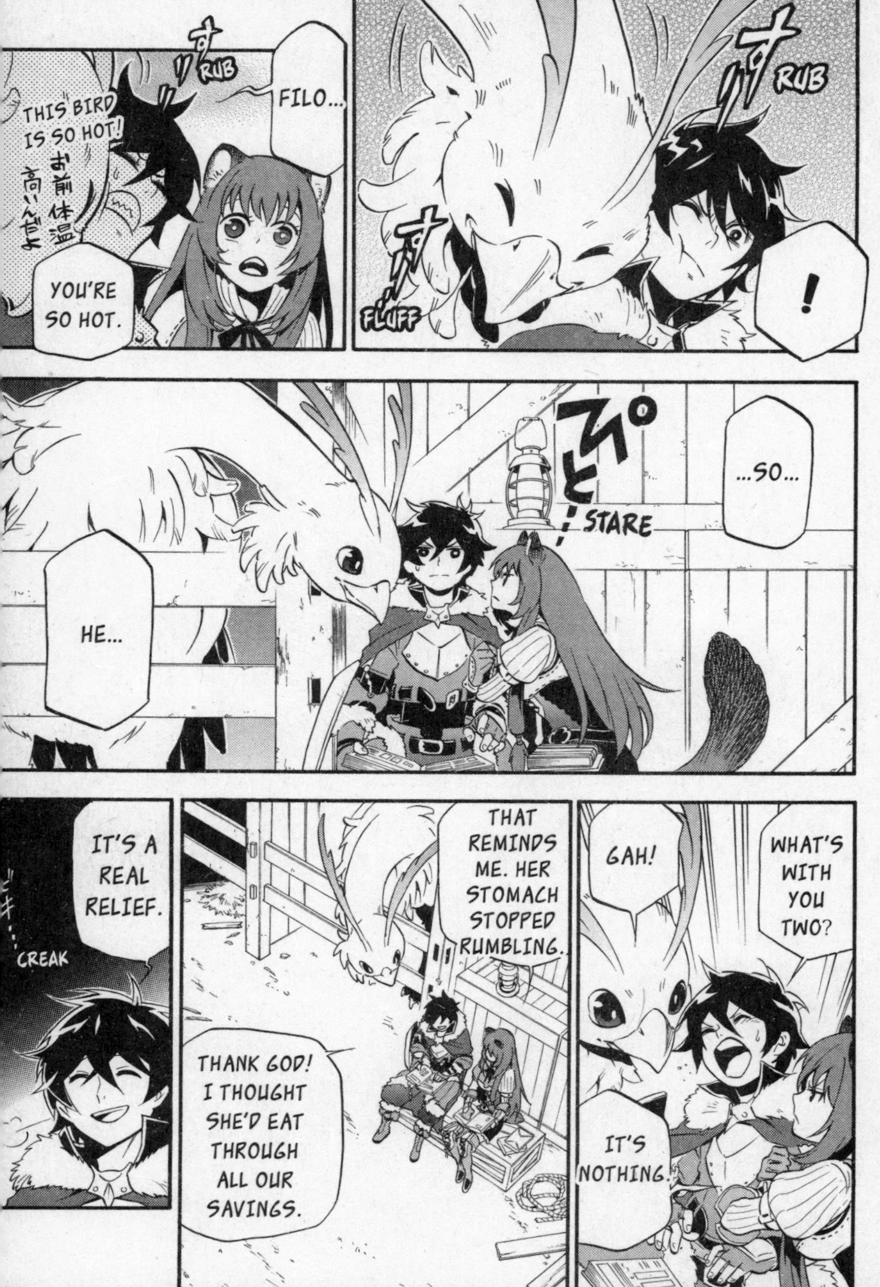
すり RUB
すり FLUFF
!
すり RUB
FILO...
THIS BIRD IS SO HOT!
お前体温高いんだよ
YOU'RE SO HOT.
...SO...
ぴと STARE
HE...
WHAT'S WITH YOU TWO?
GAH!
IT'S NOTHING.
THAT REMINDS ME. HER STOMACH STOPPED RUMBLING.
THANK GOD! I THOUGHT SHE'D EAT THROUGH ALL OUR SAVINGS.
IT'S A REAL RELIEF.
ギ... CREAK

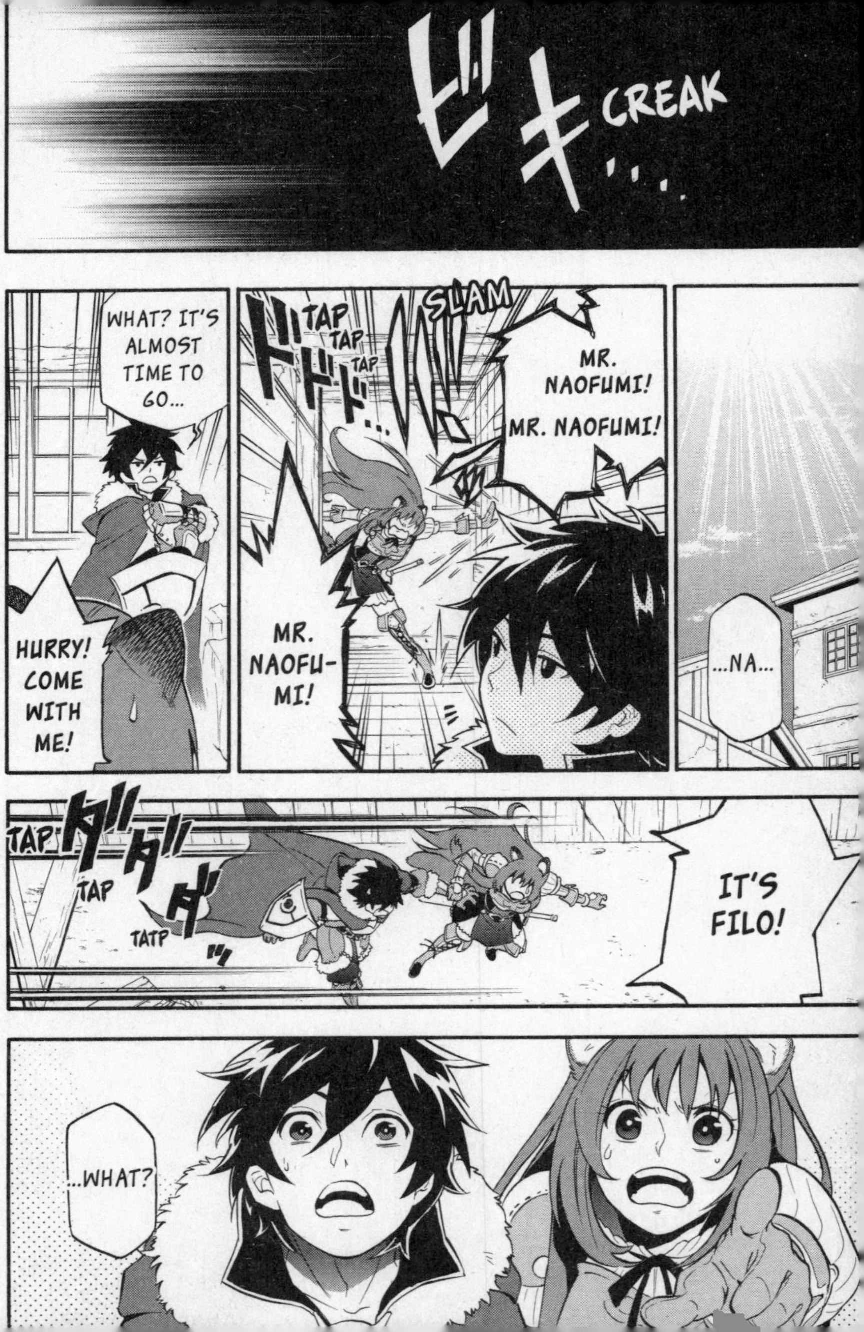

ビキ
CREAK
...
...NA...
TAP
TAP
TAP
ドドド...
SLAM
MR. NAOFUMI!
MR. NAOFUMI!
MR. NAOFU-MI!
WHAT? IT'S ALMOST TIME TO GO...
HURRY! COME WITH ME!
IT'S FILO!
TAP
ダダダ
TAP
TATP
...WHAT?

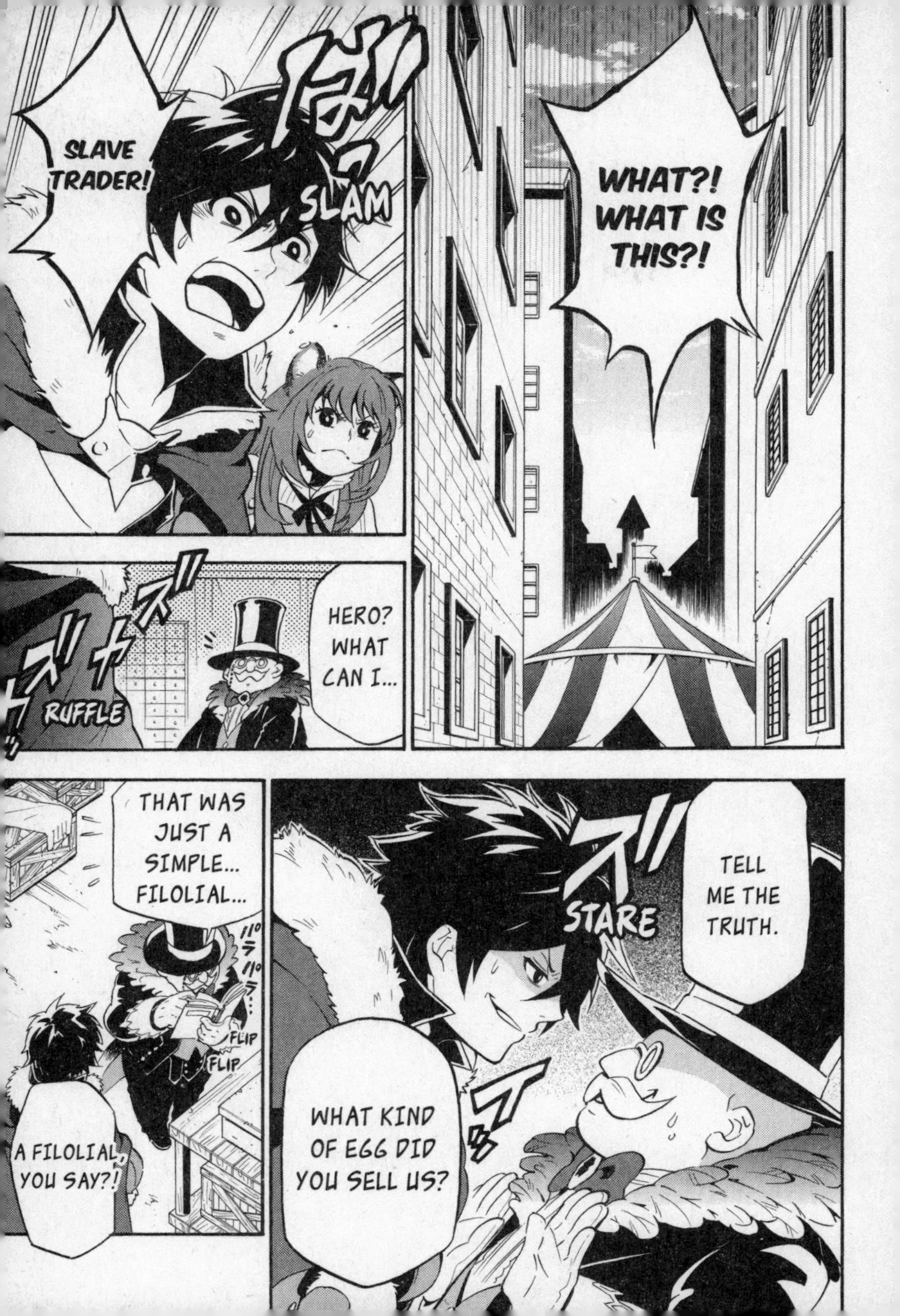
WHAT?! WHAT IS THIS?!
SLAM
SLAVE TRADER!
HERO? WHAT CAN I...
RUFFLE
TELL ME THE TRUTH.
STARE
WHAT KIND OF EGG DID YOU SELL US?
THAT WAS JUST A SIMPLE... FILOLIAL...
FLIP
FLIP
A FILOLIAL, YOU SAY?!

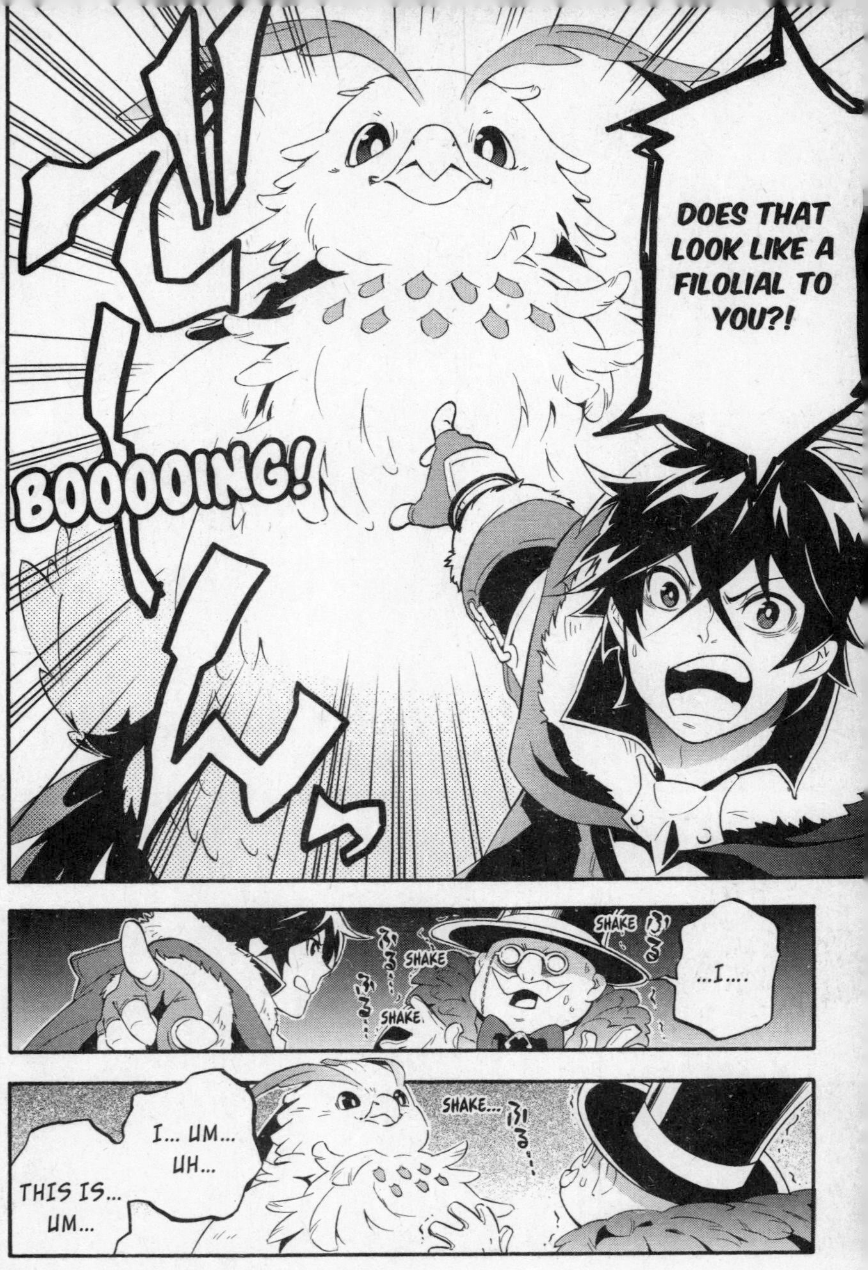
DOES THAT LOOK LIKE A FILOLIAL TO YOU?!
BOOOOING!
...I....
SHAKE
SHAKE
SHAKE
SHAKE...
I... UM... UH...
THIS IS... UM...

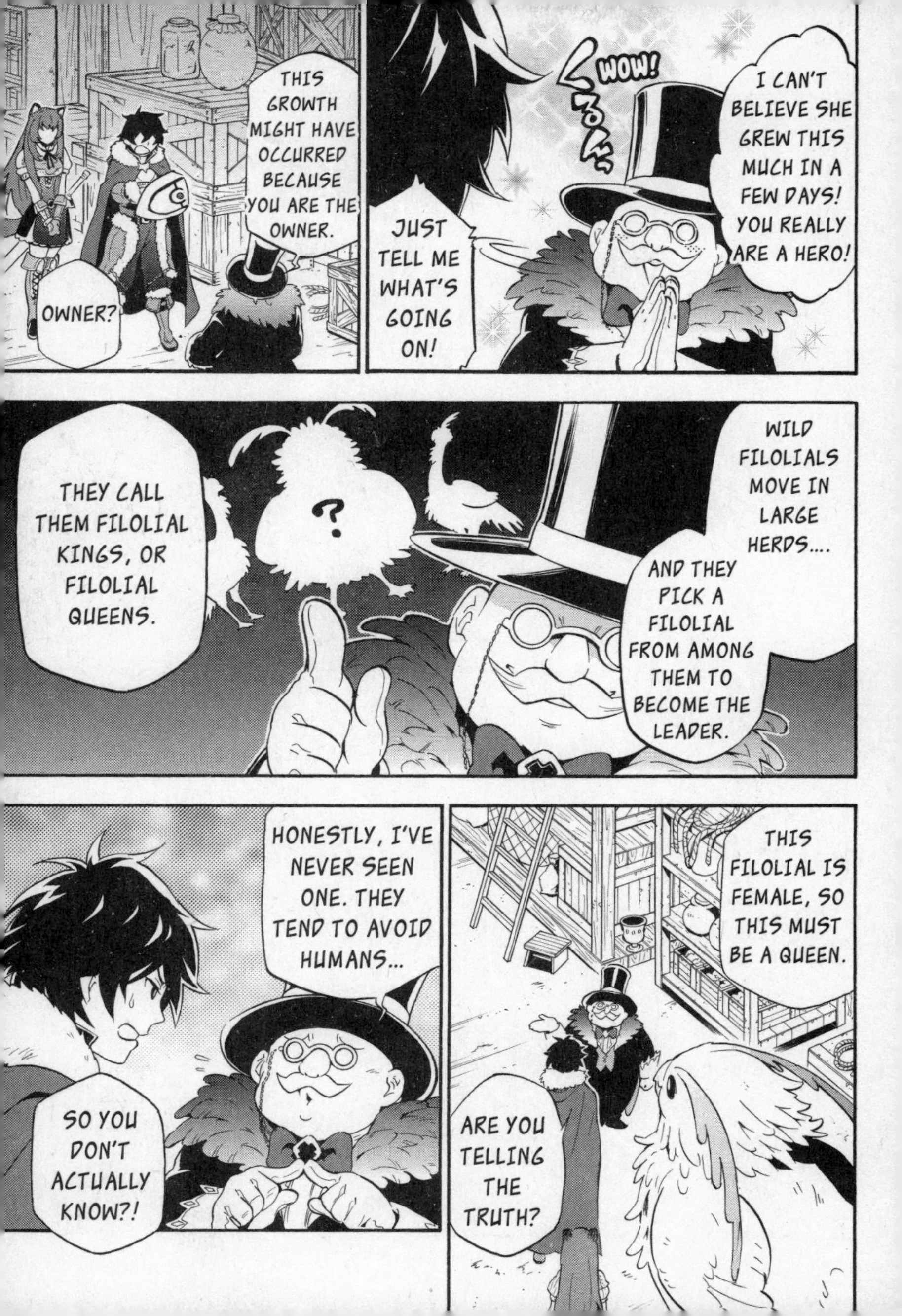
WOW!
くるん
I CAN'T BELIEVE SHE GREW THIS MUCH IN A FEW DAYS! YOU REALLY ARE A HERO!
JUST TELL ME WHAT'S GOING ON!
THIS GROWTH MIGHT HAVE OCCURRED BECAUSE YOU ARE THE OWNER.
OWNER?
WILD FILOLIALS MOVE IN LARGE HERDS....
AND THEY PICK A FILOLIAL FROM AMONG THEM TO BECOME THE LEADER.
THEY CALL THEM FILOLIAL KINGS, OR FILOLIAL QUEENS.
?
THIS FILOLIAL IS FEMALE, SO THIS MUST BE A QUEEN.
ARE YOU TELLING THE TRUTH?
HONESTLY, I'VE NEVER SEEN ONE. THEY TEND TO AVOID HUMANS...
SO YOU DON'T ACTUALLY KNOW?!

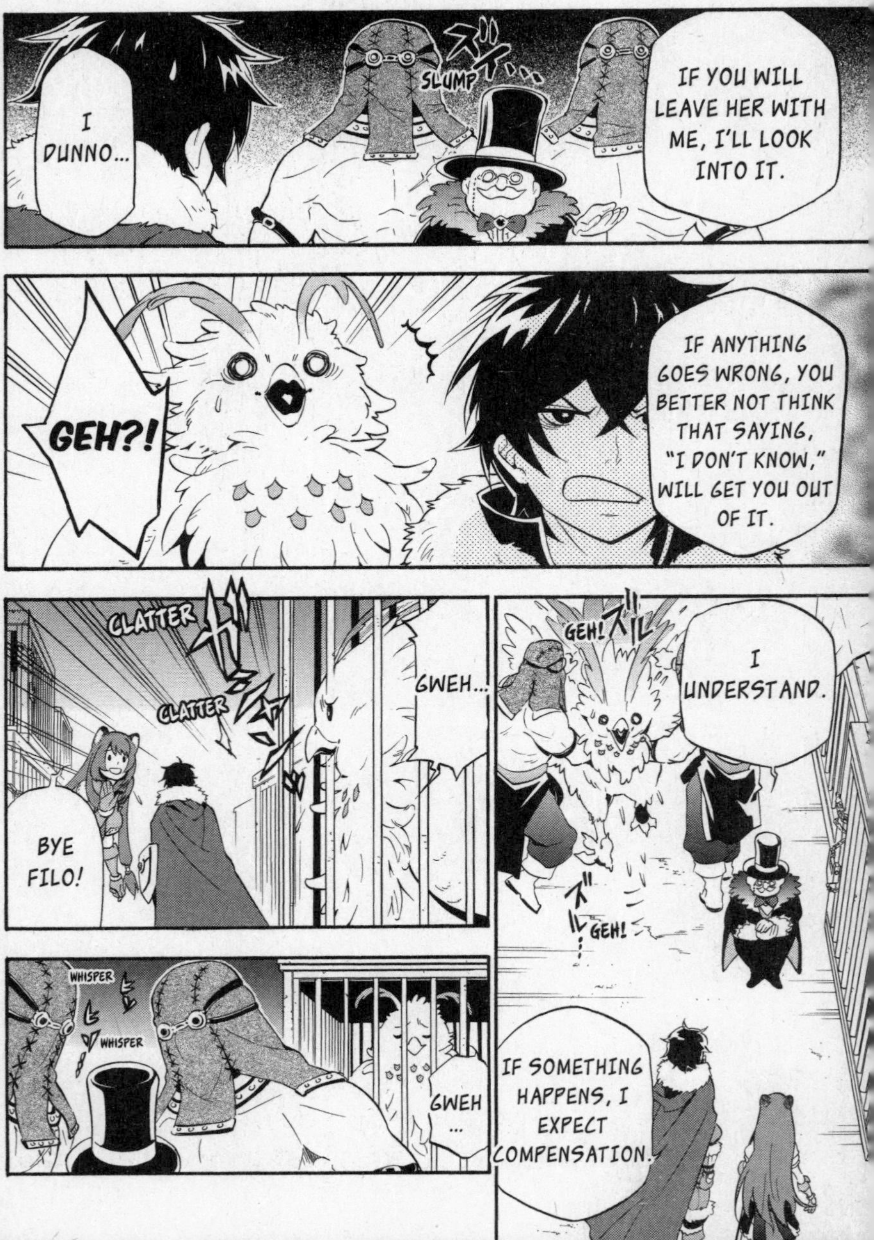
IF YOU WILL LEAVE HER WITH ME, I'LL LOOK INTO IT.
SLUMP
I DUNNO...
IF ANYTHING GOES WRONG, YOU BETTER NOT THINK THAT SAYING, "I DON'T KNOW," WILL GET YOU OUT OF IT.
GEH?!
I UNDERSTAND.
GEH!
GEH!
IF SOMETHING HAPPENS, I EXPECT COMPENSATION.
GWEH...
CLATTER
CLATTER
BYE FILO!
GWEH ...
WHISPER
WHISPER

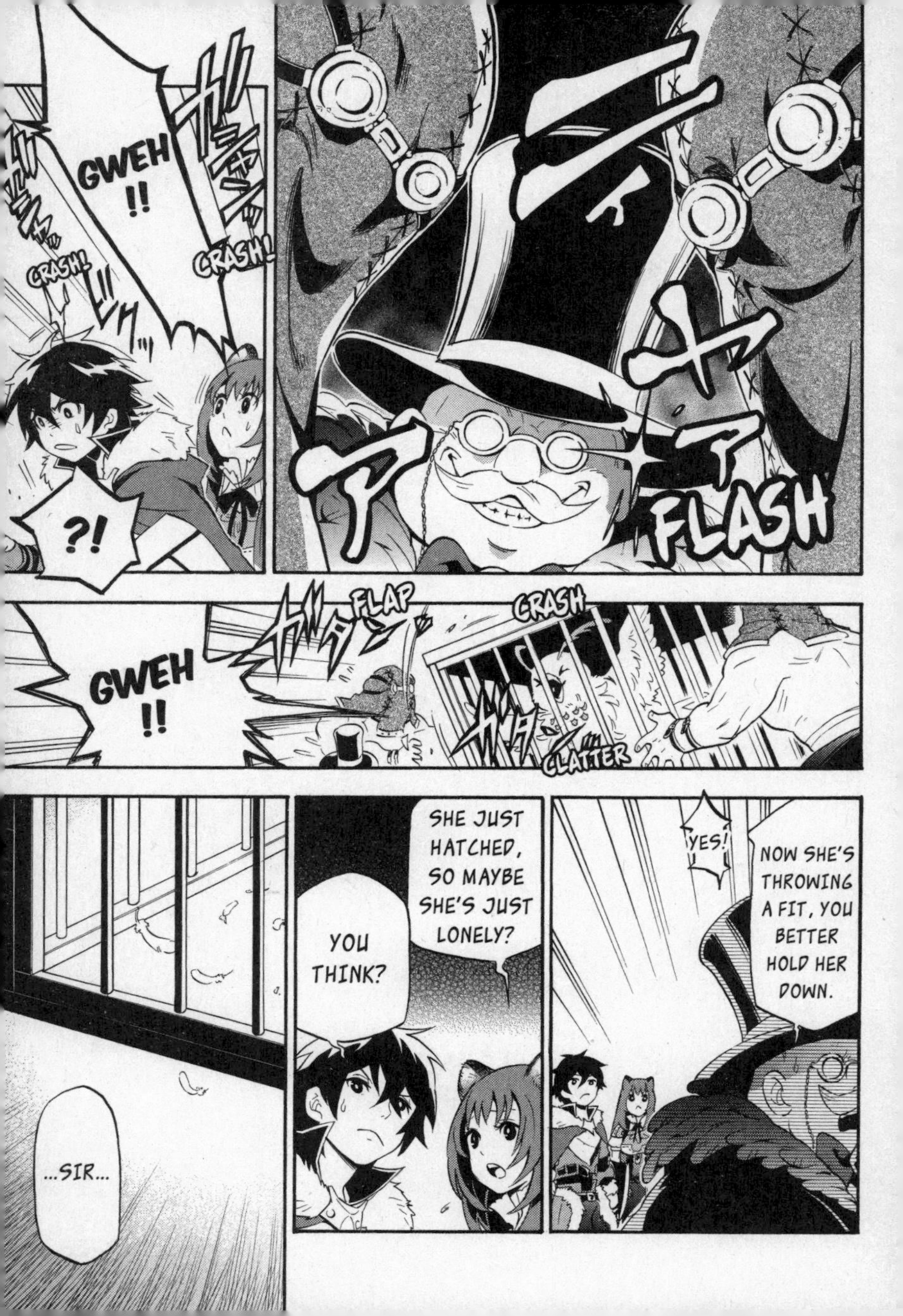
FLASH
GWEH!!
CRASH!
CRASH!
?!
CRASH
FLAP
GWEH!!
CLATTER
YES!
NOW SHE'S THROWING A FIT, YOU BETTER HOLD HER DOWN.
SHE JUST HATCHED, SO MAYBE SHE'S JUST LONELY?
YOU THINK?
...SIR...

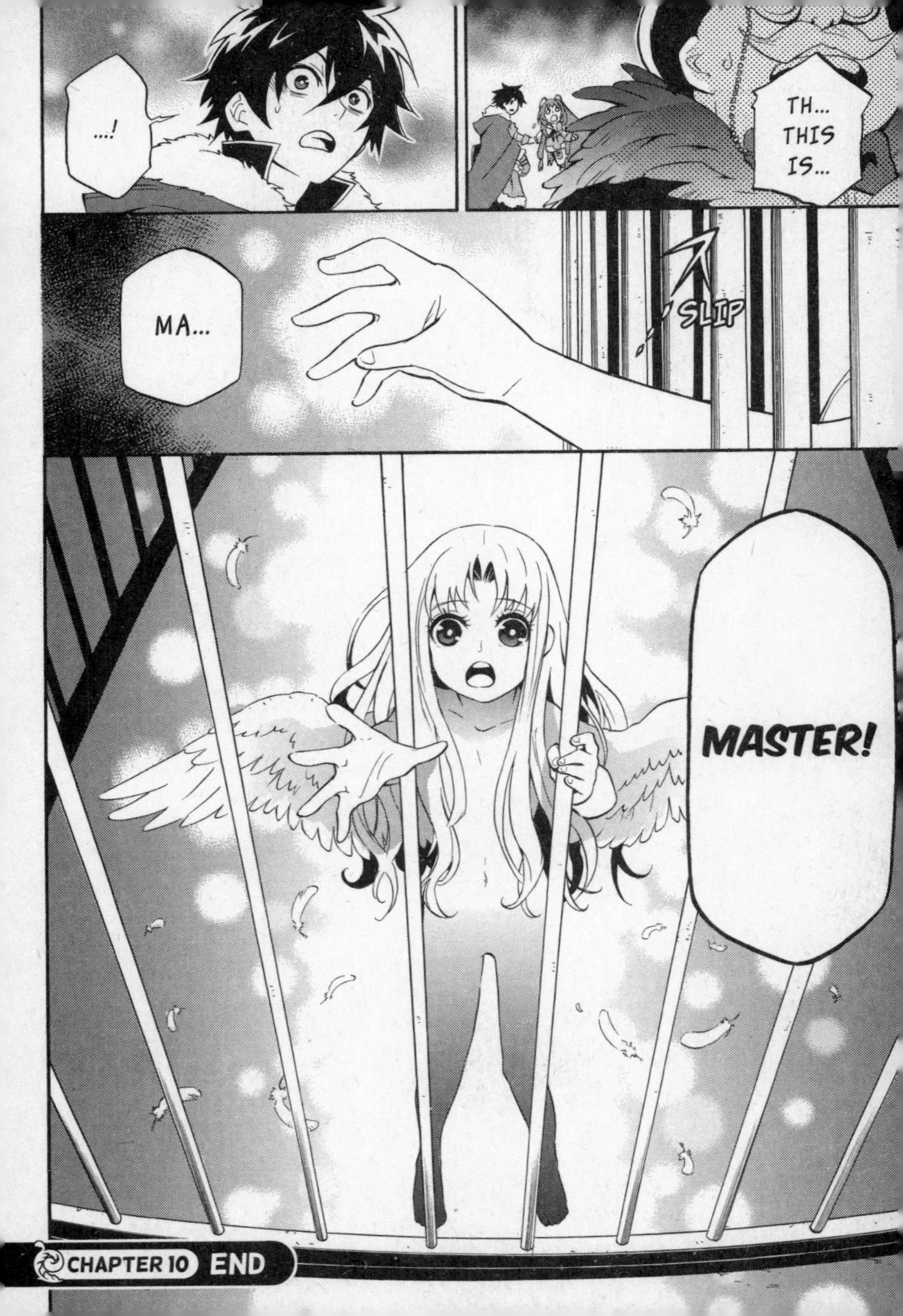
TH... THIS IS...
...!
SLIP
MA...
MASTER!
CHAPTER 10 END

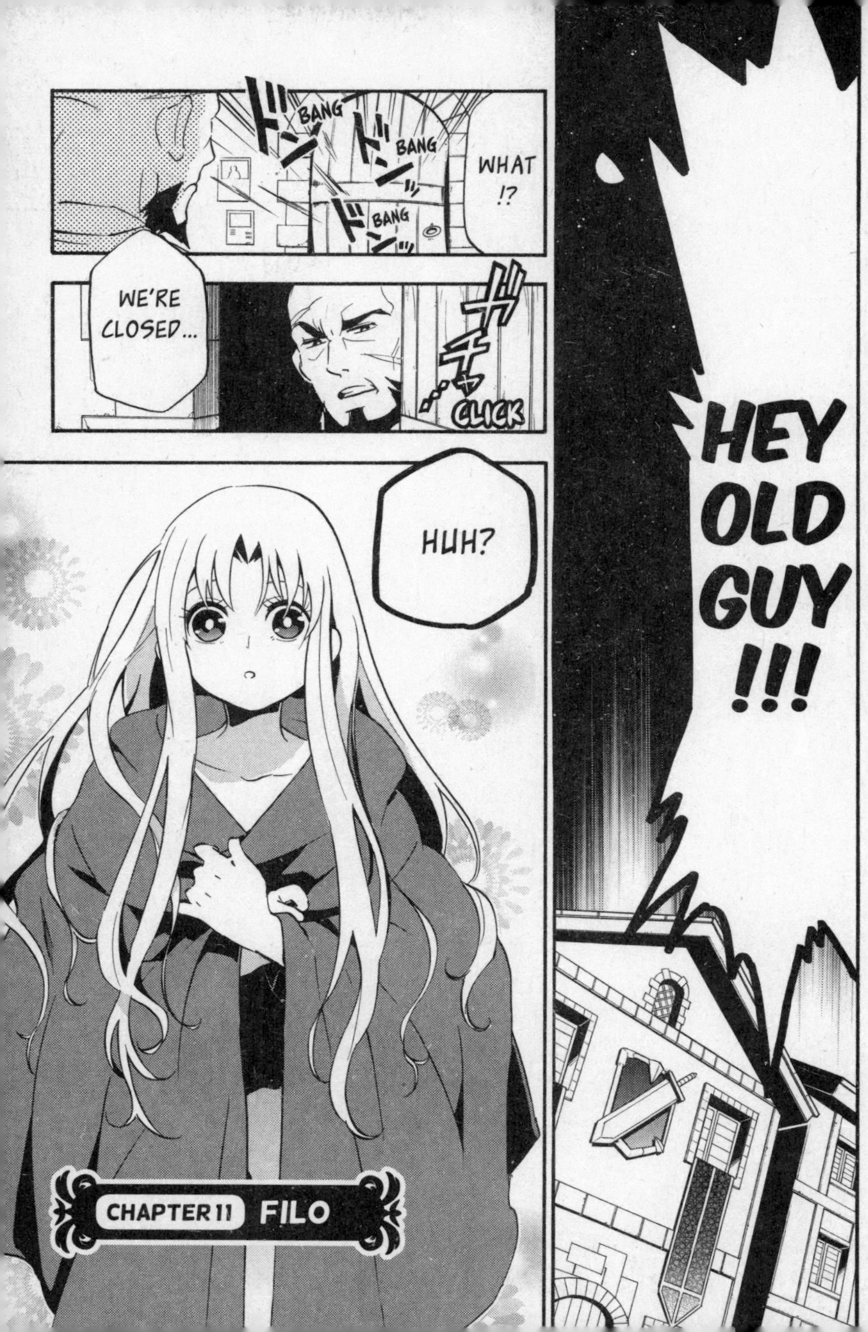
HEY OLD GUY !!!
BANG
BANG
BANG
WHAT !?
CLICK
WE'RE CLOSED...
HUH?
CHAPTER 11 FILO

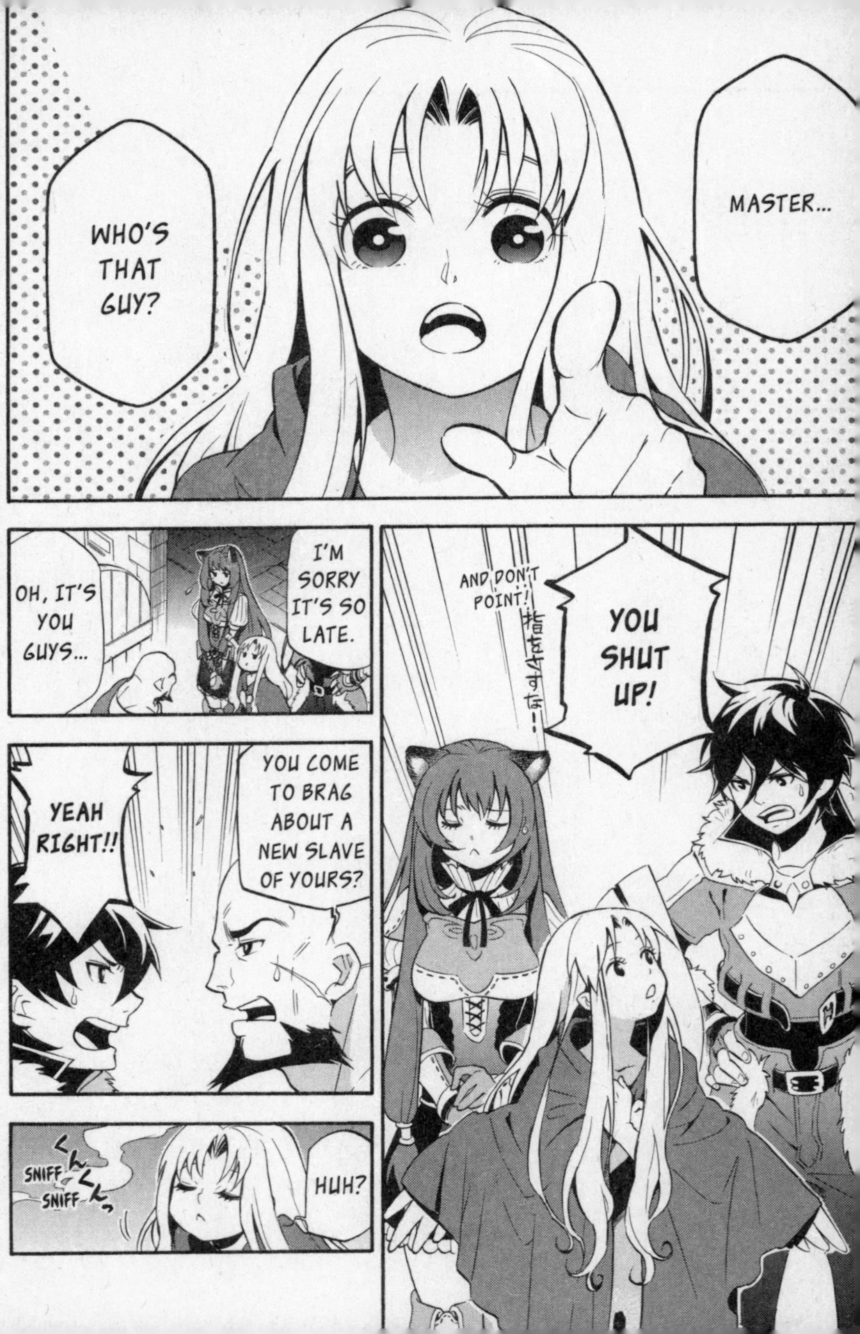
MASTER...
WHO'S THAT GUY?
YOU SHUT UP!
AND DON'T POINT!
指をさすな!
I'M SORRY IT'S SO LATE.
OH, IT'S YOU GUYS...
YOU COME TO BRAG ABOUT A NEW SLAVE OF YOURS?
YEAH RIGHT!!
HUH?
くんくん
SNIFF SNIFF

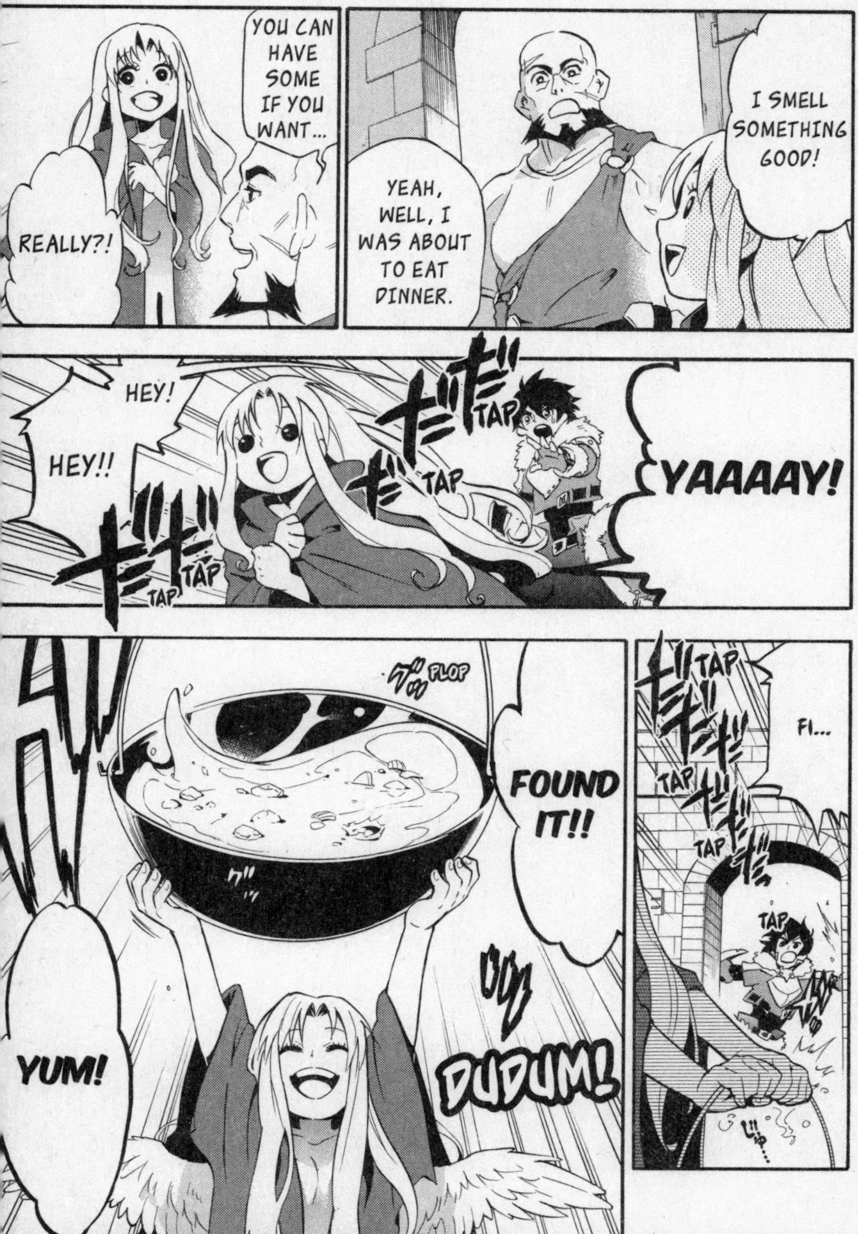
I SMELL SOMETHING GOOD!
YEAH, WELL, I WAS ABOUT TO EAT DINNER.
YOU CAN HAVE SOME IF YOU WANT...
REALLY?!
YAAAAY!
TAP
TAP
HEY!
HEY!!
TAP
TAP
TAP
FI...
TAP
TAP
TAP
FOUND IT!!
PLOP
DUDUM!
YUM!

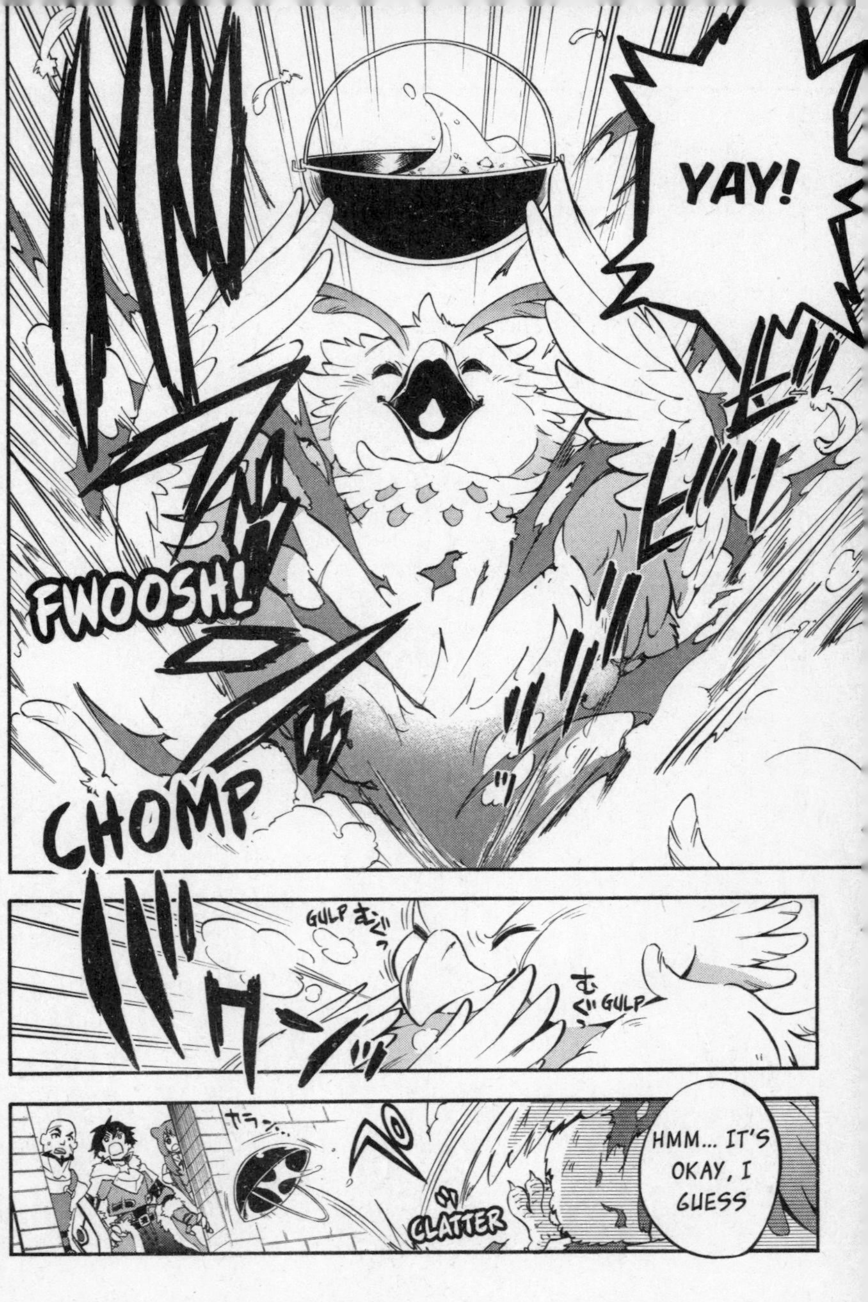
YAY!
FWOOSH!
CHOMP
むぐ GULP
GULP むぐっ
HMM... IT'S OKAY, I GUESS
CLATTER
カラン…

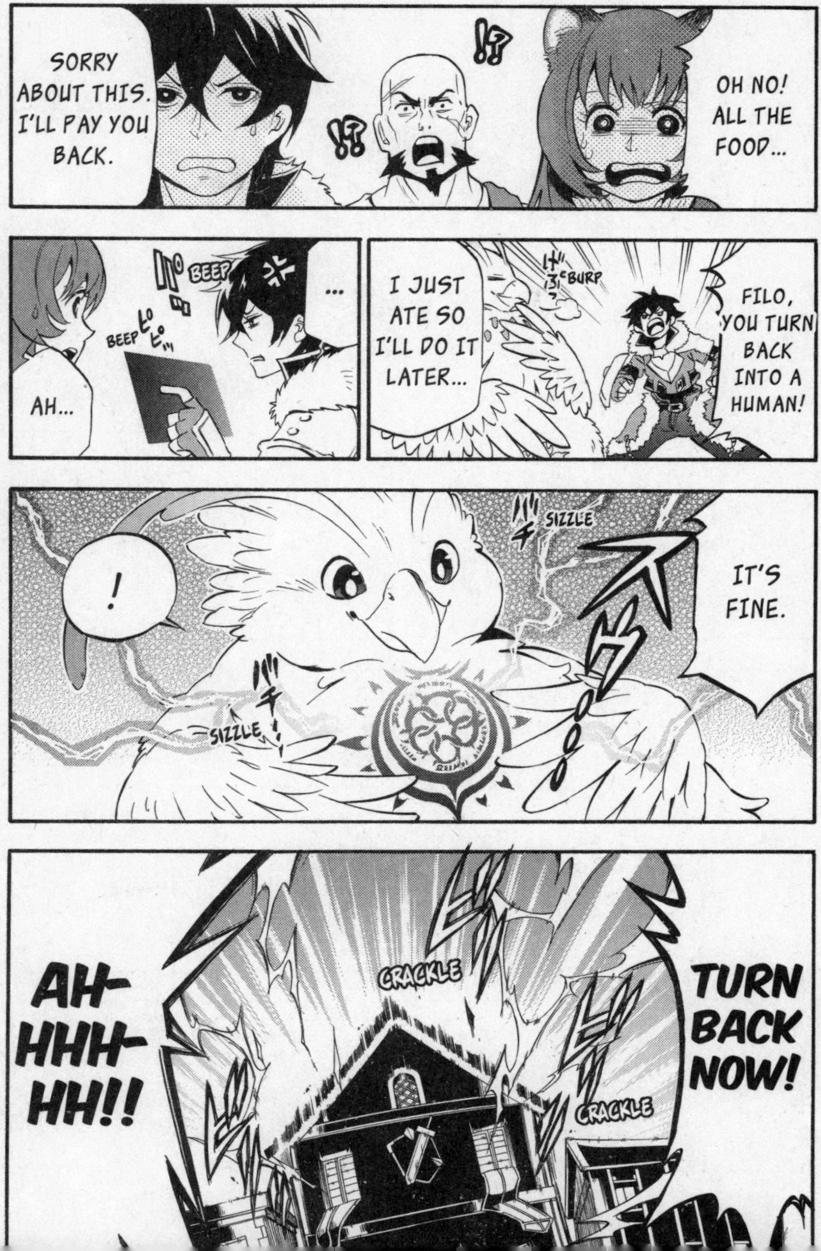
OH NO! ALL THE FOOD...
!?
!?
SORRY ABOUT THIS. I'LL PAY YOU BACK.
FILO, YOU TURN BACK INTO A HUMAN!
BURP
I JUST ATE SO I'LL DO IT LATER...
...
BEEP
BEEP
AH...
IT'S FINE.
SIZZLE
!
SIZZLE
TURN BACK NOW!
CRACKLE
CRACKLE
AH-HHH-HH!!

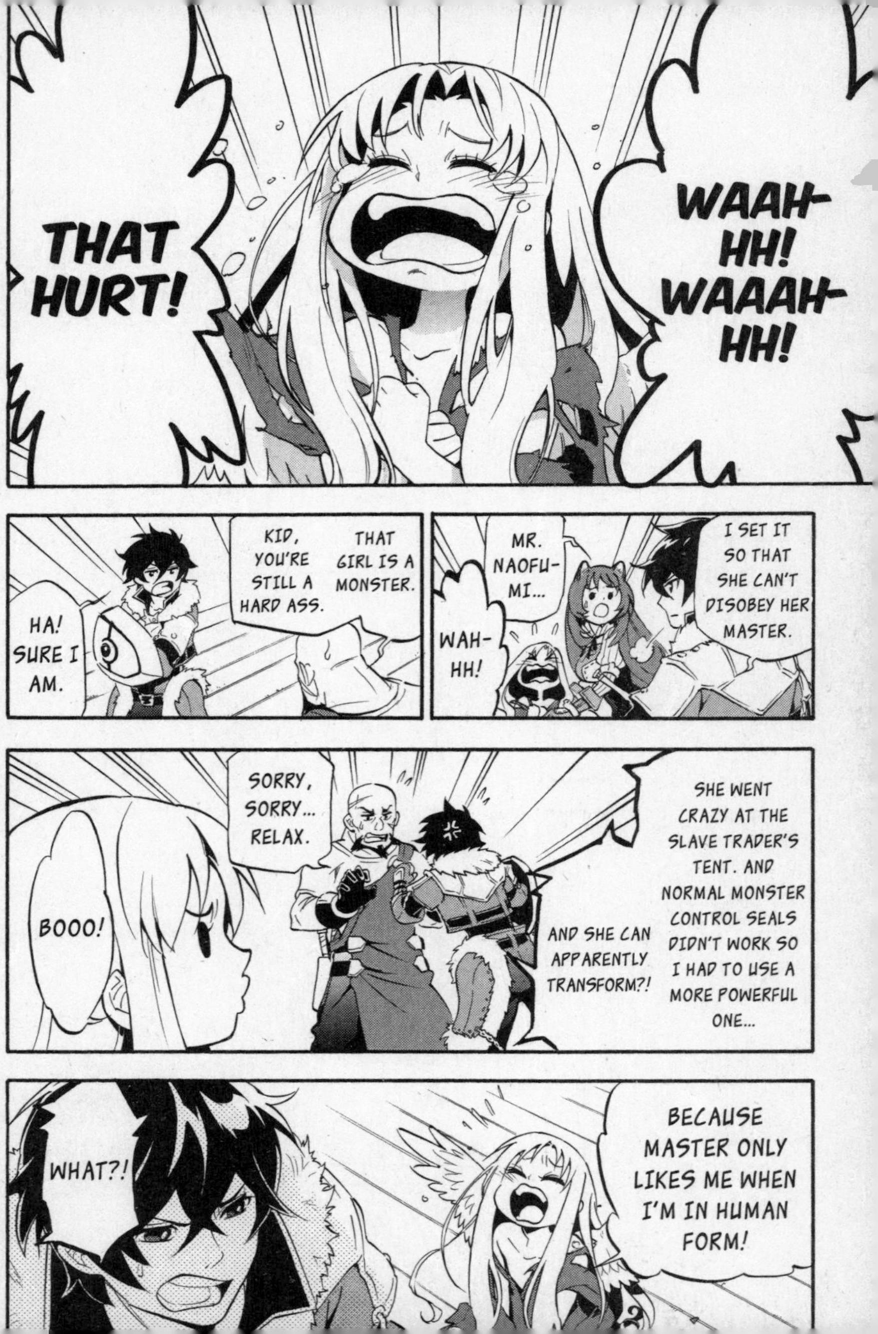

WAAHHH! WAAAHHH!
THAT HURT!
I SET IT SO THAT SHE CAN'T DISOBEY HER MASTER.
MR. NAOFUMI...
WAHHH!
THAT GIRL IS A MONSTER.
KID, YOU'RE STILL A HARD ASS.
HA! SURE I AM.
SHE WENT CRAZY AT THE SLAVE TRADER'S TENT. AND NORMAL MONSTER CONTROL SEALS DIDN'T WORK SO I HAD TO USE A MORE POWERFUL ONE...
AND SHE CAN APPARENTLY TRANSFORM?!
SORRY, SORRY... RELAX.
BOOO!
BECAUSE MASTER ONLY LIKES ME WHEN I'M IN HUMAN FORM!
WHAT?!

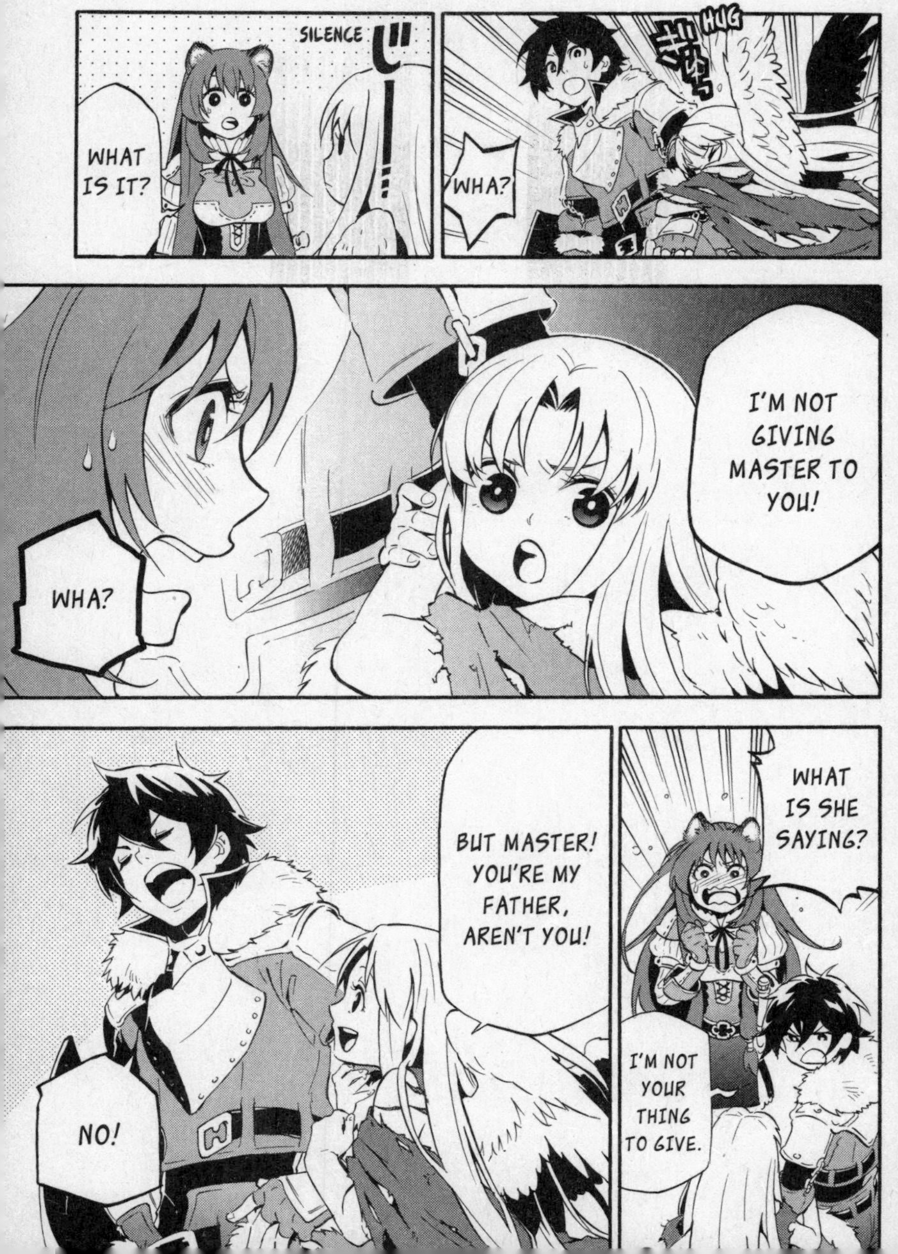
HUG
WHA?
SILENCE
WHAT IS IT?
I'M NOT GIVING MASTER TO YOU!
WHA?
WHAT IS SHE SAYING?
I'M NOT YOUR THING TO GIVE.
BUT MASTER! YOU'RE MY FATHER, AREN'T YOU!
NO!

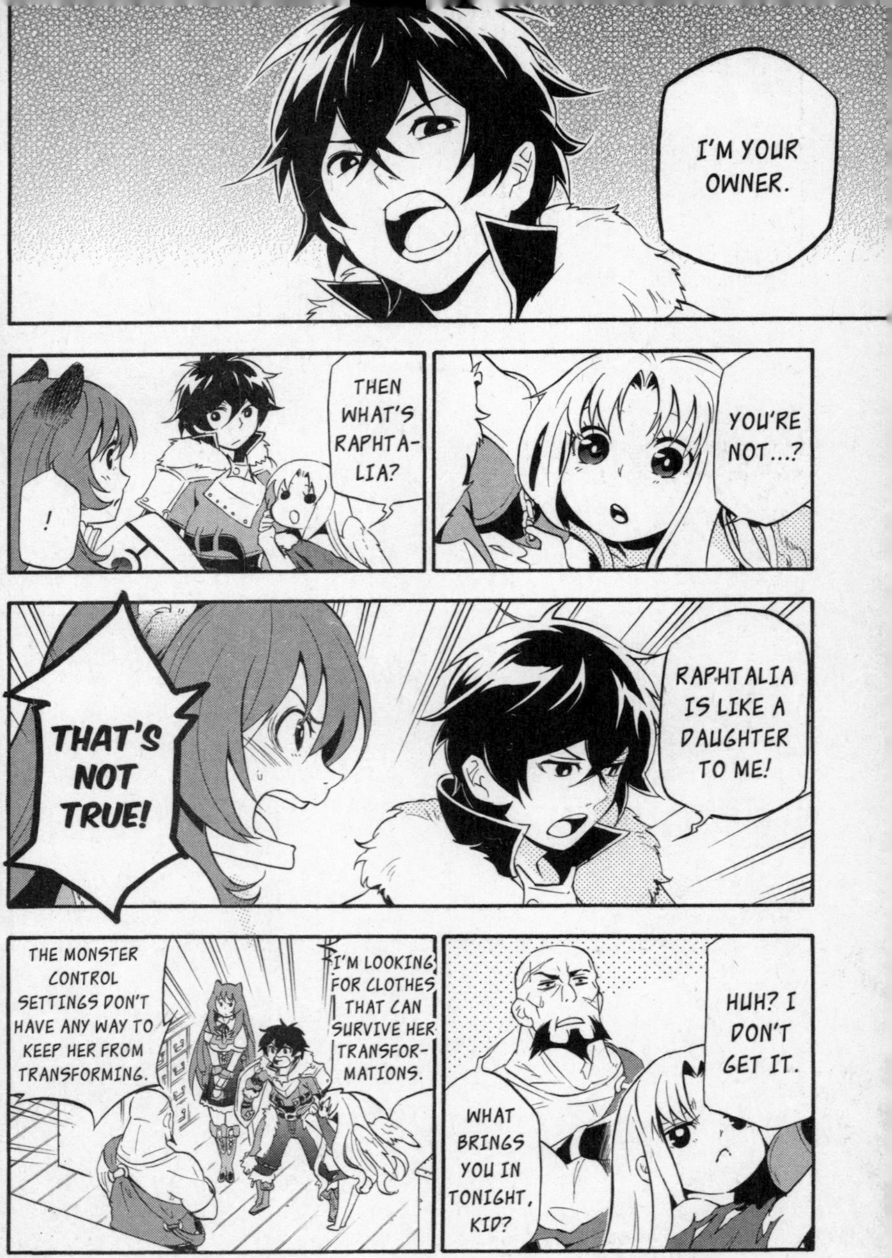
I'M YOUR OWNER.
YOU'RE NOT...?
THEN WHAT'S RAPHTA-LIA?
!
RAPHTALIA IS LIKE A DAUGHTER TO ME!
THAT'S NOT TRUE!
HUH? I DON'T GET IT.
WHAT BRINGS YOU IN TONIGHT, KID?
I'M LOOKING FOR CLOTHES THAT CAN SURVIVE HER TRANSFOR-MATIONS.
THE MONSTER CONTROL SETTINGS DON'T HAVE ANY WAY TO KEEP HER FROM TRANSFORMING.

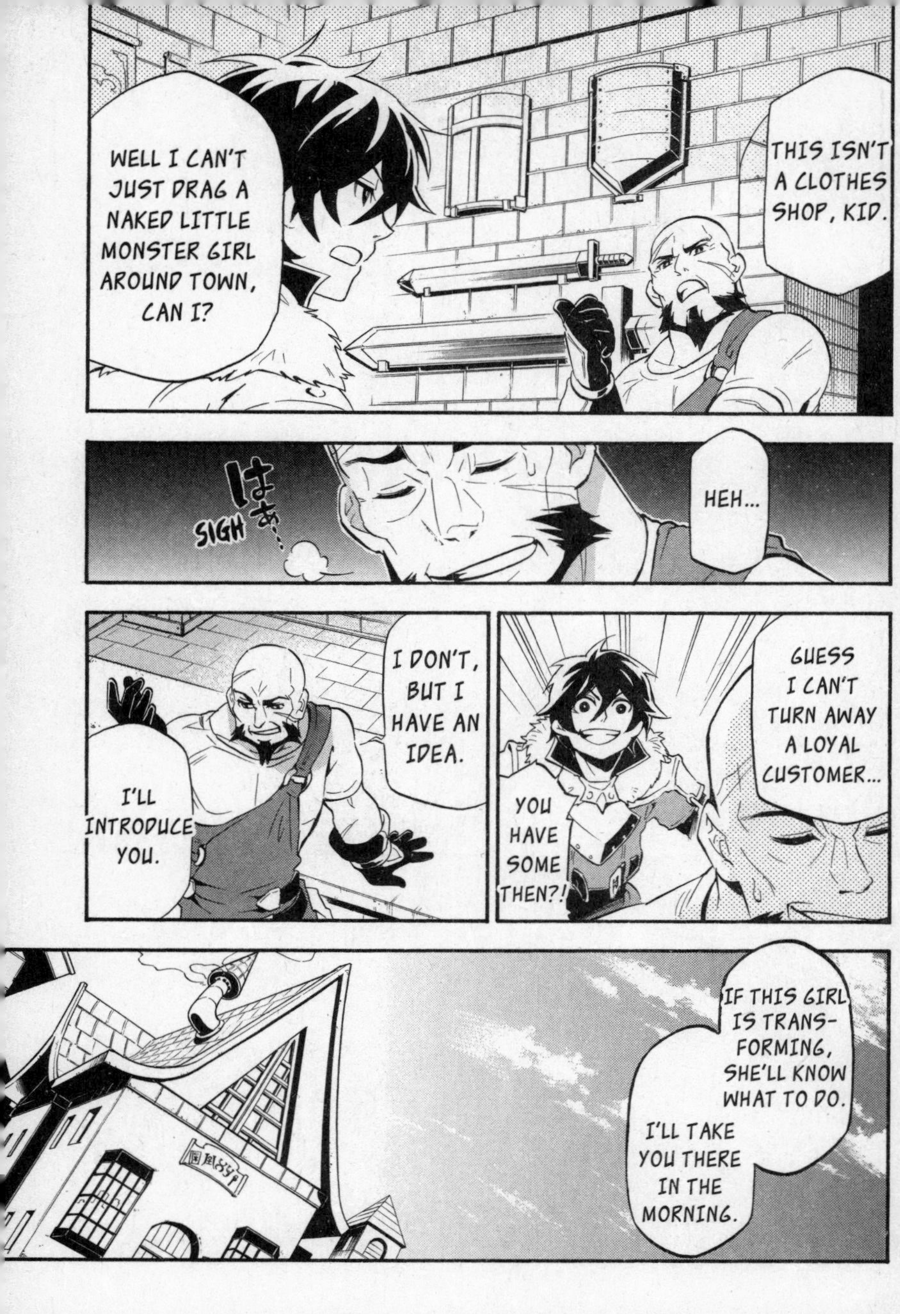
THIS ISN'T A CLOTHES SHOP, KID.
WELL I CAN'T JUST DRAG A NAKED LITTLE MONSTER GIRL AROUND TOWN, CAN I?
HEH...
はぁ…
SIGH
GUESS I CAN'T TURN AWAY A LOYAL CUSTOMER...
YOU HAVE SOME THEN?!
I DON'T, BUT I HAVE AN IDEA.
I'LL INTRODUCE YOU.
IF THIS GIRL IS TRANS-FORMING, SHE'LL KNOW WHAT TO DO.
I'LL TAKE YOU THERE IN THE MORNING.

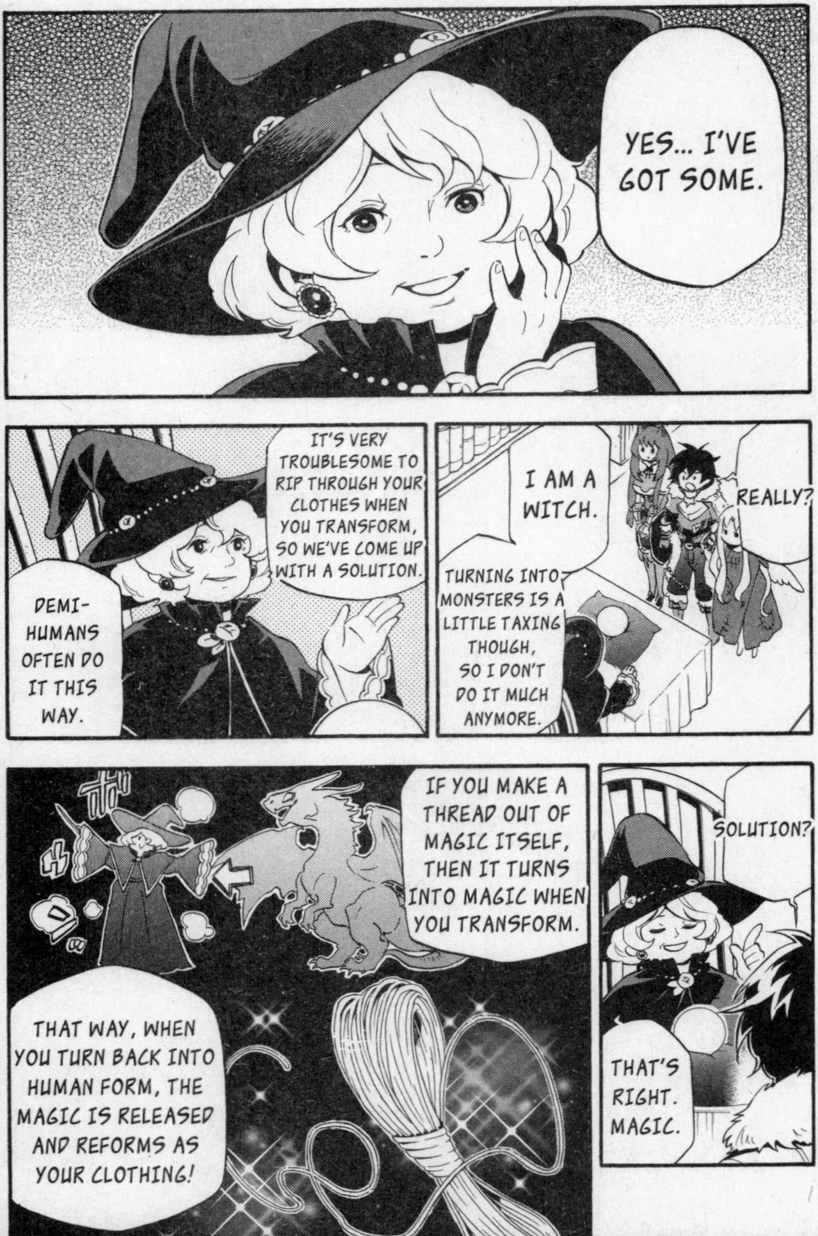
YES... I'VE GOT SOME.
REALLY?
I AM A WITCH.
TURNING INTO MONSTERS IS A LITTLE TAXING THOUGH, SO I DON'T DO IT MUCH ANYMORE.
IT'S VERY TROUBLESOME TO RIP THROUGH YOUR CLOTHES WHEN YOU TRANSFORM, SO WE'VE COME UP WITH A SOLUTION.
DEMI-HUMANS OFTEN DO IT THIS WAY.
SOLUTION?
THAT'S RIGHT. MAGIC.
IF YOU MAKE A THREAD OUT OF MAGIC ITSELF, THEN IT TURNS INTO MAGIC WHEN YOU TRANSFORM.
THAT WAY, WHEN YOU TURN BACK INTO HUMAN FORM, THE MAGIC IS RELEASED AND REFORMS AS YOUR CLOTHING!

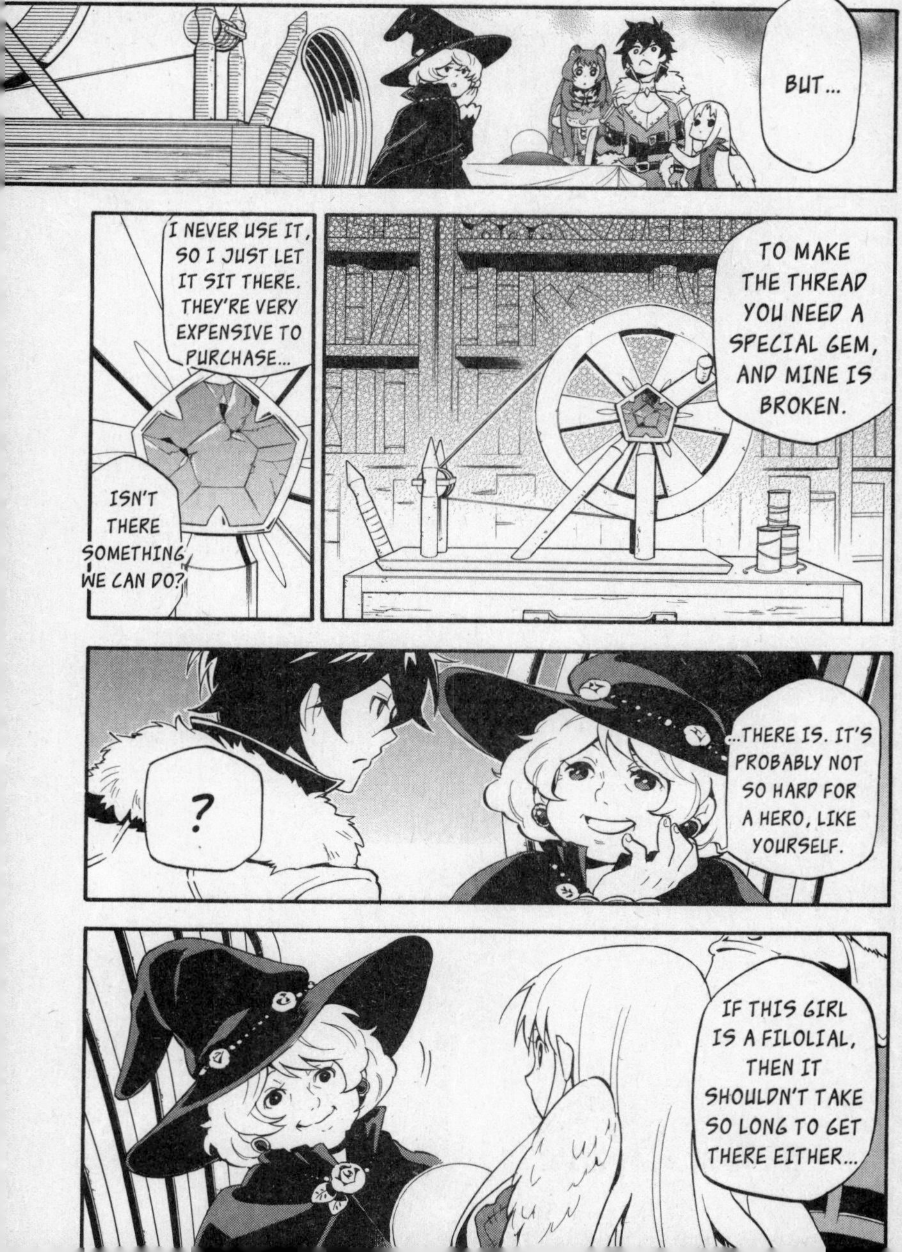
BUT...
TO MAKE THE THREAD YOU NEED A SPECIAL GEM, AND MINE IS BROKEN.
I NEVER USE IT, SO I JUST LET IT SIT THERE. THEY'RE VERY EXPENSIVE TO PURCHASE...
ISN'T THERE SOMETHING WE CAN DO?
...THERE IS. IT'S PROBABLY NOT SO HARD FOR A HERO, LIKE YOURSELF.
?
IF THIS GIRL IS A FILOLIAL, THEN IT SHOULDN'T TAKE SO LONG TO GET THERE EITHER...

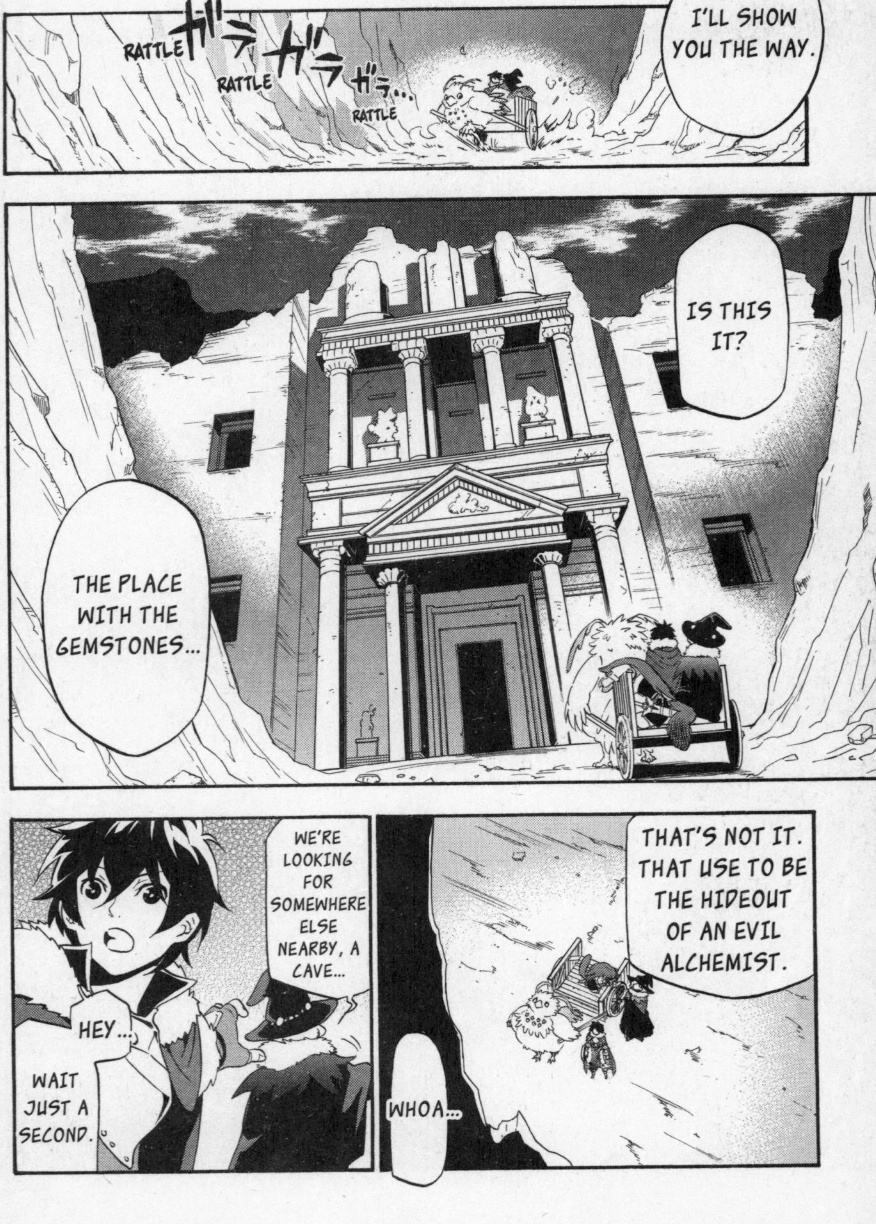
I'LL SHOW YOU THE WAY.
RATTLE ガラ
RATTLE ガラ
RATTLE ガラ…
IS THIS IT?
THE PLACE WITH THE GEMSTONES...
THAT'S NOT IT. THAT USE TO BE THE HIDEOUT OF AN EVIL ALCHEMIST.
WHOA...
WE'RE LOOKING FOR SOMEWHERE ELSE NEARBY, A CAVE...
HEY...
WAIT JUST A SECOND.

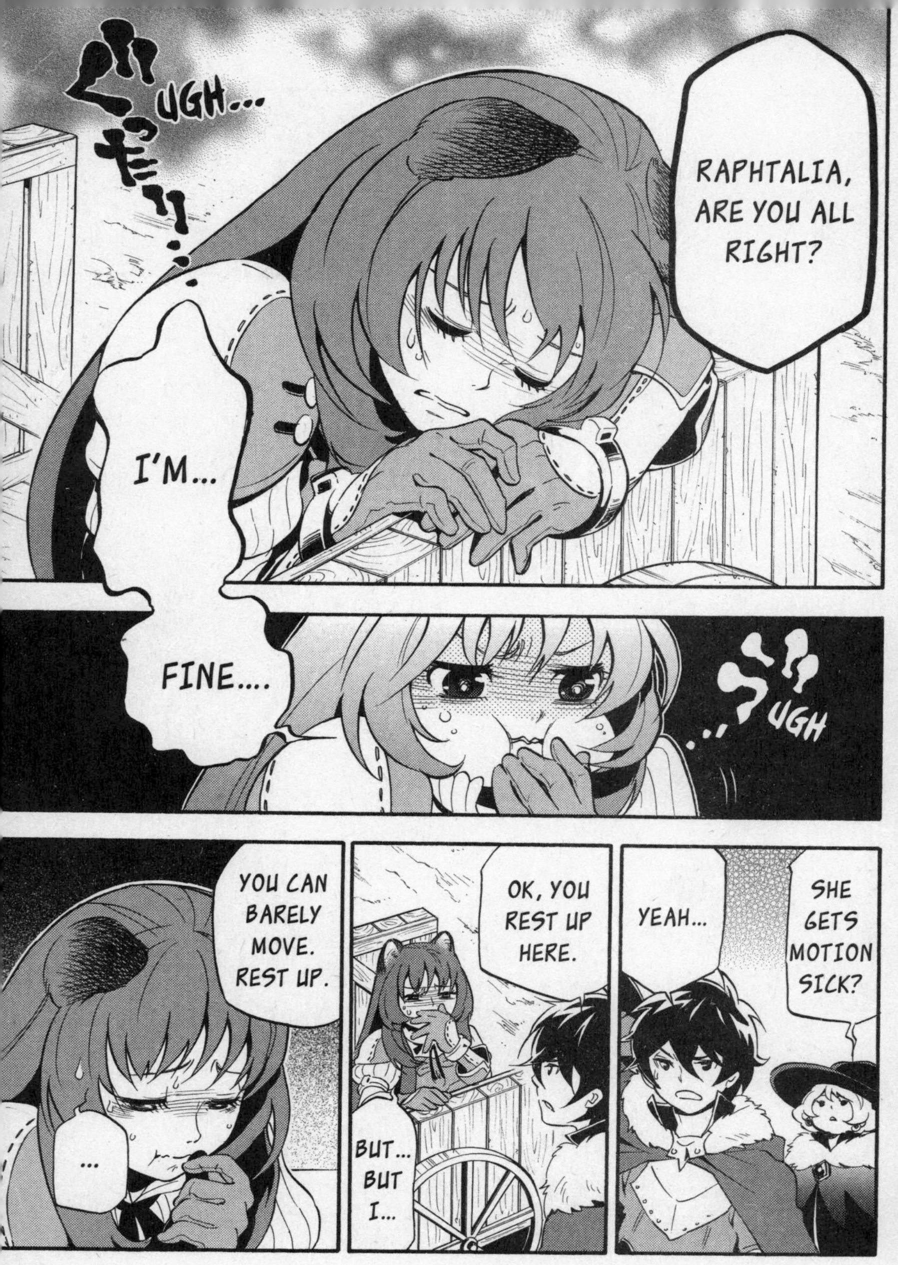
RAPHTALIA, ARE YOU ALL RIGHT?
UGH...
I'M...
FINE....
UGH
SHE GETS MOTION SICK?
YEAH...
OK, YOU REST UP HERE.
BUT... BUT I...
YOU CAN BARELY MOVE. REST UP.
...

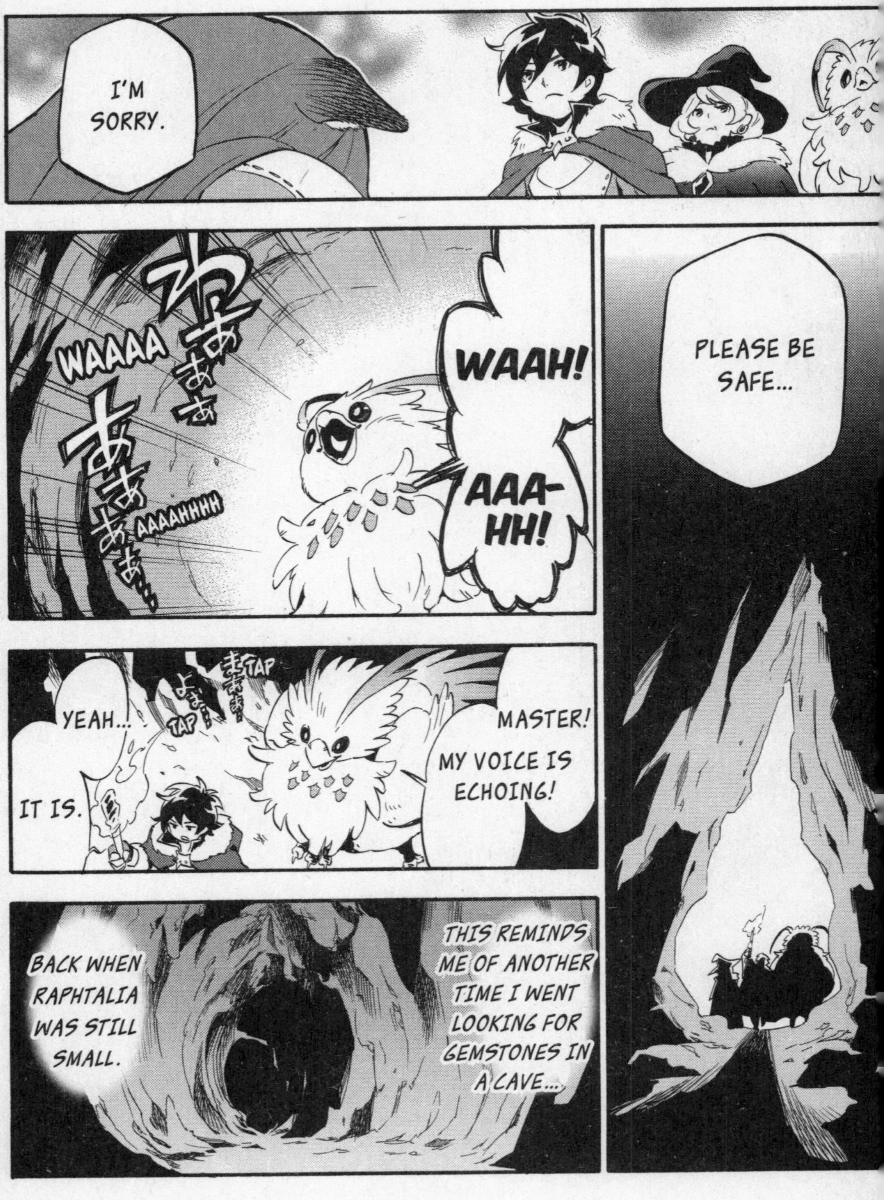
I'M SORRY.
PLEASE BE SAFE...
WAAH! AAA-HH!
WAAAA
AAAAHHHH
MASTER! MY VOICE IS ECHOING!
TAP
TAP
YEAH... IT IS.
THIS REMINDS ME OF ANOTHER TIME I WENT LOOKING FOR GEMSTONES IN A CAVE...
BACK WHEN RAPHTALIA WAS STILL SMALL.

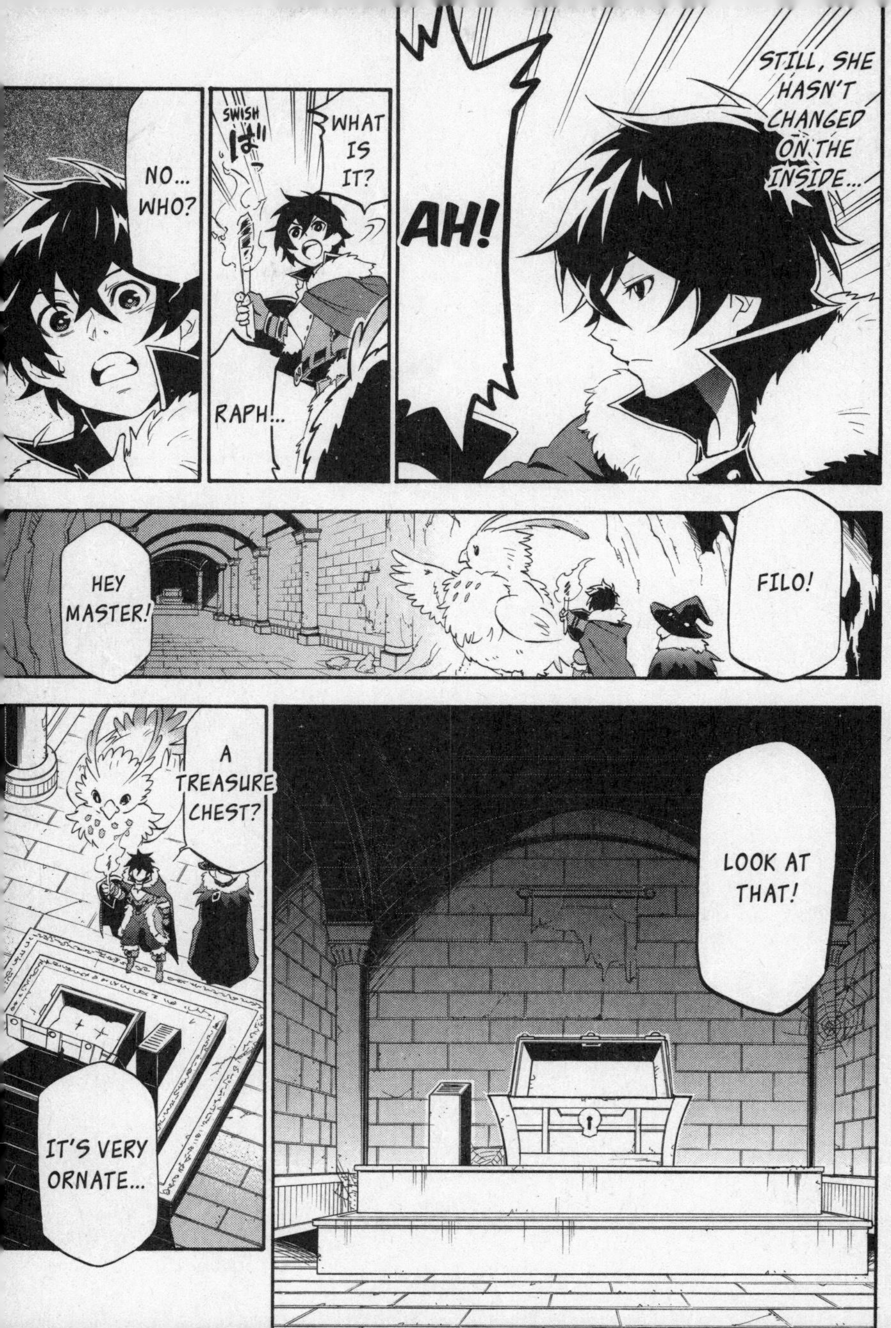
STILL, SHE HASN'T CHANGED ON THE INSIDE...
AH!
WHAT IS IT?
SWISH
ばっ
RAPH...
NO... WHO?
FILO!
HEY MASTER!
LOOK AT THAT!
A TREASURE CHEST?
IT'S VERY ORNATE...

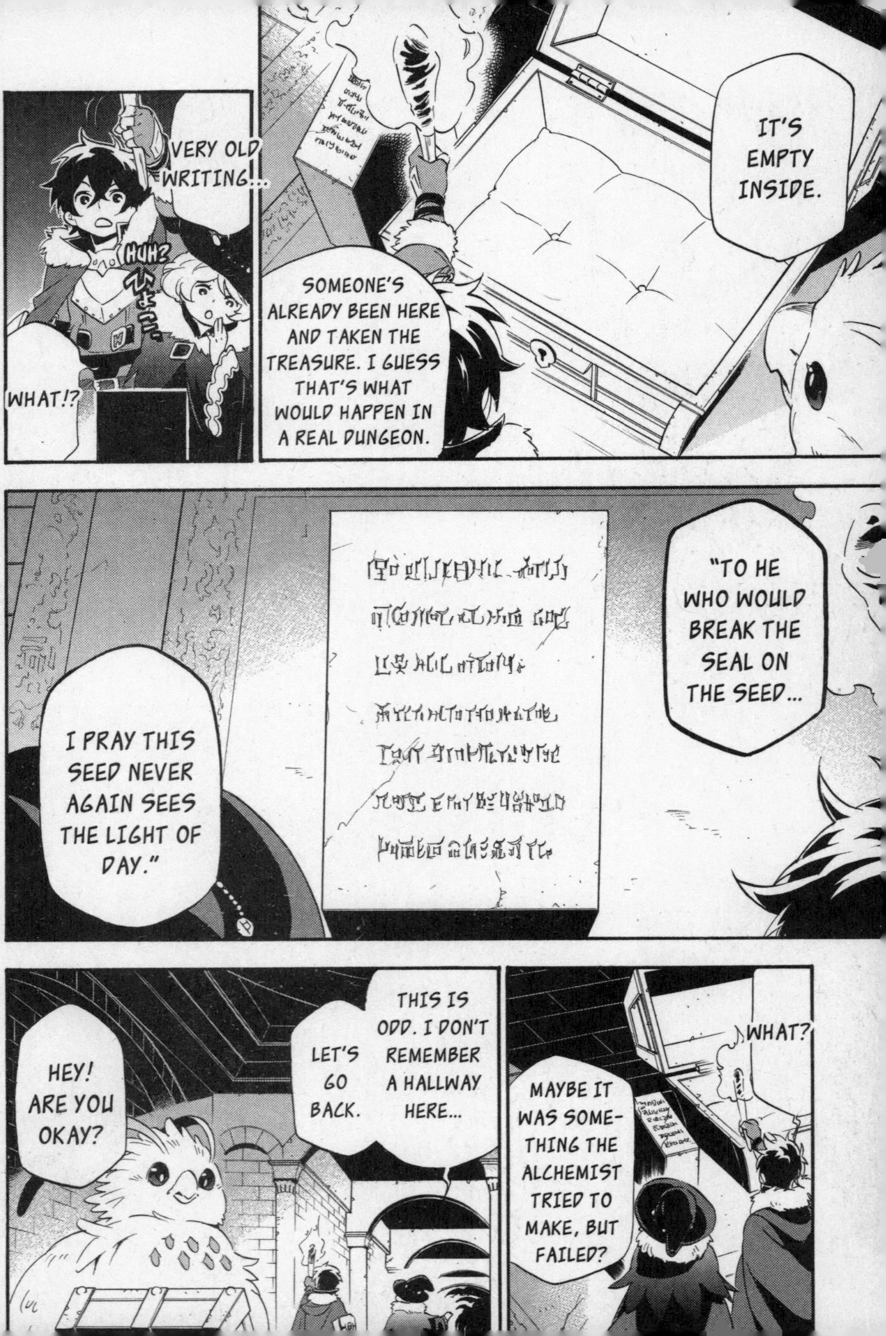
IT'S EMPTY INSIDE.
SOMEONE'S ALREADY BEEN HERE AND TAKEN THE TREASURE. I GUESS THAT'S WHAT WOULD HAPPEN IN A REAL DUNGEON.
VERY OLD WRITING...
HUH?
ひょこっ
WHAT!?
"TO HE WHO WOULD BREAK THE SEAL ON THE SEED...
I PRAY THIS SEED NEVER AGAIN SEES THE LIGHT OF DAY."
WHAT?
MAYBE IT WAS SOME-THING THE ALCHEMIST TRIED TO MAKE, BUT FAILED?
THIS IS ODD. I DON'T REMEMBER A HALLWAY HERE...
LET'S GO BACK.
HEY! ARE YOU OKAY?

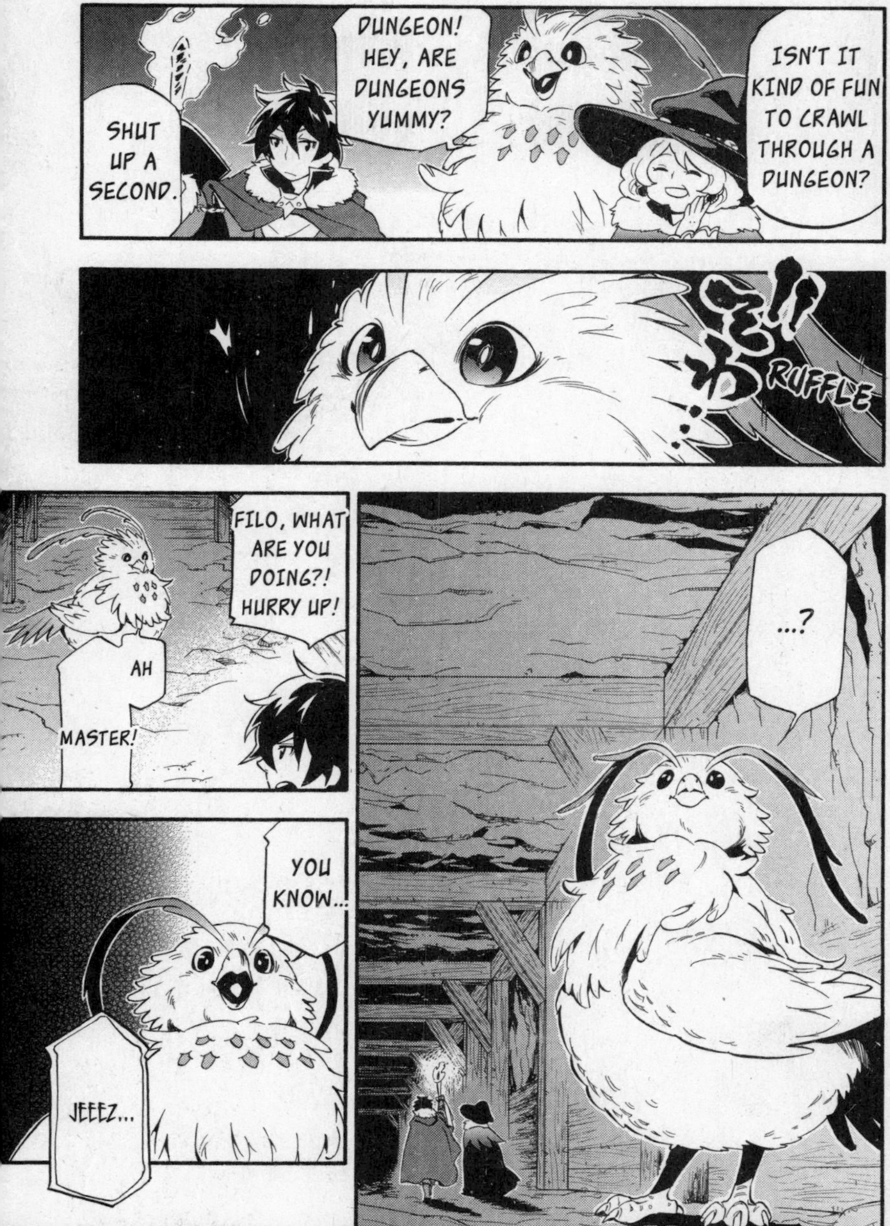
ISN'T IT KIND OF FUN TO CRAWL THROUGH A DUNGEON?
DUNGEON! HEY, ARE DUNGEONS YUMMY?
SHUT UP A SECOND.
RUFFLE
...?
FILO, WHAT ARE YOU DOING?! HURRY UP!
AH
MASTER!
YOU KNOW...
JEEEZ...

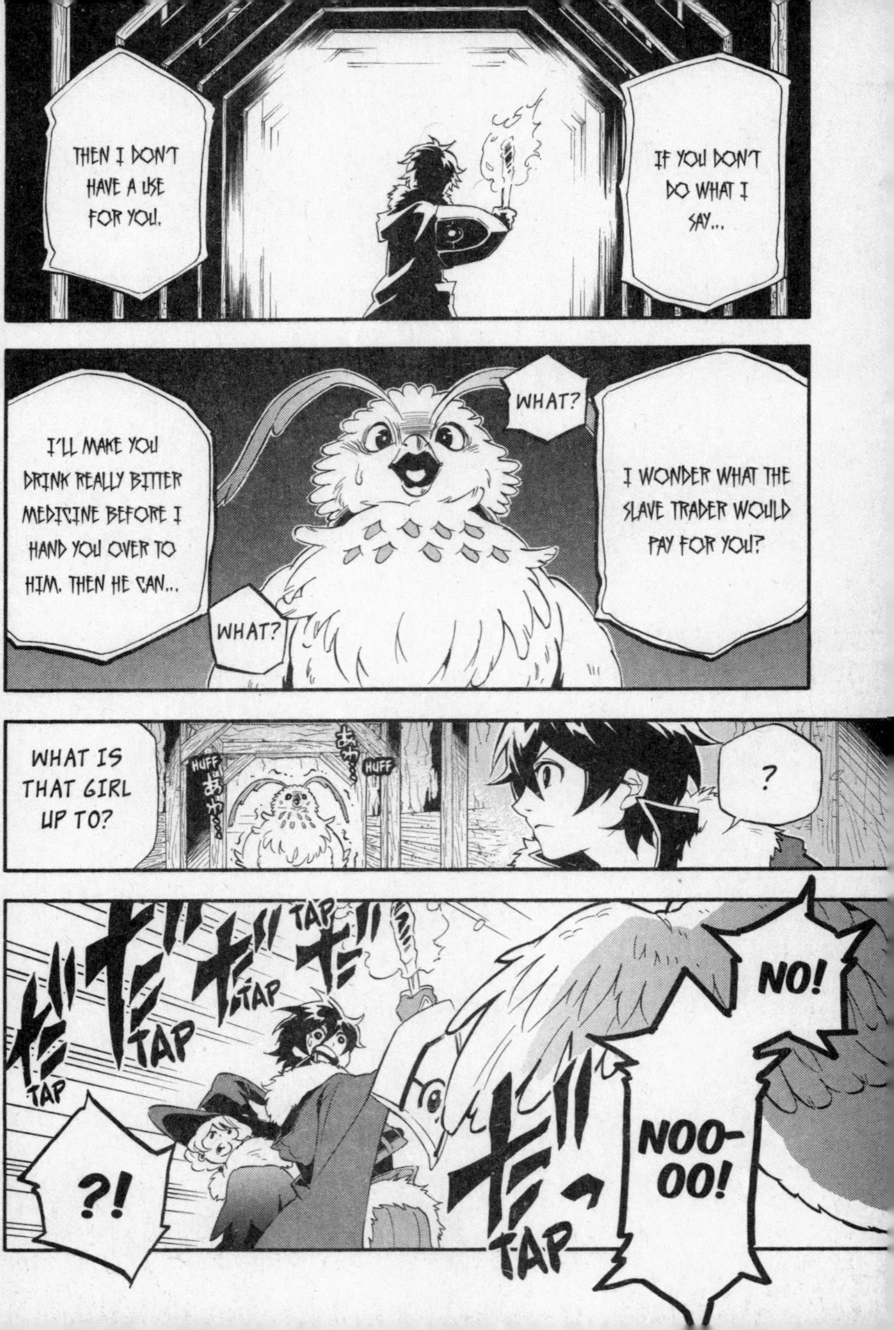
IF YOU DON'T DO WHAT I SAY...
THEN I DON'T HAVE A USE FOR YOU.
I WONDER WHAT THE SLAVE TRADER WOULD PAY FOR YOU?
WHAT?
I'LL MAKE YOU DRINK REALLY BITTER MEDICINE BEFORE I HAND YOU OVER TO HIM. THEN HE CAN...
WHAT?
?
HUFF
HUFF
WHAT IS THAT GIRL UP TO?
NO!
TAP
TAP
TAP
TAP
NOOO-OO!
TAP
?!

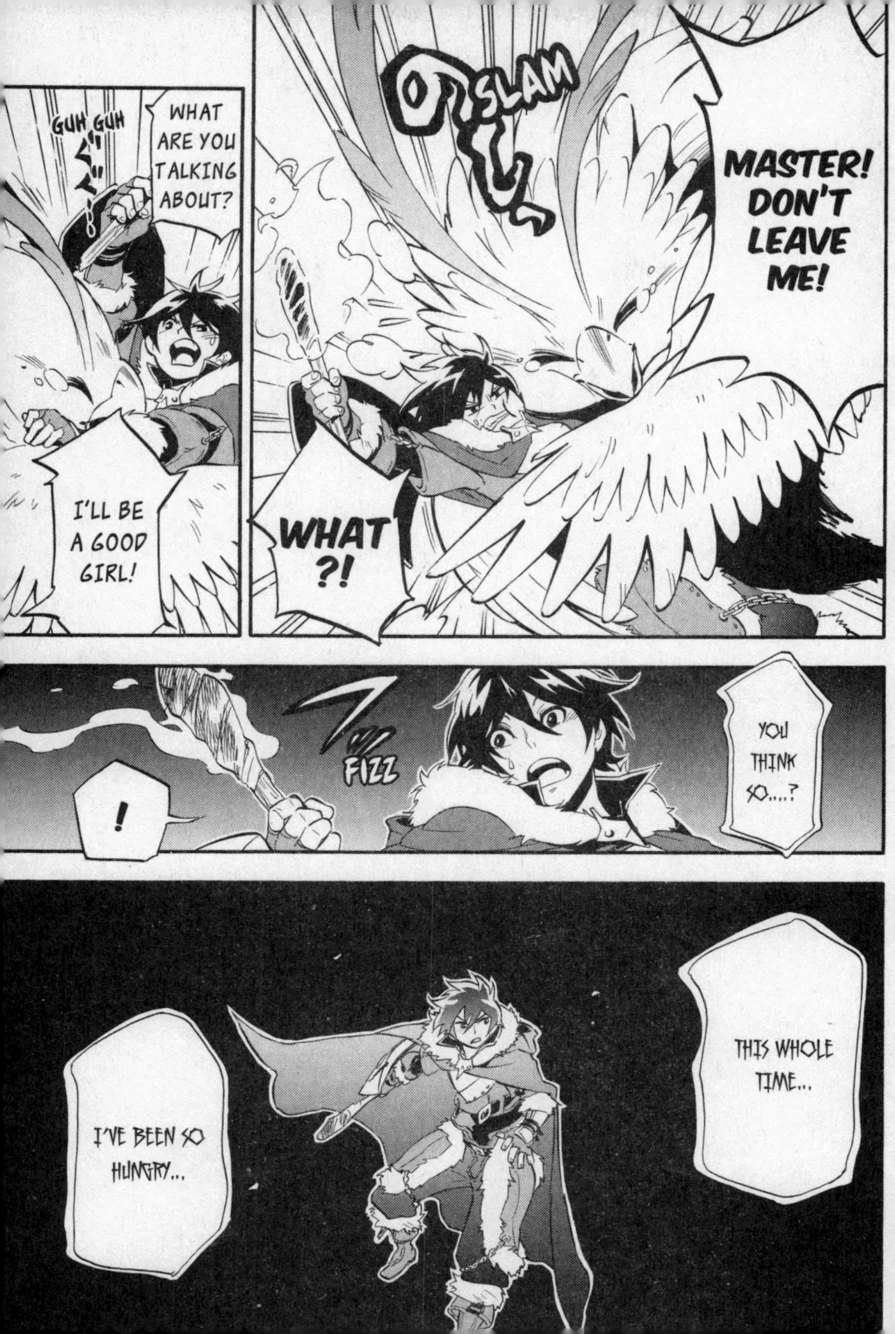
SLAM
MASTER! DON'T LEAVE ME!
WHAT ?!
GUH GUH
WHAT ARE YOU TALKING ABOUT?
I'LL BE A GOOD GIRL!
YOU THINK SO....?
FIZZ
!
THIS WHOLE TIME...
I'VE BEEN SO HUNGRY...

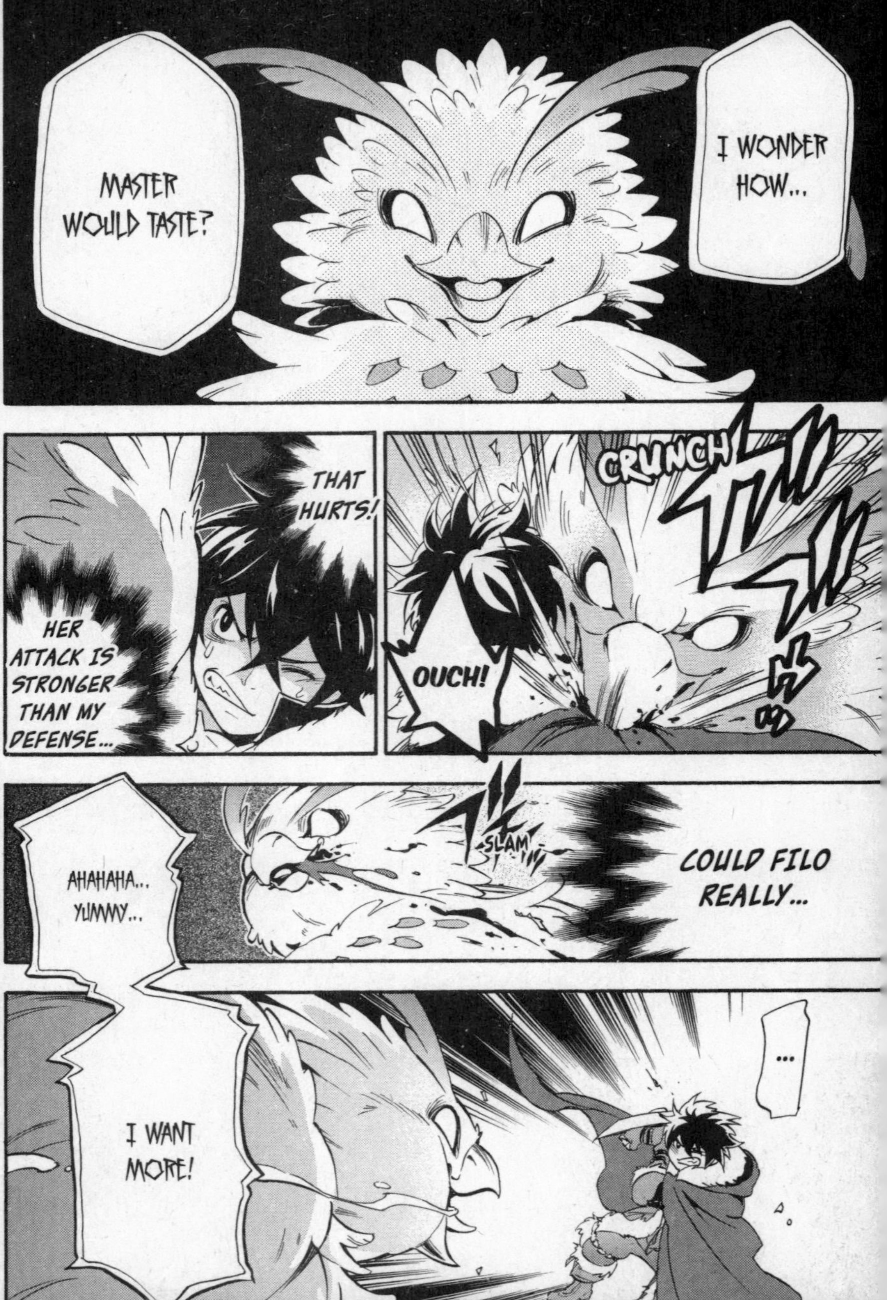
I WONDER HOW...
MASTER WOULD TASTE?
CRUNCH
OUCH!
THAT HURTS!
HER ATTACK IS STRONGER THAN MY DEFENSE...
COULD FILO REALLY...
SLAM
AHAHAHA... YUMMY...
...
I WANT MORE!

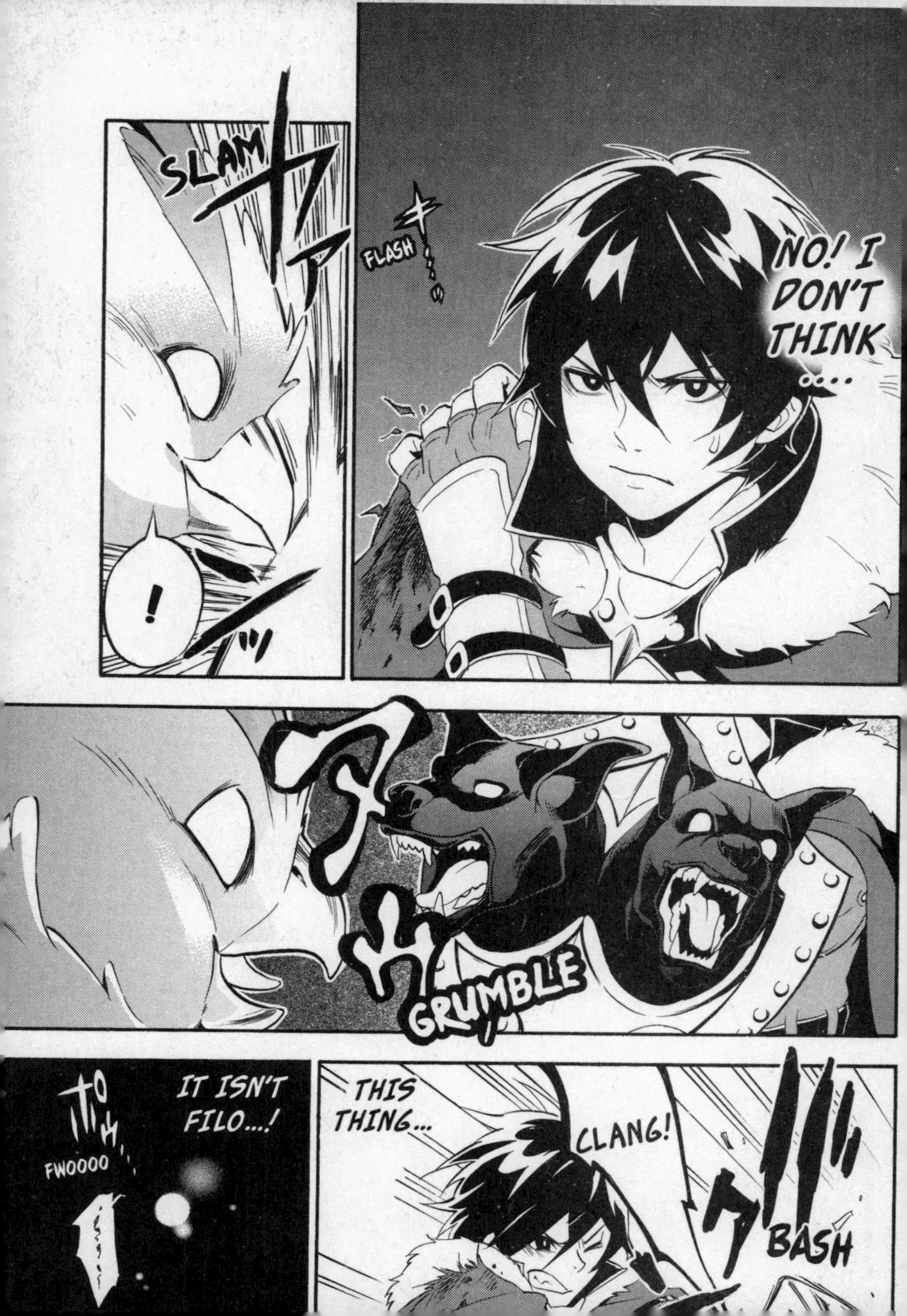
NO! I DON'T THINK....
FLASH
SLAM
!
GRUMBLE
THIS THING...
CLANG!
BASH
IT ISN'T FILO...!
FWOOOO

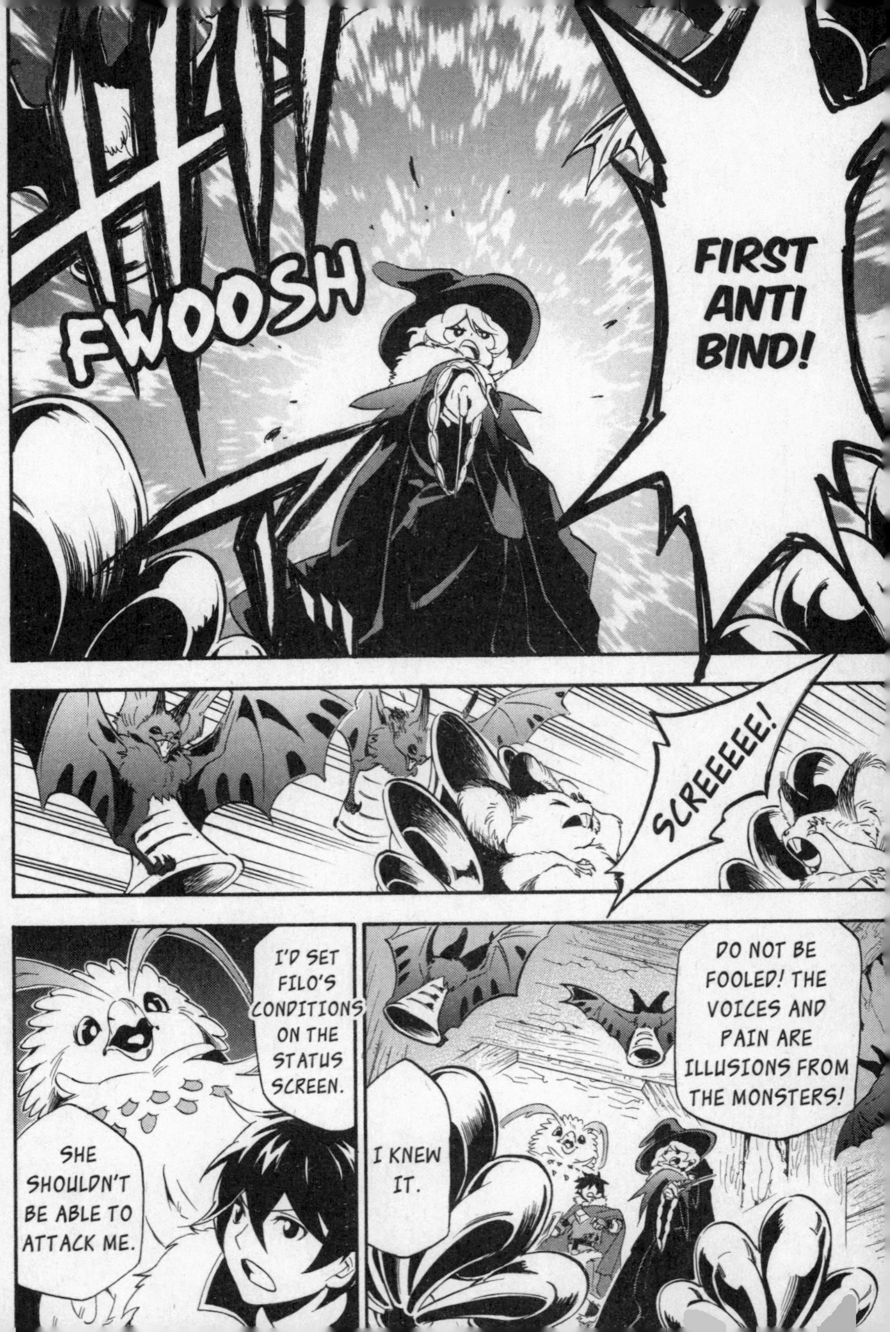
FIRST ANTI BIND!
FWOOSH
SCREEEEEE!
DO NOT BE FOOLED! THE VOICES AND PAIN ARE ILLUSIONS FROM THE MONSTERS!
I KNEW IT.
I'D SET FILO'S CONDITIONS ON THE STATUS SCREEN.
SHE SHOULDN'T BE ABLE TO ATTACK ME.

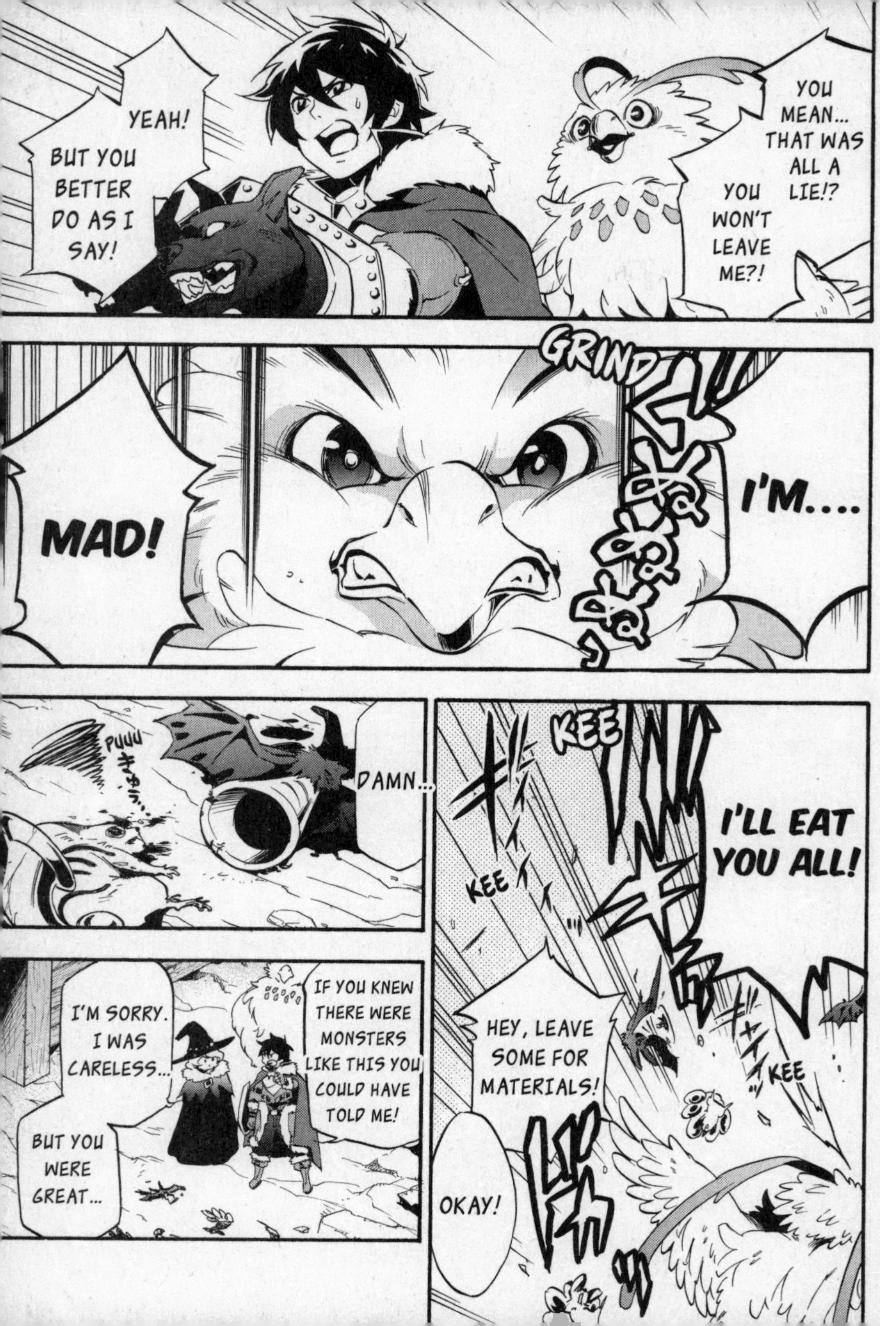
YOU MEAN... THAT WAS ALL A LIE!?
YOU WON'T LEAVE ME?!
YEAH!
BUT YOU BETTER DO AS I SAY!
GRIND
I'M....
MAD!
KEE
I'LL EAT YOU ALL!
KEE
HEY, LEAVE SOME FOR MATERIALS!
KEE
OKAY!
PUUU
DAMN...
IF YOU KNEW THERE WERE MONSTERS LIKE THIS YOU COULD HAVE TOLD ME!
I'M SORRY. I WAS CARELESS...
BUT YOU WERE GREAT...

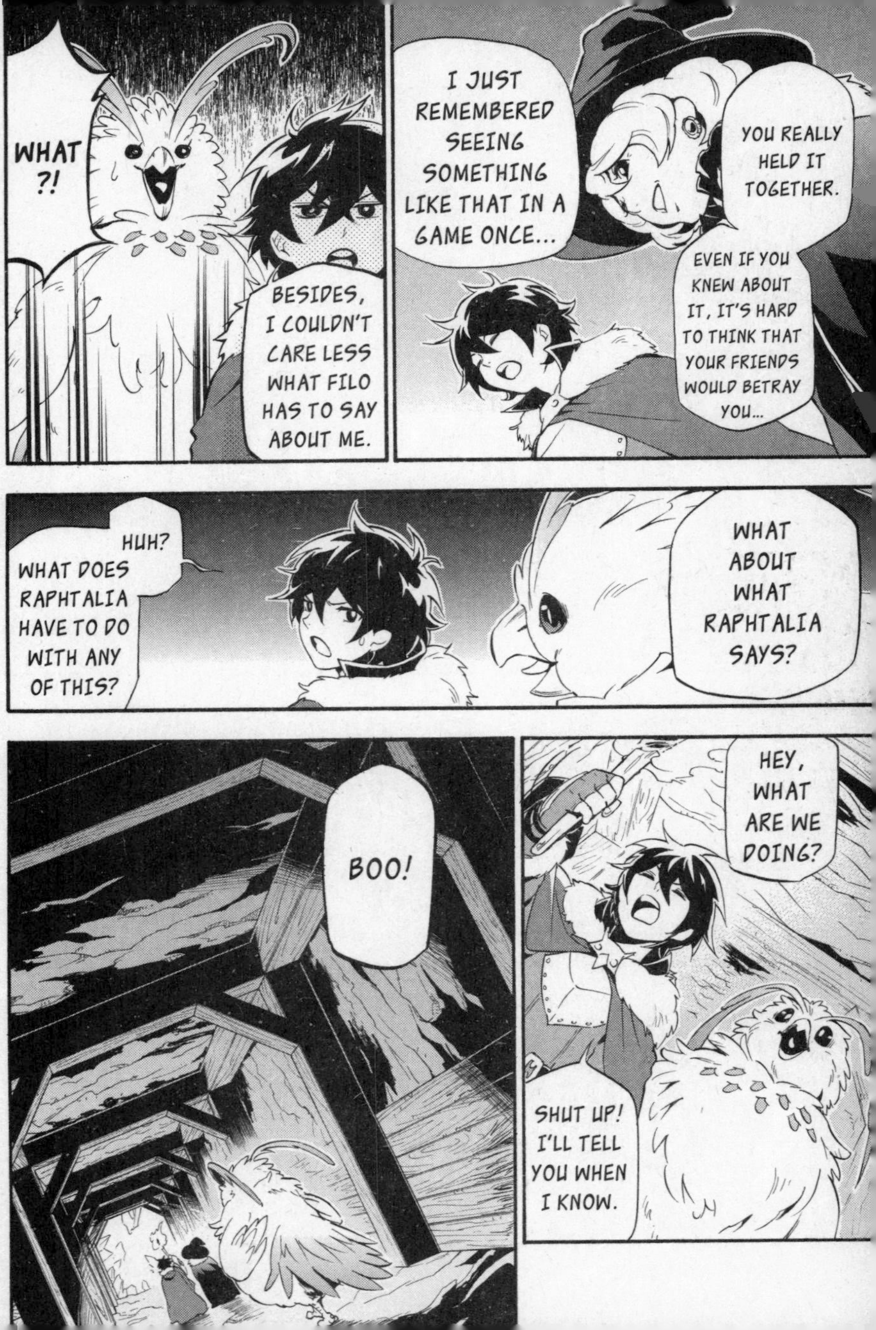
YOU REALLY HELD IT TOGETHER.
EVEN IF YOU KNEW ABOUT IT, IT'S HARD TO THINK THAT YOUR FRIENDS WOULD BETRAY YOU...
I JUST REMEMBERED SEEING SOMETHING LIKE THAT IN A GAME ONCE...
BESIDES, I COULDN'T CARE LESS WHAT FILO HAS TO SAY ABOUT ME.
WHAT ?!
WHAT ABOUT WHAT RAPHTALIA SAYS?
HUH? WHAT DOES RAPHTALIA HAVE TO DO WITH ANY OF THIS?
HEY, WHAT ARE WE DOING?
SHUT UP! I'LL TELL YOU WHEN I KNOW.
BOO!

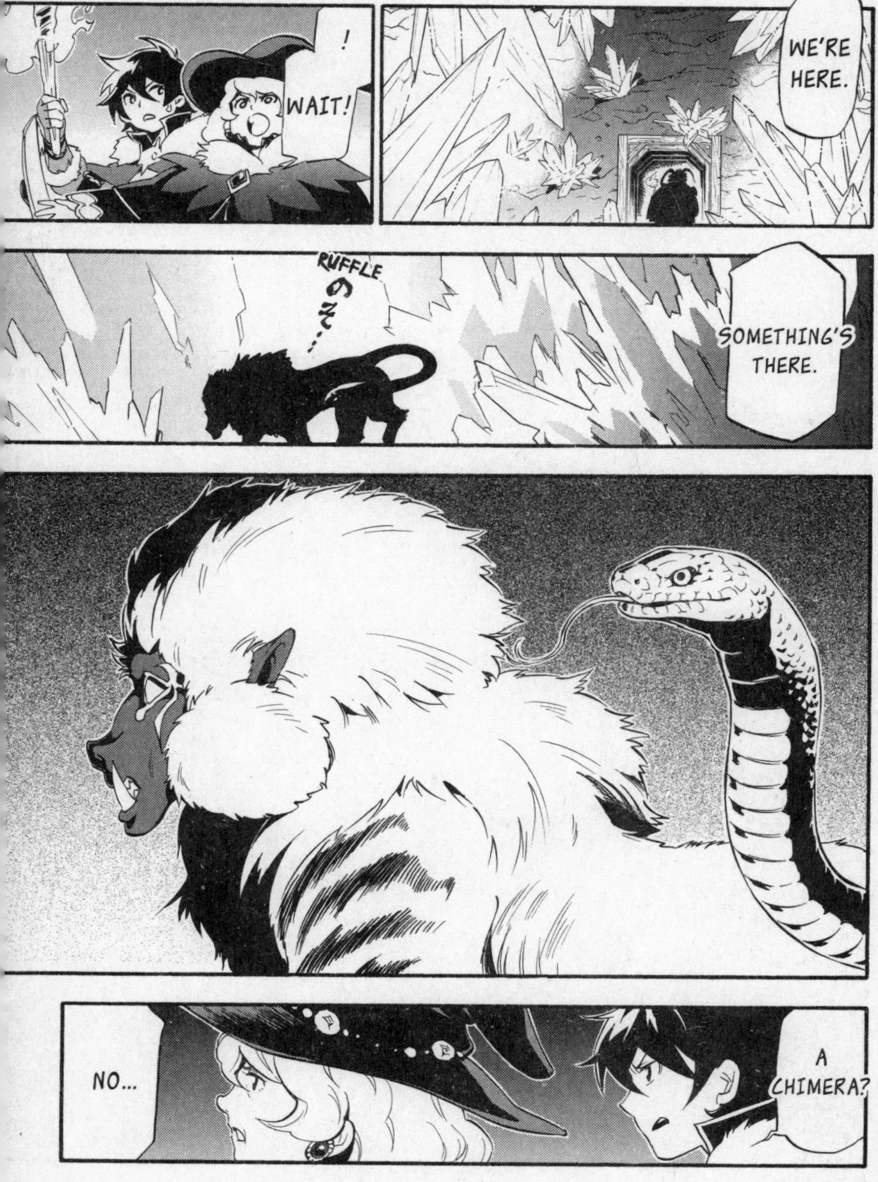
WE'RE HERE.
!
WAIT!
SOMETHING'S THERE.
RUFFLE
のそ…
A CHIMERA?
NO...

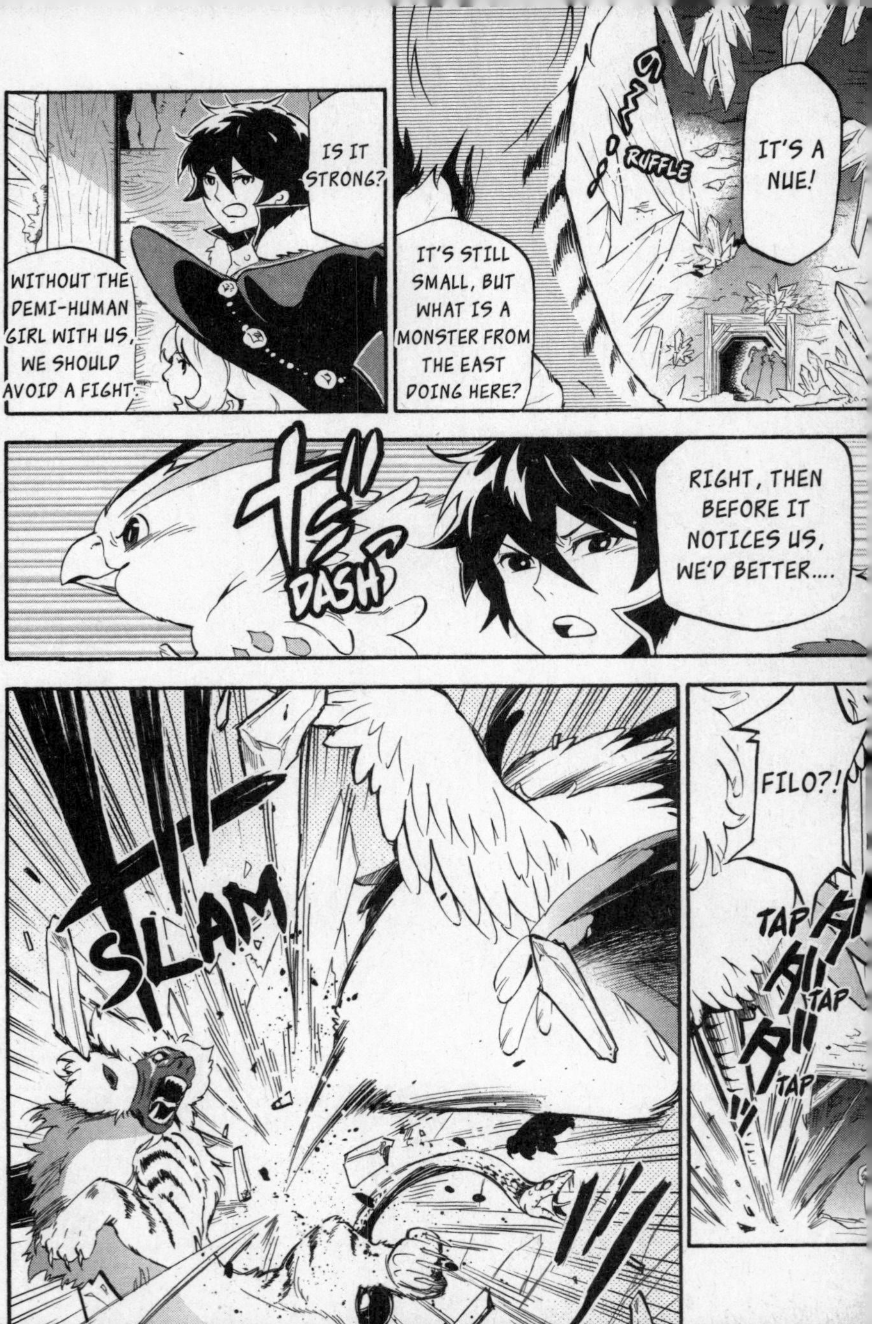
IT'S A NUE!
RUFFLE
IT'S STILL SMALL, BUT WHAT IS A MONSTER FROM THE EAST DOING HERE?
IS IT STRONG?
WITHOUT THE DEMI-HUMAN GIRL WITH US, WE SHOULD AVOID A FIGHT.
RIGHT, THEN BEFORE IT NOTICES US, WE'D BETTER....
DASH
FILO?!
TAP
TAP
TAP
SLAM

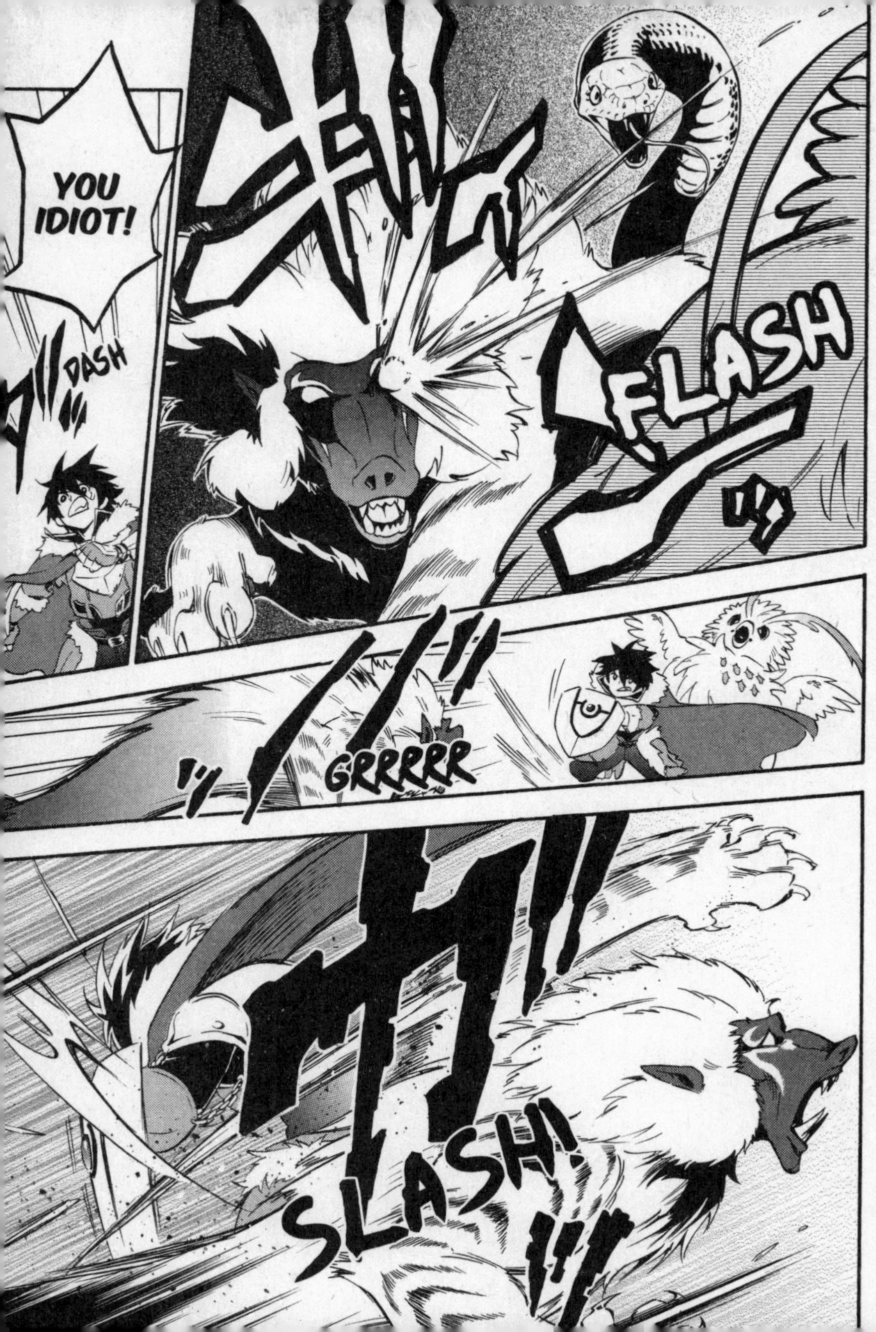
FLASH!!
YOU IDIOT!
DASH
GRRRRR
SLASH!!

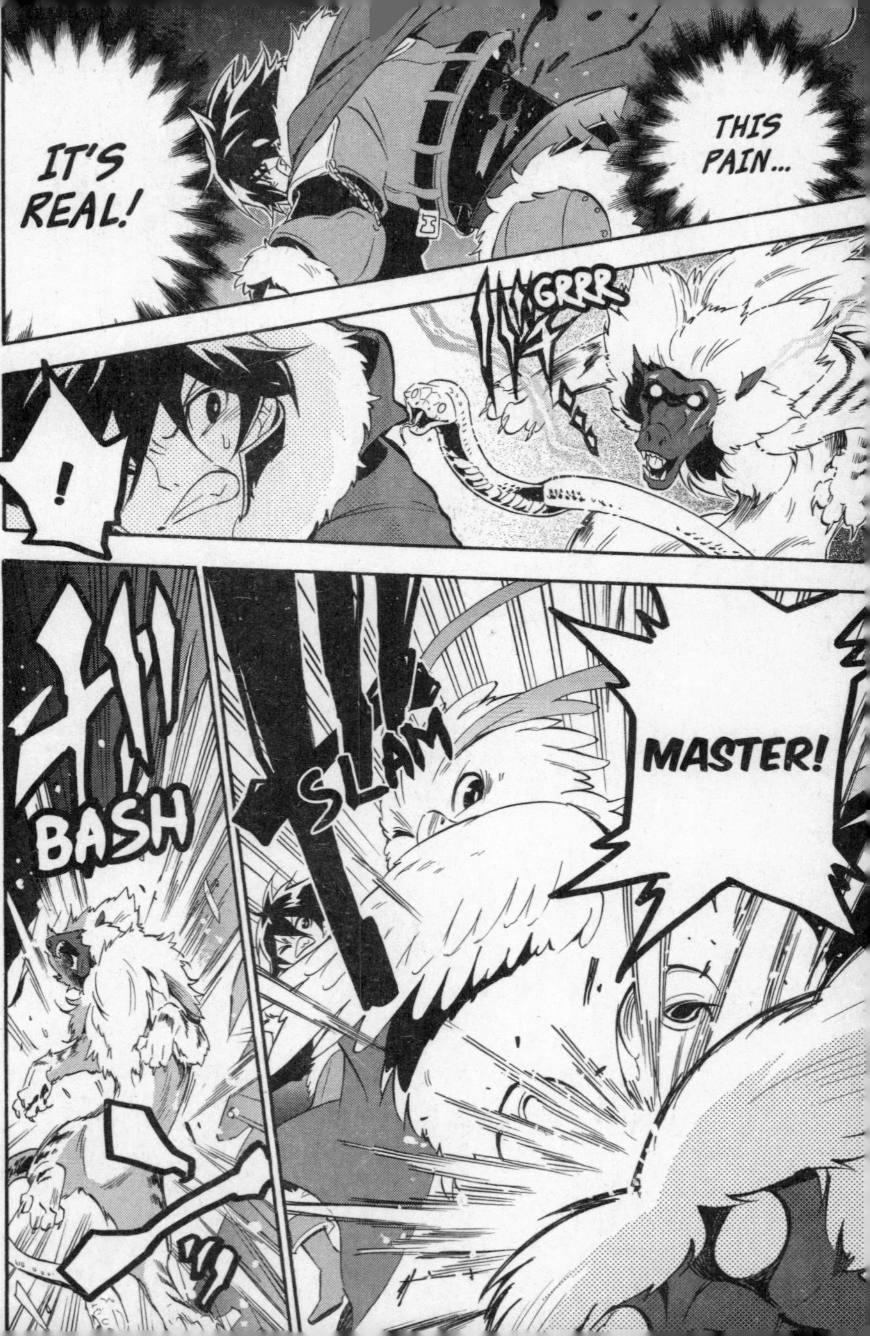
THIS PAIN...
IT'S REAL!
GRRR
!
MASTER!
SLAM
BASH

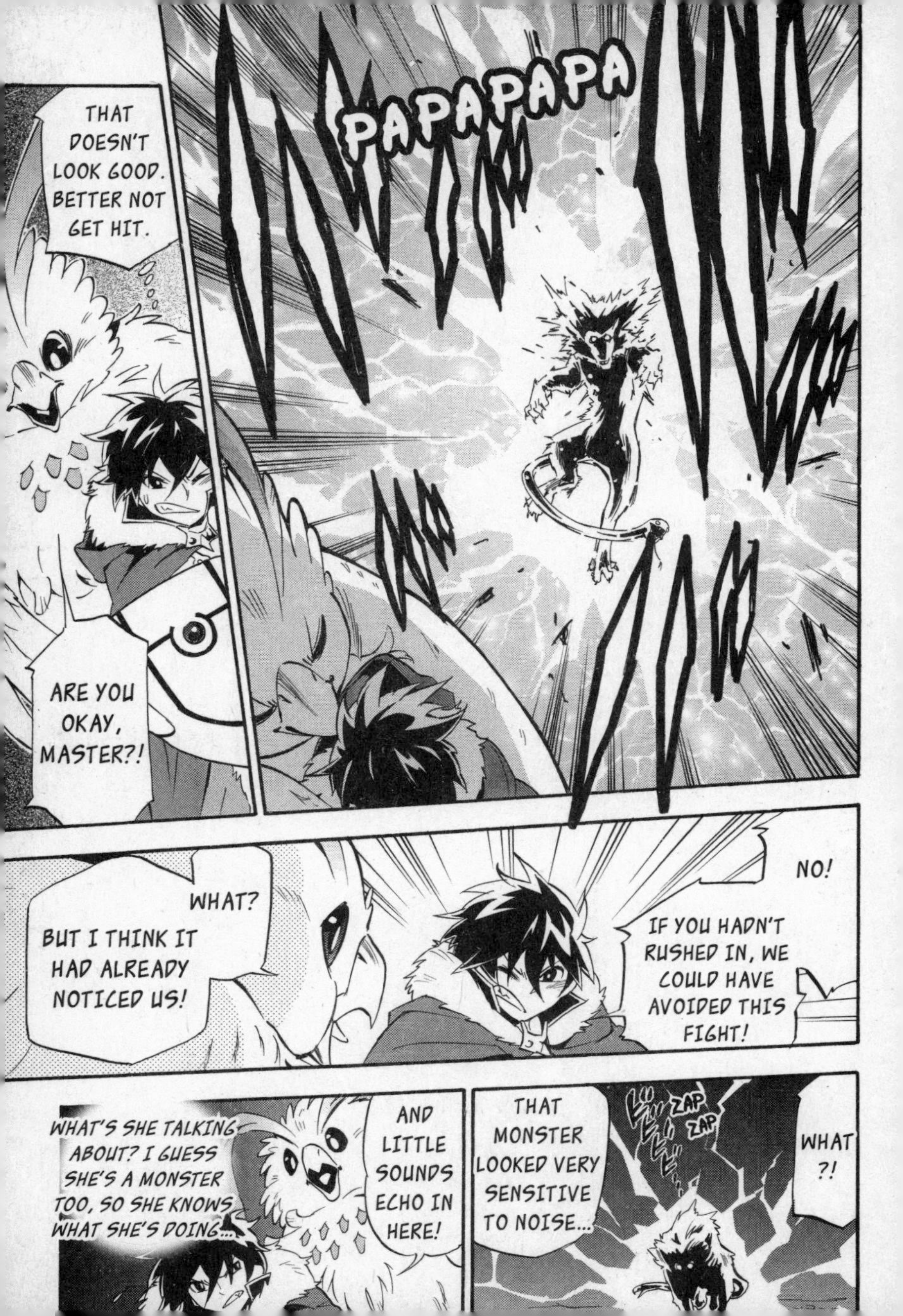

PAPAPAPA
THAT DOESN'T LOOK GOOD. BETTER NOT GET HIT.
ARE YOU OKAY, MASTER?!
NO!
IF YOU HADN'T RUSHED IN, WE COULD HAVE AVOIDED THIS FIGHT!
WHAT?
BUT I THINK IT HAD ALREADY NOTICED US!
ZAP ZAP
WHAT ?!
THAT MONSTER LOOKED VERY SENSITIVE TO NOISE...
AND LITTLE SOUNDS ECHO IN HERE!
WHAT'S SHE TALKING ABOUT? I GUESS SHE'S A MONSTER TOO, SO SHE KNOWS WHAT SHE'S DOING...

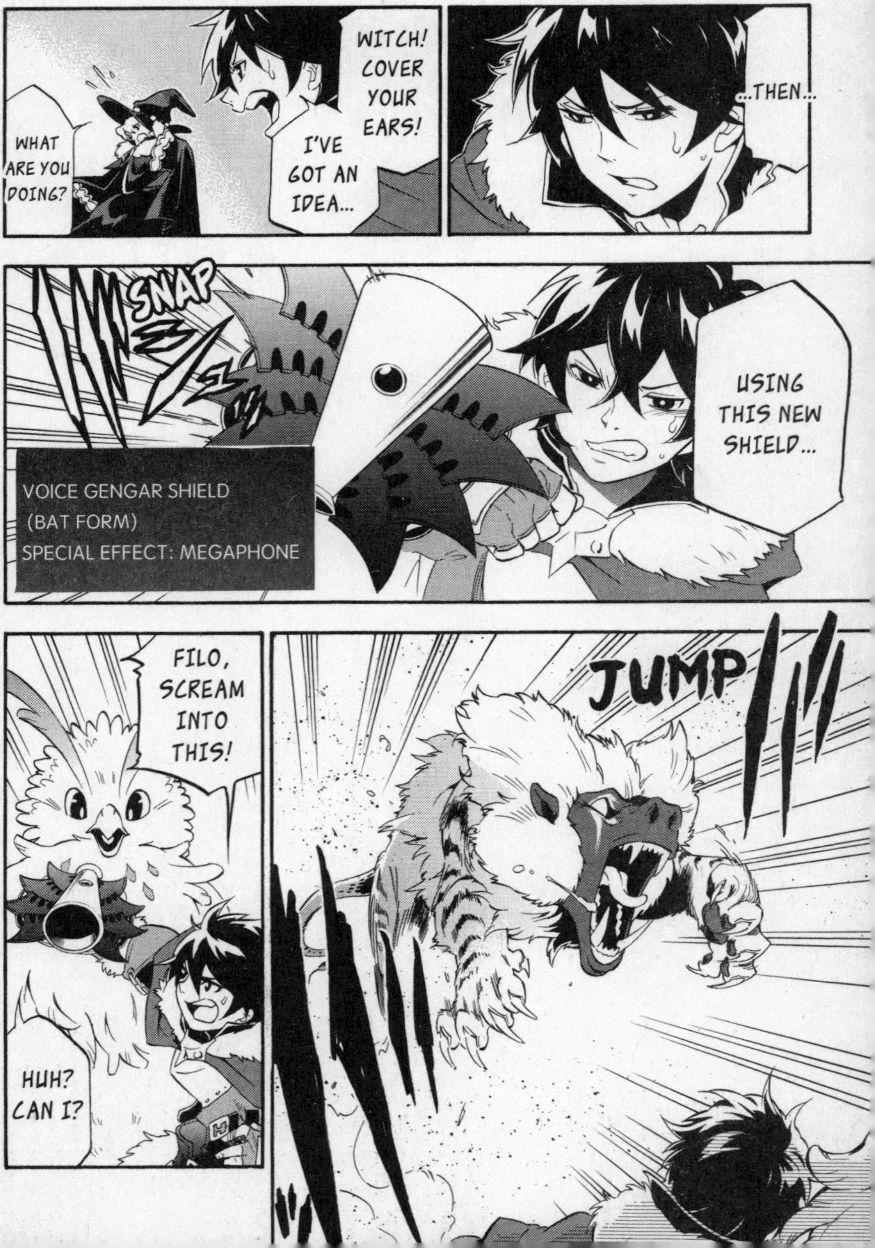
...THEN...
WITCH! COVER YOUR EARS!
I'VE GOT AN IDEA...
WHAT ARE YOU DOING?
USING THIS NEW SHIELD...
SNAP
VOICE GENGAR SHIELD (BAT FORM) SPECIAL EFFECT: MEGAPHONE
JUMP
FILO, SCREAM INTO THIS!
HUH? CAN I?

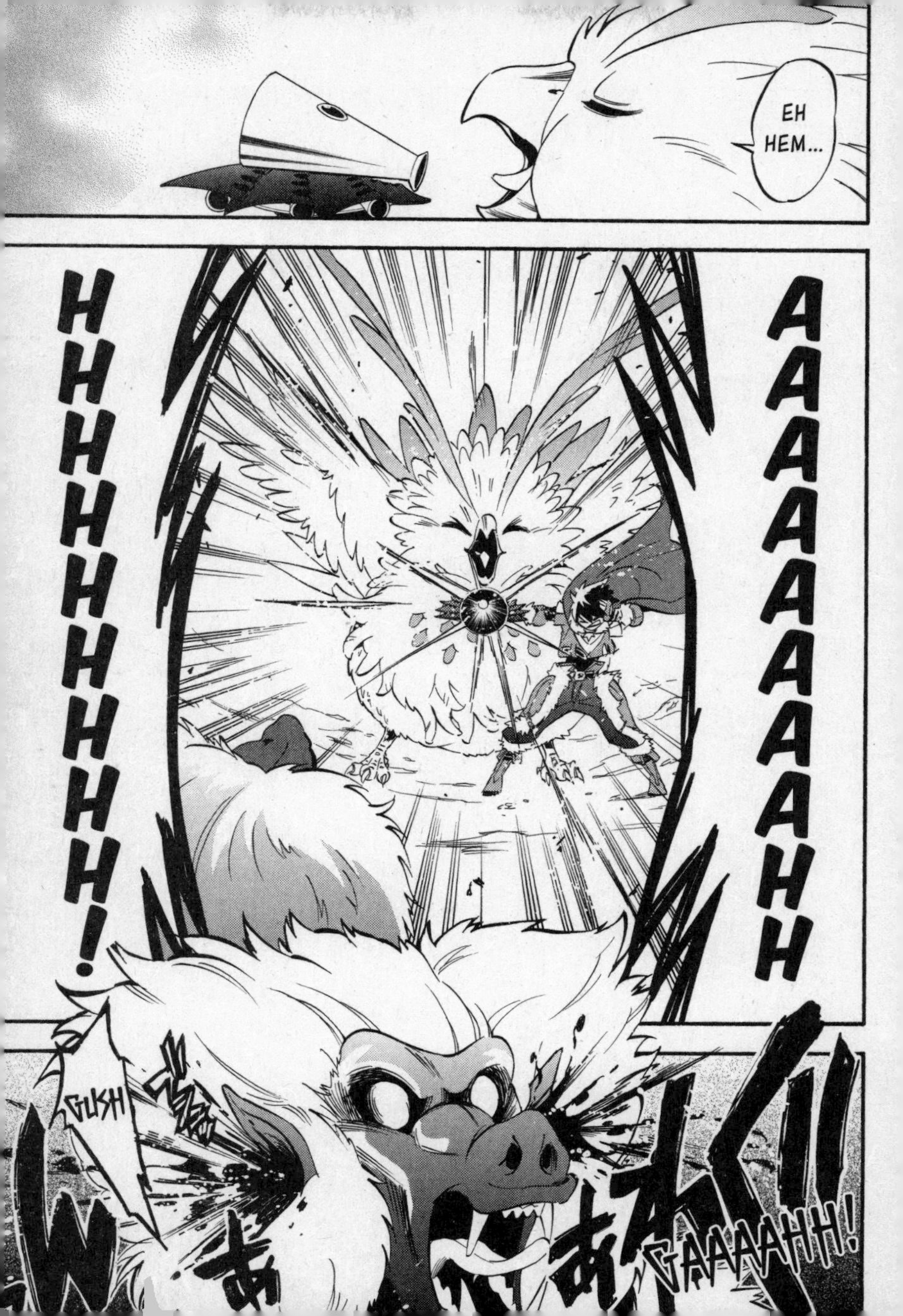
EH HEM...
AAAAAAAAHH
HHHHHHHHH!
GUSH
GAAAAAH!

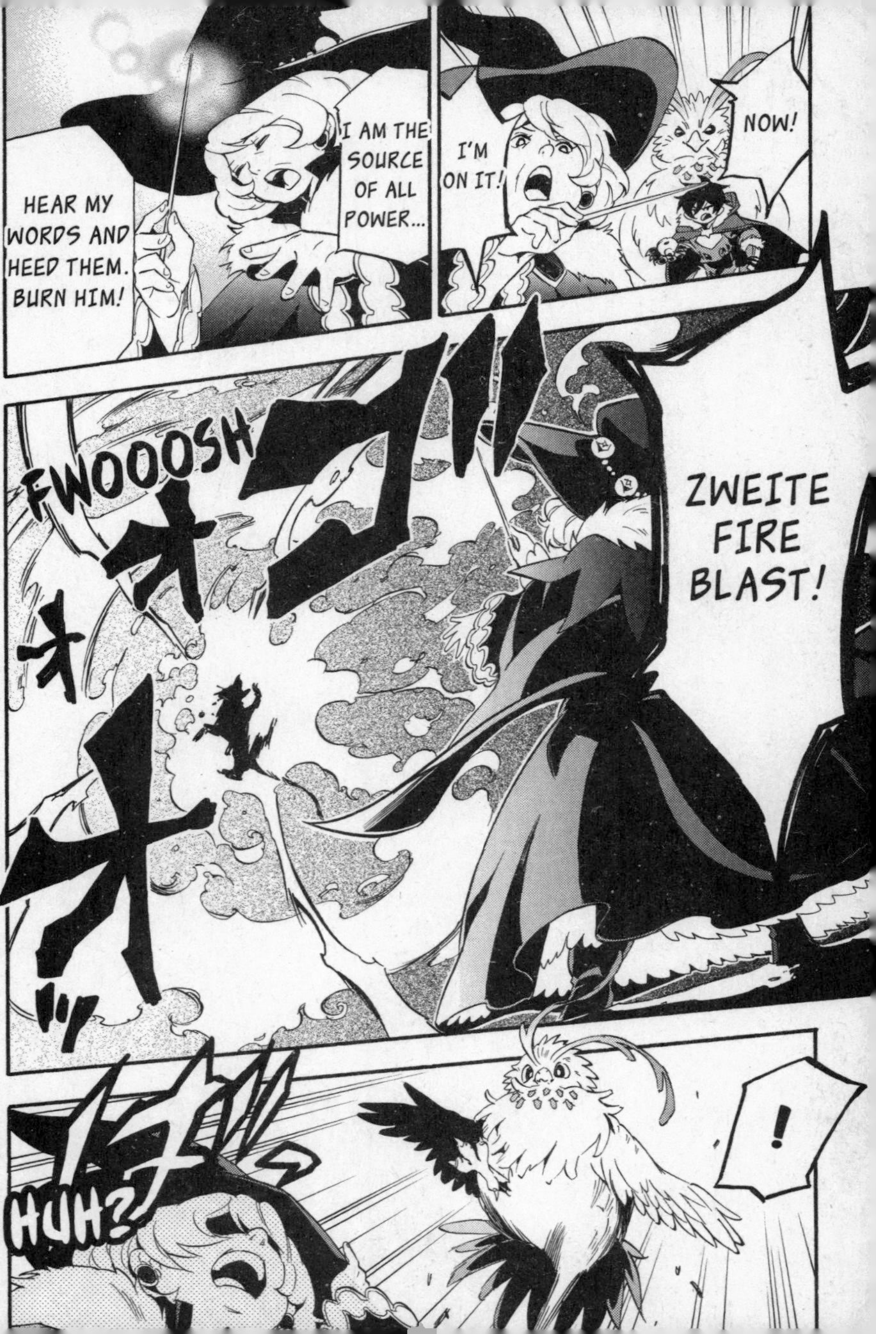
NOW!
I'M ON IT!
I AM THE SOURCE OF ALL POWER...
HEAR MY WORDS AND HEED THEM. BURN HIM!
ZWEITE FIRE BLAST!
FWOOOSH
!
HUH?

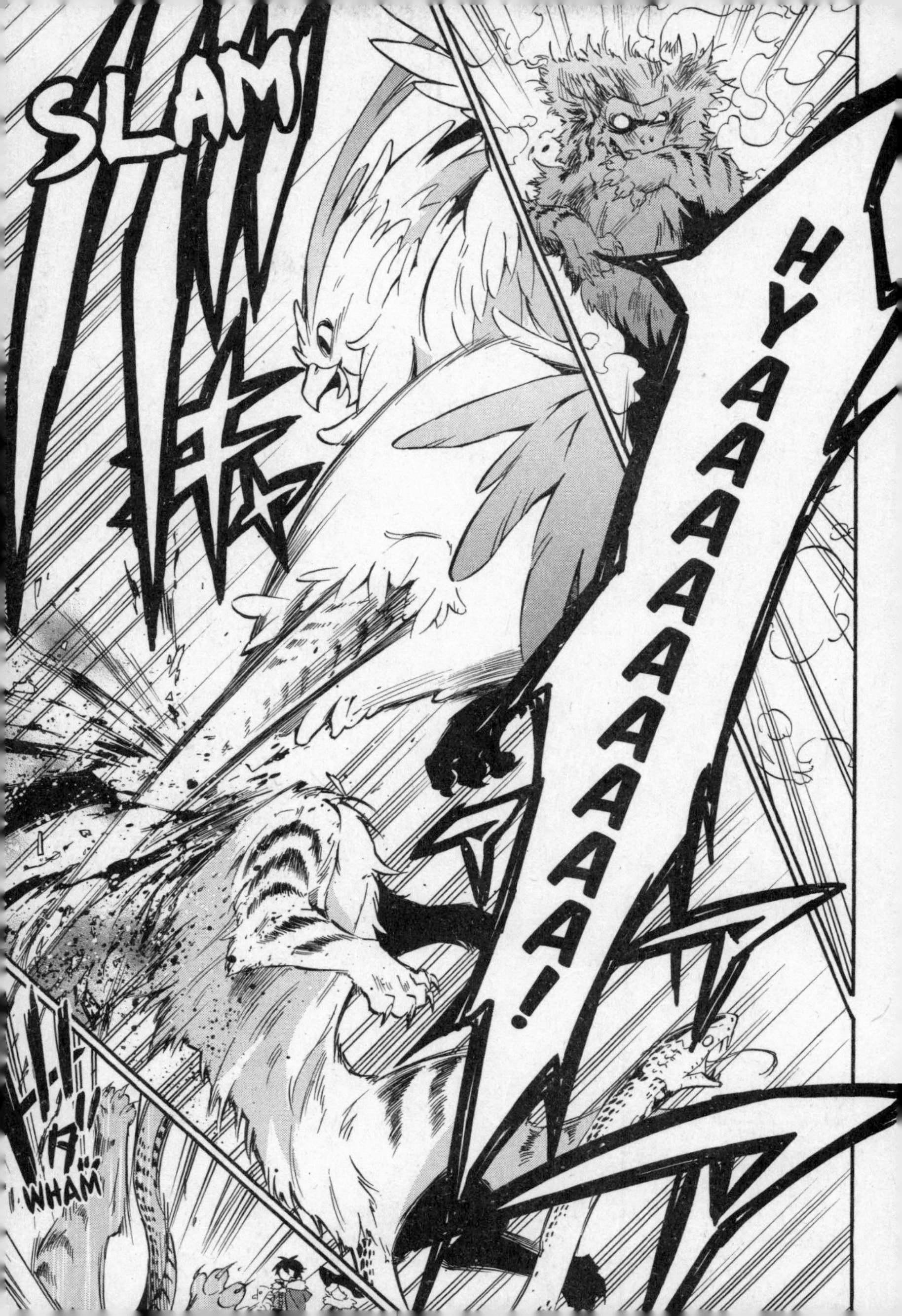
HYAAAAAAAAA!
SLAM
WHAM

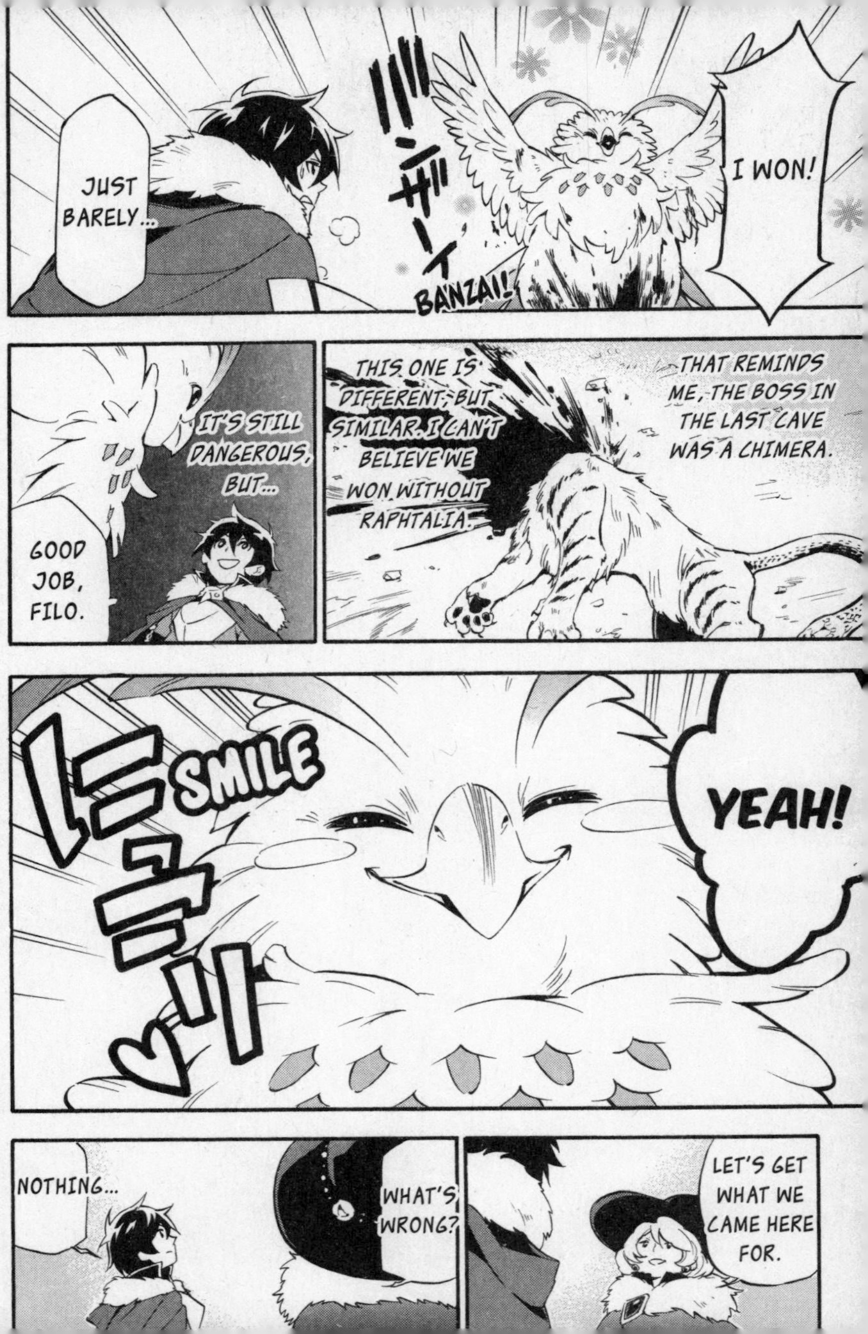
I WON!
BANZAI!
JUST BARELY...
THAT REMINDS ME, THE BOSS IN THE LAST CAVE WAS A CHIMERA.
THIS ONE IS DIFFERENT, BUT SIMILAR. I CAN'T BELIEVE WE WON WITHOUT RAPHTALIA.
IT'S STILL DANGEROUS, BUT...
GOOD JOB, FILO.
YEAH!
SMILE
LET'S GET WHAT WE CAME HERE FOR.
WHAT'S WRONG?
NOTHING...

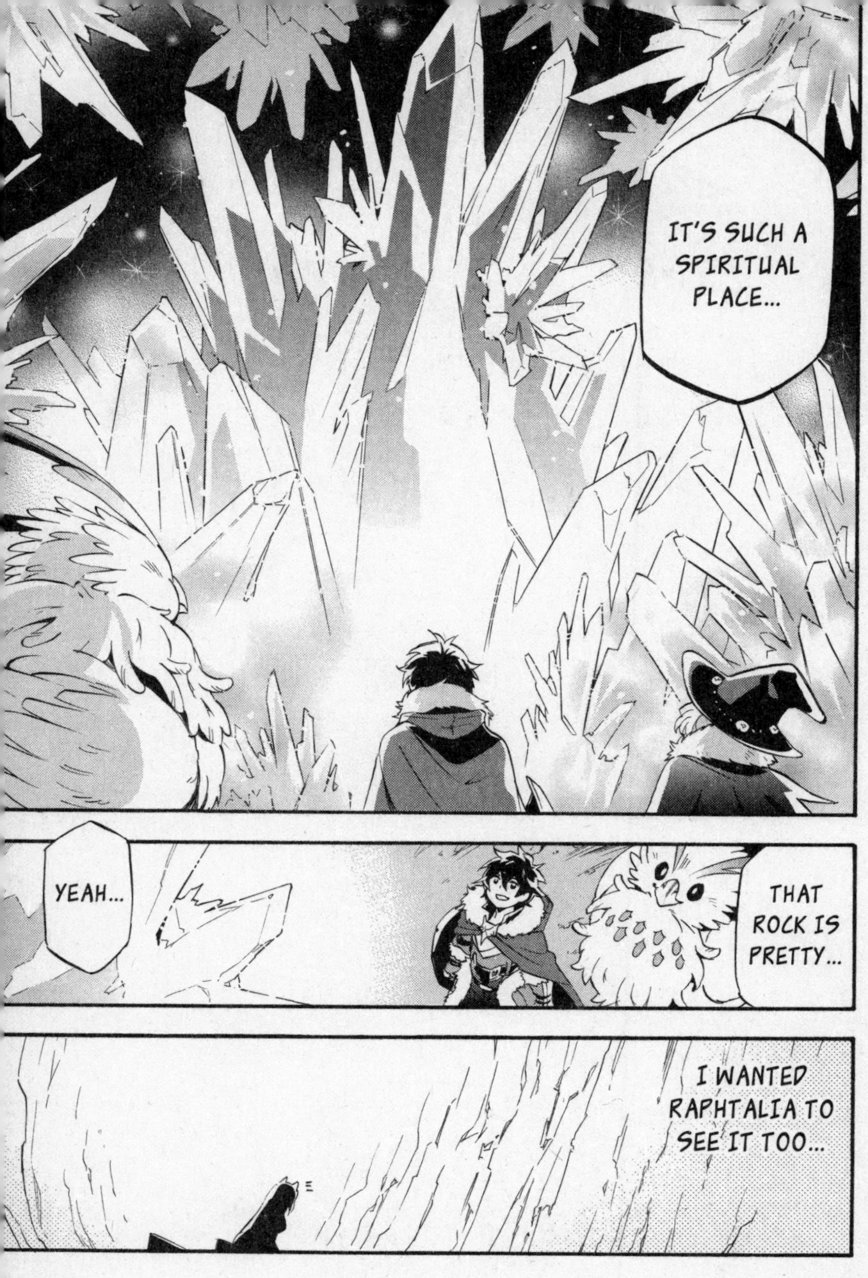
IT'S SUCH A SPIRITUAL PLACE...
THAT ROCK IS PRETTY...
YEAH...
I WANTED RAPHTALIA TO SEE IT TOO...

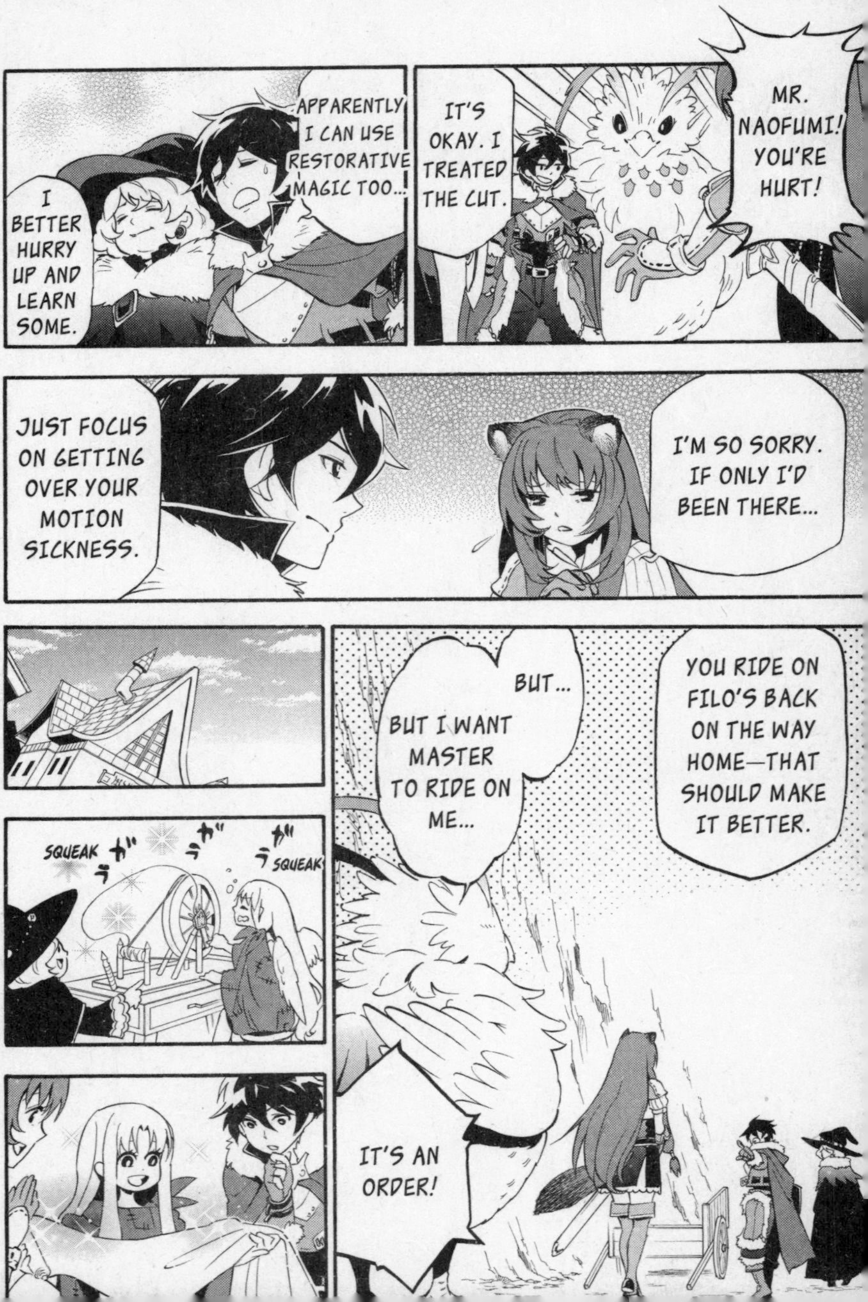
MR. NAOFUMI! YOU'RE HURT!
IT'S OKAY. I TREATED THE CUT.
APPARENTLY I CAN USE RESTORATIVE MAGIC TOO...
I BETTER HURRY UP AND LEARN SOME.
I'M SO SORRY. IF ONLY I'D BEEN THERE...
JUST FOCUS ON GETTING OVER YOUR MOTION SICKNESS.
YOU RIDE ON FILO'S BACK ON THE WAY HOME—THAT SHOULD MAKE IT BETTER.
BUT...
BUT I WANT MASTER TO RIDE ON ME...
IT'S AN ORDER!
SQUEAK
ガラ
ガラ
SQUEAK

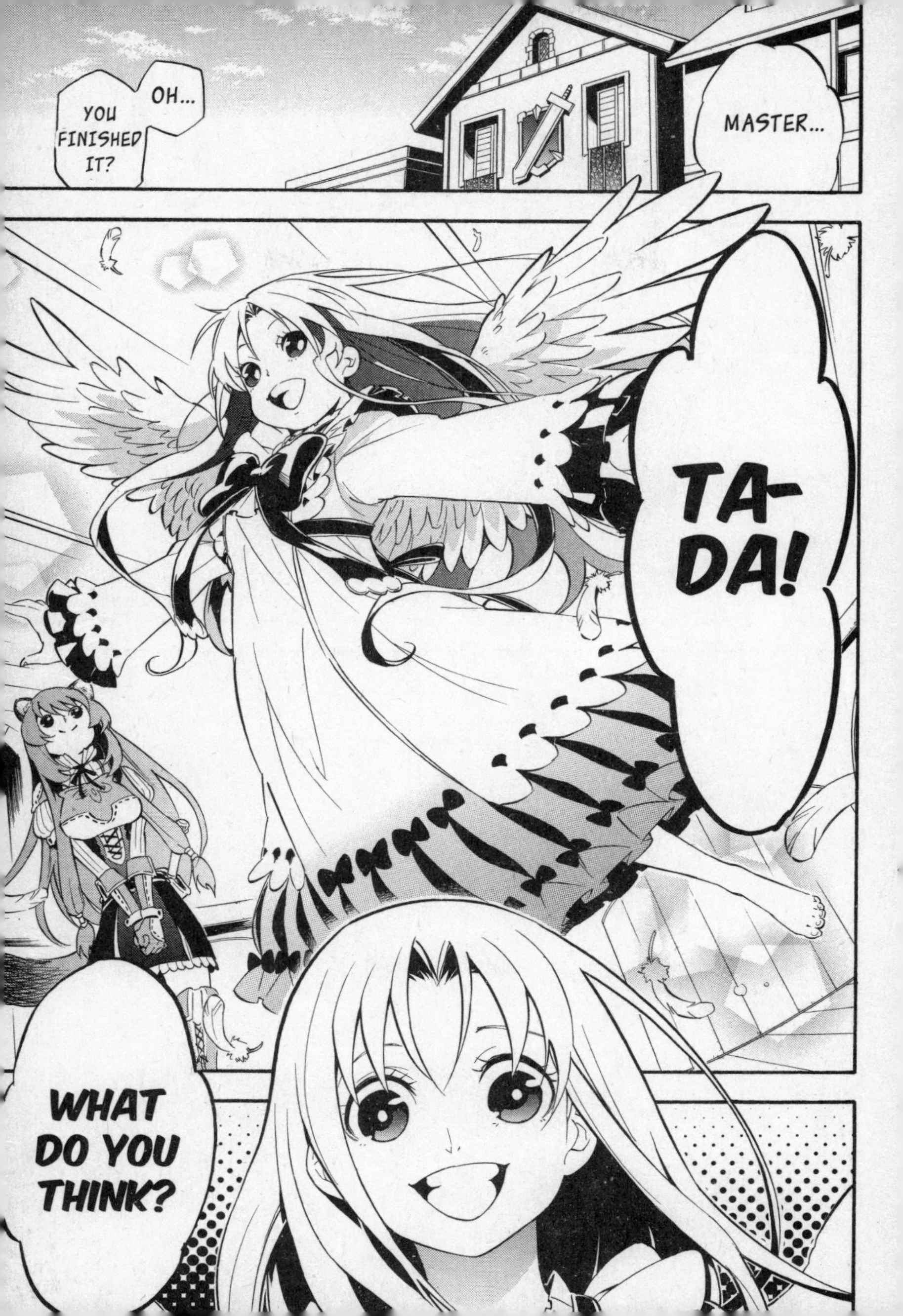
MASTER...
OH...
YOU FINISHED IT?
TA-DA!
WHAT DO YOU THINK?

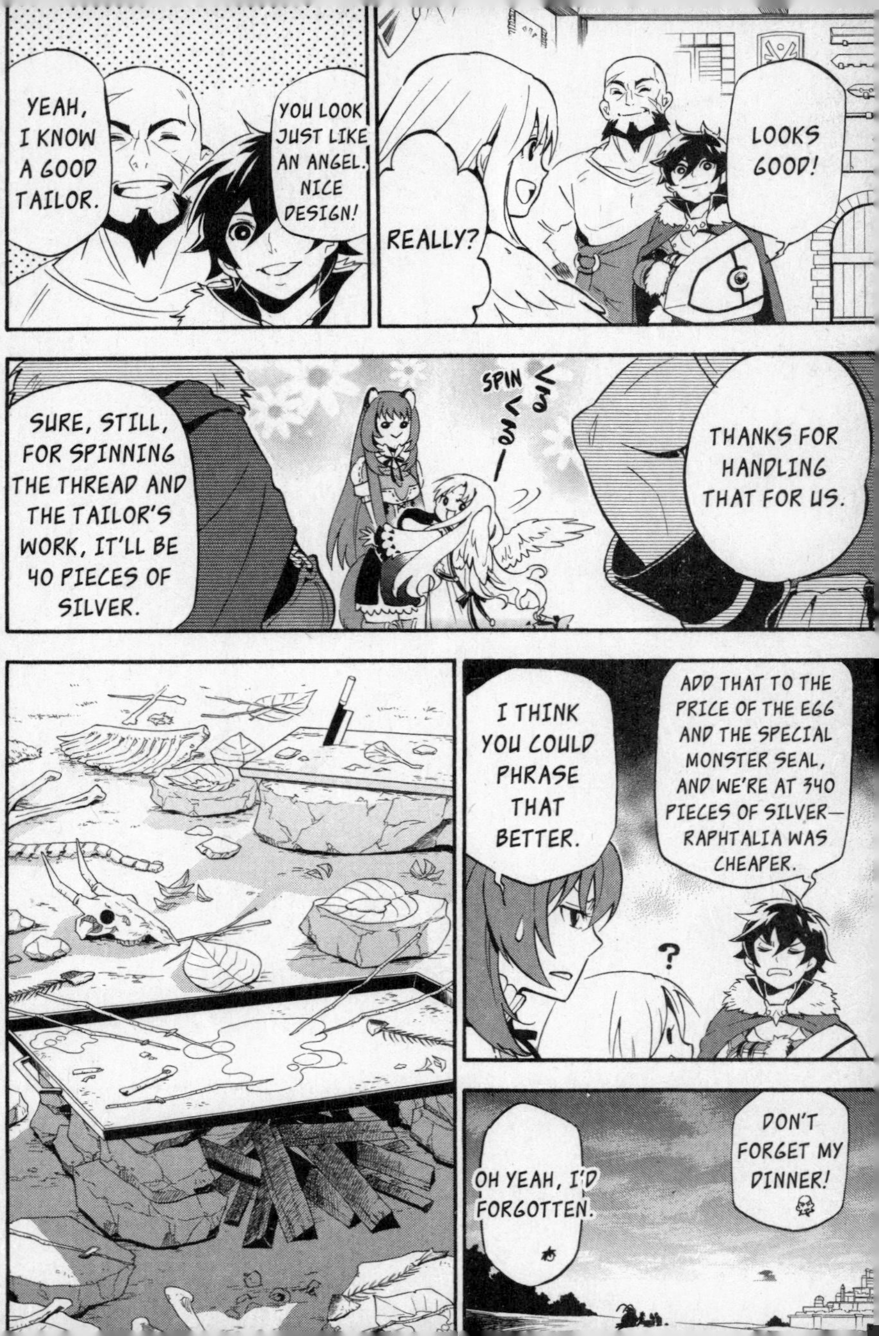
LOOKS GOOD!
REALLY?
YOU LOOK JUST LIKE AN ANGEL. NICE DESIGN!
YEAH, I KNOW A GOOD TAILOR.
THANKS FOR HANDLING THAT FOR US.
SPIN
SURE, STILL, FOR SPINNING THE THREAD AND THE TAILOR'S WORK, IT'LL BE 40 PIECES OF SILVER.
ADD THAT TO THE PRICE OF THE EGG AND THE SPECIAL MONSTER SEAL, AND WE'RE AT 340 PIECES OF SILVER—RAPHTALIA WAS CHEAPER.
I THINK YOU COULD PHRASE THAT BETTER.
?
DON'T FORGET MY DINNER!
OH YEAH, I'D FORGOTTEN.

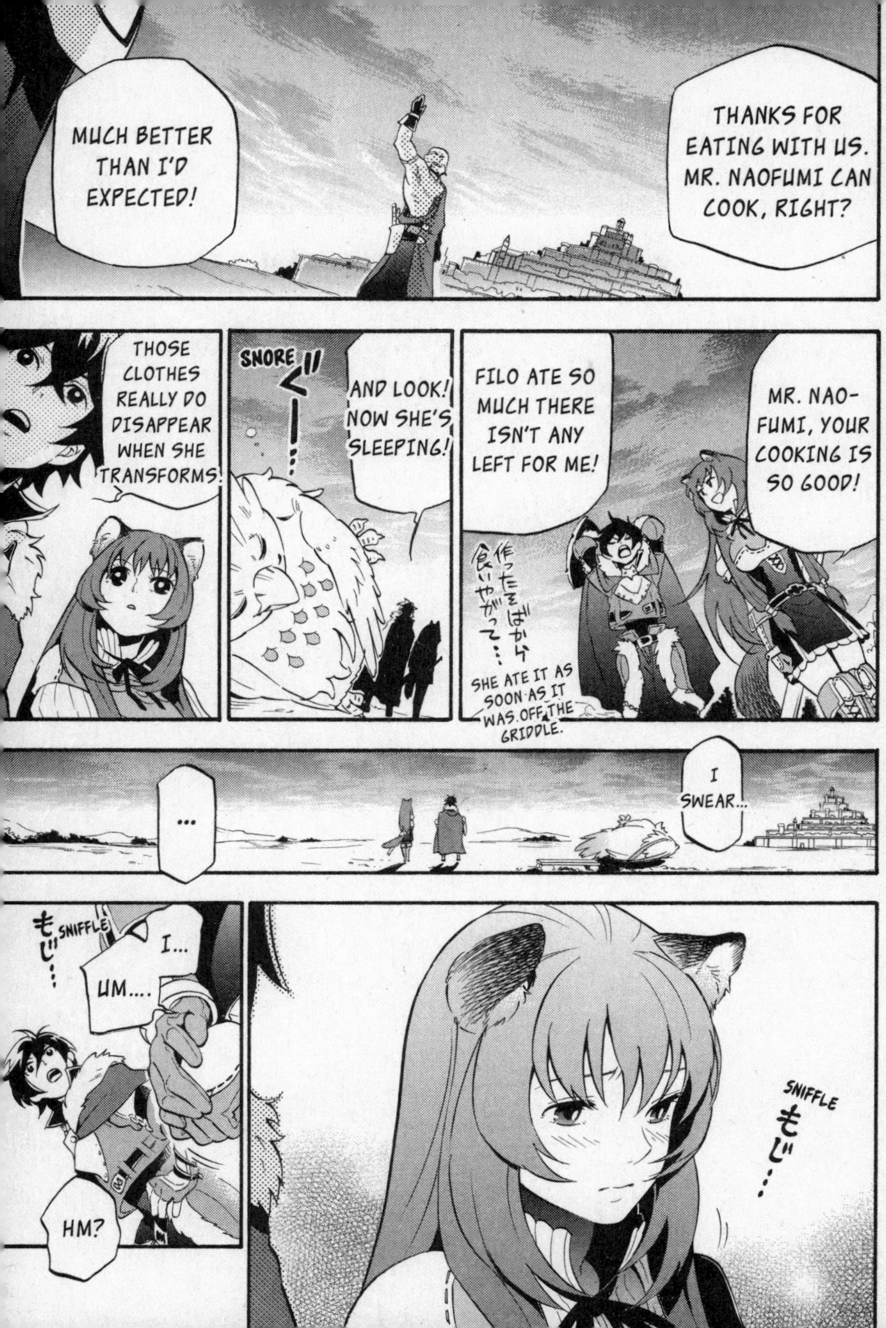
THANKS FOR EATING WITH US. MR. NAOFUMI CAN COOK, RIGHT?
MUCH BETTER THAN I'D EXPECTED!
MR. NAO-FUMI, YOUR COOKING IS SO GOOD!
FILO ATE SO MUCH THERE ISN'T ANY LEFT FOR ME!
作ったそばから食いやがって…
SHE ATE IT AS SOON AS IT WAS OFF THE GRIDDLE.
SNORE
ぐー…
AND LOOK! NOW SHE'S SLEEPING!
THOSE CLOTHES REALLY DO DISAPPEAR WHEN SHE TRANSFORMS.
I SWEAR...
...
SNIFFLE
もじ…
もじ…
SNIFFLE
I...
UM....
HM?

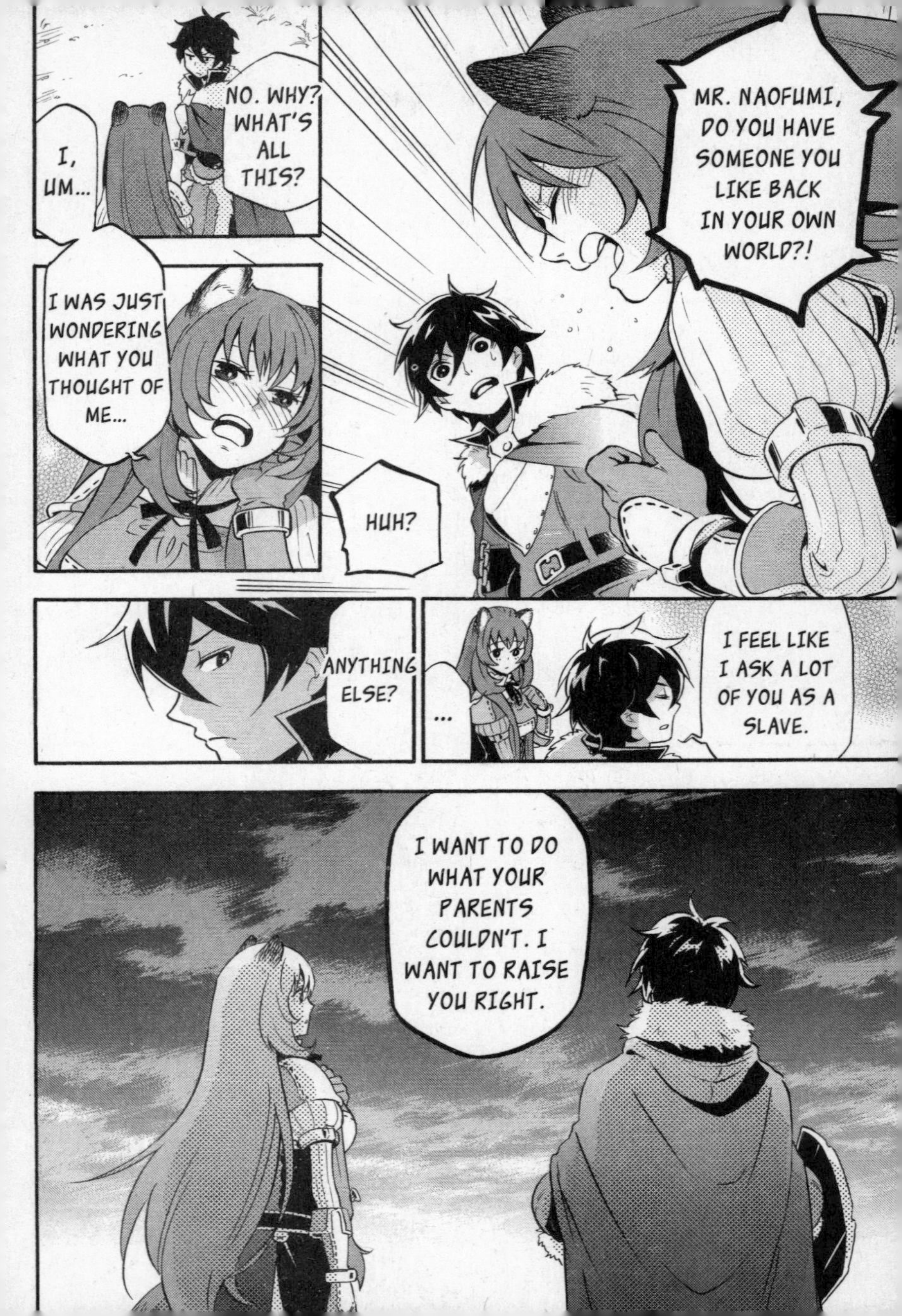
MR. NAOFUMI, DO YOU HAVE SOMEONE YOU LIKE BACK IN YOUR OWN WORLD?!
NO. WHY? WHAT'S ALL THIS?
I, UM...
I WAS JUST WONDERING WHAT YOU THOUGHT OF ME...
HUH?
I FEEL LIKE I ASK A LOT OF YOU AS A SLAVE.
...
ANYTHING ELSE?
I WANT TO DO WHAT YOUR PARENTS COULDN'T. I WANT TO RAISE YOU RIGHT.

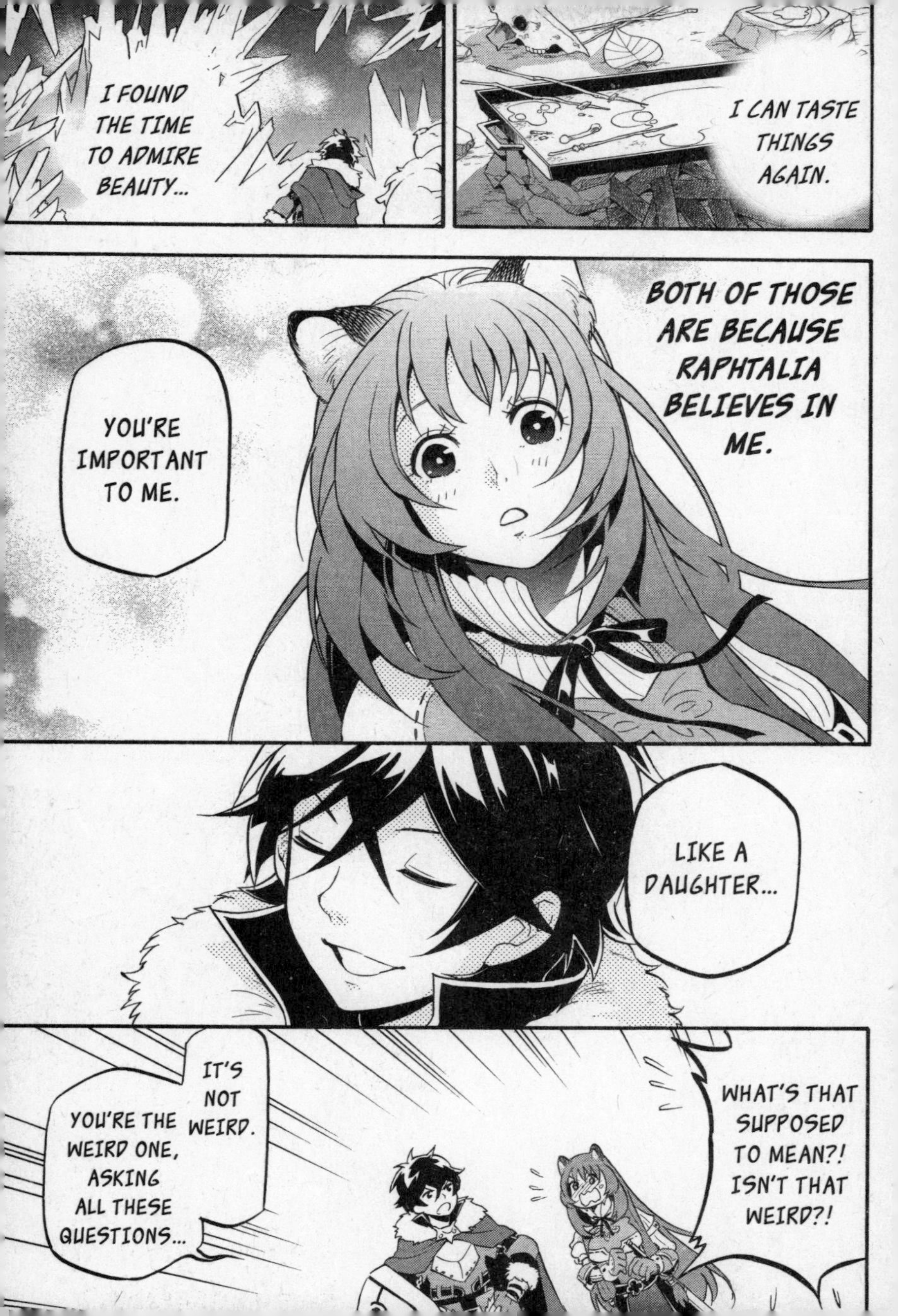
I CAN TASTE THINGS AGAIN.
I FOUND THE TIME TO ADMIRE BEAUTY...
BOTH OF THOSE ARE BECAUSE RAPHTALIA BELIEVES IN ME.
YOU'RE IMPORTANT TO ME.
LIKE A DAUGHTER...
WHAT'S THAT SUPPOSED TO MEAN?! ISN'T THAT WEIRD?!
IT'S NOT WEIRD.
YOU'RE THE WEIRD ONE, ASKING ALL THESE QUESTIONS...

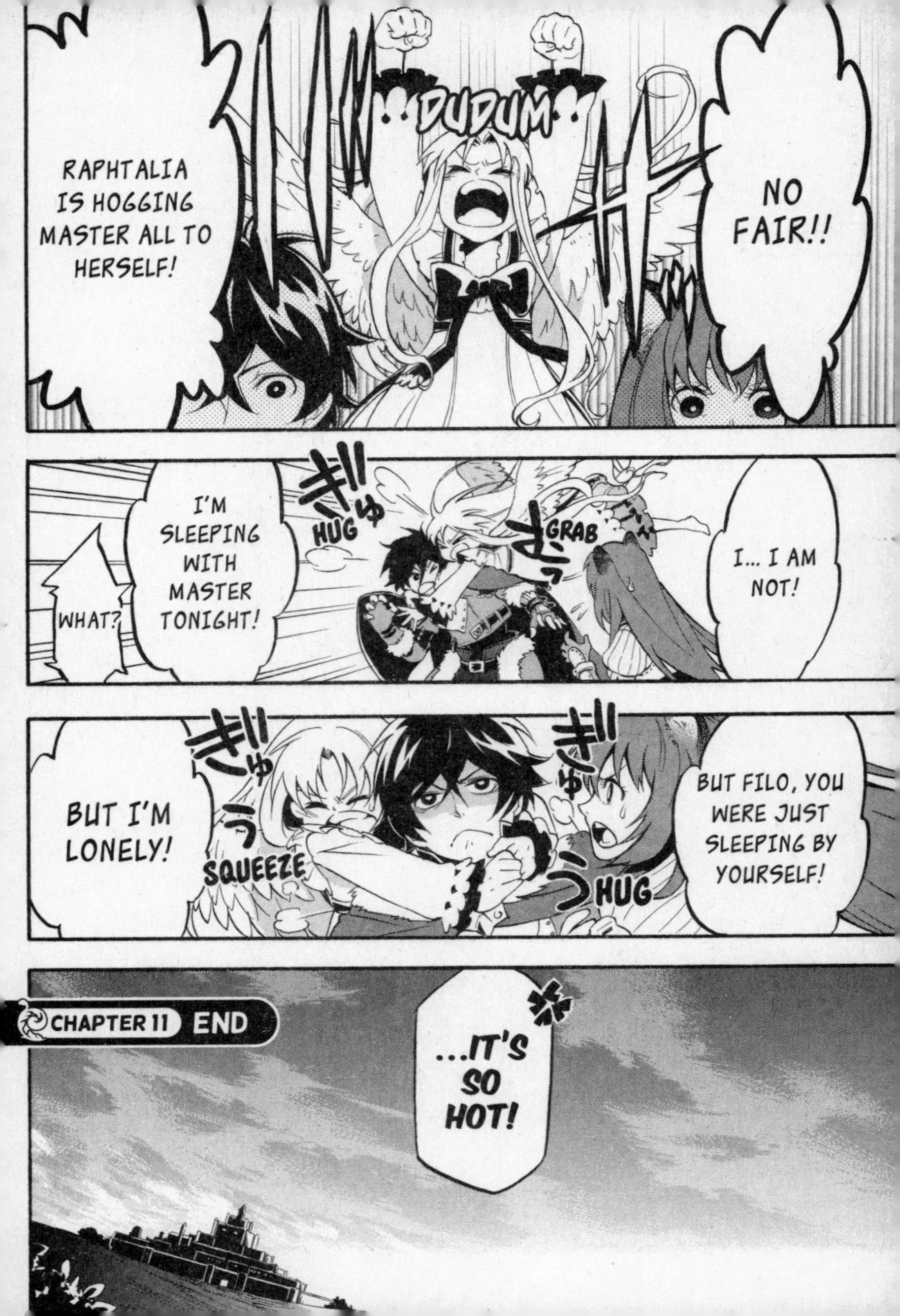
DUDUM
NO FAIR!!
RAPHTALIA IS HOGGING MASTER ALL TO HERSELF!
I... I AM NOT!
GRAB
HUG
I'M SLEEPING WITH MASTER TONIGHT!
WHAT?
BUT FILO, YOU WERE JUST SLEEPING BY YOURSELF!
HUG
SQUEEZE
BUT I'M LONELY!
...IT'S SO HOT!
CHAPTER 11 END

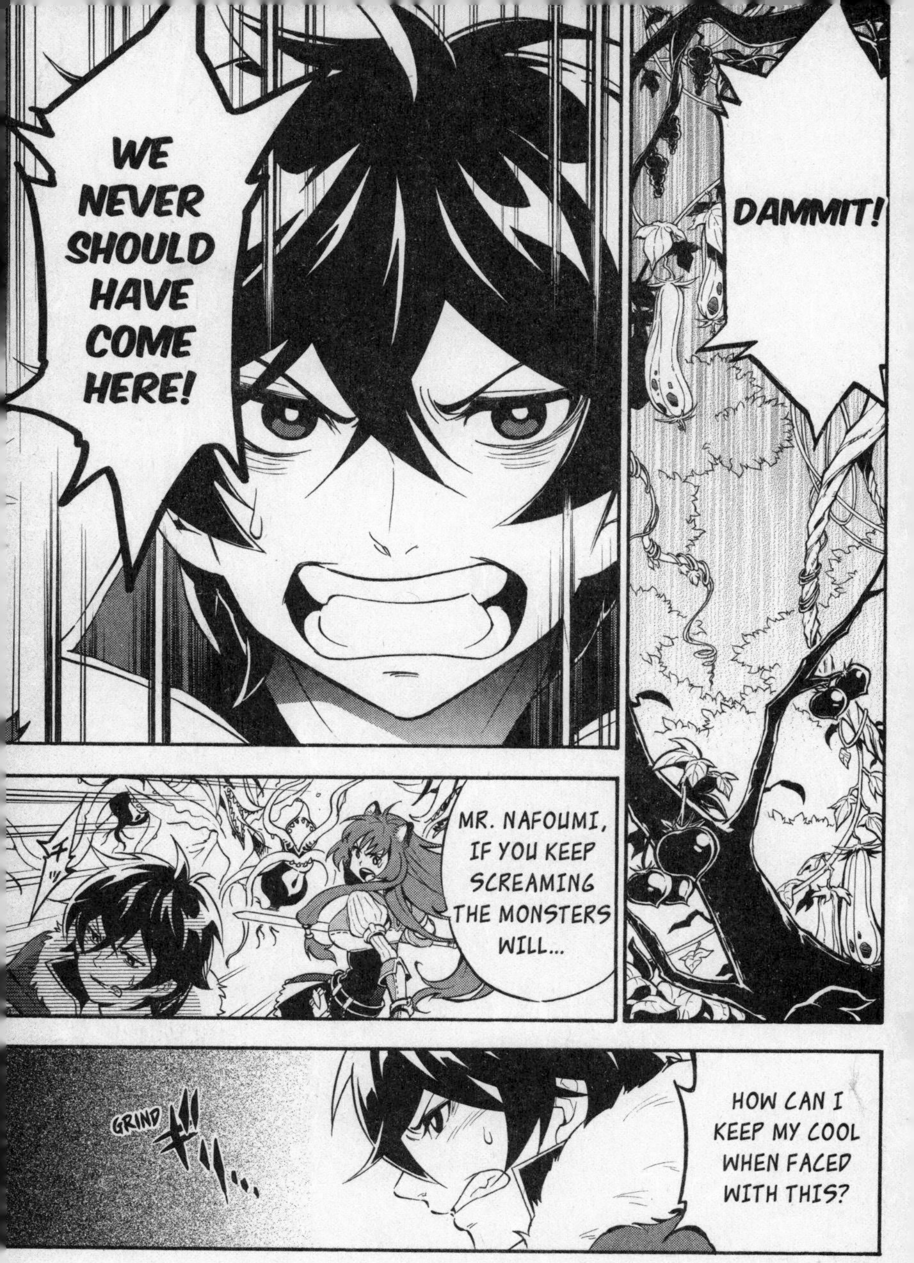
DAMMIT!
WE NEVER SHOULD HAVE COME HERE!
MR. NAFOUMI, IF YOU KEEP SCREAMING THE MONSTERS WILL...
HOW CAN I KEEP MY COOL WHEN FACED WITH THIS?
GRIND

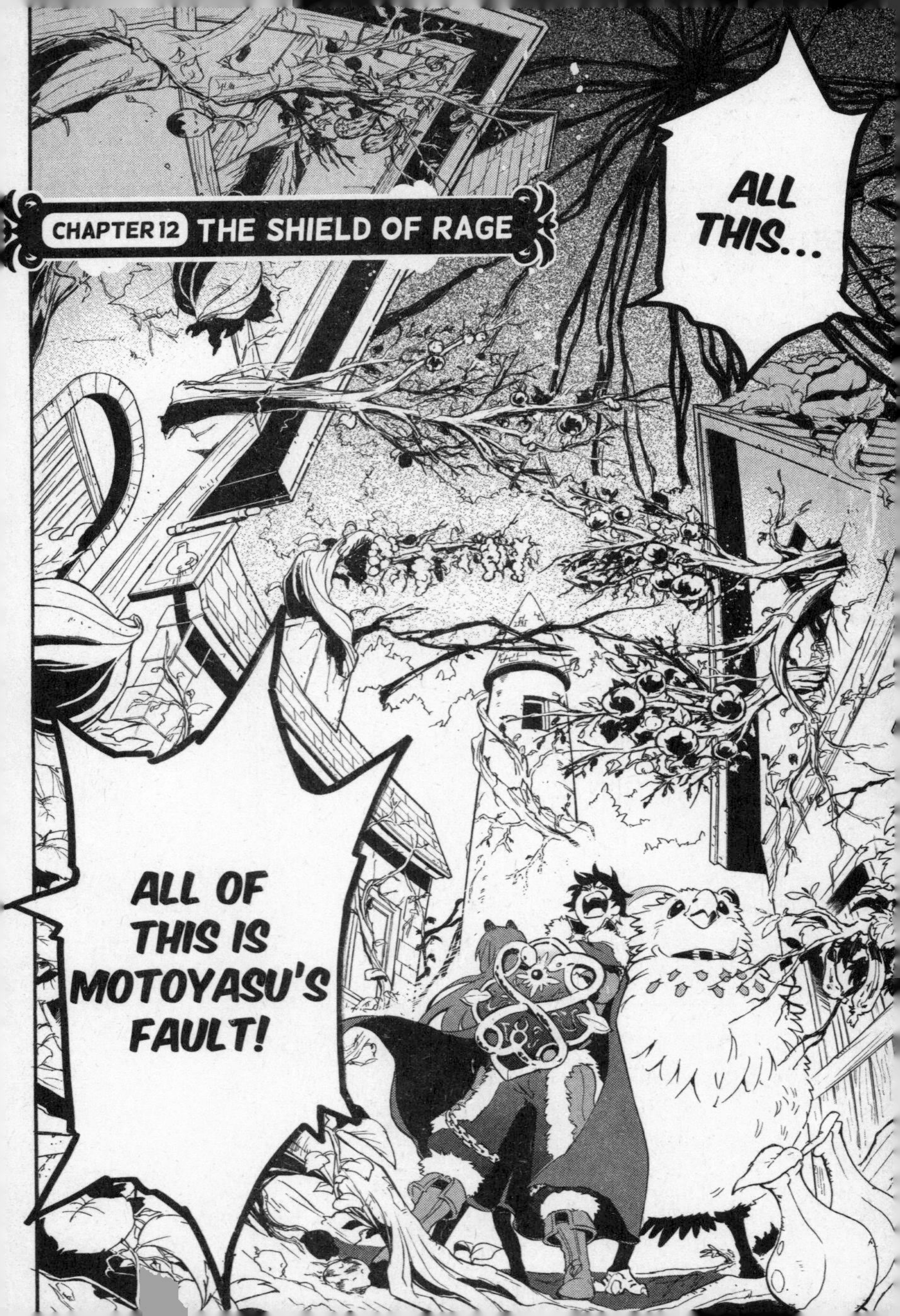
CHAPTER 12 THE SHIELD OF RAGE
ALL THIS...
ALL OF THIS IS MOTOYASU'S FAULT!

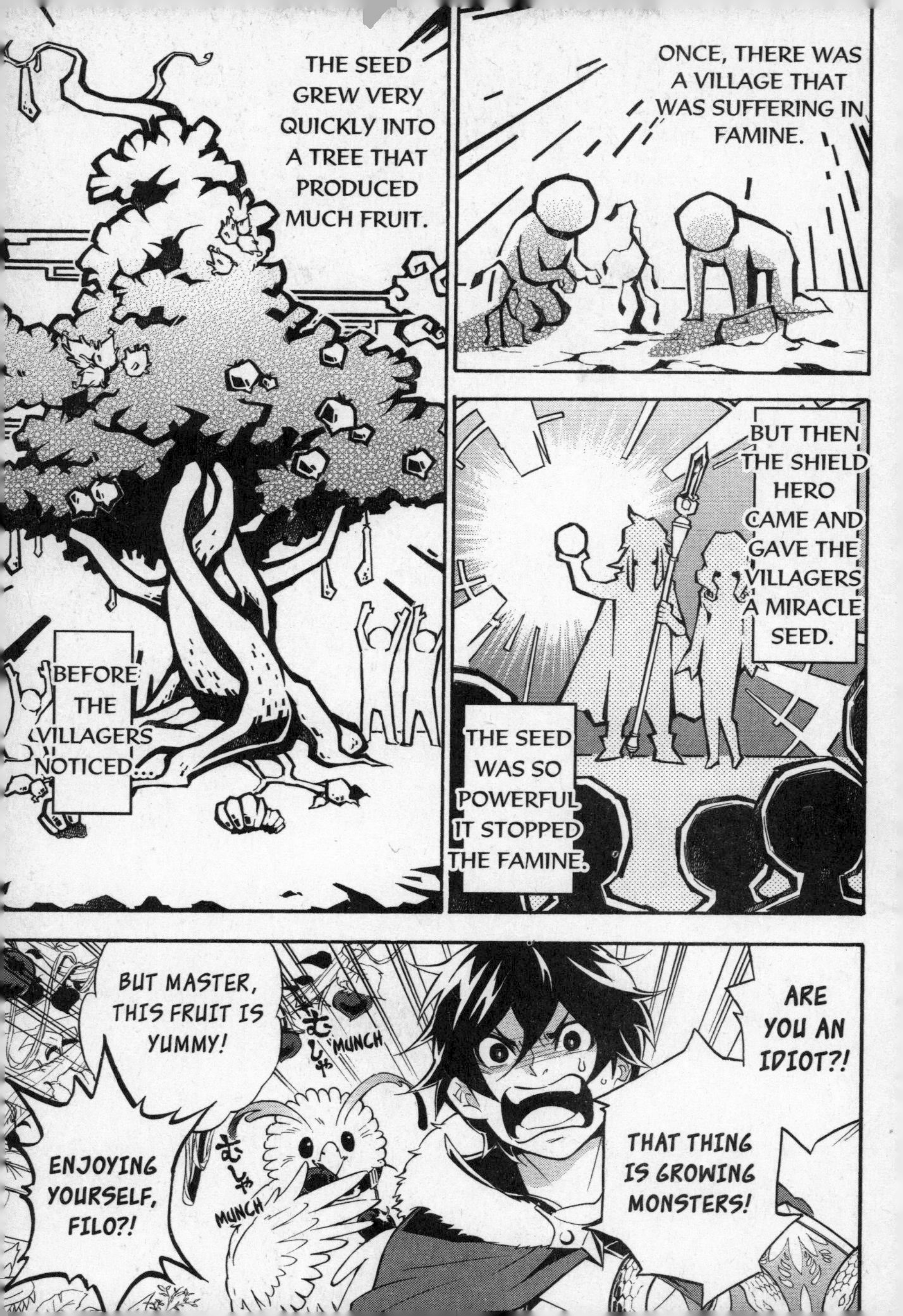
ONCE, THERE WAS A VILLAGE THAT WAS SUFFERING IN FAMINE.
BUT THEN THE SHIELD HERO CAME AND GAVE THE VILLAGERS A MIRACLE SEED.
THE SEED WAS SO POWERFUL IT STOPPED THE FAMINE.
THE SEED GREW VERY QUICKLY INTO A TREE THAT PRODUCED MUCH FRUIT.
BEFORE THE VILLAGERS NOTICED...
ARE YOU AN IDIOT?!
BUT MASTER, THIS FRUIT IS YUMMY!
MUNCH
THAT THING IS GROWING MONSTERS!
ENJOYING YOURSELF, FILO?!
MUNCH

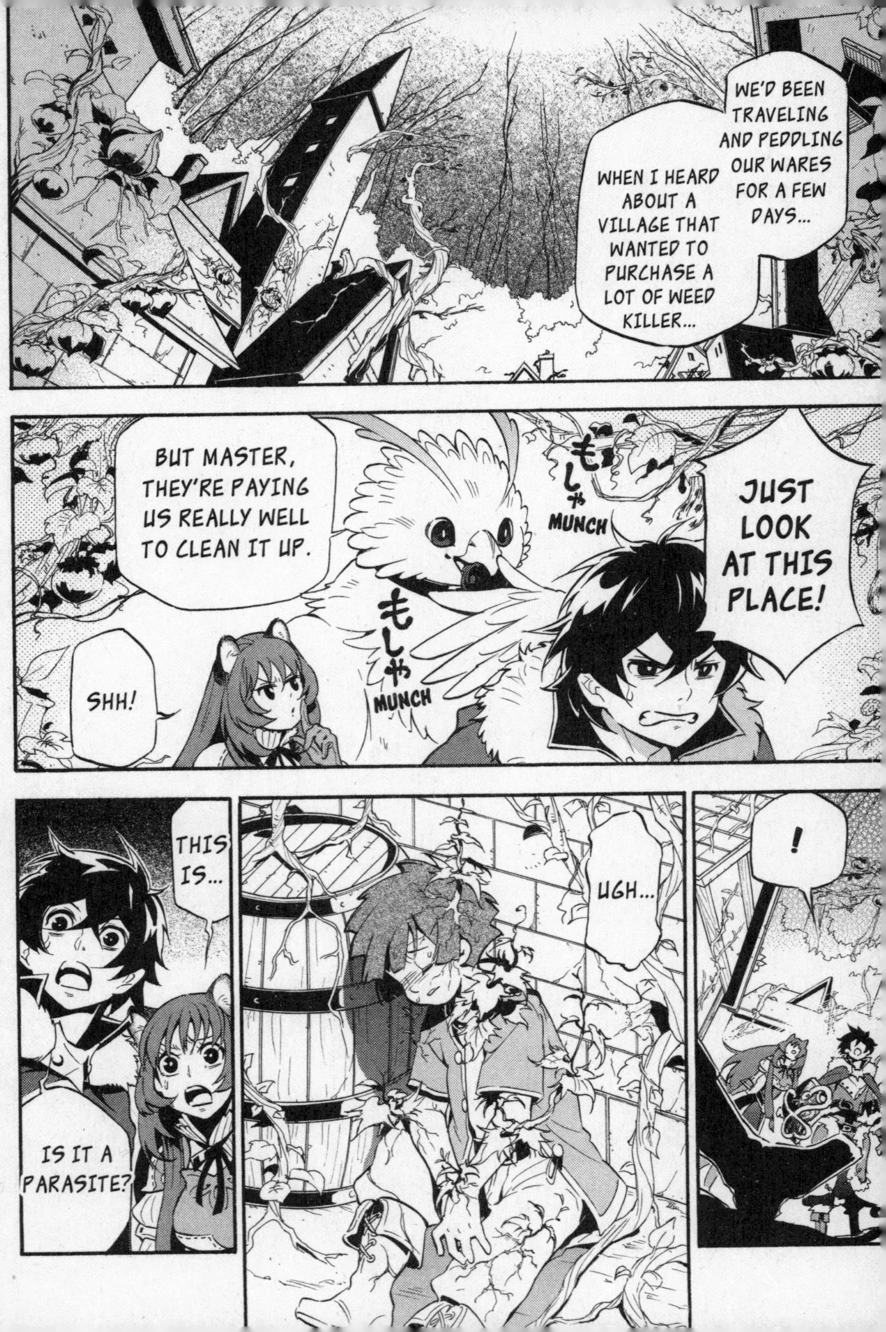
WE'D BEEN TRAVELING AND PEDDLING OUR WARES FOR A FEW DAYS...
WHEN I HEARD ABOUT A VILLAGE THAT WANTED TO PURCHASE A LOT OF WEED KILLER...
JUST LOOK AT THIS PLACE!
もしゃ MUNCH
BUT MASTER, THEY'RE PAYING US REALLY WELL TO CLEAN IT UP.
もしゃ MUNCH
SHH!
!
UGH...
THIS IS...
IS IT A PARASITE?

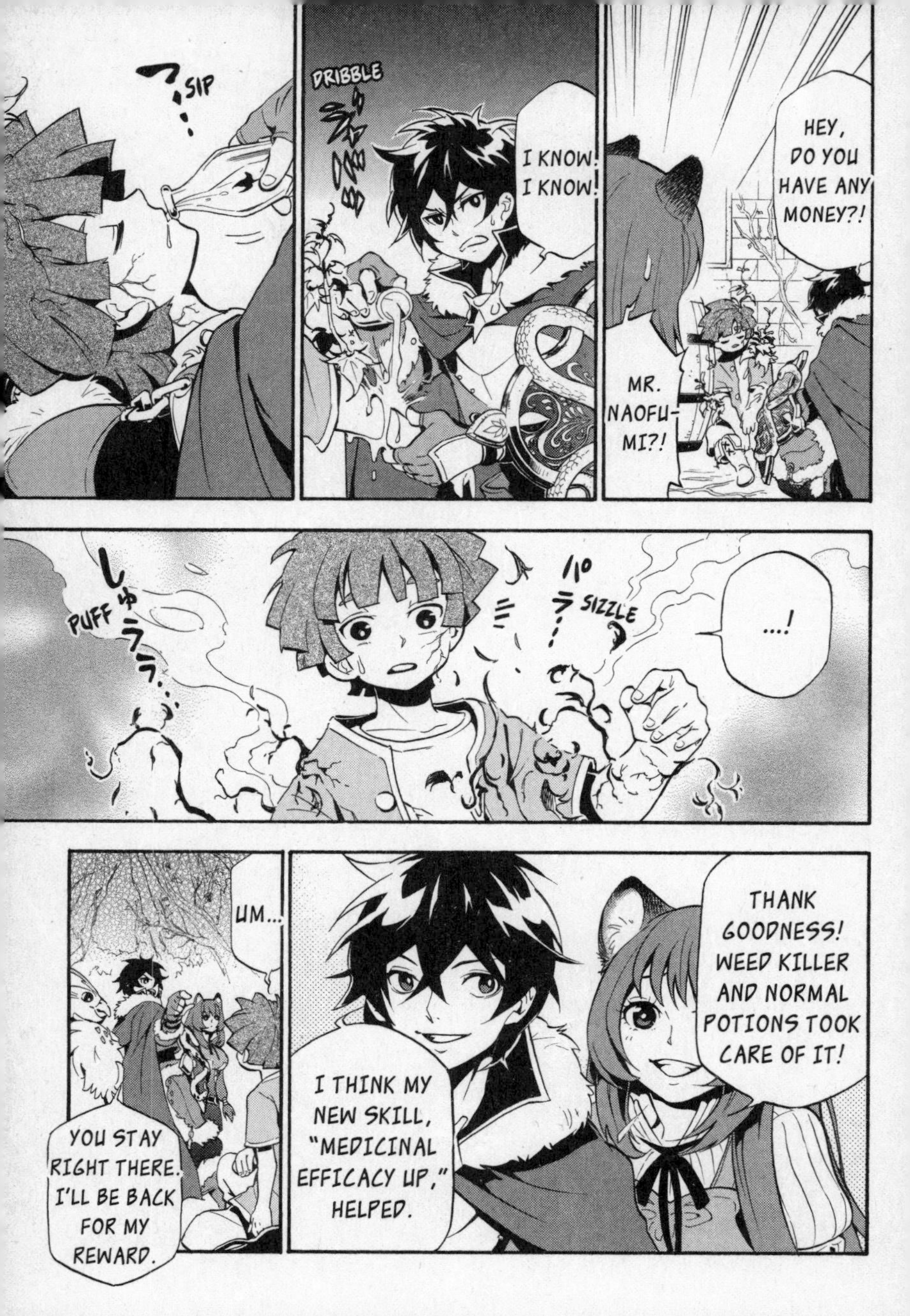
HEY, DO YOU HAVE ANY MONEY?!
MR. NAOFUMI?!
I KNOW! I KNOW!
DRIBBLE
SIP
...!
SIZZLE
PUFF
THANK GOODNESS! WEED KILLER AND NORMAL POTIONS TOOK CARE OF IT!
I THINK MY NEW SKILL, "MEDICINAL EFFICACY UP," HELPED.
UM...
YOU STAY RIGHT THERE. I'LL BE BACK FOR MY REWARD.

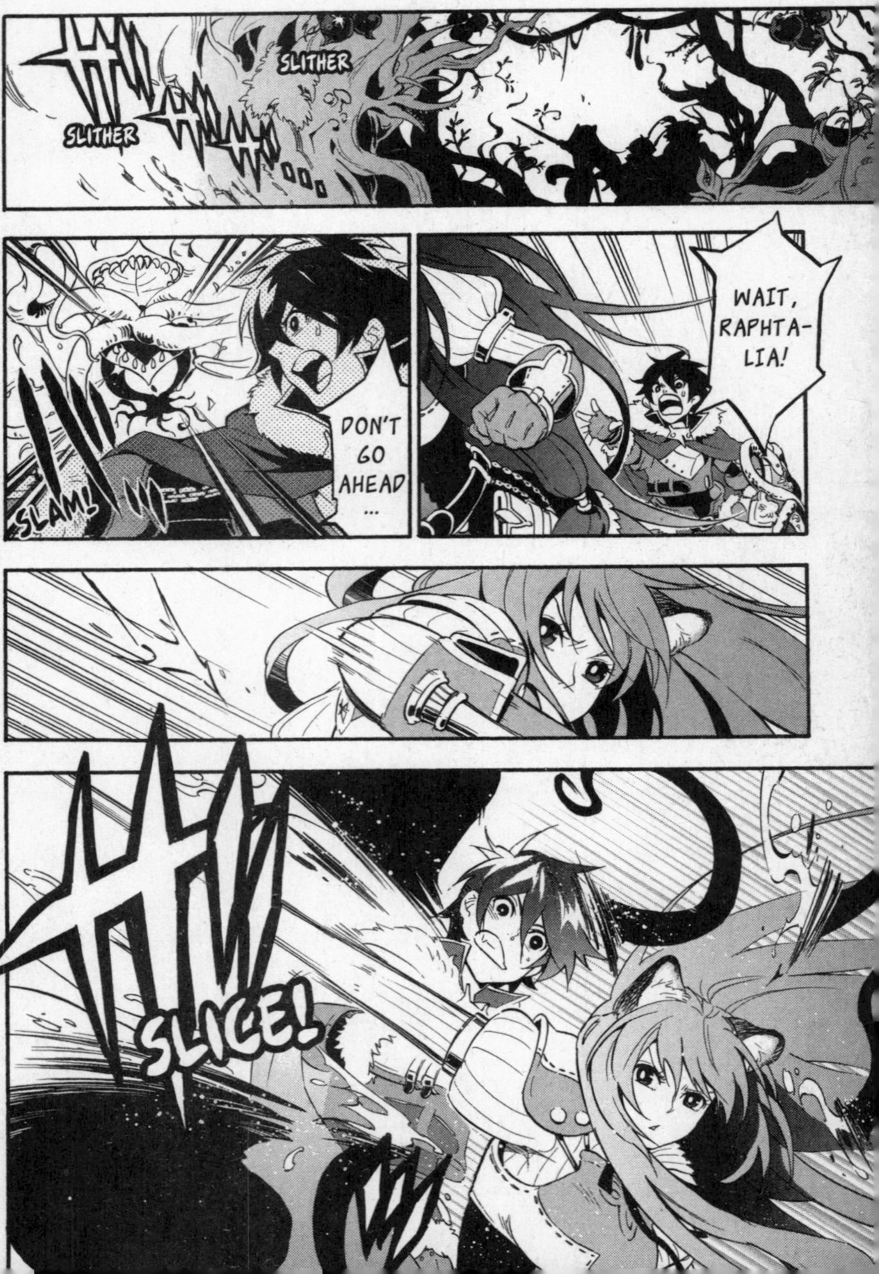
SLITHER
SLITHER
WAIT, RAPHTA-LIA!
DON'T GO AHEAD ...
SLAM!
SLICE!

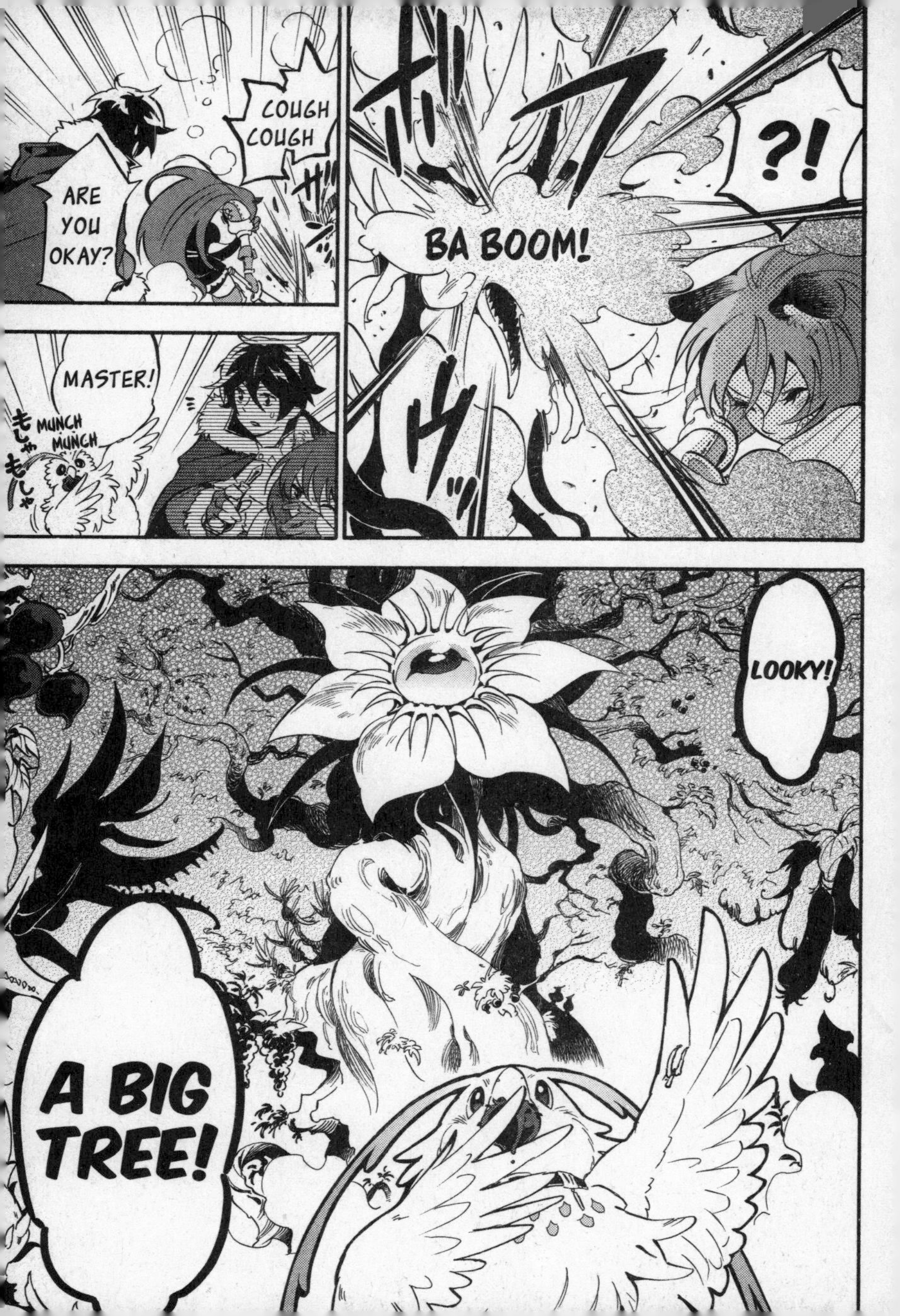
?!
BA BOOM!
COUGH COUGH
ARE YOU OKAY?
MASTER!
MUNCH MUNCH
もしゃもしゃ
LOOKY!
A BIG TREE!

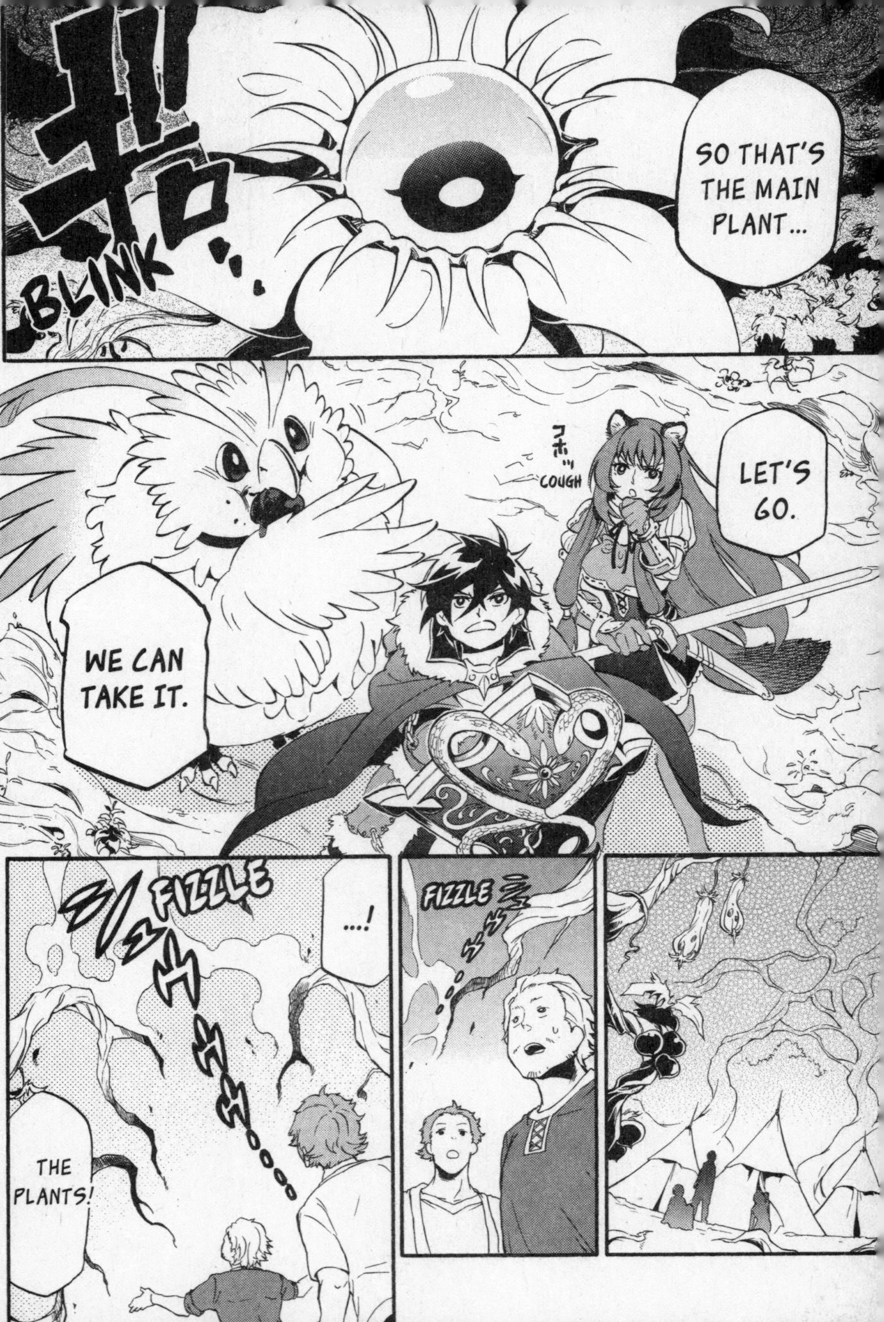
SO THAT'S THE MAIN PLANT...
ギロ
BLINK...
LET'S GO.
コホッ
COUGH
WE CAN TAKE IT.
FIZZLE
...!
FIZZLE
THE PLANTS!

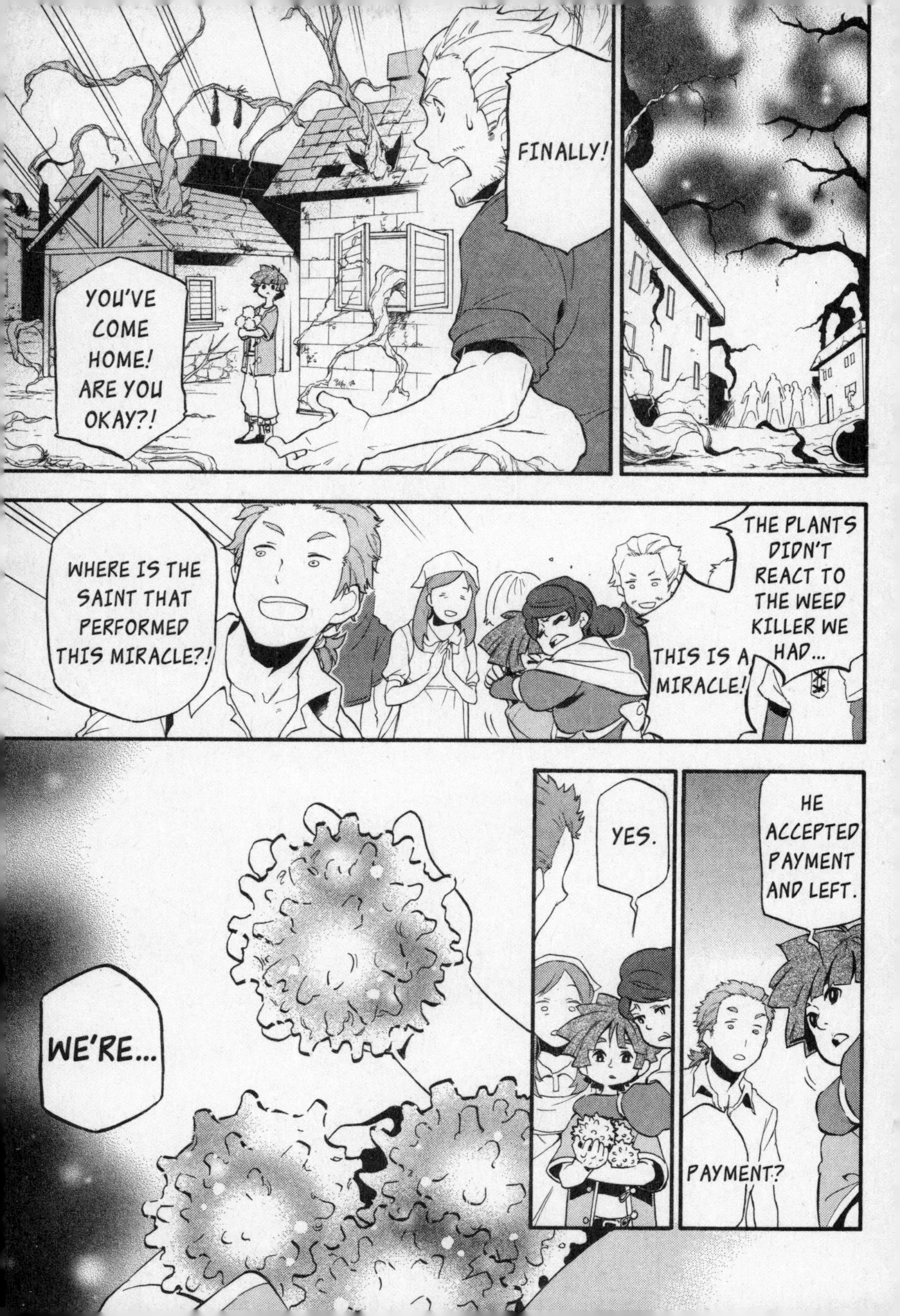
FINALLY!
YOU'VE COME HOME! ARE YOU OKAY?!
THE PLANTS DIDN'T REACT TO THE WEED KILLER WE HAD...
THIS IS A MIRACLE!
WHERE IS THE SAINT THAT PERFORMED THIS MIRACLE?!
HE ACCEPTED PAYMENT AND LEFT.
PAYMENT?
YES.
WE'RE...

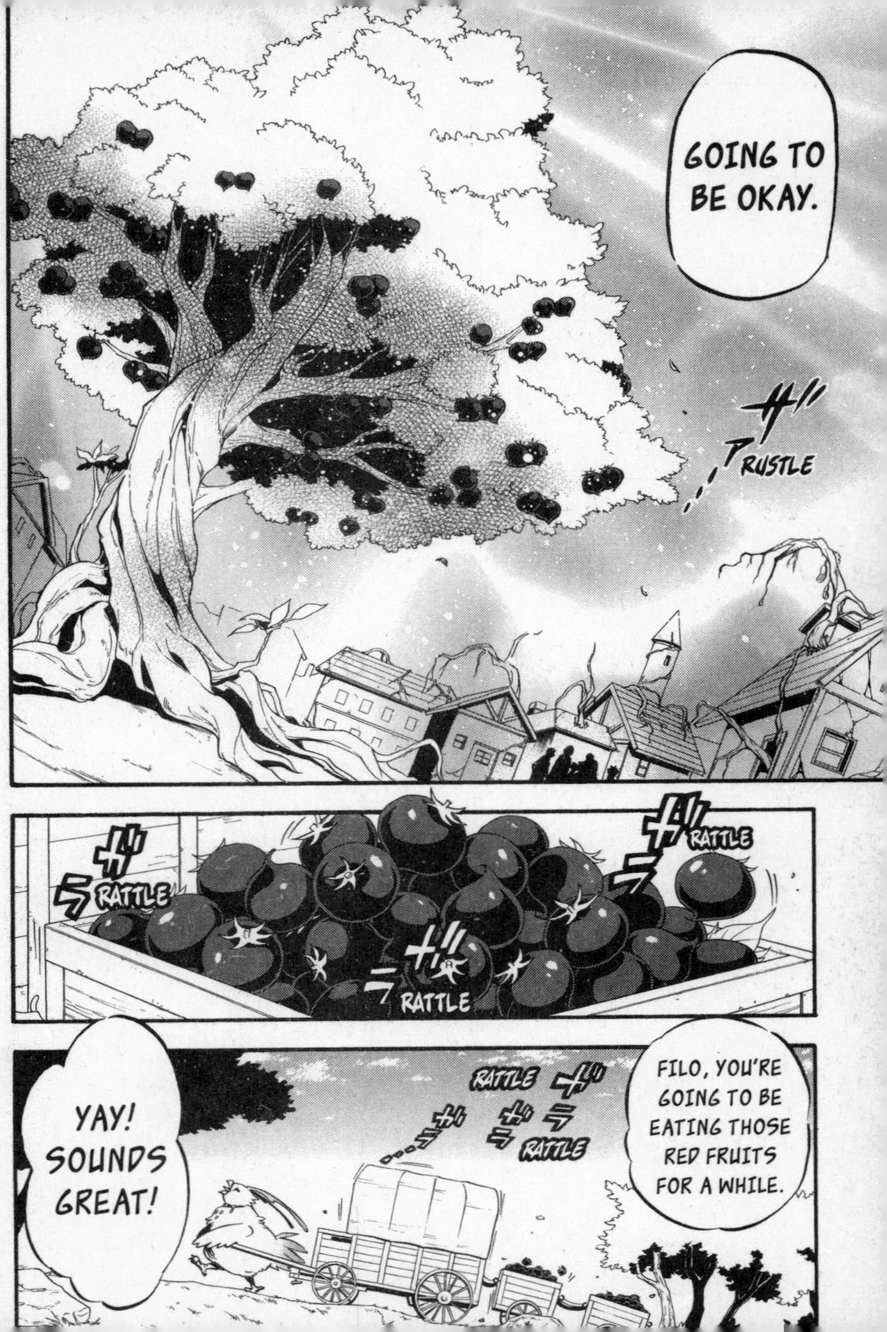
GOING TO BE OKAY.
RUSTLE
RATTLE
RATTLE
RATTLE
FILO, YOU'RE GOING TO BE EATING THOSE RED FRUITS FOR A WHILE.
RATTLE
RATTLE
YAY! SOUNDS GREAT!

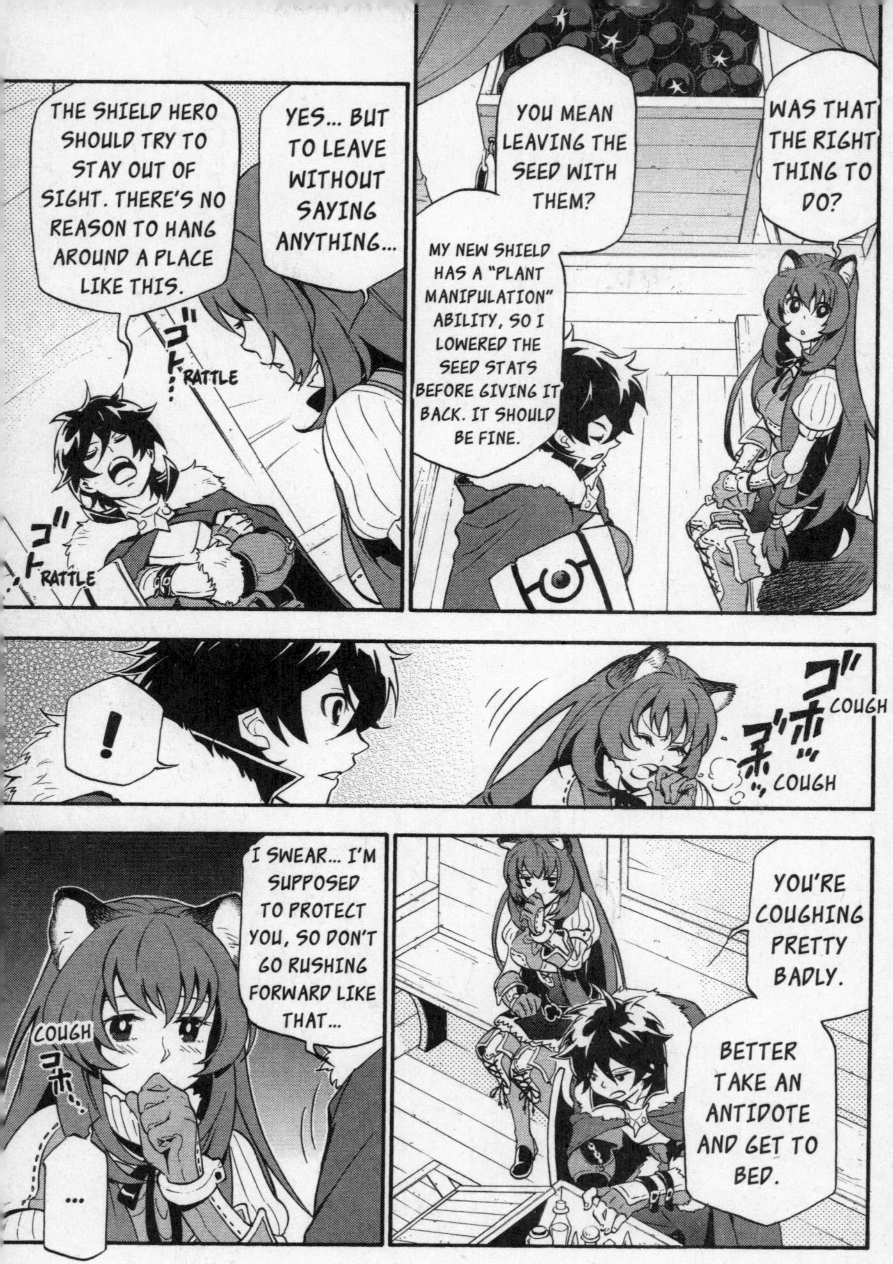
WAS THAT THE RIGHT THING TO DO?
YOU MEAN LEAVING THE SEED WITH THEM?
MY NEW SHIELD HAS A "PLANT MANIPULATION" ABILITY, SO I LOWERED THE SEED STATS BEFORE GIVING IT BACK. IT SHOULD BE FINE.
YES... BUT TO LEAVE WITHOUT SAYING ANYTHING...
THE SHIELD HERO SHOULD TRY TO STAY OUT OF SIGHT. THERE'S NO REASON TO HANG AROUND A PLACE LIKE THIS.
ゴト… RATTLE
ゴト… RATTLE
ゴホ COUGH
ゴホ… COUGH
!
YOU'RE COUGHING PRETTY BADLY.
BETTER TAKE AN ANTIDOTE AND GET TO BED.
I SWEAR... I'M SUPPOSED TO PROTECT YOU, SO DON'T GO RUSHING FORWARD LIKE THAT...
COUGH コホ…
...

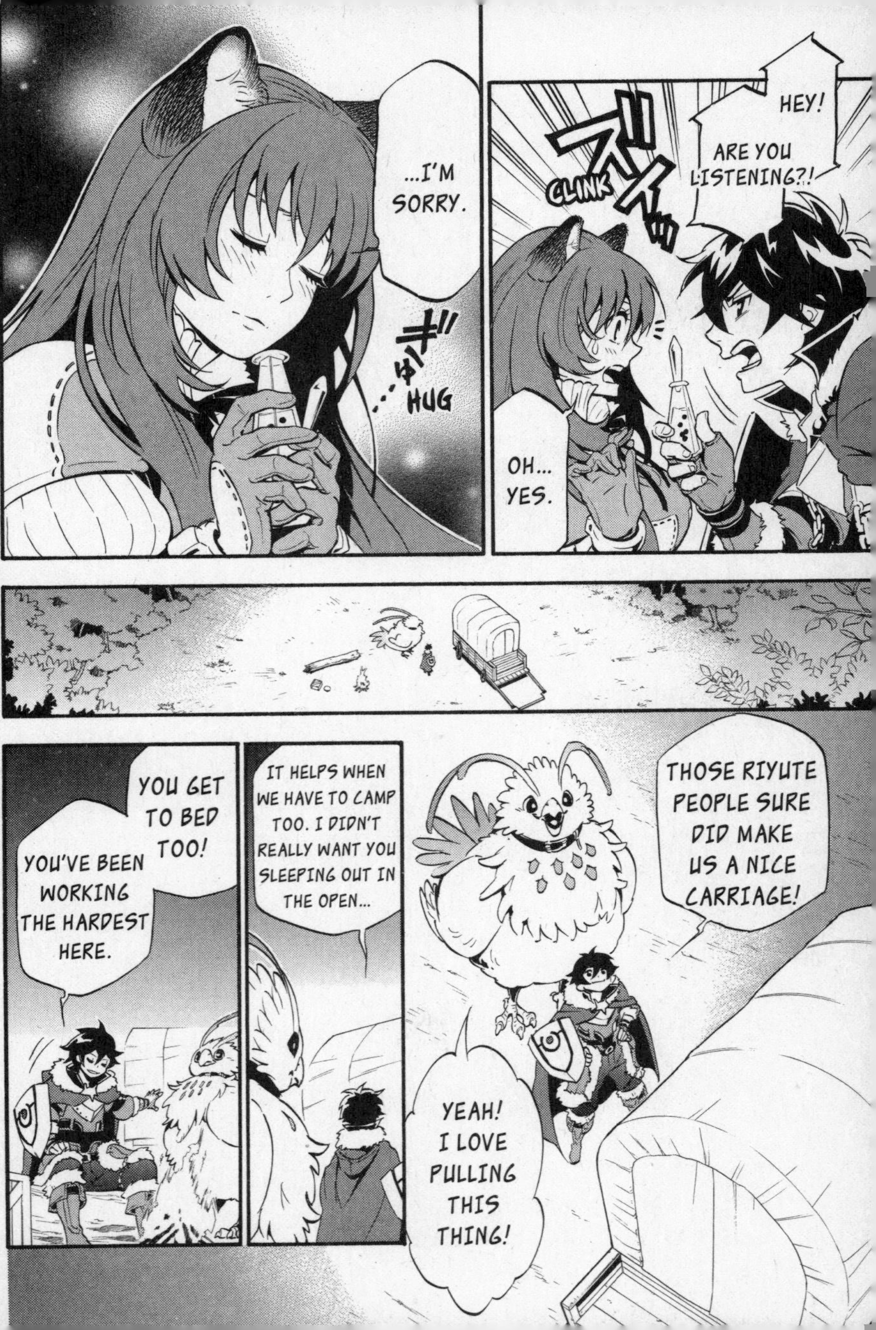
HEY!
ARE YOU LISTENING?!
CLINK
OH... YES.
...I'M SORRY.
HUG
THOSE RIYUTE PEOPLE SURE DID MAKE US A NICE CARRIAGE!
YEAH! I LOVE PULLING THIS THING!
IT HELPS WHEN WE HAVE TO CAMP TOO. I DIDN'T REALLY WANT YOU SLEEPING OUT IN THE OPEN...
YOU GET TO BED TOO!
YOU'VE BEEN WORKING THE HARDEST HERE.

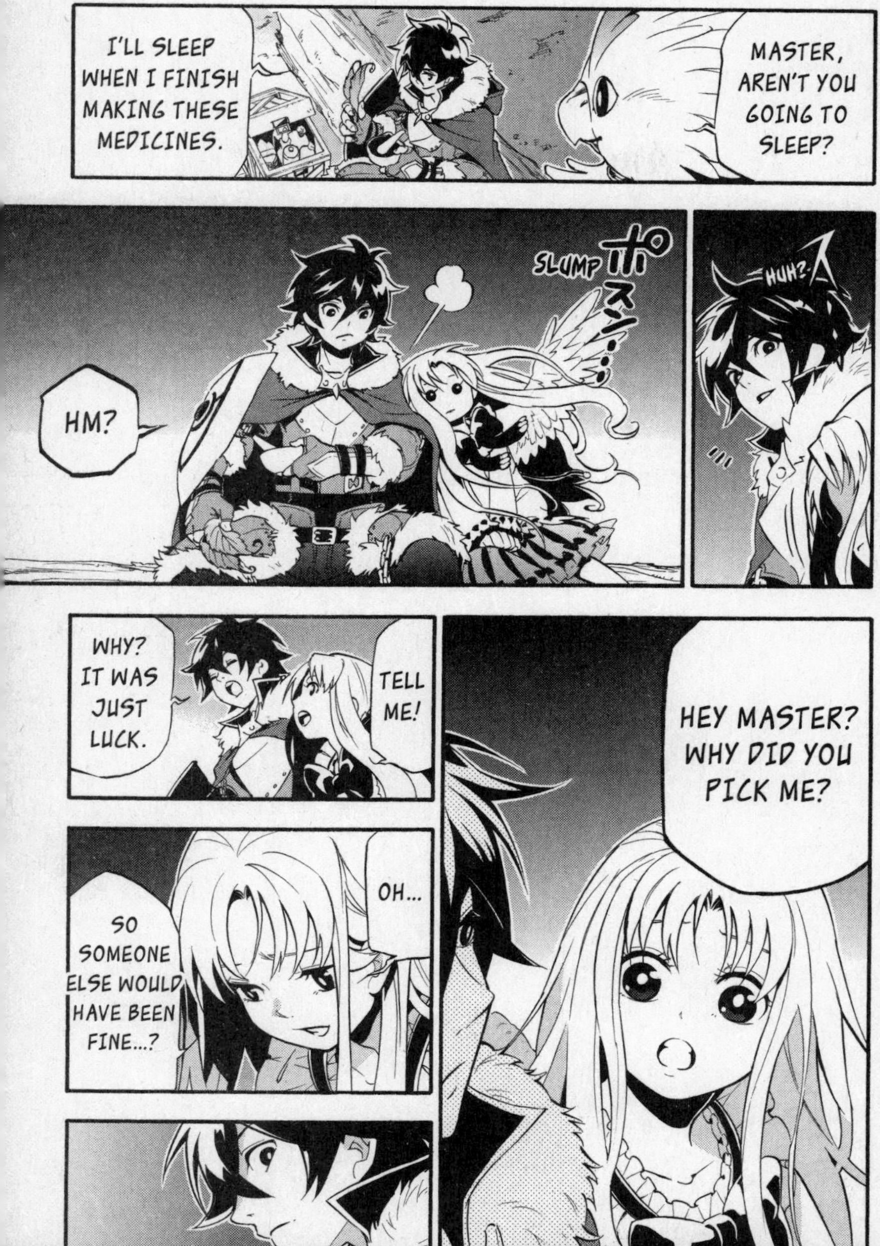
MASTER, AREN'T YOU GOING TO SLEEP?
I'LL SLEEP WHEN I FINISH MAKING THESE MEDICINES.
HUH?
SLUMP
ポスン…
HM?
HEY MASTER? WHY DID YOU PICK ME?
TELL ME!
WHY? IT WAS JUST LUCK.
OH...
SO SOMEONE ELSE WOULD HAVE BEEN FINE...?

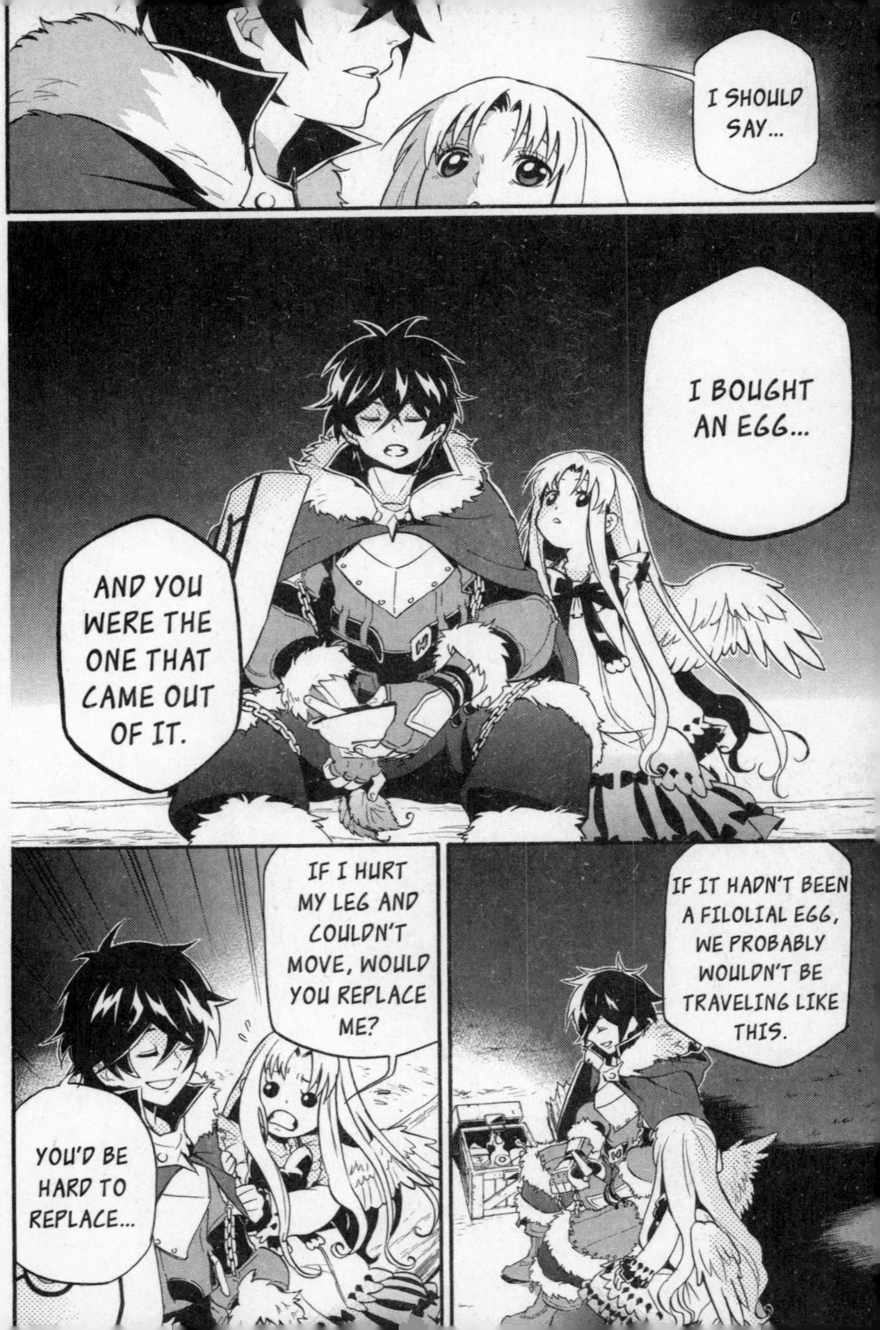
I SHOULD SAY...
I BOUGHT AN EGG...
AND YOU WERE THE ONE THAT CAME OUT OF IT.
IF IT HADN'T BEEN A FILOLIAL EGG, WE PROBABLY WOULDN'T BE TRAVELING LIKE THIS.
IF I HURT MY LEG AND COULDN'T MOVE, WOULD YOU REPLACE ME?
YOU'D BE HARD TO REPLACE...

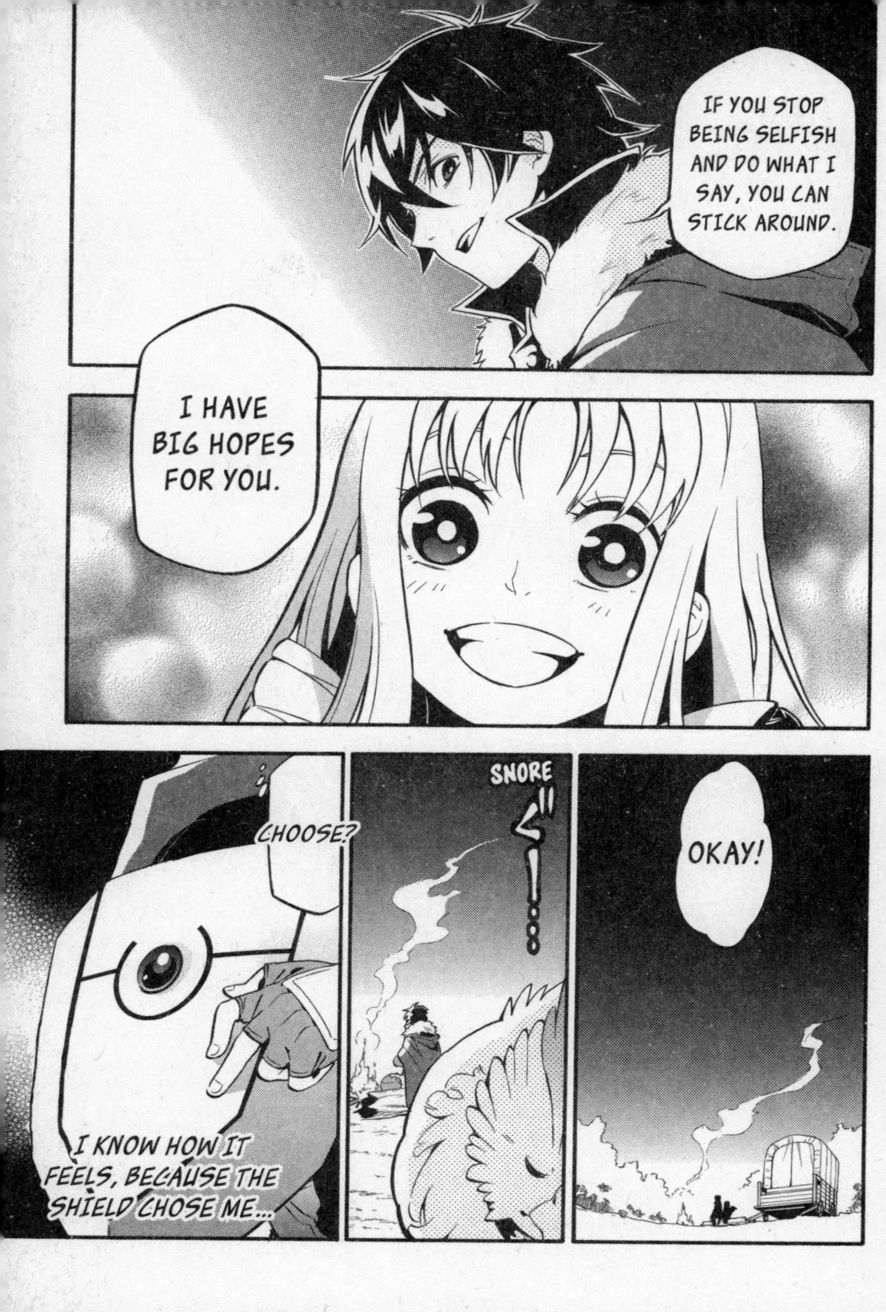
IF YOU STOP BEING SELFISH AND DO WHAT I SAY, YOU CAN STICK AROUND.
I HAVE BIG HOPES FOR YOU.
OKAY!
SNORE
CHOOSE?
I KNOW HOW IT FEELS, BECAUSE THE SHIELD CHOSE ME...

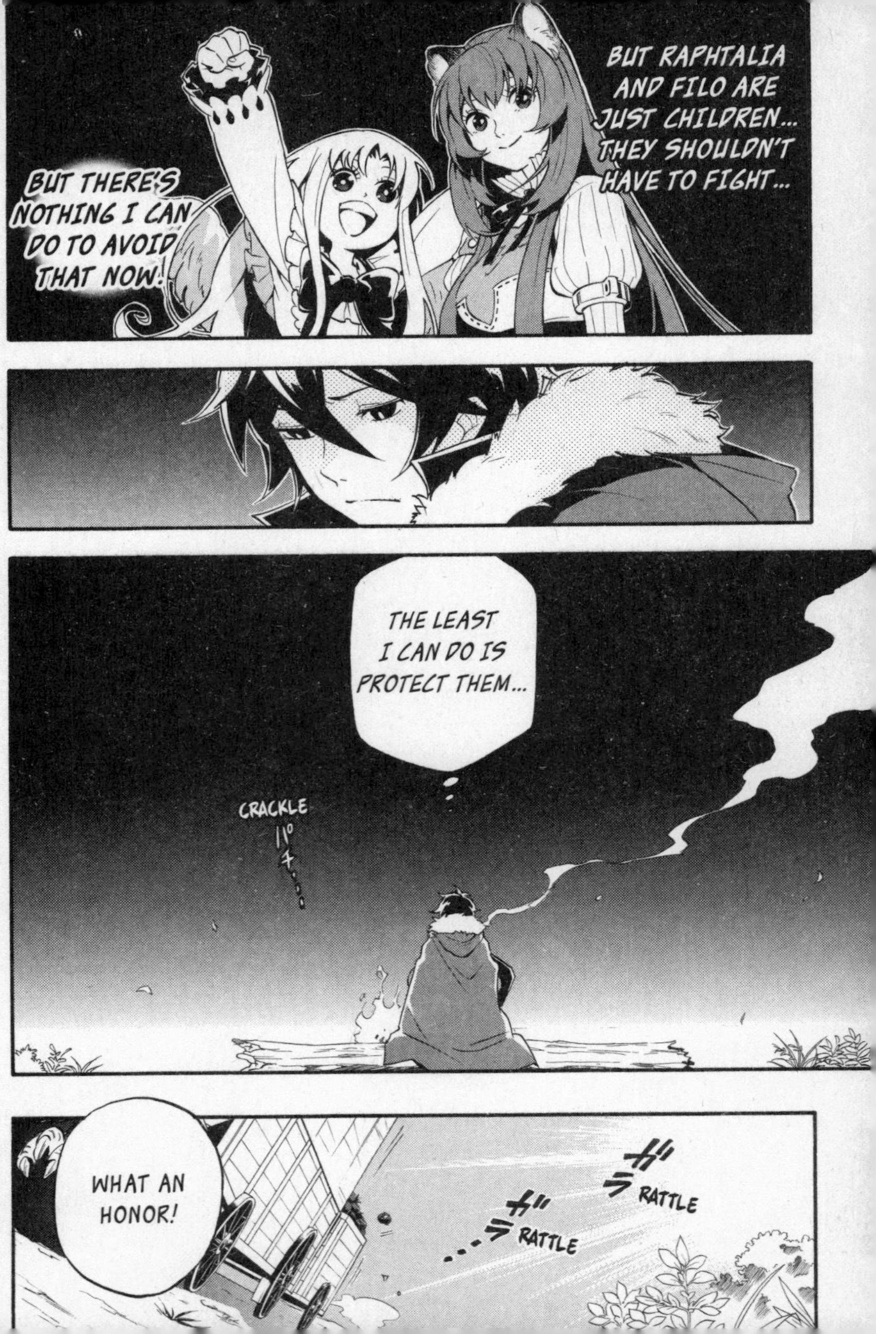
BUT RAPHTALIA AND FILO ARE JUST CHILDREN... THEY SHOULDN'T HAVE TO FIGHT...
BUT THERE'S NOTHING I CAN DO TO AVOID THAT NOW!
THE LEAST I CAN DO IS PROTECT THEM...
CRACKLE
RATTLE
RATTLE
WHAT AN HONOR!

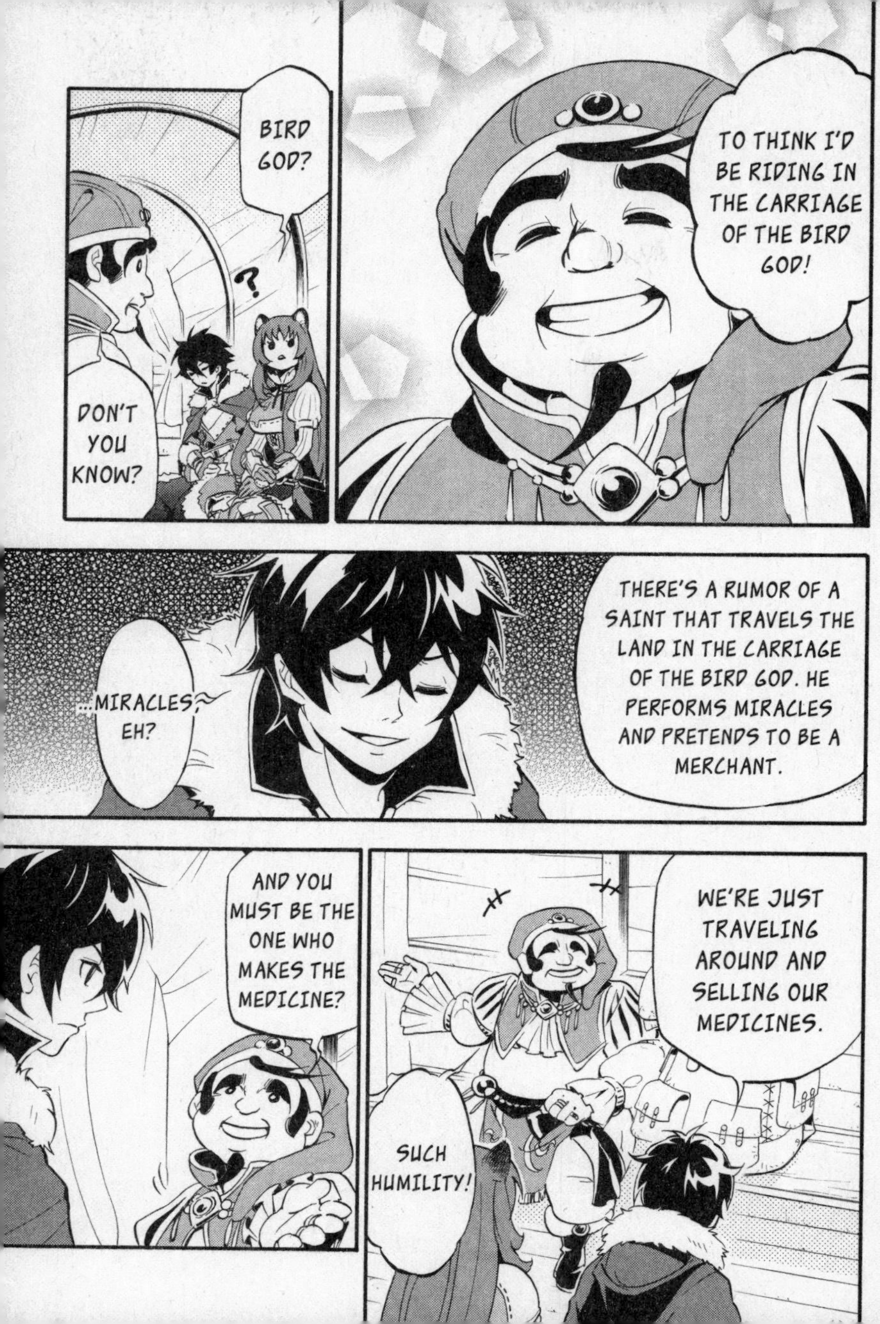
TO THINK I'D BE RIDING IN THE CARRIAGE OF THE BIRD GOD!
BIRD GOD?
?
DON'T YOU KNOW?
THERE'S A RUMOR OF A SAINT THAT TRAVELS THE LAND IN THE CARRIAGE OF THE BIRD GOD. HE PERFORMS MIRACLES AND PRETENDS TO BE A MERCHANT.
...MIRACLES~, EH?
WE'RE JUST TRAVELING AROUND AND SELLING OUR MEDICINES.
SUCH HUMILITY!
AND YOU MUST BE THE ONE WHO MAKES THE MEDICINE?

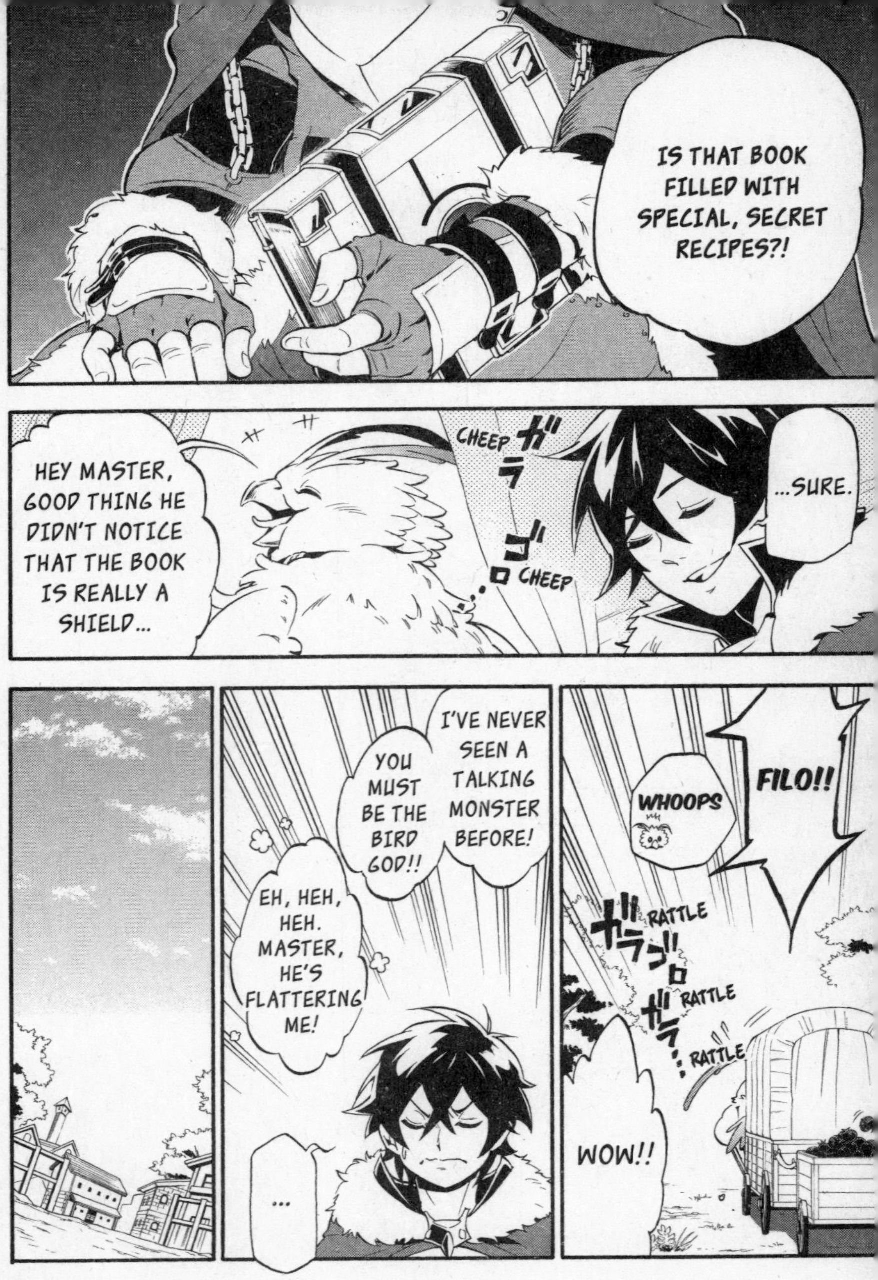
IS THAT BOOK FILLED WITH SPECIAL, SECRET RECIPES?!
...SURE.
CHEEP
CHEEP
HEY MASTER, GOOD THING HE DIDN'T NOTICE THAT THE BOOK IS REALLY A SHIELD...
FILO!!
WHOOPS
RATTLE
RATTLE
RATTLE
WOW!!
I'VE NEVER SEEN A TALKING MONSTER BEFORE!
YOU MUST BE THE BIRD GOD!!
EH, HEH, HEH. MASTER, HE'S FLATTERING ME!
...

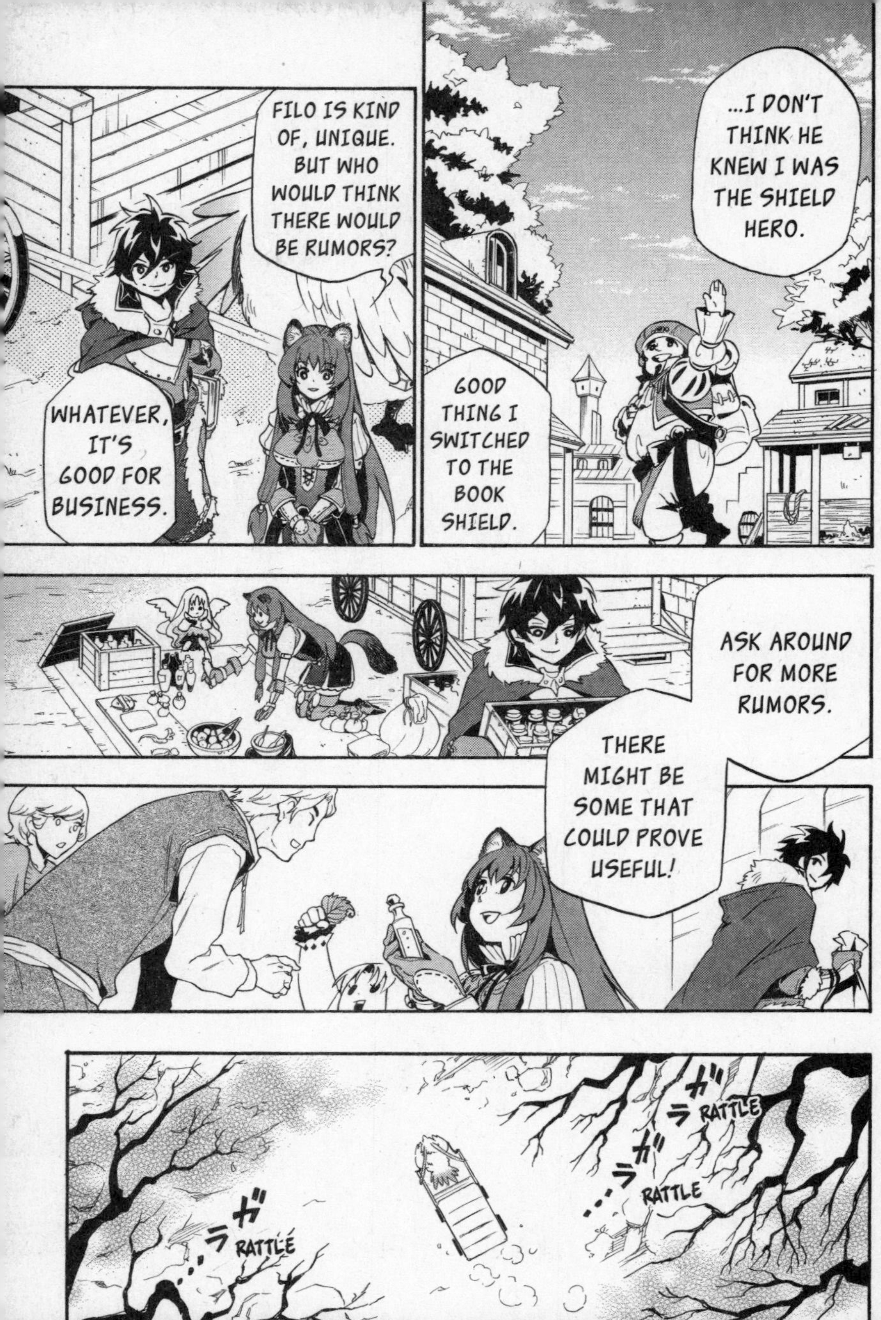
...I DON'T THINK HE KNEW I WAS THE SHIELD HERO.
GOOD THING I SWITCHED TO THE BOOK SHIELD.
FILO IS KIND OF, UNIQUE. BUT WHO WOULD THINK THERE WOULD BE RUMORS?
WHATEVER, IT'S GOOD FOR BUSINESS.
ASK AROUND FOR MORE RUMORS.
THERE MIGHT BE SOME THAT COULD PROVE USEFUL!
ガラ RATTLE
...ガラ RATTLE
...ガラ RATTLE

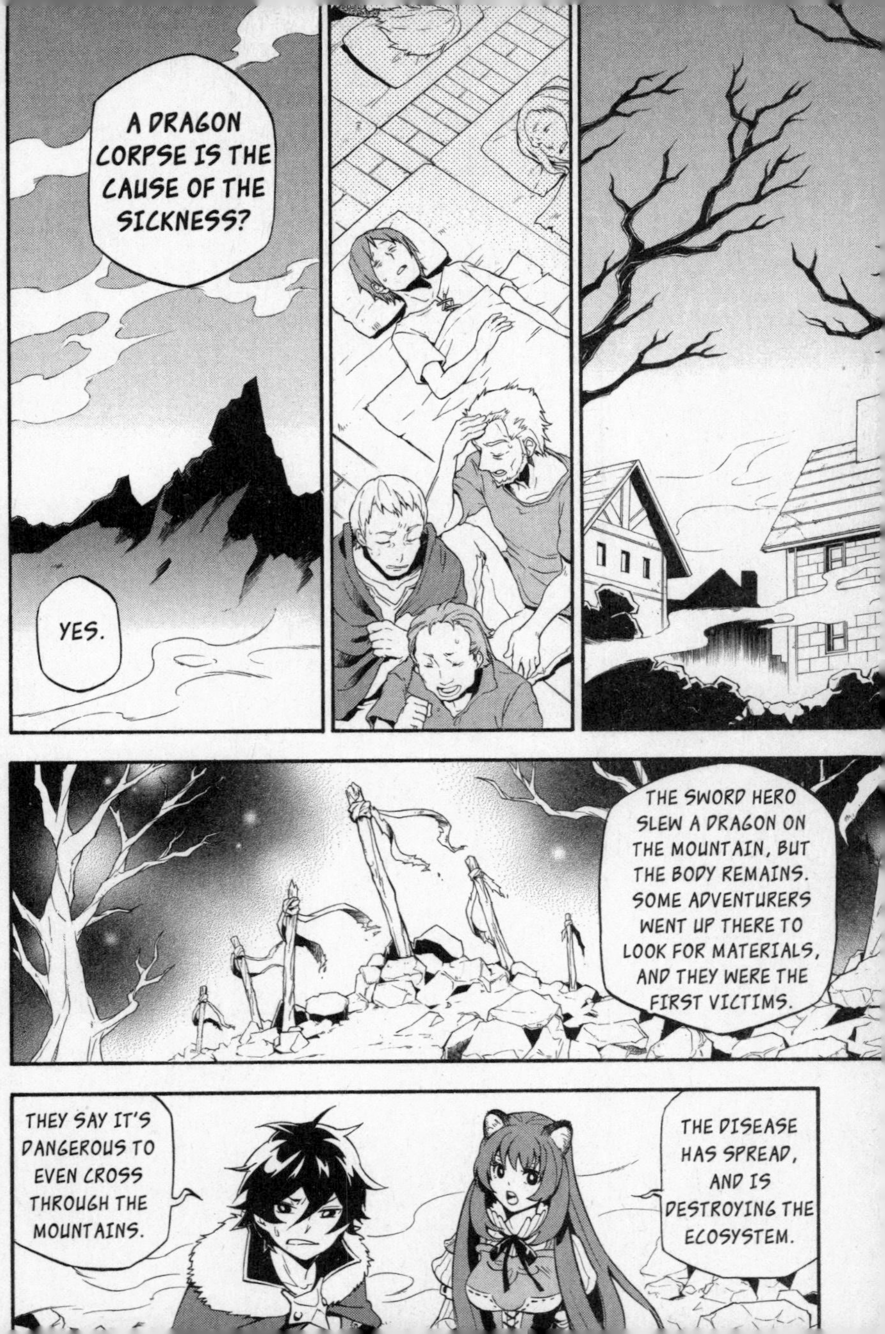
A DRAGON CORPSE IS THE CAUSE OF THE SICKNESS?
YES.
THE SWORD HERO SLEW A DRAGON ON THE MOUNTAIN, BUT THE BODY REMAINS. SOME ADVENTURERS WENT UP THERE TO LOOK FOR MATERIALS, AND THEY WERE THE FIRST VICTIMS.
THE DISEASE HAS SPREAD, AND IS DESTROYING THE ECOSYSTEM.
THEY SAY IT'S DANGEROUS TO EVEN CROSS THROUGH THE MOUNTAINS.

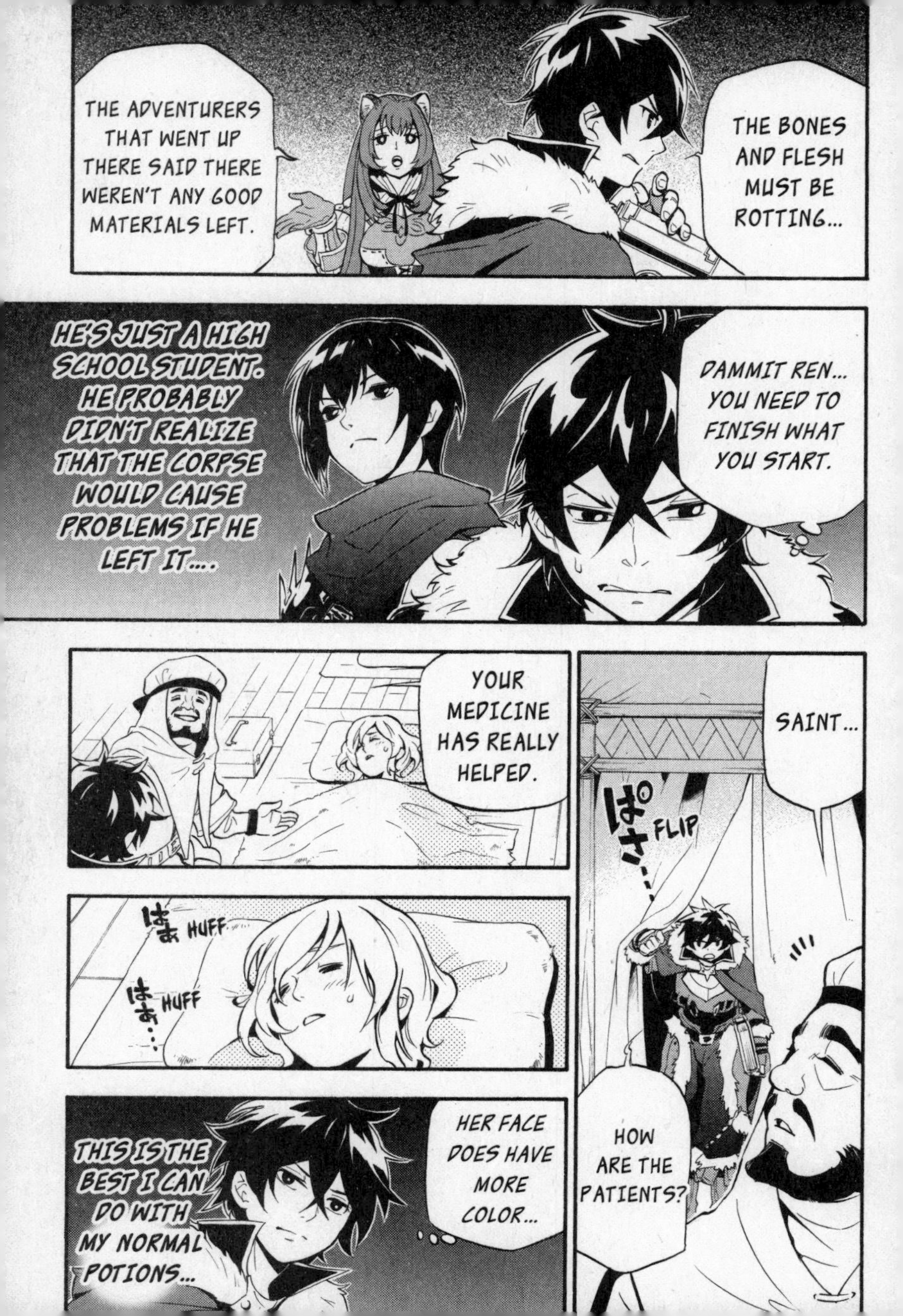
THE BONES AND FLESH MUST BE ROTTING...
THE ADVENTURERS THAT WENT UP THERE SAID THERE WEREN'T ANY GOOD MATERIALS LEFT.
DAMMIT REN... YOU NEED TO FINISH WHAT YOU START.
HE'S JUST A HIGH SCHOOL STUDENT. HE PROBABLY DIDN'T REALIZE THAT THE CORPSE WOULD CAUSE PROBLEMS IF HE LEFT IT....
SAINT...
ぱさ FLIP
HOW ARE THE PATIENTS?
YOUR MEDICINE HAS REALLY HELPED.
はぁ HUFF
はぁ... HUFF
HER FACE DOES HAVE MORE COLOR...
THIS IS THE BEST I CAN DO WITH MY NORMAL POTIONS...

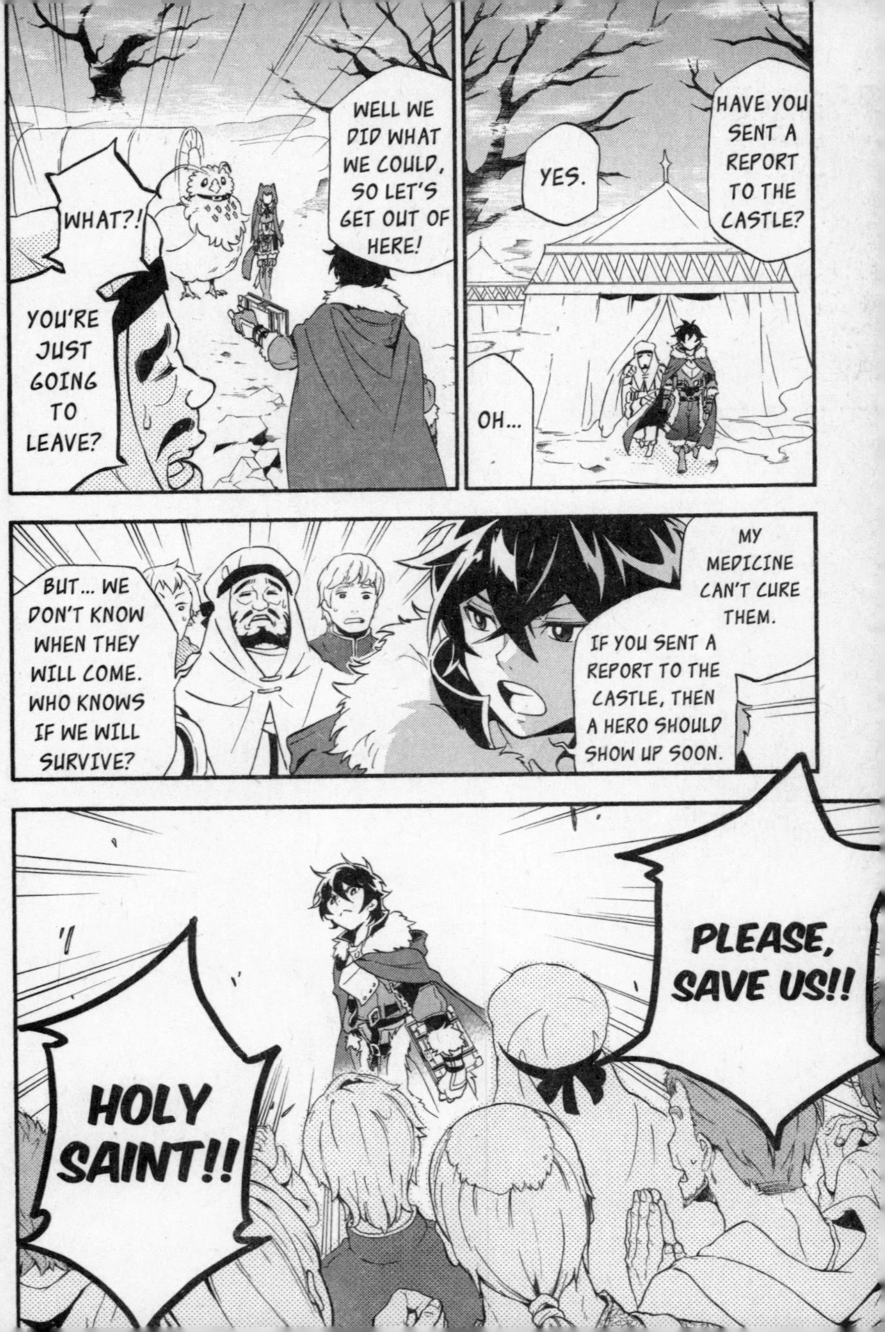
HAVE YOU SENT A REPORT TO THE CASTLE?
YES.
OH...
WELL WE DID WHAT WE COULD, SO LET'S GET OUT OF HERE!
WHAT?!
YOU'RE JUST GOING TO LEAVE?
MY MEDICINE CAN'T CURE THEM.
IF YOU SENT A REPORT TO THE CASTLE, THEN A HERO SHOULD SHOW UP SOON.
BUT... WE DON'T KNOW WHEN THEY WILL COME. WHO KNOWS IF WE WILL SURVIVE?
PLEASE, SAVE US!!
HOLY SAINT!!

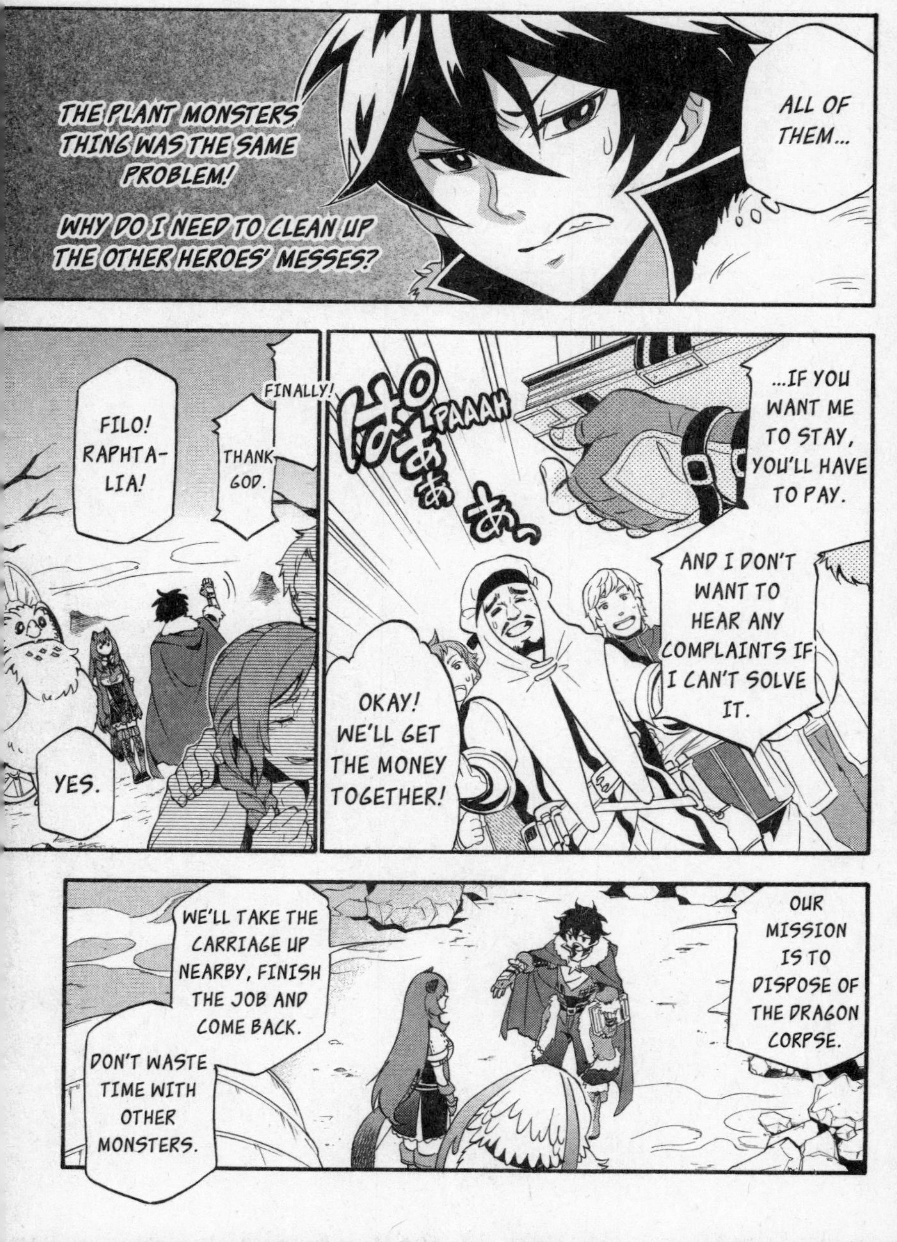
ALL OF THEM...
THE PLANT MONSTERS THING WAS THE SAME PROBLEM!
WHY DO I NEED TO CLEAN UP THE OTHER HEROES' MESSES?
...IF YOU WANT ME TO STAY, YOU'LL HAVE TO PAY.
はぁぁぁ PAAAH
AND I DON'T WANT TO HEAR ANY COMPLAINTS IF I CAN'T SOLVE IT.
OKAY! WE'LL GET THE MONEY TOGETHER!
FINALLY!
THANK GOD.
FILO! RAPHTA-LIA!
YES.
OUR MISSION IS TO DISPOSE OF THE DRAGON CORPSE.
WE'LL TAKE THE CARRIAGE UP NEARBY, FINISH THE JOB AND COME BACK.
DON'T WASTE TIME WITH OTHER MONSTERS.

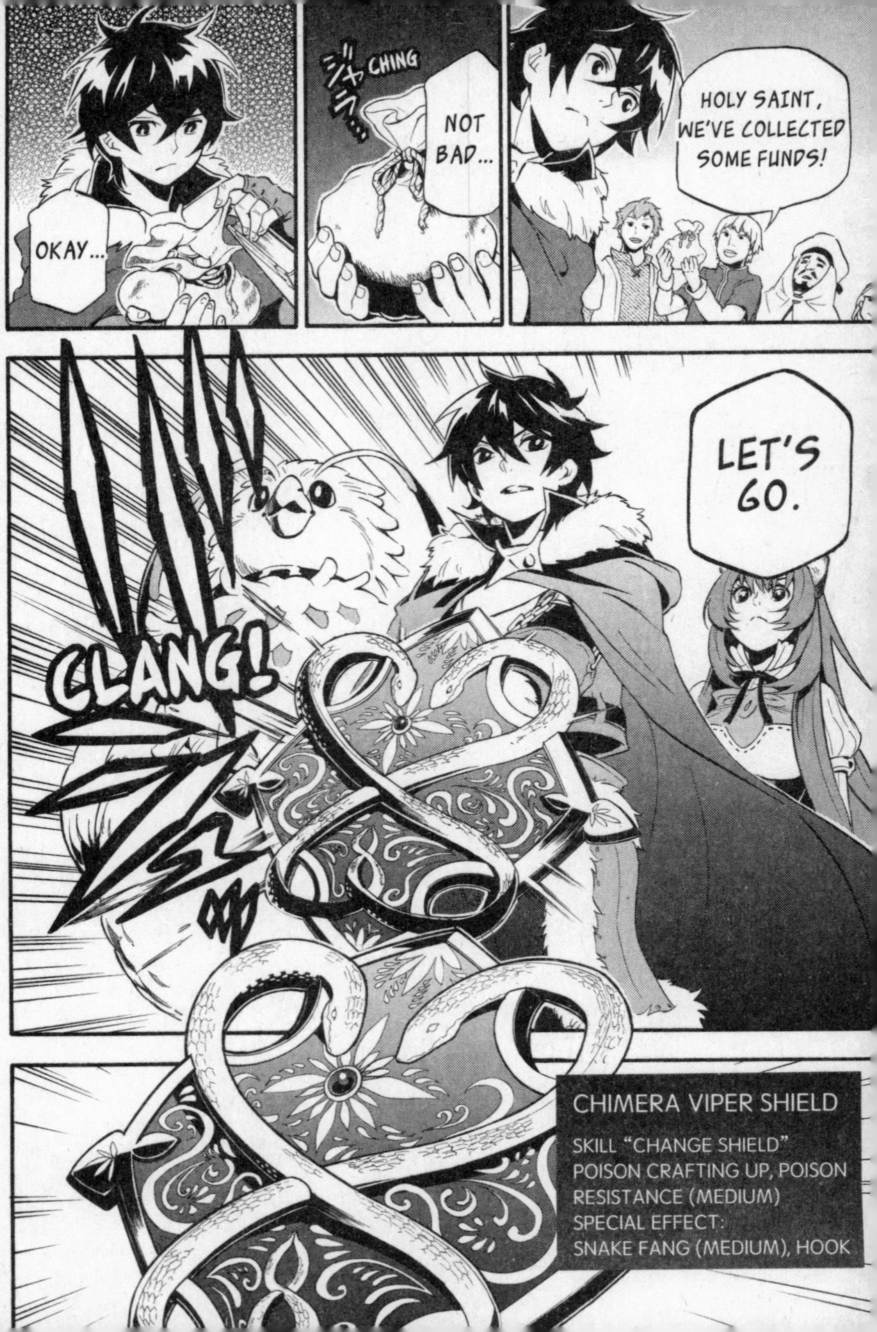
HOLY SAINT, WE'VE COLLECTED SOME FUNDS!
ジャラ…
CHING
NOT BAD...
OKAY...
LET'S GO.
CLANG!
CHIMERA VIPER SHIELD
SKILL "CHANGE SHIELD"
POISON CRAFTING UP, POISON RESISTANCE (MEDIUM)
SPECIAL EFFECT:
SNAKE FANG (MEDIUM), HOOK

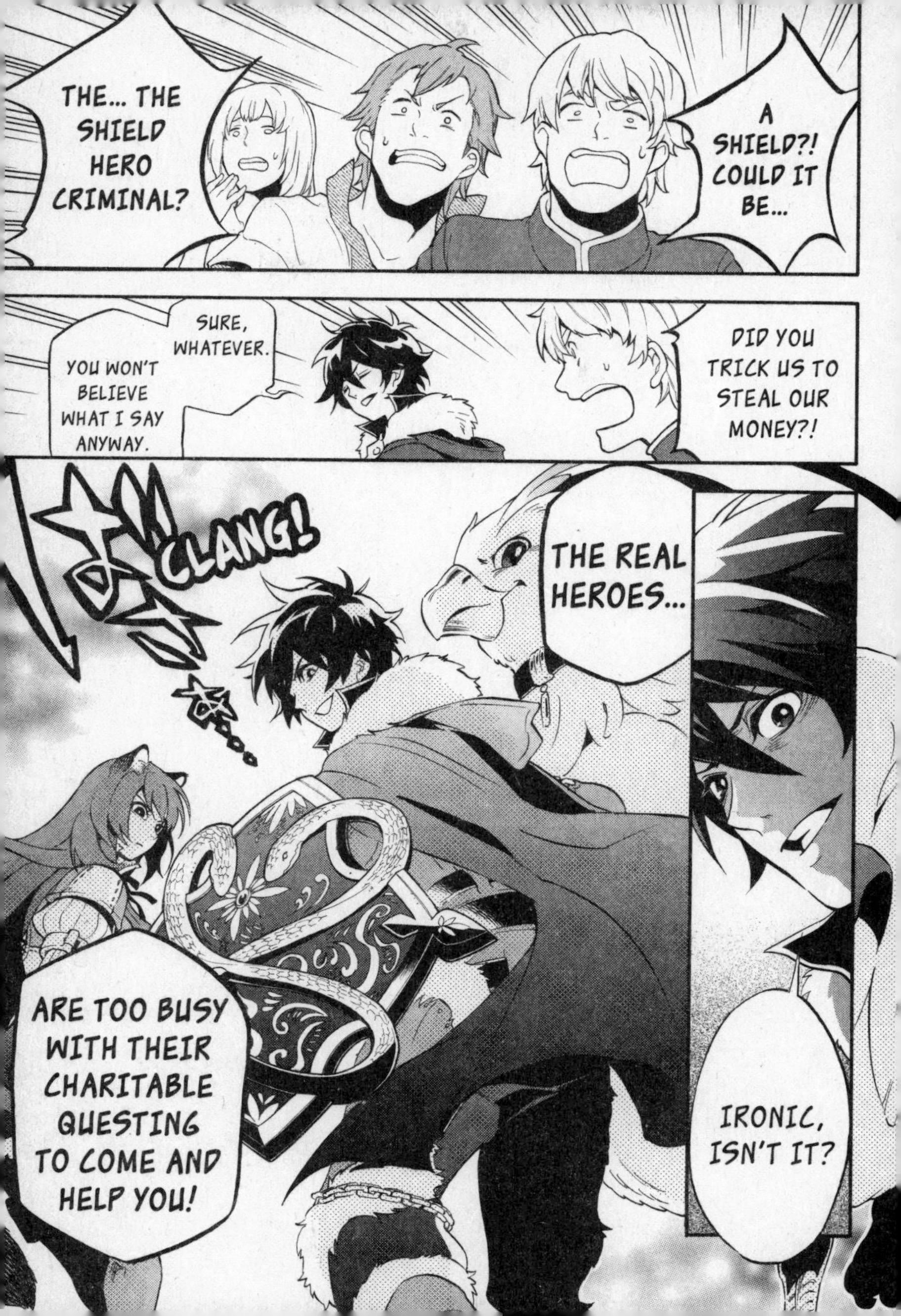
A SHIELD?! COULD IT BE...
THE... THE SHIELD HERO CRIMINAL?
DID YOU TRICK US TO STEAL OUR MONEY?!
SURE, WHATEVER.
YOU WON'T BELIEVE WHAT I SAY ANYWAY.
CLANG!
THE REAL HEROES...
ARE TOO BUSY WITH THEIR CHARITABLE QUESTING TO COME AND HELP YOU!
IRONIC, ISN'T IT?

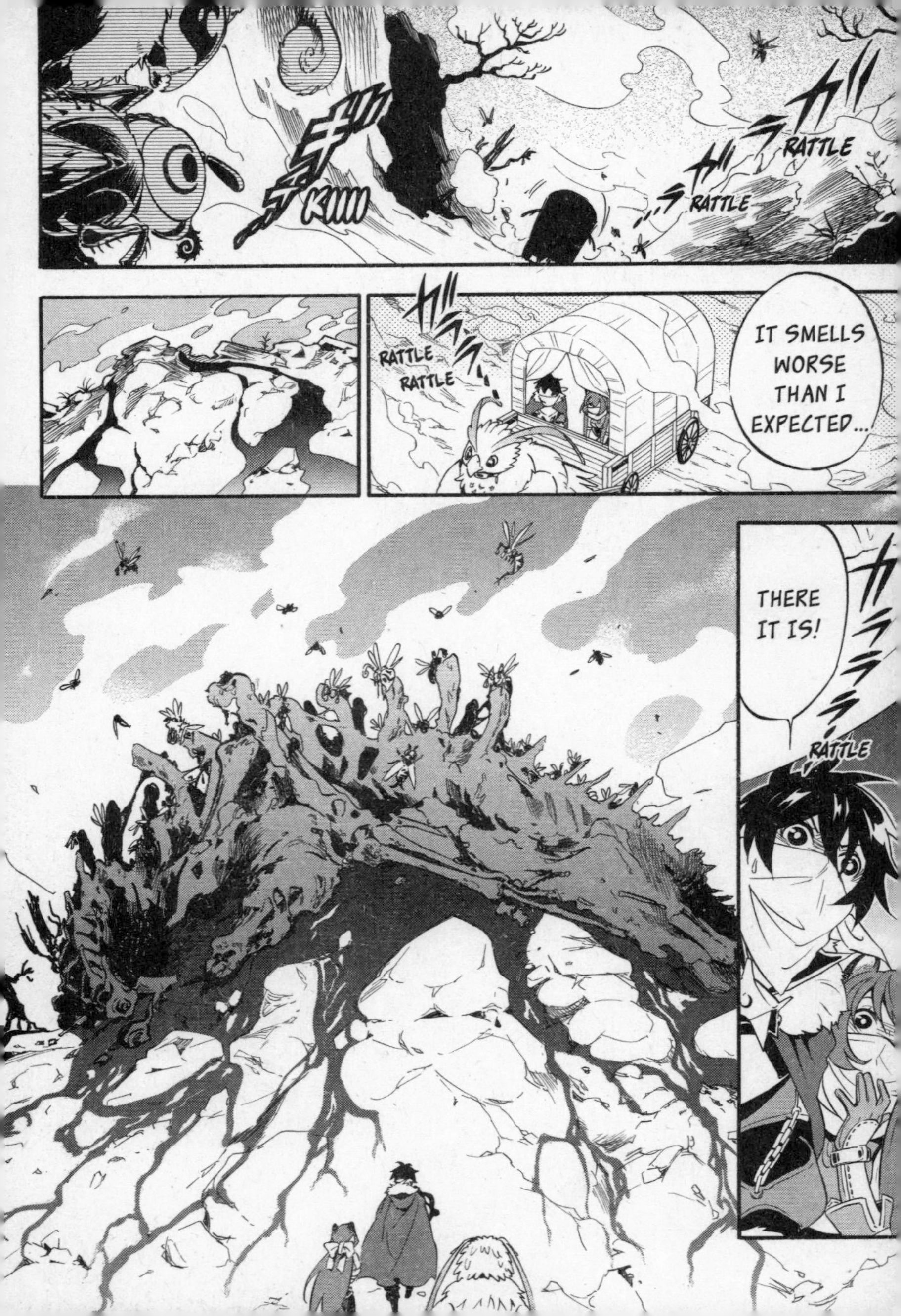
RATTLE
RATTLE
KIIII
RATTLE
RATTLE
IT SMELLS WORSE THAN I EXPECTED...
THERE IT IS!
RATTLE

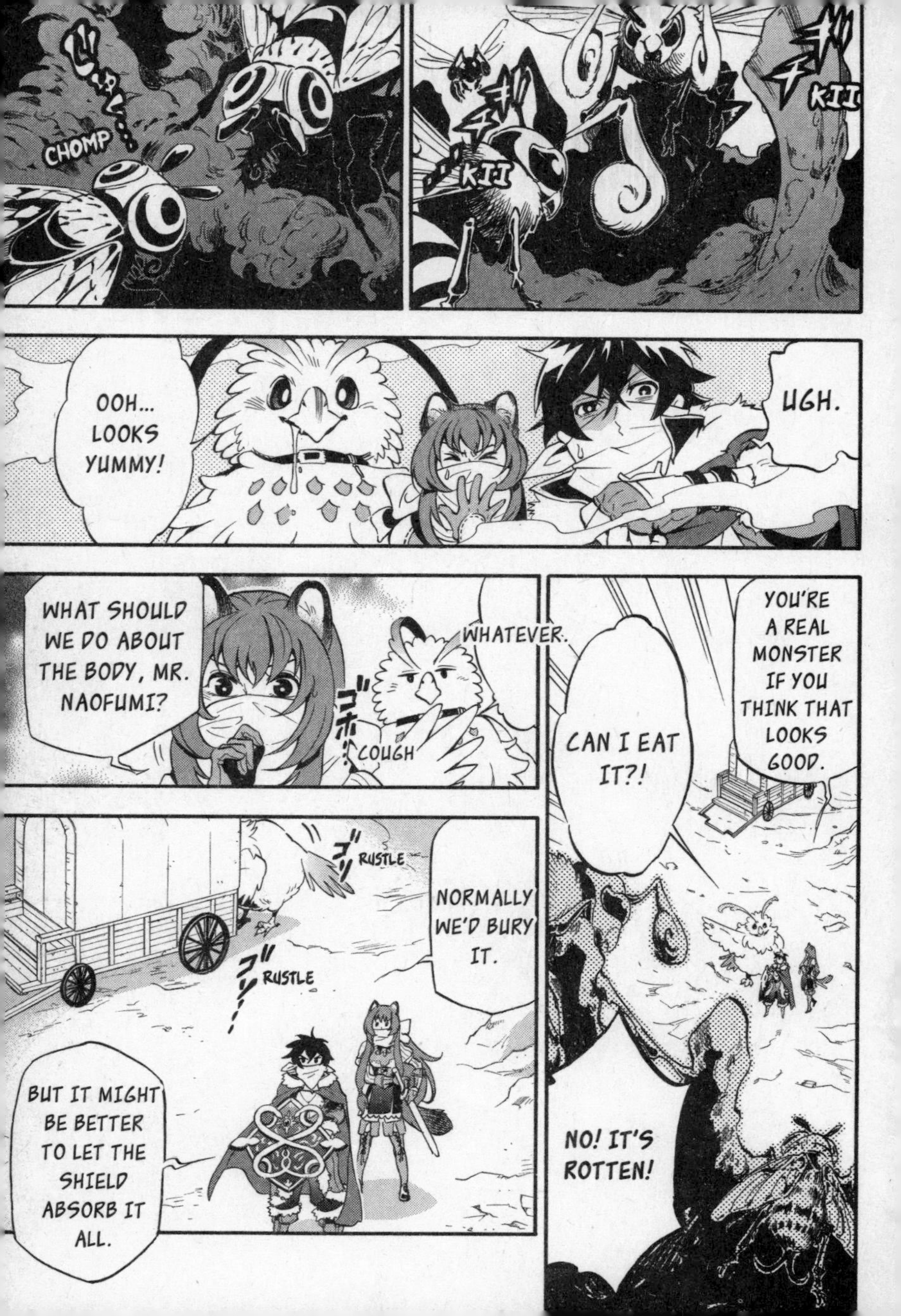
KII
KII
CHOMP
UGH.
OOH... LOOKS YUMMY!
YOU'RE A REAL MONSTER IF YOU THINK THAT LOOKS GOOD.
CAN I EAT IT?!
NO! IT'S ROTTEN!
WHAT SHOULD WE DO ABOUT THE BODY, MR. NAOFUMI?
WHATEVER.
COUGH
RUSTLE
NORMALLY WE'D BURY IT.
RUSTLE
BUT IT MIGHT BE BETTER TO LET THE SHIELD ABSORB IT ALL.

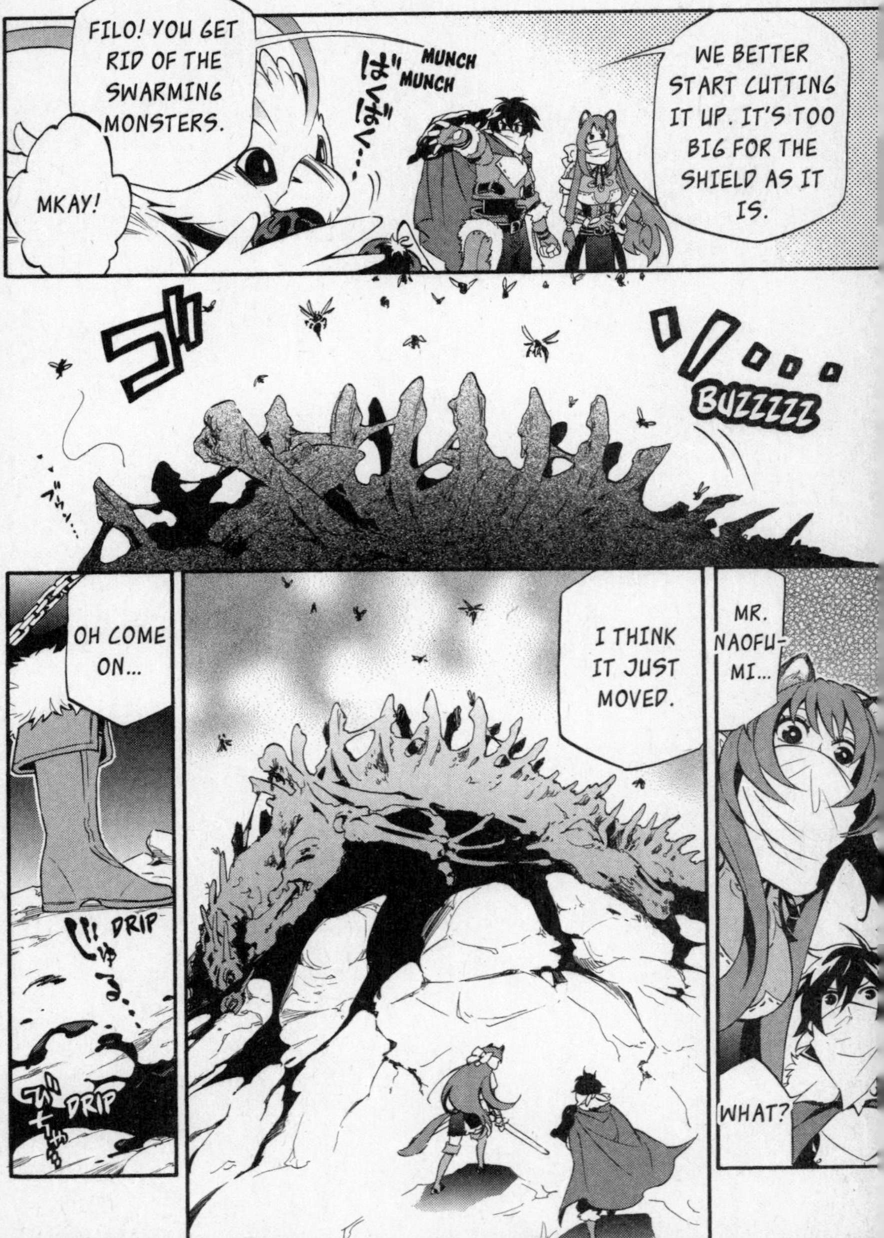
WE BETTER START CUTTING IT UP. IT'S TOO BIG FOR THE SHIELD AS IT IS.
FILO! YOU GET RID OF THE SWARMING MONSTERS.
MUNCH MUNCH
MKAY!
BUZZZZZ
MR. NAOFUMI...
WHAT?
I THINK IT JUST MOVED.
OH COME ON...
DRIP
DRIP

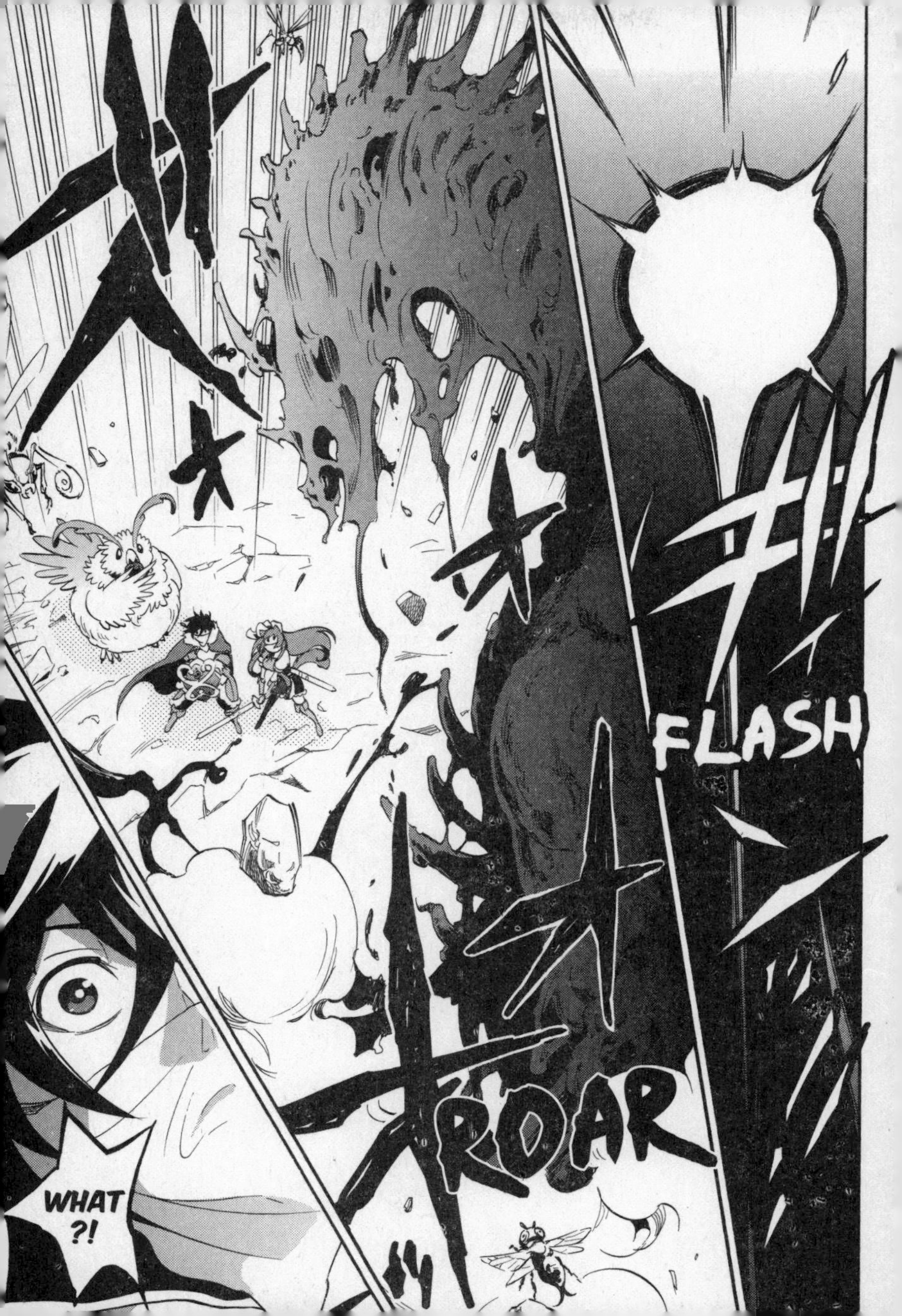
FLASH
ROAR
WHAT ?!

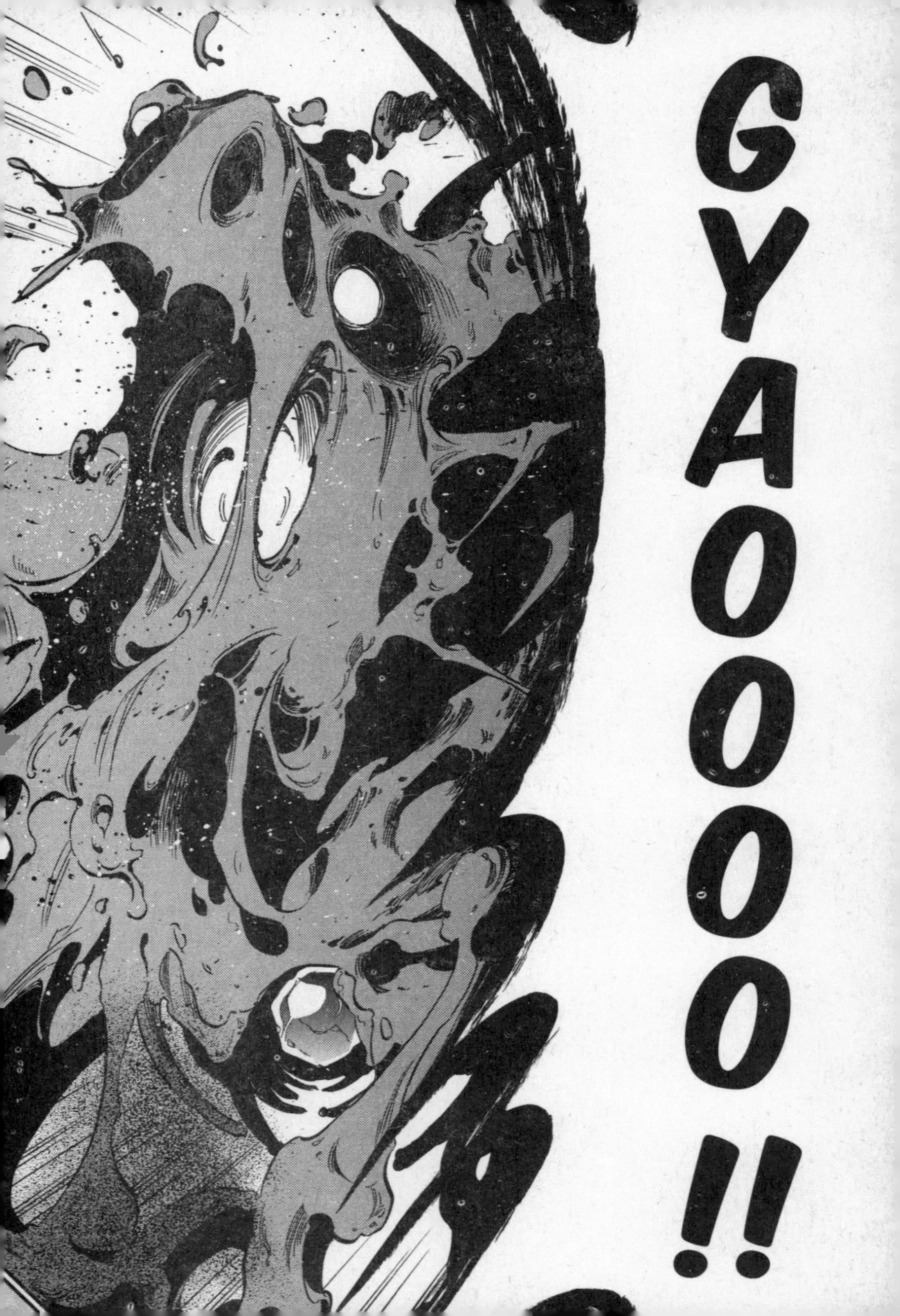
GYAOOOO!!

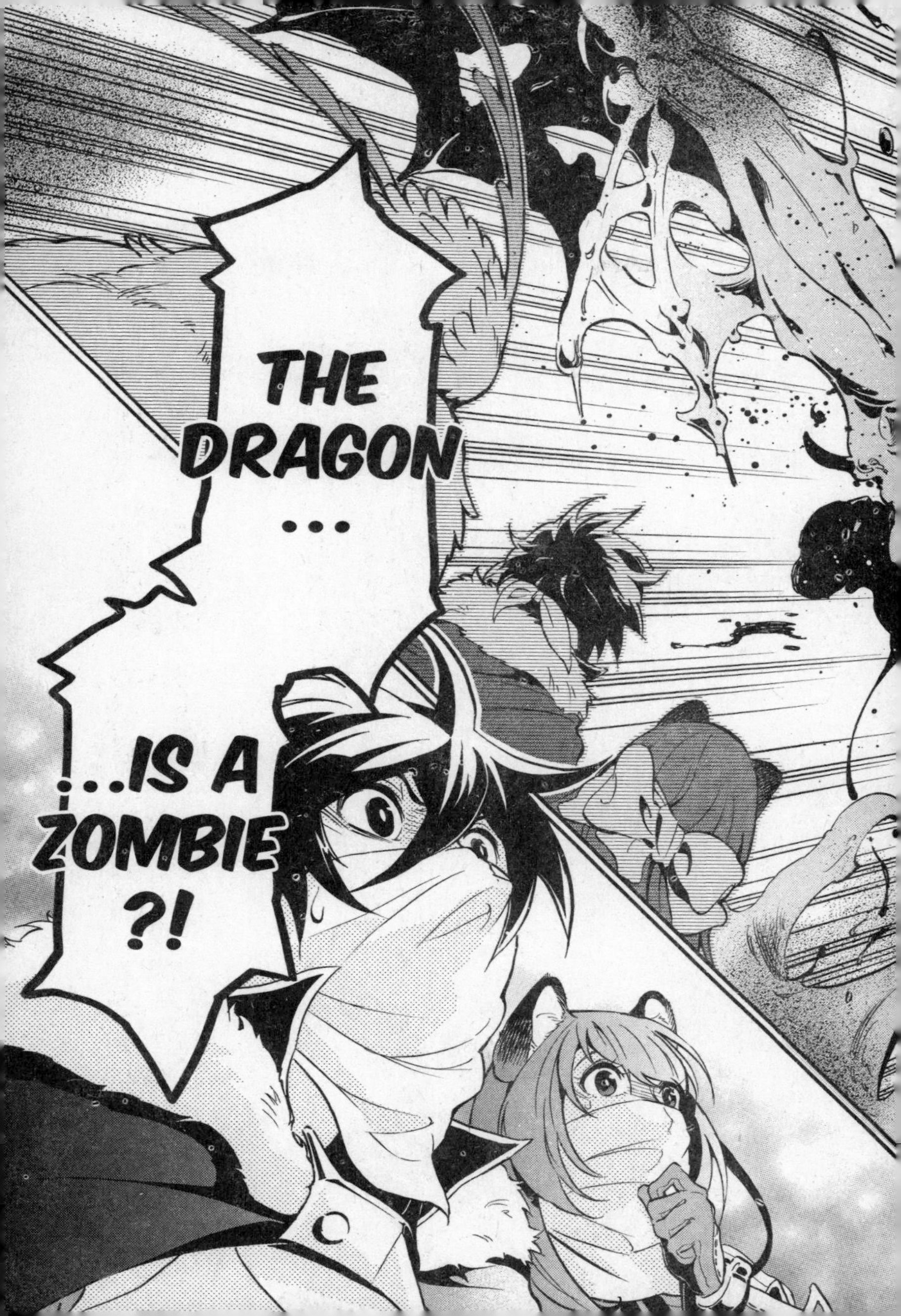
THE DRAGON ...
...IS A ZOMBIE ?!

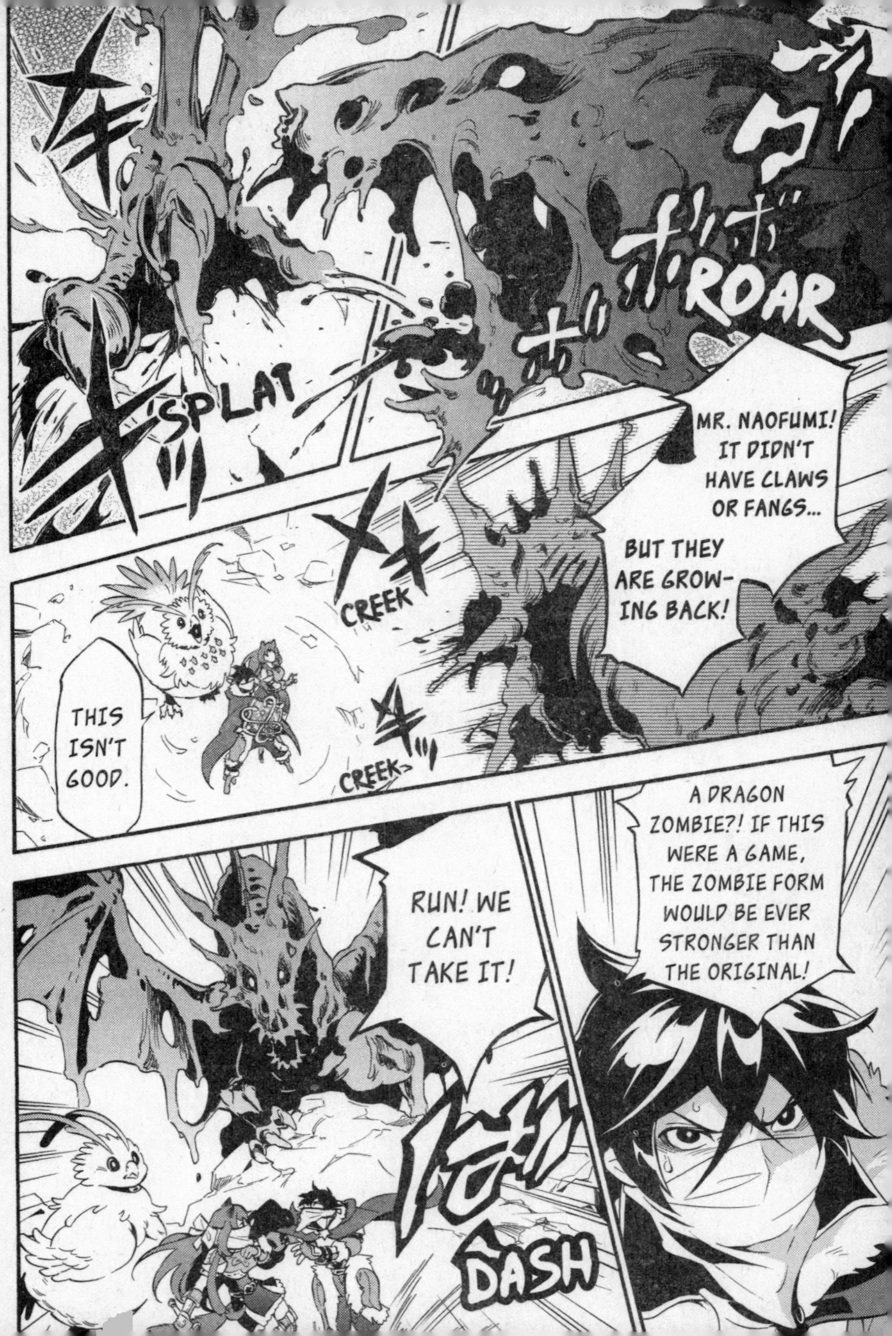
ROAR
SPLAT
MR. NAOFUMI! IT DIDN'T HAVE CLAWS OR FANGS...
BUT THEY ARE GROW-ING BACK!
CREEK
CREEK
THIS ISN'T GOOD.
A DRAGON ZOMBIE?! IF THIS WERE A GAME, THE ZOMBIE FORM WOULD BE EVER STRONGER THAN THE ORIGINAL!
RUN! WE CAN'T TAKE IT!
DASH

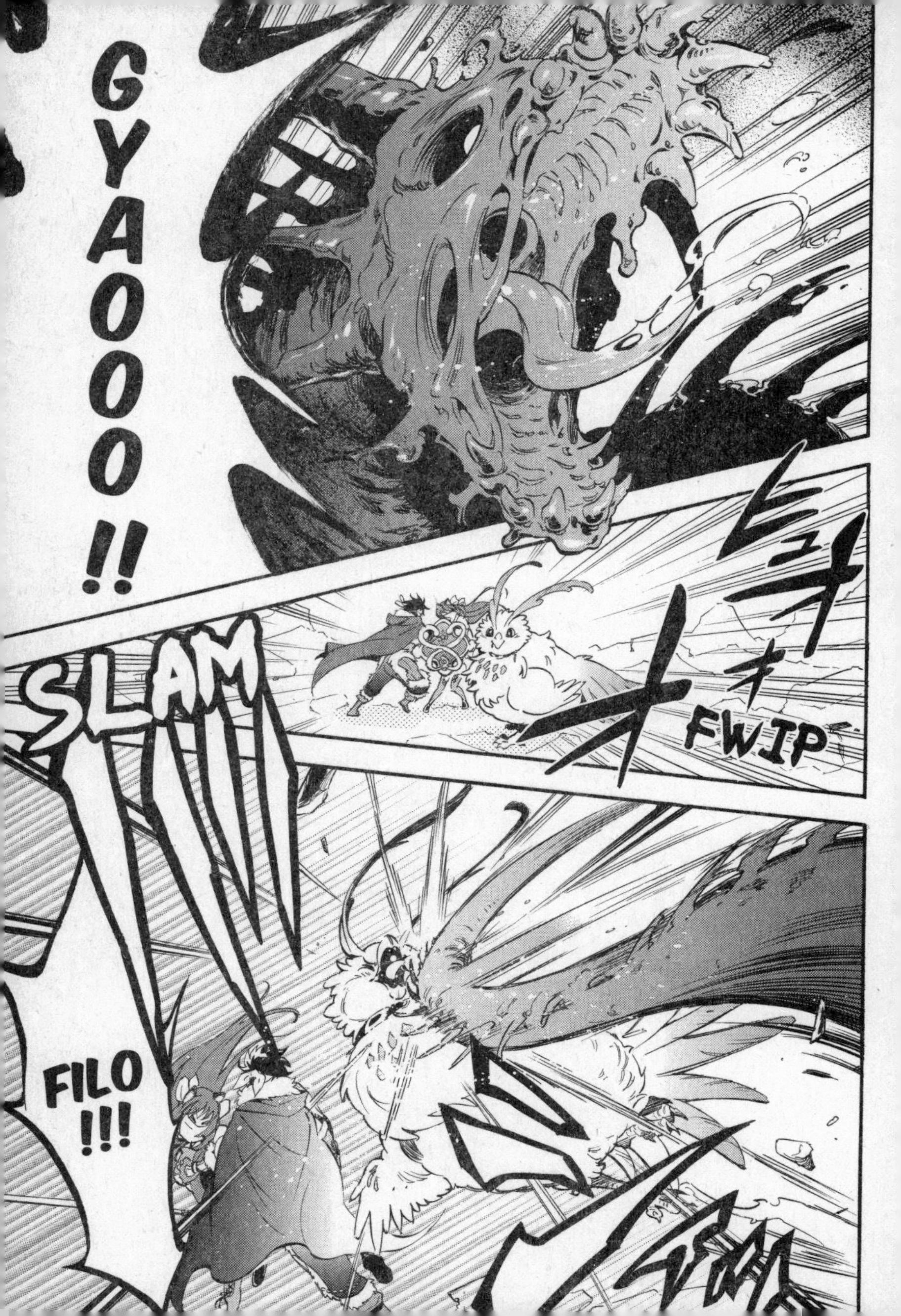
GYAOOO!!
FWIP
SLAM
FILO!!!

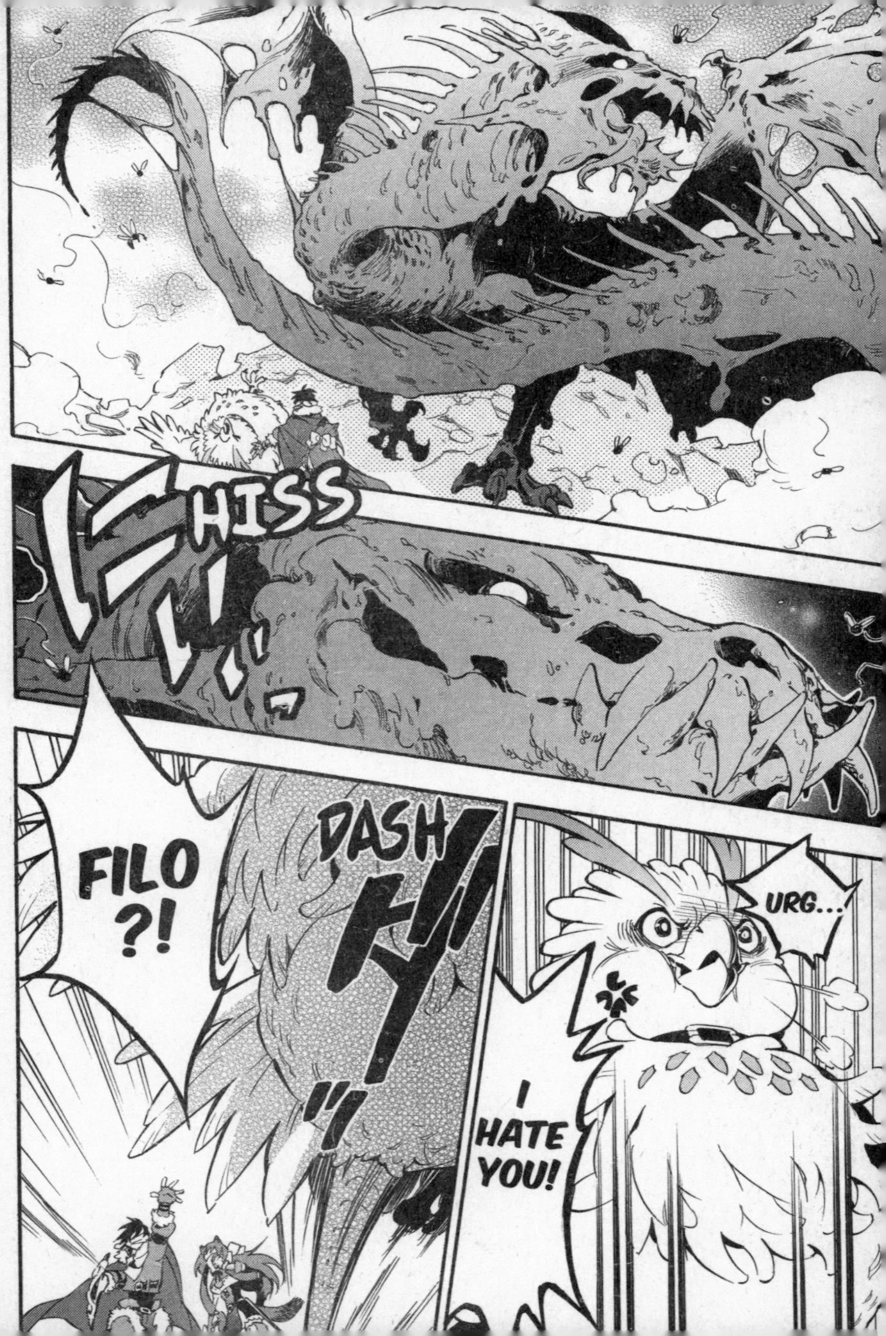
HISS
URG...
I HATE YOU!
DASH
FILO ?!

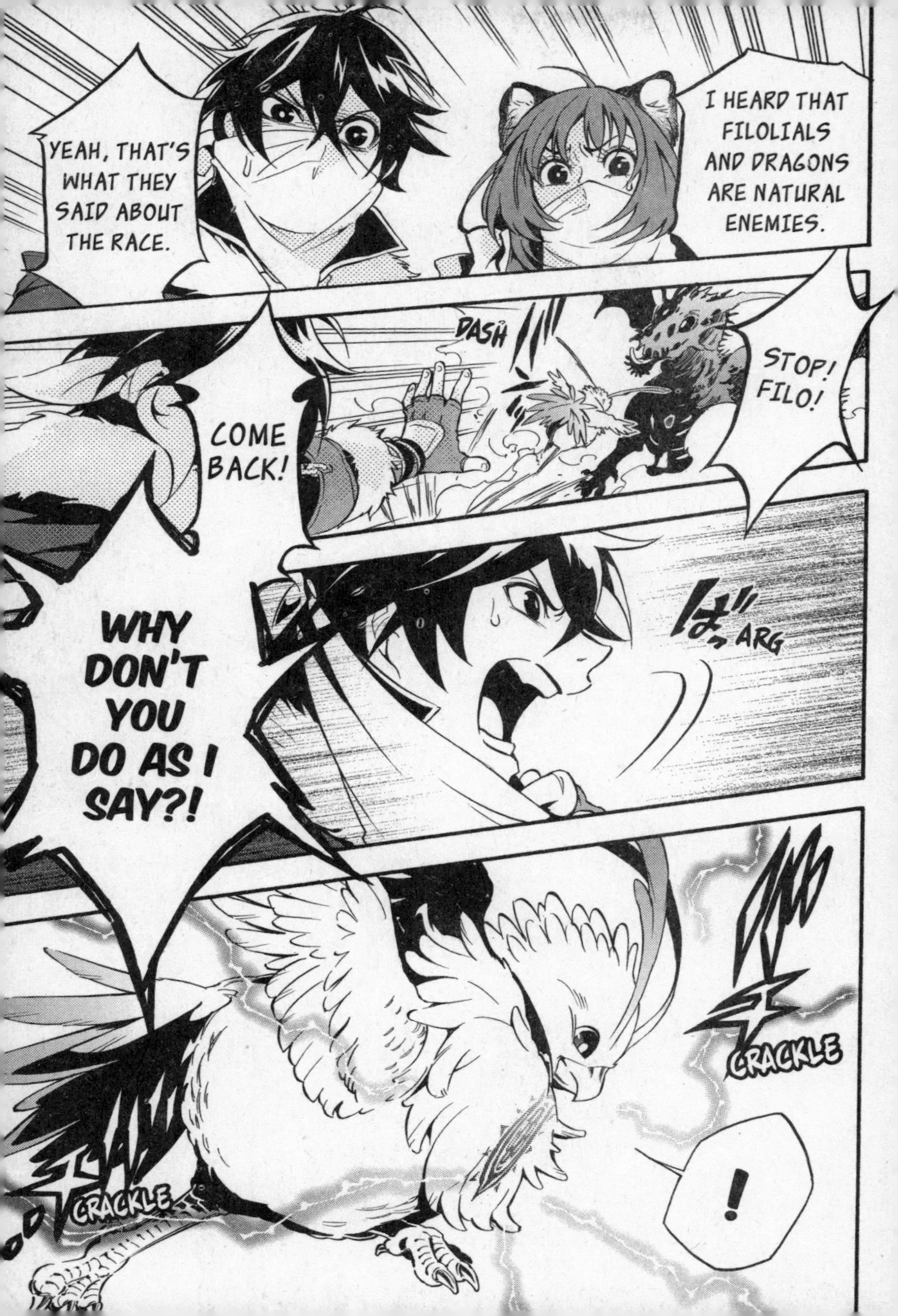
I HEARD THAT FILOLIALS AND DRAGONS ARE NATURAL ENEMIES.
YEAH, THAT'S WHAT THEY SAID ABOUT THE RACE.
STOP! FILO!
DASH
COME BACK!
ばっ ARG
WHY DON'T YOU DO AS I SAY?!
CRACKLE
!
CRACKLE

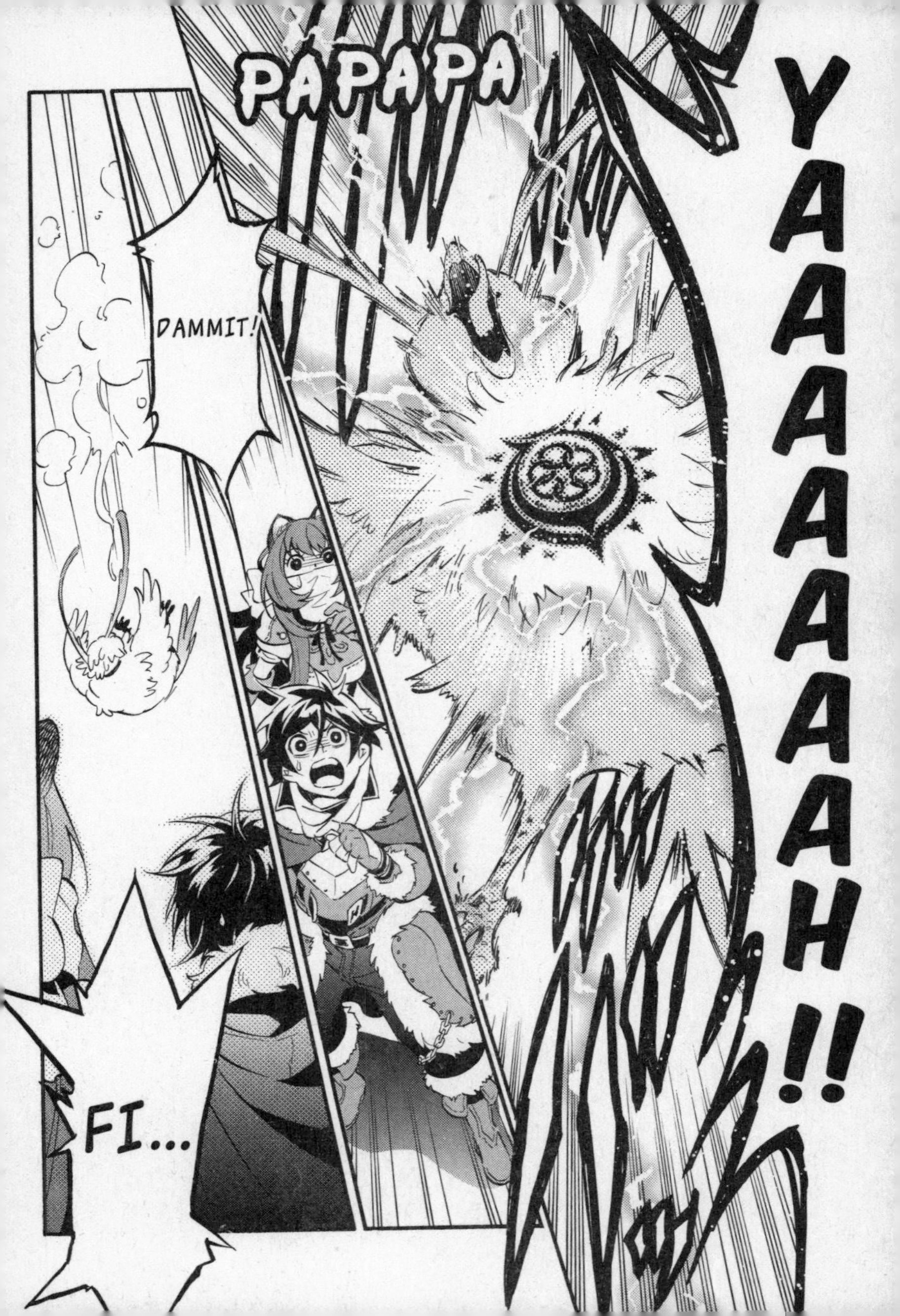
YAAAAAAH!!
PAPAPA
DAMMIT!
FI...

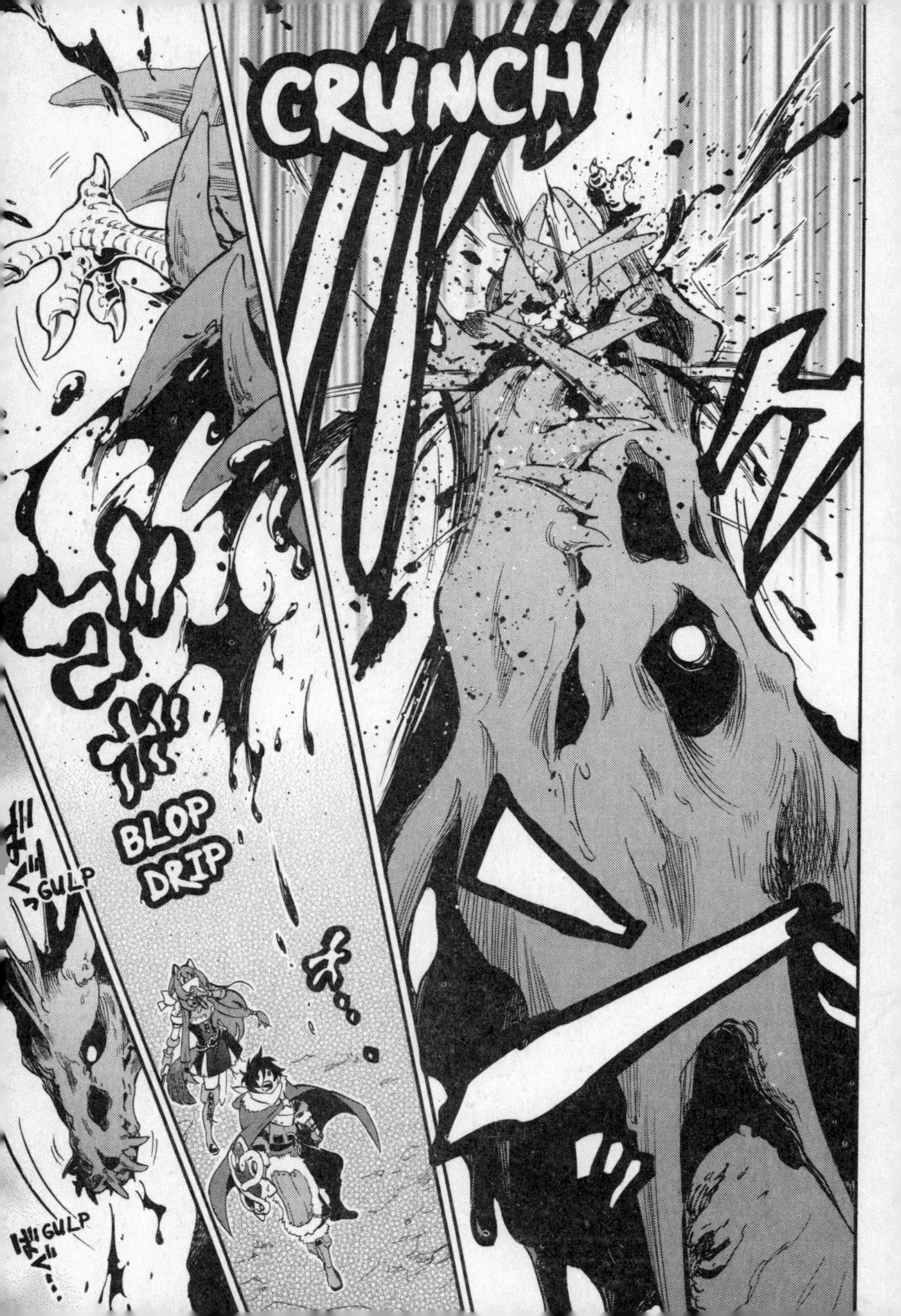
CRUNCH
BLOP
DRIP
GULP
GULP

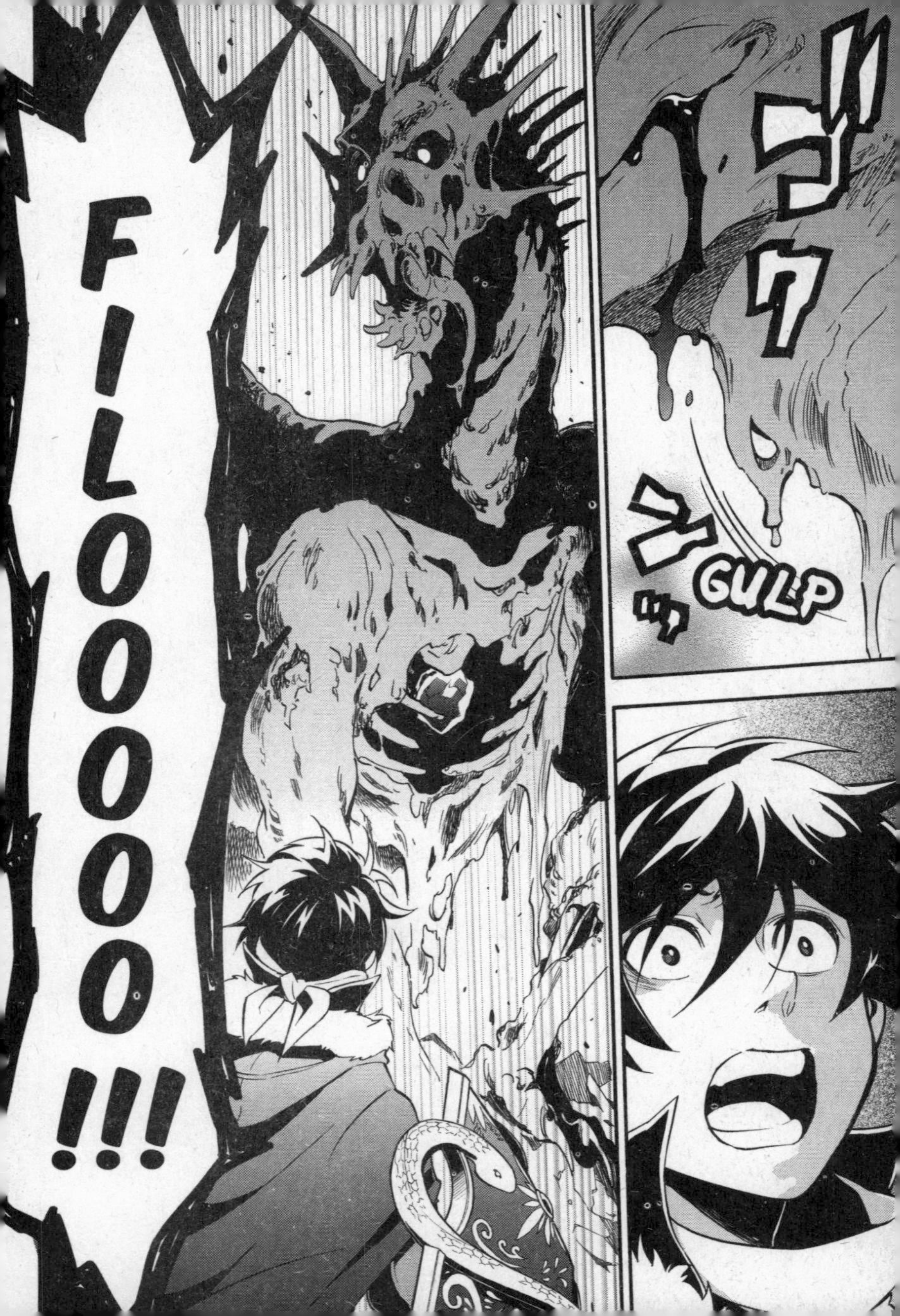
GULP
FILOOOOO!!!

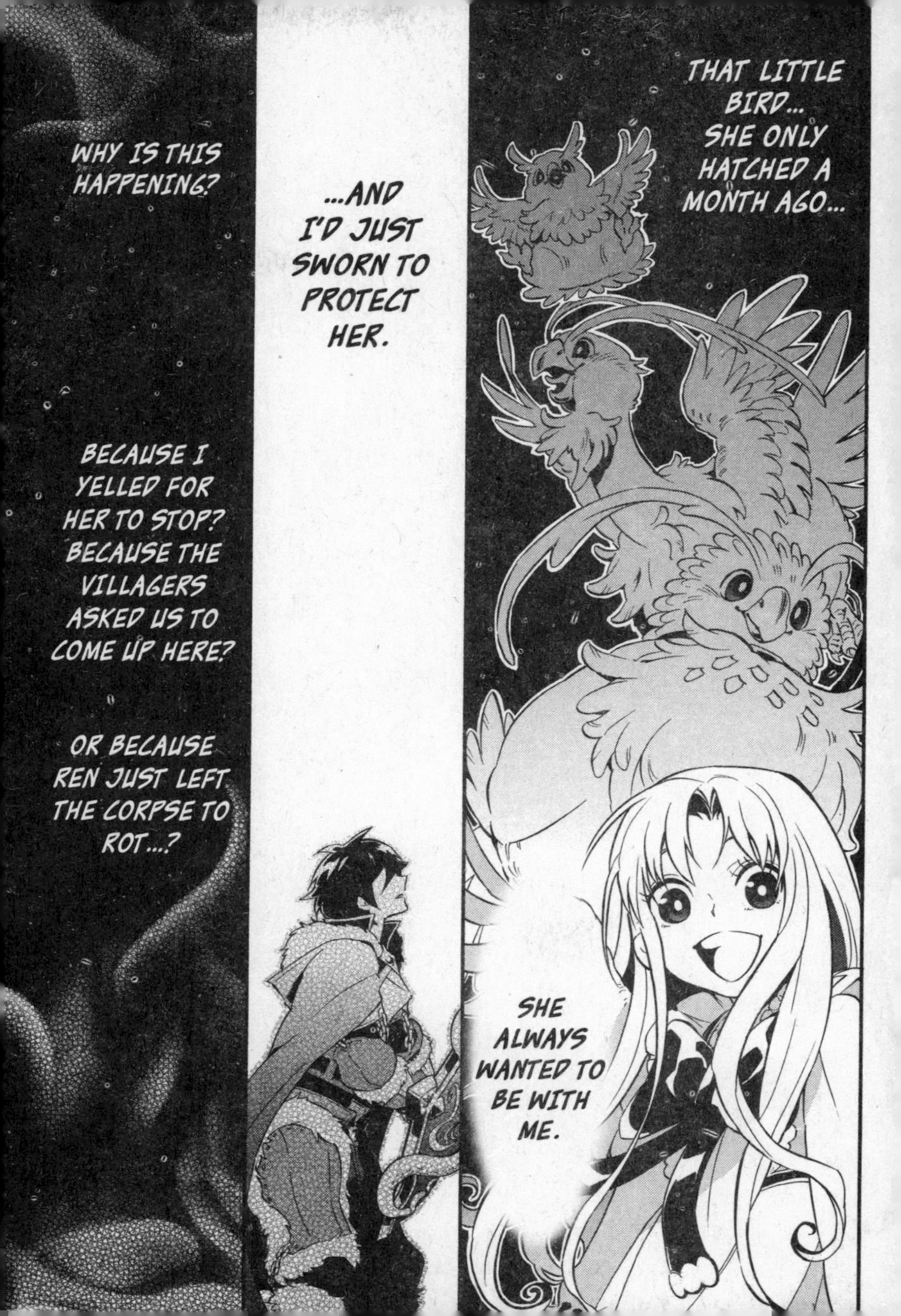
THAT LITTLE BIRD... SHE ONLY HATCHED A MONTH AGO...
SHE ALWAYS WANTED TO BE WITH ME.
...AND I'D JUST SWORN TO PROTECT HER.
WHY IS THIS HAPPENING?
BECAUSE I YELLED FOR HER TO STOP? BECAUSE THE VILLAGERS ASKED US TO COME UP HERE?
OR BECAUSE REN JUST LEFT THE CORPSE TO ROT...?

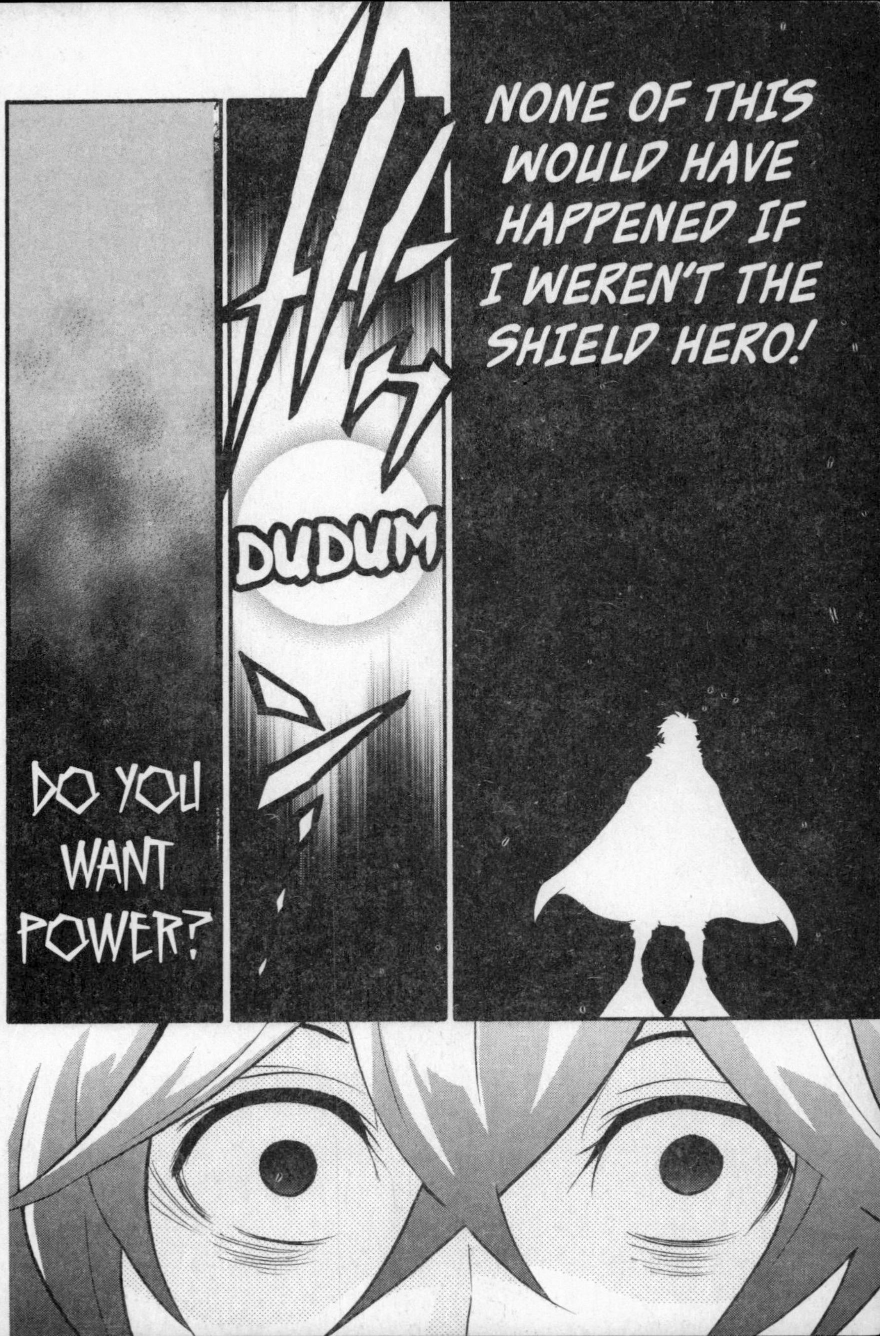
NONE OF THIS WOULD HAVE HAPPENED IF I WEREN'T THE SHIELD HERO!
DUDUM
DO YOU WANT POWER?

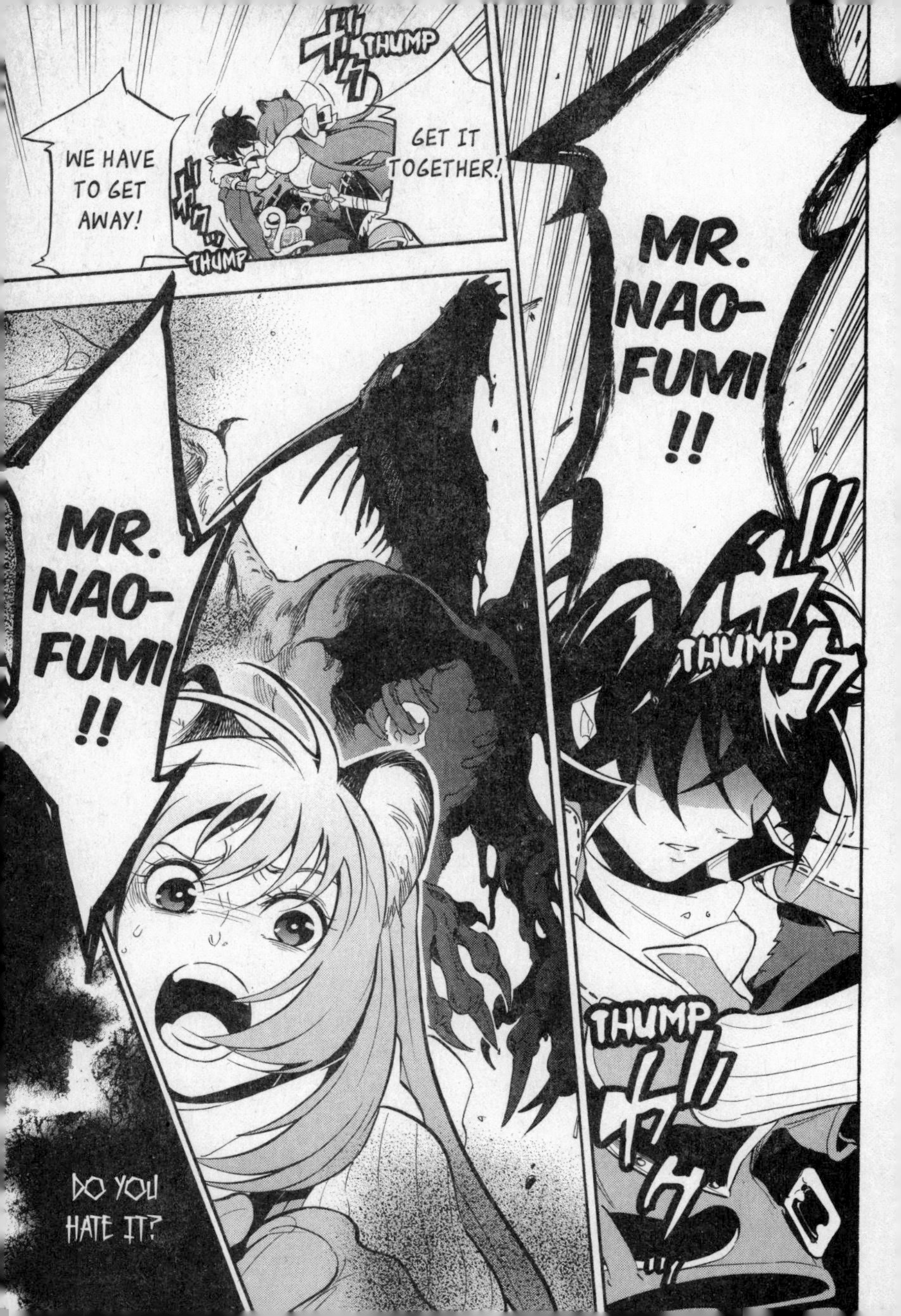
MR. NAO-FUMI!!
THUMP
THUMP
THUMP
GET IT TOGETHER!
WE HAVE TO GET AWAY!
THUMP
MR. NAO-FUMI!!
DO YOU HATE IT?

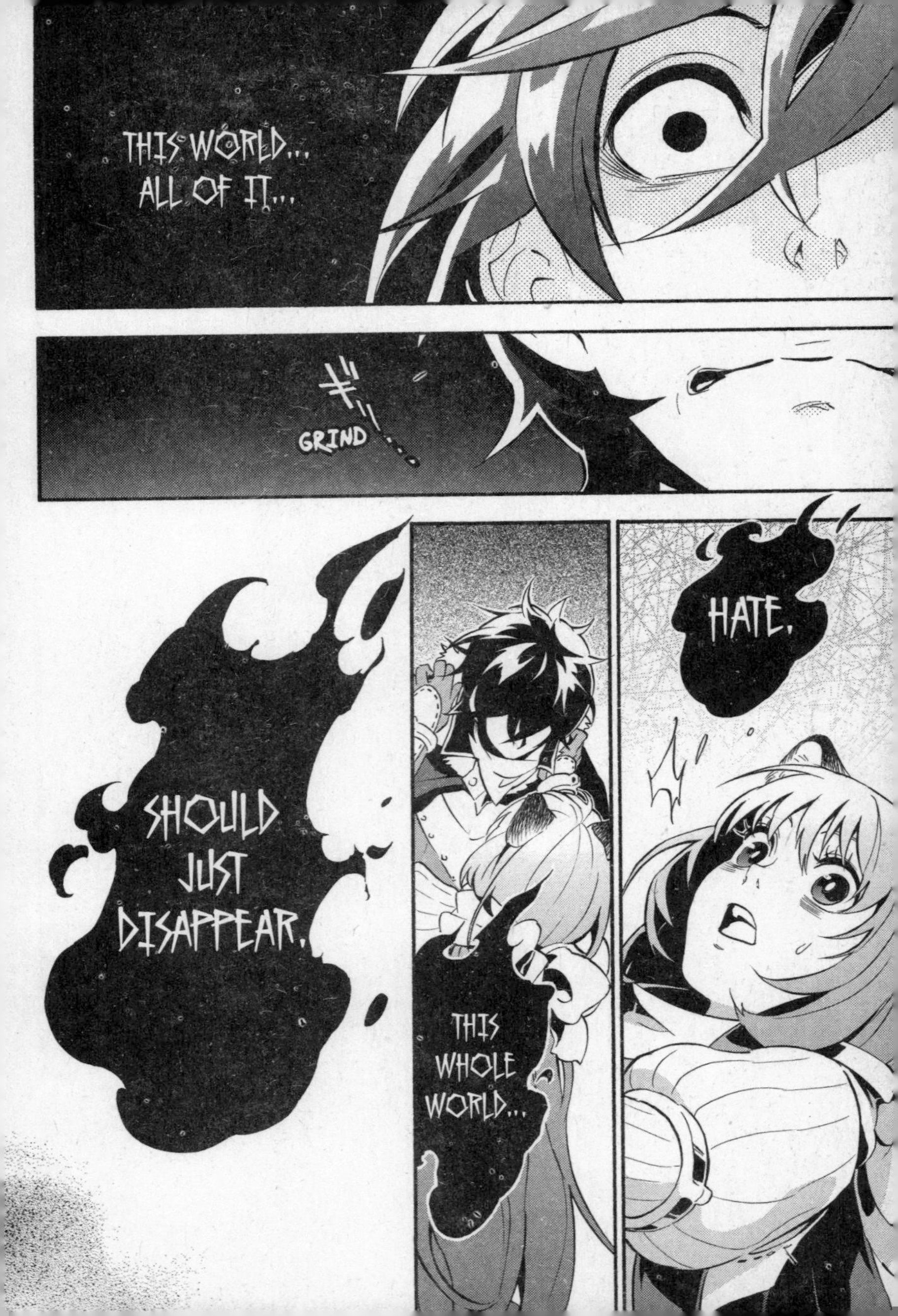
THIS WORLD... ALL OF IT...
ギ
GRIND
HATE.
THIS WHOLE WORLD...
SHOULD JUST DISAPPEAR.

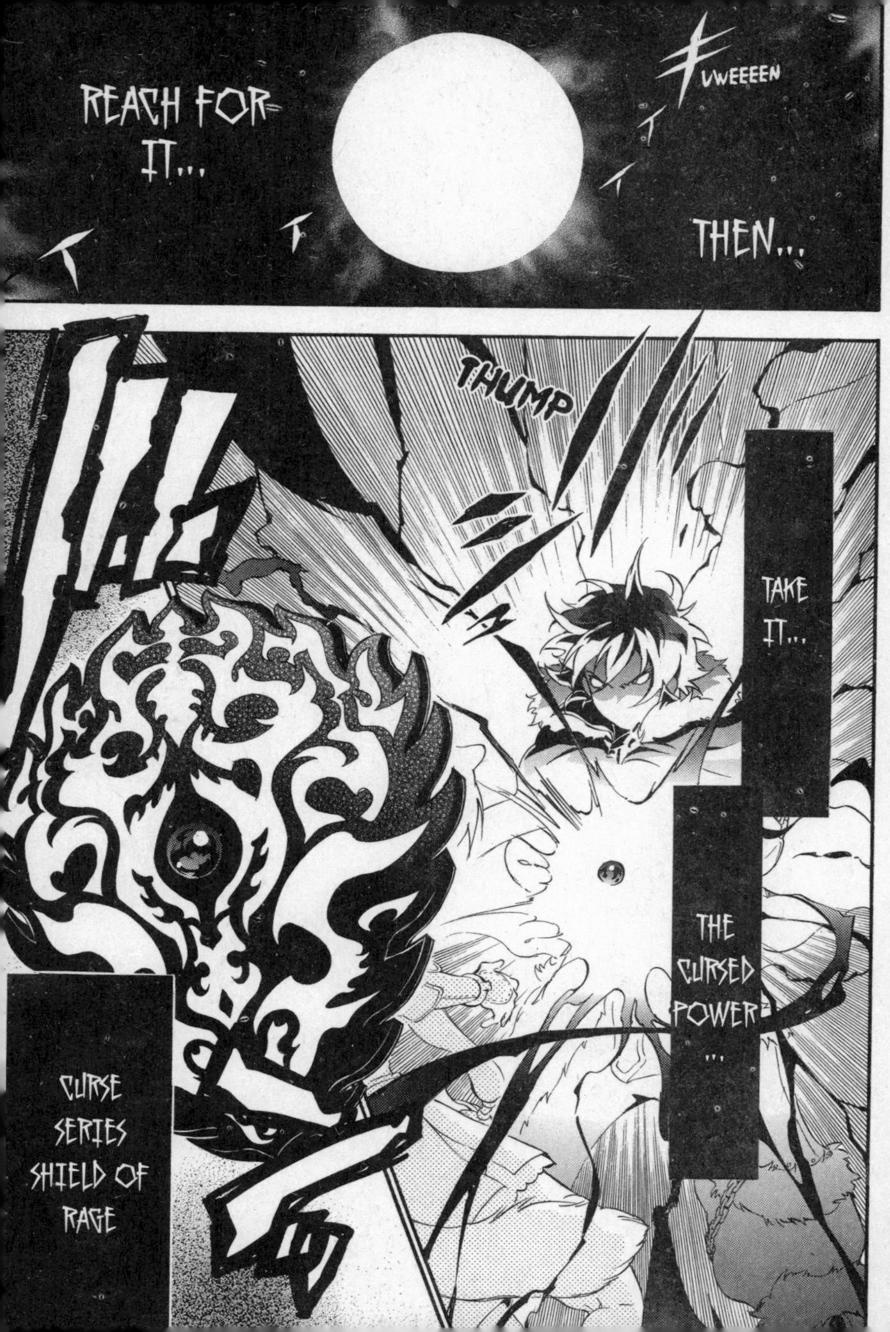
UWEEEEN
REACH FOR IT...
THEN...
THUMP
TAKE IT...
THE CURSED POWER...
CURSE SERIES SHIELD OF RAGE

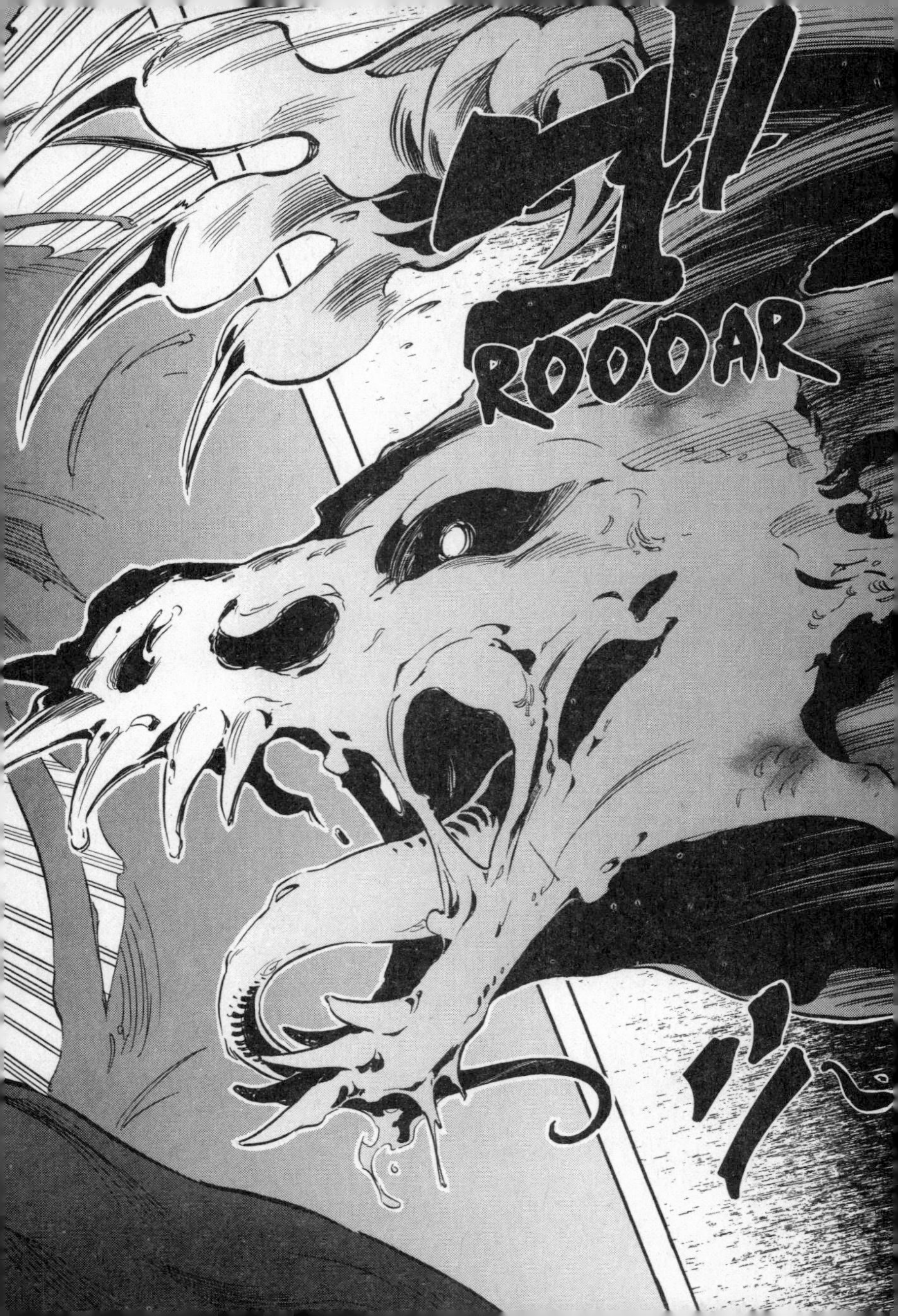
ROOOAR

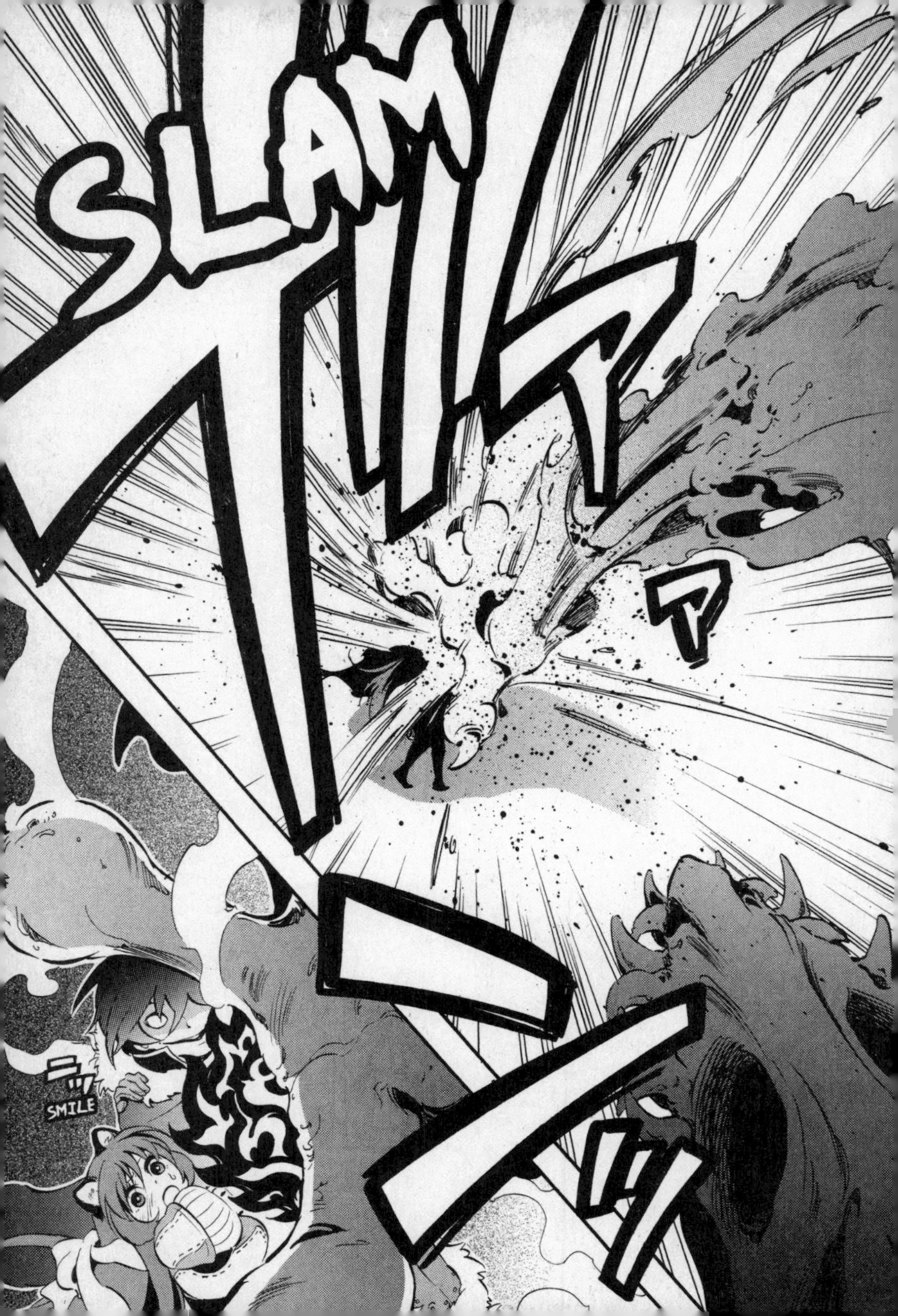
SLAM
SMILE

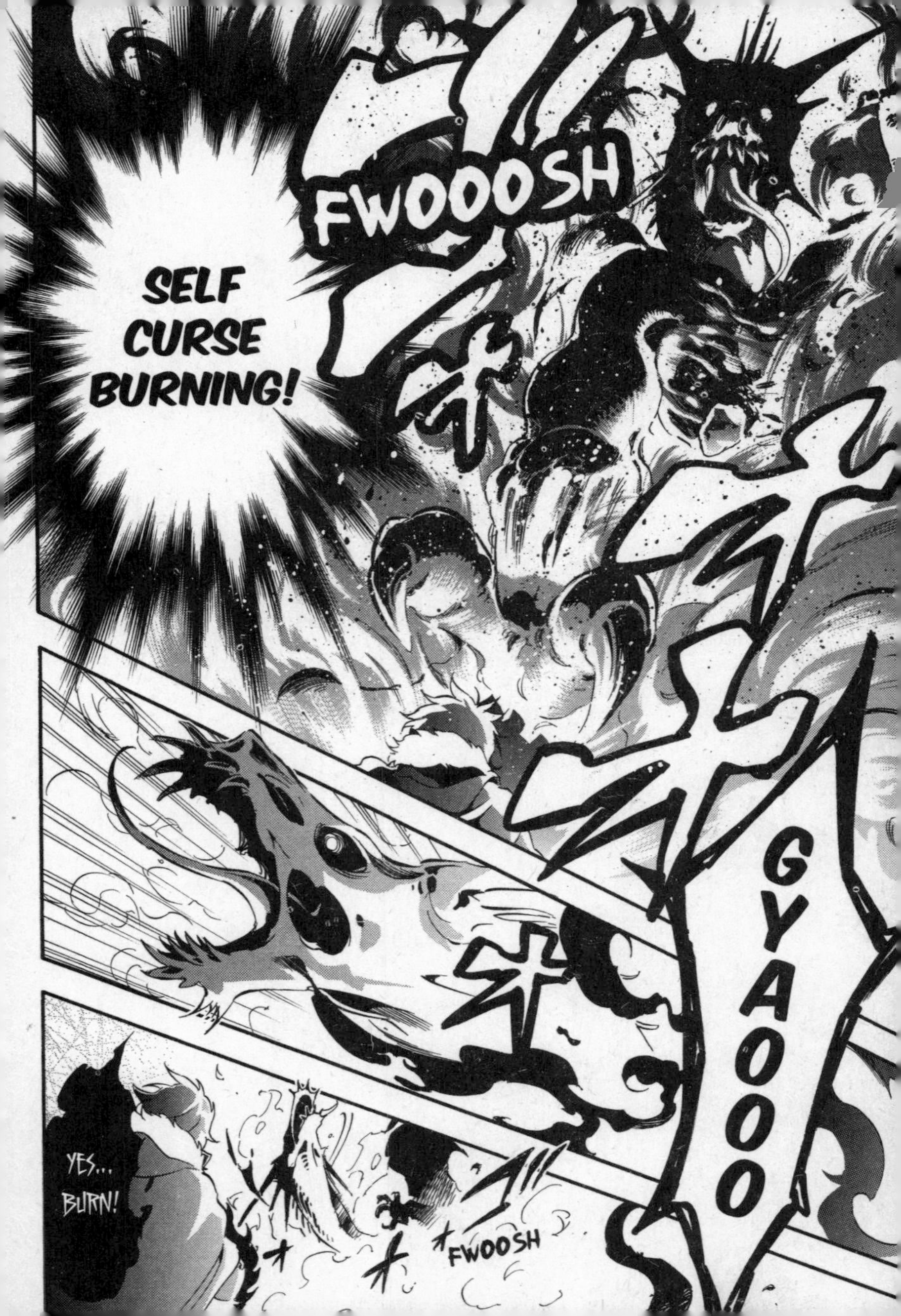
FWOOOSH
SELF CURSE BURNING!
GYAOOO
FWOOSH
YES... BURN!

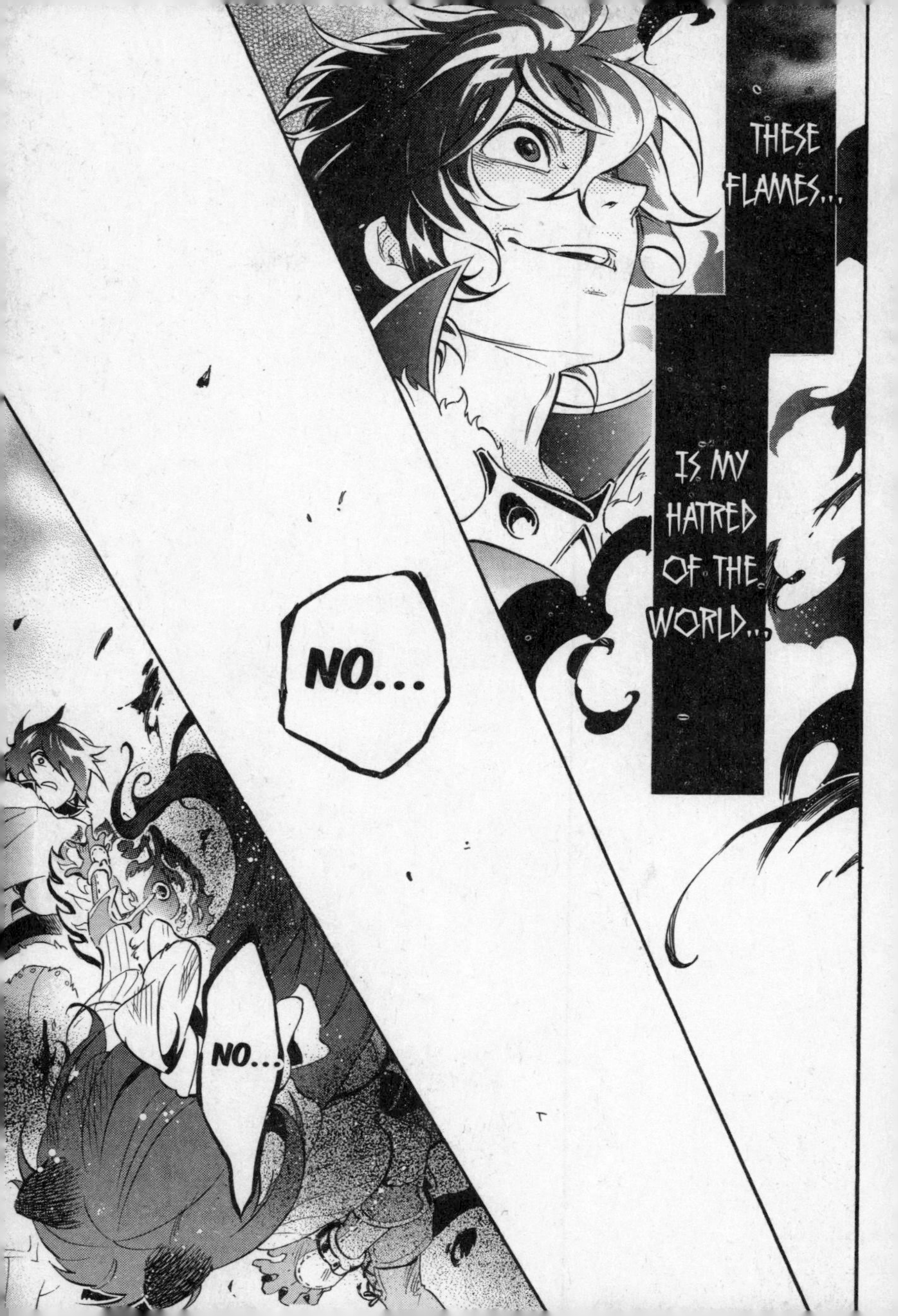
THESE FLAMES...
IS MY HATRED OF THE WORLD...
NO...
NO...

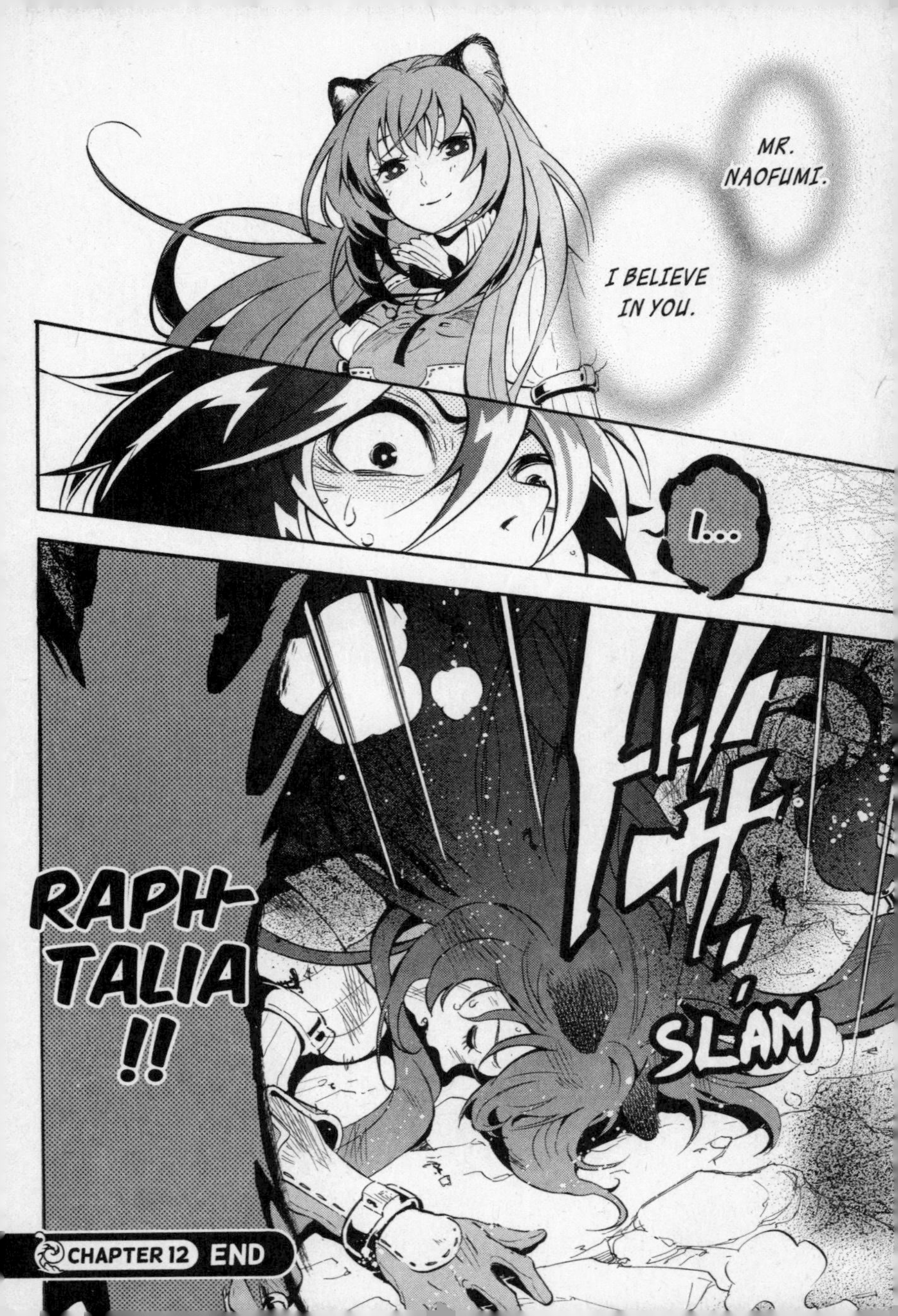
MR. NAOFUMI.
I BELIEVE IN YOU.
I...
SLAM
RAPH-TALIA!!
CHAPTER 12 END

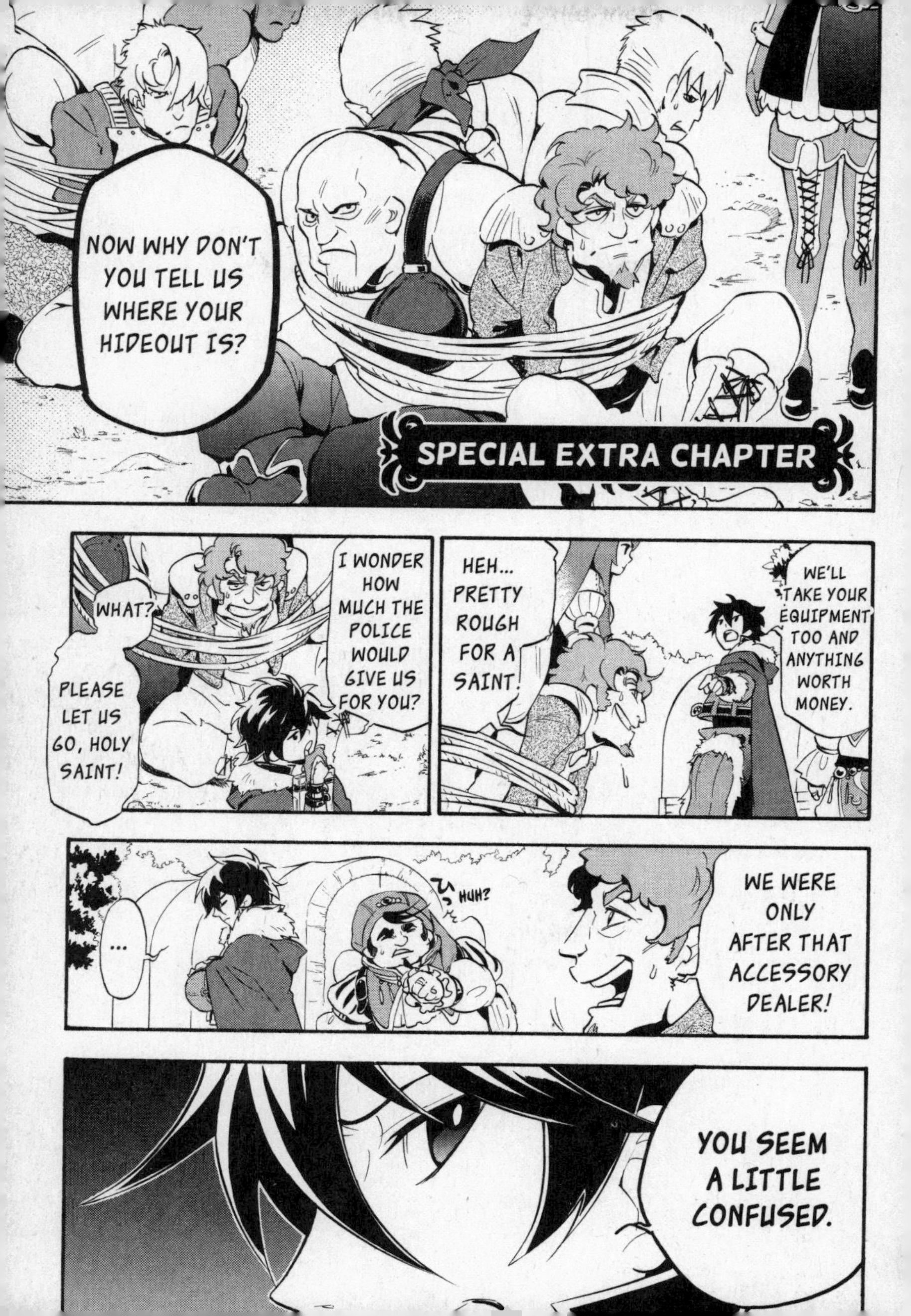
NOW WHY DON'T YOU TELL US WHERE YOUR HIDEOUT IS?
SPECIAL EXTRA CHAPTER
WE'LL TAKE YOUR EQUIPMENT TOO AND ANYTHING WORTH MONEY.
HEH... PRETTY ROUGH FOR A SAINT!
I WONDER HOW MUCH THE POLICE WOULD GIVE US FOR YOU?
WHAT?
PLEASE LET US GO, HOLY SAINT!
WE WERE ONLY AFTER THAT ACCESSORY DEALER!
HUH?
...
YOU SEEM A LITTLE CONFUSED.

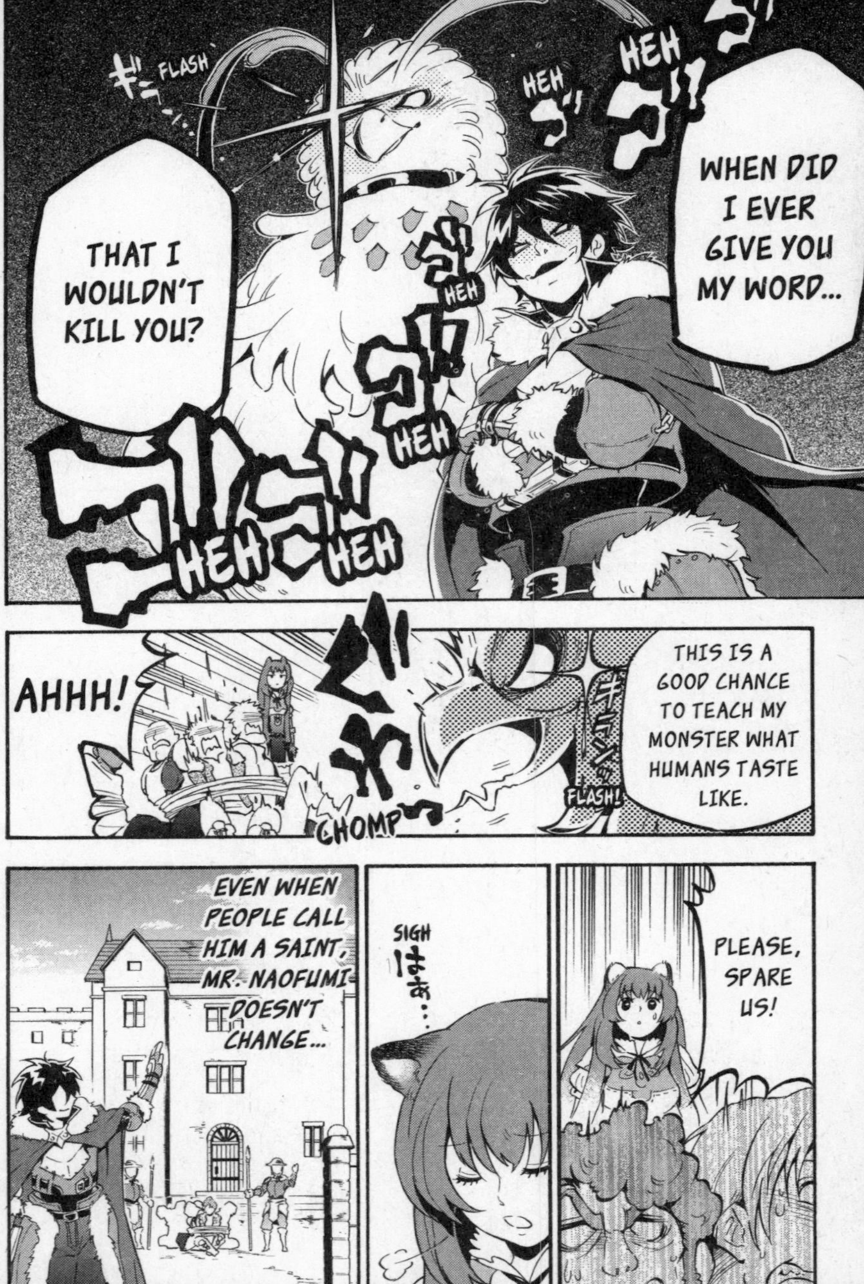
HEH
HEH
WHEN DID I EVER GIVE YOU MY WORD...
FLASH
THAT I WOULDN'T KILL YOU?
HEH
HEH
HEH HEH
THIS IS A GOOD CHANCE TO TEACH MY MONSTER WHAT HUMANS TASTE LIKE.
FLASH!
CHOMP
AHHH!
PLEASE, SPARE US!
SIGH
はぁ…
EVEN WHEN PEOPLE CALL HIM A SAINT, MR. NAOFUMI DOESN'T CHANGE...

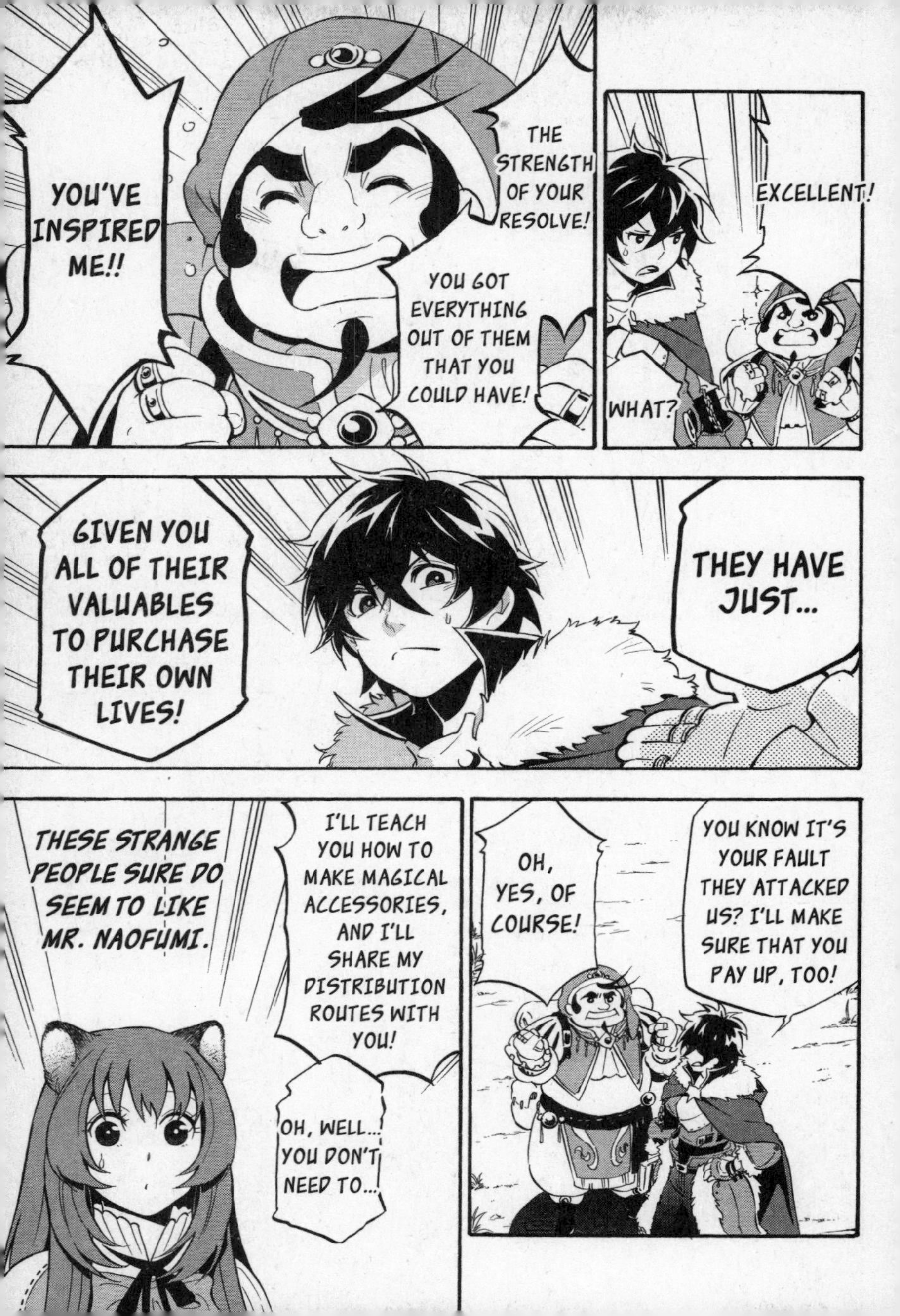
EXCELLENT!
WHAT?
THE STRENGTH OF YOUR RESOLVE!
YOU GOT EVERYTHING OUT OF THEM THAT YOU COULD HAVE!
YOU'VE INSPIRED ME!!
THEY HAVE JUST...
GIVEN YOU ALL OF THEIR VALUABLES TO PURCHASE THEIR OWN LIVES!
YOU KNOW IT'S YOUR FAULT THEY ATTACKED US? I'LL MAKE SURE THAT YOU PAY UP, TOO!
OH, YES, OF COURSE!
I'LL TEACH YOU HOW TO MAKE MAGICAL ACCESSORIES, AND I'LL SHARE MY DISTRIBUTION ROUTES WITH YOU!
THESE STRANGE PEOPLE SURE DO SEEM TO LIKE MR. NAOFUMI.
OH, WELL... YOU DON'T NEED TO...

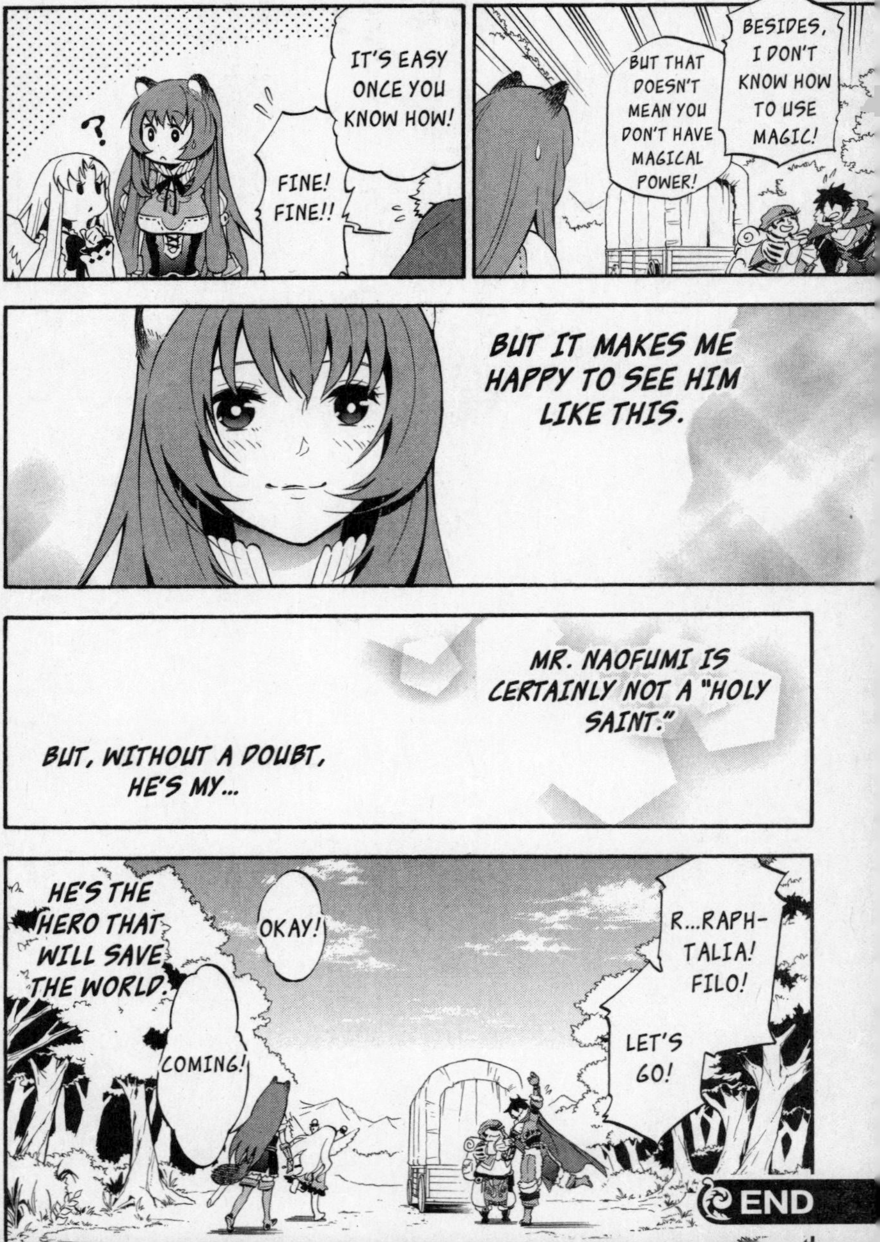
BESIDES, I DON'T KNOW HOW TO USE MAGIC!
BUT THAT DOESN'T MEAN YOU DON'T HAVE MAGICAL POWER!
IT'S EASY ONCE YOU KNOW HOW!
?
FINE! FINE!!
BUT IT MAKES ME HAPPY TO SEE HIM LIKE THIS.
MR. NAOFUMI IS CERTAINLY NOT A "HOLY SAINT."
BUT, WITHOUT A DOUBT, HE'S MY...
R...RAPH-TALIA! FILO!
LET'S GO!
OKAY!
HE'S THE HERO THAT WILL SAVE THE WORLD.
COMING!
END

AFTERWORD

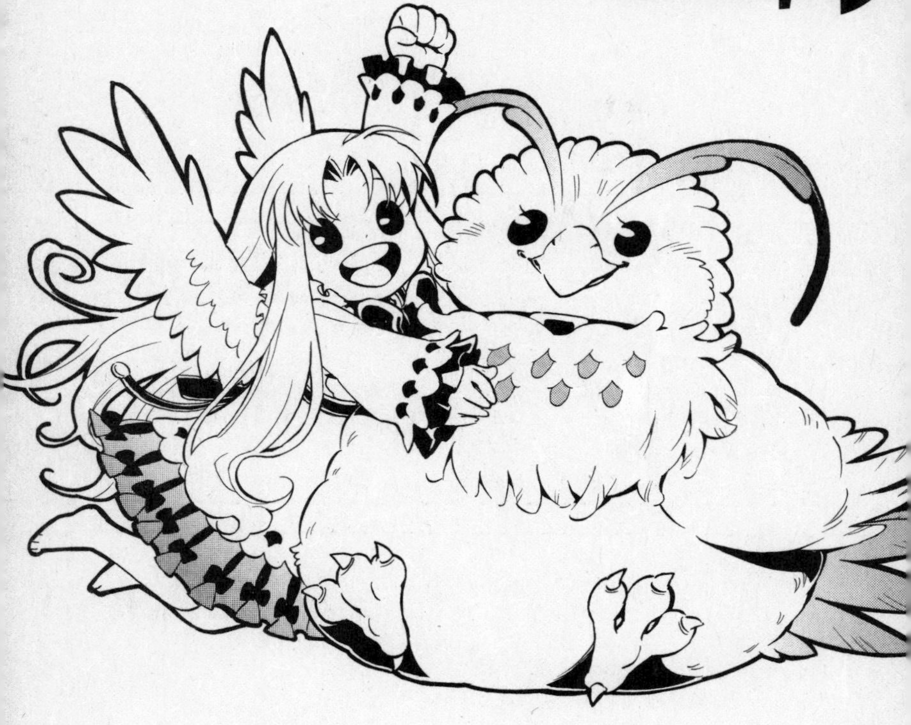

I CAN'T BELIEVE THE THIRD VOLUME IS ALREADY OVER!
FILO HAS BEEN SO MUCH FUN TO DRAW, AND FOR SOME REASON THE ASSISTANTS REALLY LOVE FILO WHEN SHE IS BIG, FAT, AND ASLEEP.
I'M GOING TO KEEP WORKING ON DRAWING RAPHTALIA THE BEST I CAN. SHE'S SO CUTE!
SEE YOU NEXT VOLUME!

The Rising of the Shield Hero: The Manga Companion Volume 03

© Aiya Kyu 2014
© Aneko Yusagi   2014
First published by KADOKAWA in 2014 in Japan.
English translation rights arranged by One Peace Books
under the license from KADOKAWA CORPORATION, Japan.

ISBN 978-1-935548-90-4

Written by Aiya Kyu
Original Story by Aneko Yusagi
Character Design by Minami Seira
English Edition Published by One Peace Books 2015

Printed in Canada

1 2 3 4 5 6 7 8 9 10

One Peace Books
43-32 22nd Street STE 204 Long Island City New York 11101
www.onepeacebooks.com